MIGRATION, HUMAN CAPITAL, AND THE LABOR MARKET

RESEARCH IN LABOR ECONOMICS

Series Editors: Solomon W. Polachek and Benjamin Elsner

Recent Volumes:

Volume 37: Labor Market Issues in China
Edited by Corrado Giulietti and Klaus F. Zimmermann

Volume 38: New Analyses in Worker Well-Being
Edited by Solomon W. Polachek

Volume 39: Safety Nets and Benefit Dependence
Edited by Stéphane Carcillo, Herwig Immervoll, Stephen P. Jenkins and Sebastian Königs

Volume 40: Factors Affecting Worker Well-Being: The Impact of Change in the Labor Market
Edited by Solomon W. Polachek

Volume 41: Gender Convergence in the Labor Market
Edited by Solomon W. Polachek and Klaus F. Zimmermann

Volume 42: Gender and the Labor Market
Edited by Solomon W. Polachek and Klaus F. Zimmermann

Volume 43: Inequality: Causes and Consequences
Edited by Lorenzo Cappellari and Solomon W. Polachek

Volume 44: Income Inequality Around the World
Edited by Lorenzo Cappellari and Solomon W. Polachek

Volume 45: Skill Mismatch in Labor Markets
Edited by Solomon W. Polachek, Konstantinos Pouliakas and Giovanni Russo

Volume 46: Transitions Through the Labor Market: Work, Occupation, Earnings and Retirement
Edited by Solomon W. Polachek

Volume 47: Health and Labor Markets
Edited by Solomon W. Polachek

Volume 48: Change at Home, in the Labor Market, and On the Job
Edited by Solomon W. Polachek

Volume 49: Workplace Productivity and Management Practices
Edited by Solomon W. Polachek

Volume 50: Fiftieth Celebratory Volume
Edited by Solomon W. Polachek

Volume 51: Time Use in Economics
Edited by Daniel S. Hamermesh and Solomon W. Polachek

Volume 52A: Big Data Applications in Labor Economics, Part A
Edited by Benjamin Elsner and Solomon W. Polachek

Volume 52B: Big Data Applications in Labor Economics, Part B
Edited by Benjamin Elsner and Solomon W. Polachek

EDITORIAL ADVISORY BOARD

RESEARCH IN LABOR ECONOMICS VOLUME 53A

MIGRATION, HUMAN CAPITAL AND THE LABOR MARKET

EDITED BY

BENJAMIN ELSNER
University College Dublin, Ireland and IZA, Germany

AND

SOLOMON W. POLACHEK
State University of New York at Binghamton, USA and IZA, Germany

emerald PUBLISHING

United Kingdom – North America – Japan
India – Malaysia – China

Emerald Publishing Limited
Emerald Publishing, Floor 5, Northspring, 21–23 Wellington Street, Leeds LS1 4DL

First edition 2026

British Library Cataloguing in Publication Data
A catalogue record for this book is available from the British Library

ISBN: 978-1-80592-632-0 (Print)
ISBN: 978-1-80592-631-3 (Online)
ISBN: 978-1-80592-633-7 (Epub)

ISSN: 0147-9121 (Series)

Printed and bound by CPI Group (UK) Ltd, Croydon, CR0 4YY

CONTENTS

PREFACE

Migration is among the most controversial topics of our time. In many countries, it pervades public debates and electoral campaigns and remains a polarizing issue. For some, immigration is a solution to labor shortages due to demographic decline and a welcome source of innovation and inspiration. For others, immigration is seen as the root of many societal problems such as unemployment, the sustainability of welfare states, housing shortages, or high crime rates. Although people often overstate the scale and impacts of immigration (see, for example, Alesina et al., 2023), empirical research documents manifold and often unexpected impacts of immigration. Understanding who migrates, what drives their decisions, how policies can help their integration into the host societies, and the impact on the labor market is essential for designing effective immigration policies and labor market institutions and for informing the public debate through credible evidence.

This volume contains 16 new studies that shed light on key aspects of immigration: the drivers of immigration, the factors fostering or hindering immigrant integration in the host country, and the impact of immigration in the host countries. The studies span a wide range of countries in Europe and North and South America and use novel administrative, regional, and survey data to offer insights into historical and contemporary episodes of migration. Together, they enrich our understanding of the determinants and consequences of migration and provide an evidence base for policy discussions.

The volume covers three broad themes. The first part examines the drivers of migration decisions, exploring why people move, and if so, where they choose to move. The second part contains eight papers on the integration of immigrants in the host society, focusing on the acquisition of human capital, labor supply, family formation, and returns to skills. The third part studies the impact of immigration on outcomes that often dominate the public debate, namely employment, education, and crime.

The first two papers explore the drivers of international migration. Ismael Gálvez-Iniesta and Cem Özgüzel examine the extent to which migrants respond to regional labor market shocks across European countries between 2003 and 2017. They distinguish between natives and immigrants and between economic expansions and recessions. Using an instrumental variable strategy, they show that foreigners respond strongly to economic downturns by reducing inflows into high-unemployment regions, while outflows remain stable. By contrast, natives are largely immobile. Their findings point to the role of migration as a shock absorber in the labor market and to the cyclical nature of migration flows. These findings are particularly important for large and diverse labor markets such as the United States or the European Union. When regional shocks hit these markets, the geographic mobility of immigrants can cushion the negative impact of shocks for natives.

The second paper, by Joanna Clifton-Sprigg, Ines Homburg, Anneleen Huyghe, and Sunčica Vujić, investigates how Brexit—the United Kingdom's exit from the European Union (EU) in 2016—affected international student migration from the EU to the United Kingdom. Using administrative data from higher education in the United Kingdom and a difference-in-differences strategy, they find that neither the Brexit referendum nor the introduction of visa requirements had much effect on student migration. However, the imposition of higher tuition fees—a by-product of Brexit and the ensuing political climate—triggered a sharp decline in applications, offers, and enrolments by EU students. The paper highlights that international students—by definition a highly mobile group—are sensitive to the cost of studying. The higher tuition fees, paired with the greater economic and political uncertainty after Brexit, led to a shift in student migration away from the United Kingdom and to other destinations in Europe and further afield.

Although migration decisions are shaped by pull and push factors, what happens after arrival plays a crucial role in shaping long-term outcomes. The second part of the volume brings together eight papers that examine how migrants settle into their host societies—economically, socially, and culturally. They explore what kinds of policies support integration, and what trade-offs arise between working immediately and investing in skills for the future. Some of the papers focus on labor market policies—such as refugee placement programs or tax credits—and their effects on employment and social inclusion. Others look at how language ability, legal status, or marriage shape migrants' paths after arrival. Together, these studies highlight the complex choices migrants face and the critical role of policy in shaping both their opportunities and their contributions to the host country.

The first paper, by Mette Foged, Janis Kreuder, and Giovanni Peri, looks at a Danish policy introduced in 2013 to help newly arrived refugees integrate into the labor market by matching them with occupations facing worker shortages. They use variation in how the policy was rolled out across municipalities and arrival cohorts to estimate its impact on employment outcomes. They find that the program significantly boosted employment—by 5 to 6 percentage points after one year and 10 points after two. The gains were strongest for men with secondary education, while women and those with less schooling saw little benefit. Importantly, the policy didn't reduce employment for other immigrants and had no negative effect on language course participation. These results suggest that aligning integration efforts with labor demand can pay off—at least in the short run. However, the authors also raise a note of caution: emphasizing early employment too strongly might come at the cost of long-term gains, particularly if it discourages investment in general human capital.

The papers by Barry Chiswick and RaeAnn Robinson and Harriet Duleep, Dan Dowhan, Xingfei Liu, Mark Regets, and Robert Gesumaria take a historical perspective on the human capital accumulation and labor market integration of immigrants. Barry Chiswick and RaeAnn Robinson analyze census data from 1850 and 1860 to assess occupational outcomes of white male immigrants in the antebellum United States. They find that while immigrants initially lagged behind natives in occupational status, they achieved parity within about eight years. This rapid assimilation reflects the strong labor market integration of European immigrants in the 19th century. The authors interpret this finding as evidence that the transferability of skills, the absence of immigration restrictions, and the high labor demand facilitated upward mobility among immigrants. The historical evidence highlights how the institutional and economic environment shapes the pace of immigrant assimilation. In today's world, characterized by severe migration restrictions, the upward mobility of immigrants is likely lower.

A paper by Harriet Duleep, Dan Dowhan, Xingfei Liu, Mark Regets, and Robert Gesumaria re-examines immigrant earnings trajectories before and after the 1965 U.S. immigration reform. The authors challenge previous findings of slow earnings assimilation, which they show were based on incorrect assumptions about the human capital accumulation of immigrants. In a model based on more realistic assumptions, post-1965 immigrants show high earnings growth, consistent with a model of human capital investment. The authors also challenge the Family Investment Hypothesis for immigrant women, which states that immigrant women have a slower earnings assimilation than immigrant men because families prioritize the investment in the human capital of the man over that of the women. Their findings suggest that low initial earnings are not indicative of lower quality but rather reflect high returns to human capital investment when skill transferability is limited. Overall, the paper offers a more dynamic view of immigrant success—one shaped by institutional context and long-term opportunities for economic mobility.

The paper by Eva Dziadula and Jorgen Harris turns to intermarriage as an important mechanism of immigrant integration. They study the effects of NACARA, a U.S. amnesty policy, on the marriage decisions of undocumented immigrants. They find that after gaining legal status, recipients are more likely to marry in general, less likely to marry for legal status, and more likely to marry partners from similar backgrounds. The findings point to the broader social impacts of immigrant legalization. Specifically, the authors show that legal status reduces dependence on citizen spouses; financial considerations play a lesser role in marriage decisions. These results suggest that offering pathways to legal status outside of marriage may facilitate social integration and promote more stable marriages.

An important factor for immigrant integration is language skills. The paper by Jonas Feld and Joanna Tyrowicz explores how the linguistic distance between origin and destination countries affects migrants' labor market outcomes. Using data from nine destination countries and a wide array of origin countries, they find that migrants from linguistically distant countries face larger wage penalties, especially among the highly skilled. This relationship holds even after adjusting for migrants' language proficiency and other personal characteristics. The authors argue that employers face higher costs when evaluating foreign qualifications from linguistically distant countries, which limits the returns to education for skilled migrants. Their findings highlight that improving the transparency and comparability of foreign credentials could help mitigate information frictions and enhance labor market integration for immigrants.

Occupational sorting plays a central role in shaping the long-run economic integration of immigrants. If immigrants initially sort into low-paid occupations, this may hinder their upward mobility later in their career. Agnieszka Postepska and Francis Vella document persistent occupational hierarchies among immigrant groups in the United States from 1940 to 2011. Using rich census data and the Duncan Socioeconomic Index, they show that certain immigrant groups—such as Canadians and English—consistently occupy higher-ranked occupations than others—such as Mexicans or Vietnamese—even when comparing workers with similar levels of education. The authors argue that while human capital contributes to occupation choices, the persistence of these hierarchies is primarily driven by the presence of immigrant networks and employers' perceptions of the productivity of different immigrant groups. Their findings underscore how immigrants' labor market entry can entrench inequality and limit upward mobility.

How refugees allocate time between language acquisition and work is critical for their long-term integration. Anna Piil Damm, Ahmad Hassani, Trine Skriver Høholt Jensen, Mathias Schindler, and Marie Louise Schultz-Nielsen analyze how newly arrived refugees in Denmark solve this trade-off during their first years in the country. Drawing on rich administrative data covering language course participation, completion, and labor market outcomes, they find that younger and higher-skilled refugees make faster progress in language courses and subsequently achieve better employment rates and higher earnings. These patterns align with predictions from a dynamic human capital model. Importantly, they show that the early years are key for language acquisition, and that time spent in training trades off directly against short-term work. The findings make a strong case for integration policies that prioritize early investment in language skills, even when that means a temporary dip in earnings and employment.

Tax policy can significantly influence labor market behavior, especially among low-income workers. Sakshi Bhardwaj investigates the labor supply effects of excluding undocumented immigrants from the Earned Income Tax Credit (EITC), using a policy change in 1996 that made a valid Social Security number a requirement to claim the credit. Using quasi-experimental variation in eligibility, she shows that the reform led to a 6–9 percentage point decline in labor force participation among undocumented single mothers—groups previously found to be highly responsive to EITC incentives. The study further reveals that this reduction in labor supply was not offset by other household income sources, thus leading to a drop in total family income. These findings underscore how restrictions on social benefits can produce unintended effects for the children of undocumented immigrants who—despite being U.S. citizens—bear the economic consequences of their mothers' reduced earnings.

Clearly, as we have seen in the first ten articles, migrants are affected economically, socially, and legally by migration, with outcomes shaped by language, policy, skill recognition, and the choice between immediate work and long-term investment in host-country integration. But what about spillover effects in the destination areas? Do migrants affect these communities as well? Much of the current literature focuses on economic outcomes, especially those related to labor markets. But surely, natives are affected in other dimensions, as well. The next six articles explore spillovers. Three articles examine direct economic impacts and three on social institutions.

In the first of thesem Pia Orrenius and Madeline Zavodny explore spillovers in the United States economy. They address how different immigration enforcement policies affect business dynamism, namely the creation and destruction of businesses and jobs. They ask how employer-based policies like E-Verify and police-based programs such as 287(g) and Secure Communities impact business entry and exit rates and job flows. The study also investigates the mechanisms behind these effects, including changes in labor supply, consumer demand, compliance costs, and immigrant entrepreneurship. Finally, it considers whether such enforcement policies have contributed to the long-term decline in U.S. business and job dynamism and why changes in underlying economic churn matter beyond net job or business totals.

The next two articles examine economic spillovers from the Venezuelan refugee crisis, one in Brazil's labor market and the other in Columbia's. The first, by Mrittika Shamsuddin, Pablo Ariel Acosta, Rovane Battaglin Schwengber, Jedediah Fix, and Nikolas Pirani, focuses on the Venezuelan refugee crisis and its effects on the labor market in Brazil, specifically in Roraima, the main gateway of the Venezuelan refugees entering Brazil. It explores how the arrival of Venezuelans has affected employment and wages in both the formal and informal sectors in Roraima and whether these effects differ by education level. The study also asks whether Brazilian natives in Roraima are differentially impacted compared to the overall population and how methodological differences, such as data granularity and control group selection, influence the findings. By analyzing the uniquely high concentration of refugees in Roraima and applying both synthetic control and difference-in-difference methods, the paper investigates displacement effects, changes in wage structures, and potential productivity shifts in the informal sector.

The second, by Andres García-Suaza, Angie Mondragón-Mayo, Alexander Sarango-Iturralde, Juan Miguel Gallego, Juan Diego Mayorga, and Carlos Sepúlveda, addresses several critical questions regarding the impact of Venezuelan migration on Colombia's labor market. It examines how Venezuelan immigration has affected native employment, wages, and informality rates over time and whether these impacts have changed with the onset of the COVID-19 pandemic. It asks how recent migrants differ from earlier arrivals in terms of their influence on labor outcomes and how both groups were affected during and after the lockdown period. The article also explores which native subgroups (e.g., young, female, low-educated, or informal workers) are most vulnerable to these shifts. Finally, it investigates how well Venezuelan migrants are integrating socially and economically, what factors contribute to their resilience against economic shocks, and which mechanisms might help reduce their labor market vulnerability over time.

While immigration influences host country economies, both on the macro level via business dynamism and on the micro level through the labor market, it can also impact broader social outcomes. The next article by Alejandro Iribas de la Puerta investigates whether undocumented immigration leads to higher crime rates, with a focus on Spain. Although public opinion often associates undocumented immigrants with increased criminal activity, the study challenges this perception using novel data and analysis. By combining municipal registry records with residence permit data, Iribas de la Puerta estimates the undocumented immigrant population across Spanish provinces from 2010 to 2019 and examines its relationship with crime rates. His findings reveal no significant positive link between immigration and crime; in fact, legal immigration is associated with a decline in property crimes over time. As the first long-term, macro-level study of undocumented immigration and crime in Europe, the paper offers important evidence that questions widespread concerns about immigration and public safety.

Another social outcome is education. In the next article, Town Oh addresses several key questions related to the impact of international students on domestic students in U.S. higher education, particularly in STEM fields. He explores how immigration influences the academic outcomes of domestic students, focusing on whether the growing presence of international students in STEM courses affects domestic students' grades and choices to persist in those fields. The article also investigates whether these academic effects translate into differences in early career outcomes, specifically starting salaries. Additionally, it examines whether the challenges domestic students face in STEM are due to language barriers or deeper issues like differences in math preparation. Ultimately, the article aims to provide a causal understanding of how international peer presence influences domestic students' academic performance and early labor market outcomes.

In the United States, a sanctuary city is a municipality that limits cooperation with federal immigration authorities to protect undocumented immigrants from being detained or deported. One would think a sanctuary city can help protect vulnerable immigrants and promote trust in local communities, but as Catalina Amuedo-Dorantes and Esther Arenas-Arroyo explain in the next article, this is not necessarily the case, at least for youth still at school. They explore whether sanctuary policies affect school bullying, especially with respect to Hispanic students. Among the questions they answer are do these policies help reduce bullying by building trust in local authorities and encouraging students to report incidents, or do they lead to more bullying by triggering an ethnic backlash? Finally, the article examines whether Hispanic students are uniquely affected, whether increased bullying reports reflect actual rises or improved reporting. In short, it shows how immigration policies can shape school climates and student behavior.

The contributions to this volume resulted from an open Call for Abstracts that elicited 40 responses, out of which we solicited complete articles from authors of 16 submissions. All were then refereed, each by two scholars whose identity was held anonymous from the contributors. For insightful editorial advice, we thank Gaetano Basso, Breno Braga, Justin Bucciferro, Maria Caballero, Barry Chiswick, Daria Denti, Scott Drewianka, Anthony Edo, Katherine Eriksson, Francesco Fasani, Yvonne Giesing, Rania Gihleb, Thomas Ginn, Osea Giuntella, Simon Görlach, Josh Grelewicz, Julie Hotchkiss, Guillermina Jasso, Julieth Santamaria, Claudia Smith Kelly, Dohun Kim, Parag Mahajan, Yuki Otsu, Tyler Ransom, David Ribar, Agnese Romiti, Kevin Shih, Andreas Steinmayr, Steve Stillman, Kevin Williams, Lorraine Wong, Abigail Wozniak, Bin Xie, Diego Zambiasi, and Julia Zhu. This volume would not have been possible without their thorough and expeditious help.

Benjamin Elsner
Solomon W. Polachek
Volume Editors

REFERENCE

Alesina, A., Miano, A., & Stantcheva, S. (2023, January). Immigration and redistribution. *The Review of Economic Studies*, *90*(1), 1–39.

SECTION I

MIGRATION DECISIONS

WHO IS MOVING? MOBILITY RESPONSES OF FOREIGNERS AND NATIVES TO REGIONAL SHOCKS[1]

Ismael Gálvez-Iniesta[a] and Cem Özgüzel[b]

[a]*Universitat de les Illes Balears, Spain*
[b]*Paris School of Economics, France*

ABSTRACT

Workers' geographic mobility can balance differences across labor markets facing asymmetric shocks. However, not everybody moves. This chapter provides the first cross-country evidence on the differential mobility responses of foreigners and natives to regional economic shocks in Europe (2003–2017). Unlike prior studies, we decompose net migration into inflows and outflows and distinguish responses during economic expansions and recessions. We find that foreigners' in-migration rates drive population dynamics and react strongly to rising unemployment, while natives remain largely immobile. Using an instrumental variable (IV) approach, we show that foreigners adjust to negative shocks by reducing inflows rather than increasing outflows but only during recessions. These findings highlight migration's role in labor market adjustment and its cyclical nature, offering new insights into spatial economic resilience.

Keywords: Migration; economic crisis; regional labor markets; employment; labor mobility

1. INTRODUCTION

Geographic labor mobility is key when it comes to dissipating local economic shocks and reducing differences between labor markets after a spatially asymmetric shock. However, not all workers move. As a burgeoning literature indicates, while migrants living in distressed labor markets relocate, natives tend to remain immobile (Basso & Peri, 2020). Therefore, foreign workers' mobility

Migration, Human Capital and the Labor Market
Research in Labor Economics, Volume 53A, 3–35

ISSN: 0147-9121/doi:10.1108/S0147-91212026000053A001

helps labor markets recover and provides stability for less mobile native workers (Cadena & Kovak, 2016).

The migration literature has traditionally measured migrant mobility through net changes in migrant populations. However, this approach has an important limitation: changes in migrant populations can be driven by changes in inflows, outflows, or both (Monras, 2021). Understanding which margin operates is important, as it reveals how labor markets adjust to changes in labor demand, which has significant policy implications.

This chapter fills this gap by documenting the mobility margins through which native and immigrant workers react to regional economic shocks. Specifically, we aim to answer three main questions: Do in-migration rates respond more than out-migration rates to economic shocks? Does this result differ between migrants and natives? And, finally, are these responses symmetric during economic expansions and recessions?

To answer these questions, we exploit the high level of heterogeneity in the magnitude of demand shocks across European regions. This chapter uses country-level European data to provide cross-country evidence on how foreigners and natives adjust to regional economic shocks. Unlike studies that compare the euro area or the European Union to the United States (e.g., Arpaia et al., 2016; Basso et al., 2019; Bayer & Smets, 2015; Edo & Özgüzel, 2023), our focus is not on institutional differences but on the role of migration in absorbing local labor market shocks. Europe offers a useful setting for this analysis due to its relatively low migration barriers and diverse labor markets, providing a useful source of heterogeneity to identify causality. While we pool data across countries to identify general patterns, we also acknowledge the importance of country-specific differences. To address this, we first provide descriptive evidence on the evolution of regional migration and unemployment rates, highlighting both regional and cross-country heterogeneity before conducting the empirical analysis.

We use the EU Labour Force Survey data from 2003 to 2017 to evaluate changes in mobility patterns in response to changes in regional economic conditions, measured by changes in the regional unemployment rate. To account for heterogeneous mobility responses to regional shocks during booms and recessions, we exploit the fact that the timing and severity of the Great Recession varied greatly across European countries and regions. We also decompose average effects by workers, households, and regional characteristics.

We start by providing descriptive evidence on regional migration, unemployment rates, and their interaction with the economic cycle. We document changes in the in- and out-migration rates of foreigners and natives, focusing on the differences before and after the Great Recession. We then assess how these migration patterns influence the working-age population, decomposing the change in population into net inflows of natives and foreigners. During the economic boom, most countries saw high population growth, driven primarily by foreign-born inflows, especially in Spain, Greece, and Portugal. In contrast, during the bust, population growth declined significantly, with native inflows remaining stable but immigrant inflows decreasing, particularly in southern

European countries. We also find a strong correlation between the rise in unemployment during the Great Recession and the reduction in foreigners' in-migration, suggesting migration flows react to the economic cycle.

Second, we estimate an empirical equation to assess the migration response to regional economic shocks. From a methodological point of view, we have to deal with the fact that regional unemployment and migration decisions are likely to be determined jointly. Consequently, unobservable determinants of migration rates are likely to be correlated with the unemployment rate, which would bias the raw correlation. To address these concerns, we rely on an instrumental variable (IV) approach and use a Bartik (1991) instrument that captures local sector-specific changes in labor demand, which is common in the literature (Basso et al., 2019).

We find that an increase in the local unemployment rate (i.e., a negative labor demand shock) reduces the net migration rate of foreigners mainly through a lower in-migration rate while the out-migration rate remains unaffected. In other words, an increase in a region's unemployment rate discourages workers from coming from other regions. However, foreigners who are already in the region are not more likely to leave. On average, a 1% point increase in the unemployment rate of a region decreases the in-migration rate of foreigners by 0.286% points. Most of this effect is driven by a reduction of the in-migration rate during recessions while during boom and recovery periods, the estimated coefficients are not significant. We find that men and migrants with low levels of education account for most of the labor market adjustment. Additionally, the reduction in the in-migration rate of foreigners after an increase in unemployment is stronger in smaller regions and in those with lower degree of urbanizations, especially during recessions.

This chapter contributes to two strands of literature. First, it is related to the body of literature that suggests that worker mobility is an important mechanism for balancing differences across labor markets (Bartik, 1991; Blanchard & Katz, 1992). More recently, a burgeoning body of literature has focused on the importance of migrant mobility as a channel for smoothing spatial differences across labor markets. In their seminal paper, Cadena and Kovak (2016) show that during the Great Recession Mexican-born foreigners in the United States were much more likely to react to local demand shocks through geographic mobility compared to natives. Consequently, this higher geographical mobility reduced the effect of local demand shocks on natives. Similarly, focusing on Europe Basso et al. (2019) also show that the mobility of foreign workers is very pro-cyclical and that it reduces the variation of overall employment rates throughout the business cycle. More recently, Özgüzel (2021) showed that the sharp decline in labor demand led migrants to leave Spain during the Great Recession. As a result, provinces that lost a larger number of migrants relative to the total population saw a slower decline in native employment and wages. The findings and mechanism are consistent with that found by Gálvez-Iniesta (2024) at the national level. We contribute to the literature using an alternative measure of mobility that goes beyond the changes in the net migrant population. While all the aforementioned papers look at the *net change* in the immigrant population, we explicitly decompose net migration flows into in- and out-migration rates and investigate which mobility margin is driving the changes in the foreign-born population. The uneven responsiveness of both mobility margins to demand shocks confirms the importance of differentiating these two possible drivers of population change, which is crucial for understanding the adjustment mechanism.

Second, this chapter contributes to the recent body of literature aiming to understand the mobility margins that drive population changes. Monras (2021) documents that most of the responses to internal migration are accounted for by variations in in-migration rates in the United States. We further contribute to the literature in two ways. First, unlike Monras (2021) who focuses on a single country, we look at several European countries and provide the first cross-country evidence. This allows us to examine whether foreigners' mobility responses to regional shocks vary between the United States and the European Union. Also, by looking at several countries, we exploit the heterogeneity of labor demand shocks over a long period. This gives us the variation that will help us better identify the estimated coefficient and allows us to explicitly distinguish between periods of economic expansion and a recession. Secondly, we document the responses of in- and out-migration rates *separately* for foreigners and natives. This is crucial for capturing the uneven geographical responsivity between these two groups of workers, which has been extensively documented by the literature (see e.g., Basso & Peri, 2020; Schündeln, 2014).

The rest of the chapter is organized as follows. Section 2 describes the data and provides an overview of regional migration and unemployment rates, as well as their interaction with the economic cycle. Section 3 presents our empirical and identification strategies. Section 4 discusses results, and Section 5 concludes.

2. DATA AND DESCRIPTIVE EVIDENCE

We use data from the European Labour Force Survey (EU-LFS) from 2003 to 2017. The survey provides personal characteristics, such as individuals' level of education, labor market status, sector of activity, or job occupation. Importantly, it also offers information on subjects' current region of residence (at NUTS-2 level) and their region of residence one year ago. The survey is harmonized so that it can be used to monitor the labor market situation in European countries. The sample is restricted to individuals aged 25–65.

There are two important limitations of our data. First, not all countries provide information on the region of residence the year before the survey. This limitation restricts our sample to six European countries: Belgium, France, Greece, Portugal, Spain, and Sweden. Secondly, we are not able to measure outflows directed abroad. This is because the survey sample is composed of individuals currently residing in the country where the survey is being conducted. Consequently, if a person is residing in a given country in the current year and the following year she moves out of that country, she will not be part of the survey sample next year. Therefore, the dataset cannot capture individuals who move abroad. The difficulty of inaccurately measuring worker outflows abroad is a common problem in the literature (Monras, 2021; Yu, 2023) and is one of the reasons for which the literature has traditionally focused on net flows or changes in stocks. Therefore, when computing the out-migration rate in a given region, we restrict ourselves to internal outflows (i.e., movements from one region to another within the country). Finally, French overseas regions and Ceuta and Melilla (autonomous Spanish cities on the African continent) have been excluded from our analysis.

We define the in-migration rate to region r at time t as the number of people that live in region r at time t but who were living somewhere else at time $t-1$ (within the same country or abroad), divided by the number of people that live in region r at time t. This rate is then defined for different groups, e.g., foreigners and natives, males and females, college and non-college graduates, and so forth. Similarly, the out-migration rate from a region r at time t is defined as the number of people that lived in region r at time $t-1$, and who live in another region (in the same country) at time t, divided again by the number of people that live in region r at time t.

2.1 A First Look at the Evolution of Regional Migration Rates and Unemployment Rate

We start by documenting migration flows for our sample of countries for natives and foreigners and how they changed over the sample period. Fig. 1 summarizes the average rates for each country, splitting the sample period into two subperiods: 2003–2008 (to capture the pre-Great Recession period) and 2009–2017 (to capture the crisis and recovery period). Before the Great Recession (2003–2008), the average in-migration rate of foreigners was around 4.6%, while for natives it was 1.1%. For the same period, the out-migration rate was also higher for foreigners than for natives: 2.3% and 1.1%, respectively. These raw numbers indicate the well-documented higher propensity to move among foreigners. With the onset of the crisis, foreigners' in-migration and out-migration rates declined. The in-migration rate fell to 3.5% in post-crisis period (2009–2017) while the out-migration rate dropped to 1.5%. This pattern is observed in all the countries, except for Sweden, and it is particularly strong in Portugal, France, or Spain. For natives, changes are less striking. These raw time trends provide preliminary evidence on the key margin of adjustment in terms of labor mobility: in-migration rates seem to be more responsive to changes in the economic conditions.

How important are foreign and native migration patterns in explaining the evolution of a region's working-age population? To explore this, we decompose the change in the working-age population for each region into the sum of the net inflow of natives and foreigners:

$$\Delta\text{Population}_{t,r} = \text{Inflow}^{N}_{r,t} + \text{Inflow}^{M}_{r,t} - \text{outflow}^{N}_{r,t} - \text{outflow}^{M}_{r,t} + \text{resid}^{N}_{r,t} + \text{resid}^{M}_{r,t} \tag{1}$$

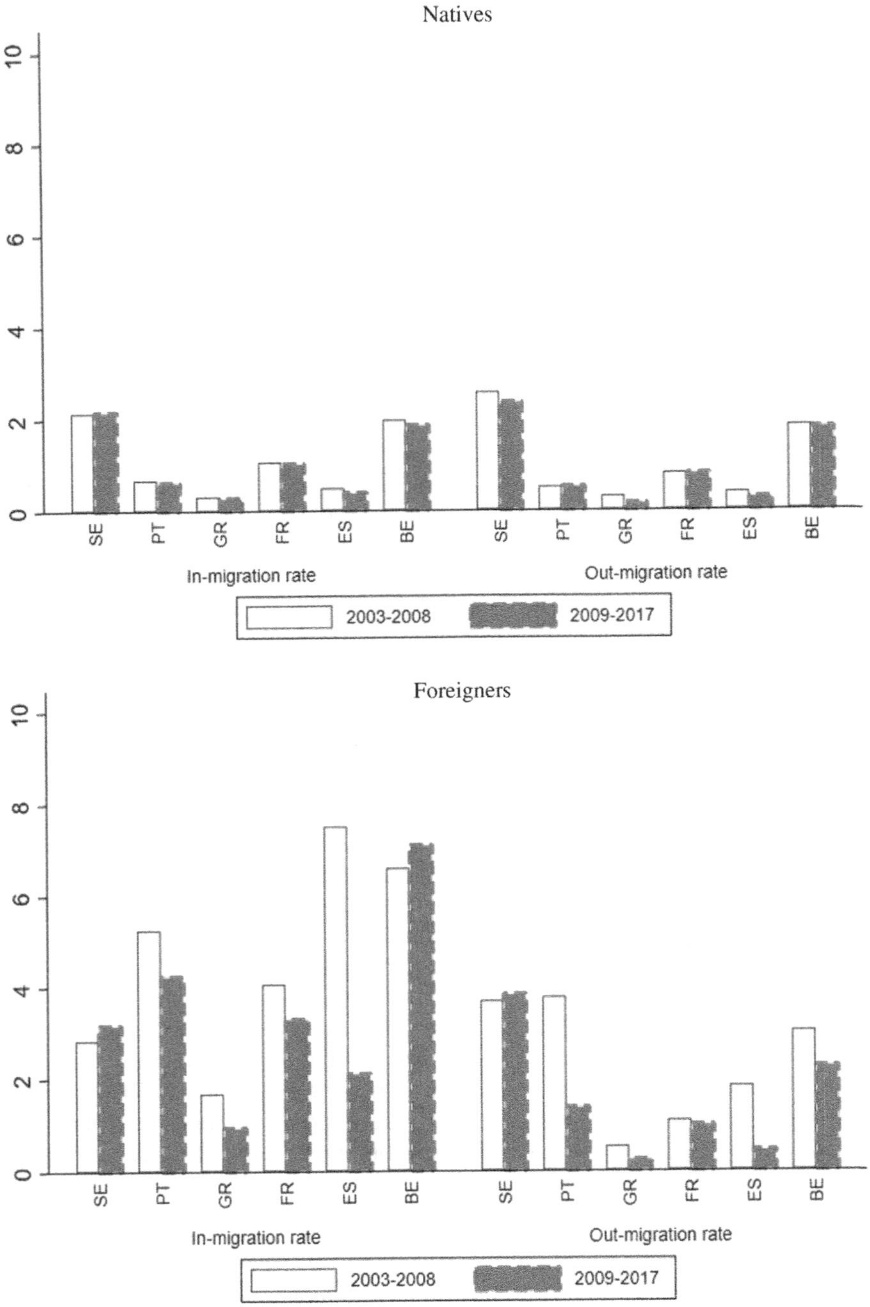

Fig. 1. Migration Rates by Nationality and Years. *Source*: EU-LFS (2003–2017), authors' own calculations. *Note:* The native (foreigner) in-migration rate to region r at time t is defined as the number of natives (foreigners) that live in region r at time t and were living somewhere else at time $t-1$ (within the same country or abroad), divided by the number of natives (foreigners) that live in region r in time t. The out-migration rate from a region r at time t is defined as the number of natives (foreigners) that were living in region in region r at time $t-1$ and were living in another region (and in the same country) at time t, again divided by the number of natives (foreigners) that live in region r in time t. Each bar displays the simple national average across regions. Sample of countries: Belgium, Greece, France, Portugal, Spain, and Sweden.

where the change in population (total, native and foreign) is calculated as the difference between the population in region r at year t and the population in region r at year $t - 1$. The inflow of natives (foreigners) is measured as the number of natives (foreigners) residing in region r at year t who did not live in region r in year $t - 1$. Outflows account only for internal outflows (see the text for details). The residual is determined by subtracting inflows from the observed change in population and adding outflows. Therefore, the residual captures external outflows, aging affects, and potential data mismeasurement.

Table 1 presents the decomposition. To make them more readable, we divide (1) by the total population of region r at year t and we express the numbers as a percentage of total population. We present the decomposition for two sub periods: 2002–2008, which we interpret as the boom period, and 2009–2013, which we consider the bust period (see Table A1 in the Appendix for the decomposition using the whole period). During the boom, most countries experienced relatively high population growth, with Belgium, Spain, and Sweden seeing increases of 0.5%, 1.4%, and 1.8%, respectively. Foreigners played a significant role in population growth in Spain (37.3%) and Belgium (25.7%) while countries like Sweden (6.2%) and France (14.2%) relied more on native population growth. Analyzing the balance between inflows and outflows, we observe that both native and foreign inflows were high during this period, while outflows remained modest. Consequently, foreign inflows were the primary driver of population growth, particularly in Spain, Greece, and Portugal.

In contrast, during the bust period, population growth declined significantly, with some countries such as Spain, Belgium, and Greece even experiencing negative growth. While native inflows remained relatively stable, foreign inflows saw a marked decrease, especially in southern European countries like Spain and Greece, making this drop in immigration the key factor behind the decline in population growth. For instance, in Spain, the decrease in foreign inflows accounted for 87.5% of the total population decline, with similar patterns observed in France (65.0%) and Portugal (12.6%). Additionally, while outflows of both natives and foreigners generally increased during the bust period, the change in outflows was less pronounced compared to the sharp drop in inflows.

To understand the effect of the economic cycle on the estimated responses of the migration rates, in the estimations we split the entire period (2003–2017) into three subperiods: the first before the Great Recession, the second during the recession, and the last during the recovery. Some papers in the literature split the subperiods by years, with 2008 or 2009 being the year marking the beginning of the Great Recession (Basso et al., 2019; Jauer et al. 2019). However, given that our sample is made up of countries that experienced very different economic conditions during the Great Recession (e.g., Spain and Sweden),[2] and because there is a high level of heterogeneity across regions within a country, we take an alternative approach. We construct a dummy capturing the start and the end of the Great Recession: it starts when the yearly increase in the unemployment rate is higher than $\widehat{x}$ per cent (%), where $\widehat{x}$ is a threshold value (10% in the baseline estimation). And it ends when there is a drop in the yearly change in the unemployment rate.

Table 1. Decomposition of Change in Population Between Natives and Foreigners Inflows and Outflows.

	Belgium	Spain	France	Greece	Portugal	Sweden
			All Periods			
Δ Population	0.294	0.468	−0.025	−0.315	−0.193	0.488
Δ Natives	0.190	−0.056	−0.080	−0.456	−0.204	0.177
Δ Foreigners	0.083	0.427	0.148	0.094	0.005	0.286
Inflow Natives	1.846	0.344	0.923	0.205	0.596	2.090
Inflow Foreigners	0.359	0.278	0.145	0.035	0.097	0.151
Outflow Natives	1.573	0.226	0.741	0.125	0.415	2.191
Outflow Foreigners	0.133	0.006	0.037	0.000	0.007	0.141
Residual Natives	0.021	−0.106	−0.139	−0.581	−0.393	0.203
Residual Foreigners	−0.187	0.241	0.045	0.081	−0.108	0.264
			Boom (2001–2008)			
Δ Population	0.504	1.421	0.730	0.287	0.354	1.802
Δ Natives	0.566	0.025	0.598	−0.282	0.081	1.546
Δ Foreigners	−0.033	1.497	0.214	0.544	0.264	0.056
Inflow Native	1.342	0.357	1.039	0.261	0.581	2.093
Inflow Foreigners	0.345	0.530	0.148	0.064	0.102	0.130
Outflow Natives	1.393	0.251	0.840	0.185	0.440	2.147
Outflow Foreigners	0.145	0.056	0.037	0.000	0.021	0.089
Resid Natives	0.375	0.013	0.556	−0.276	−0.095	1.240
Resid Foreigners	−0.303	1.002	0.060	0.486	0.097	0.141
			Bust (2009–2012)			
Δ Population	0.351	−0.282	−0.223	−0.593	−0.634	0.226
Δ Natives	0.422	0.126	−0.374	−0.839	0.148	0.213
Δ Foreigners	0.044	−0.237	0.113	−0.044	−0.300	0.137
Inflow Natives	1.647	0.371	0.895	0.156	0.596	2.017
Inflow Foreigners	0.439	0.247	0.145	0.049	0.080	0.127
Outflow Natives	0.923	0.145	0.670	0.039	0.384	1.646
Outflow Foreigners	0.096	0.000	0.039	0.000	0.000	0.122
Resid Natives	−0.041	−0.029	−0.599	−0.864	−0.137	0.196
Resid Foreigners	−0.309	−0.558	0.045	−0.137	−0.371	0.118

Source: EU-LFS (2003–2017), authors' own calculations.

Note: The change in population (both total, native and foreigner population) is calculated as the difference between the population in region r at year t and the population in region r at year $t-1$. The inflow of natives (foreigners) is measured as the number of natives (foreigners) residing in region r at year t who did not live in region r in year $t-1$. Outflows account only for internal outflows (see the text for details). The residual is determined by subtracting inflows from the observed change in population and adding outflows. Therefore, the residual captures for external outflows, aging affects, and potential data mismeasurement. All components are expressed as percentage of total population.

The left panel of Fig. 2 presents a map showing the change in the unemployment rate across regions before and after the Great Recession, based on the dummy variable we constructed. The map categorizes regions into nine quintiles according to the increase in unemployment, using different shades of gray, with darker shades representing larger increases. The map highlights significant regional disparities in how unemployment evolved during the crisis. Spain experienced the sharpest increase, with most of its regions falling into the top two quintiles (more than a 9% point rise). The southern and Mediterranean regions, along with the islands, were particularly affected, largely due to their dependence on construction and tourism – two sectors that collapsed during the downturn. Additionally, the prevalence of temporary contracts in these areas led to more immediate and widespread job losses. In Portugal, the most significant rise occurred in the Centro and Algarve regions, which also had a strong reliance on construction and tourism, making them highly vulnerable to the economic downturn. In France, unemployment increased more in the center and northern regions, such as Alsace, Haute-Normandie, and Lorraine, where manufacturing industries were hit hard by declining demand. Meanwhile, Sweden saw the most pronounced impact in its southern regions, which were more exposed to international trade, particularly in industries that suffered from falling exports. In contrast, countries such as France and Belgium experienced a more moderate rise in unemployment across all regions, likely due to their more regulated labor markets and stronger social protection systems, which helped cushion the effects of the crisis.

The right panel of Fig. 2 shows the reduction in the foreign in-migration rate, also categorized in nine quintiles. In this case, the darker gray is associated with the largest reduction in the migration rate. Spanish regions lead the reduction in the foreign in-migration rate, followed by Portugal (Lisbon, Madeira and the

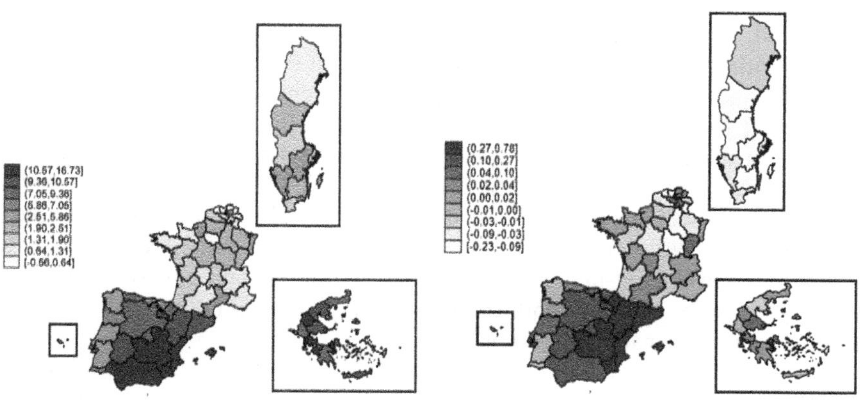

Fig. 2. Change in the Unemployment Rate and Foreign In-Migration Rate From the Boom to the Bust. *Source*: EU-LFS (2003–2017), authors' own calculations. *Note:* The left-hand panel displays the increase in the region unemployment rate from the boom to the bust period, where the subperiods are defined according to the dummy crisis. The right hand displays the reduction in the region foreign in-migration rate from the boom to the bust.

center) and Greece. In contrast, all regions in Sweden fall into the lowest two quintiles of regions with the smallest change in migration rates. The south and East of France (Midi-Pyrenees, Franche-Comté, and Limousin) also experienced large reductions in the foreign in-migration rates, as well as the center of Belgium (Wallonia or Brussel).

A quick comparison between the two panels suggests a positive correlation between the increase in unemployment and the reduction of the foreigners in-migration rates: This correlation can be clearly seen in Spain, with the most affected regions showing the largest reduction in the foreign in-migration rate (south and Mediterranean cost), as well as in Greece. In France, Sweden and Portugal, the correlation is less evident. We will elaborate more on this in the next subsection.

2.2 Migration Rates and the Economic Cycle

The previous subsection suggests that migration flows react to the economic cycle and that they explain a substantial amount of the drop in population growth. It also shows a great deal of heterogeneity in the impact of the Great Recession across countries and regions.

We dig into the relationship between the evolution of migration rates and the economic cycle by exploiting the correlation between the changes in unemployment rates and the changes in migration flows. Fig. 3 displays the relationship between changes in migration flow rates (both in- and out-migration in the *y*-axis) and changes in the unemployment rate (*x*-axis) across 76 regions from 2003 to 2017. The left and right panels of the figure represent in-migration and out-migration rates, respectively. Each marker represents a single region over the period. For foreigners, the left panel illustrates a strong negative correlation: regions with a greater increase in the unemployment rate during the period saw a larger decline in in-migration. This suggests that higher unemployment acted as a deterrent to foreigners' inflows. The right panel for out-migration shows a small negative correlation, indicating that regions with rising unemployment also experienced a slight increase in the out-migration of foreigners, though the relationship is weaker. For natives, the graphs reveal very weak correlations. The change in the unemployment rate had almost no effect on native in-migration, while out-migration for natives showed a slight positive trend, but the slope is close to zero in both cases, indicating minimal influence of regional unemployment on native migration patterns.

One of the limitations of the last figure is that it pools all years, ignoring the possibility that the relationship (slope) differs by the economic cycle. We expect the mobility responses to differ across the economic cycle because foreign-born workers are more severely affected by negative shocks than their native counterparts (Dustmann et al., 2010; Lessem & Nakajima, 2019; Orrenius & Zavodny, 2010). Part of the vulnerability to the economic cycle is also due to the sectoral composition of foreigners. Table A2 in the Appendix displays the share of foreigners employed in each sector over the full sample period. It shows that a large share of foreign workers are employed in wholesale, retail trade, and

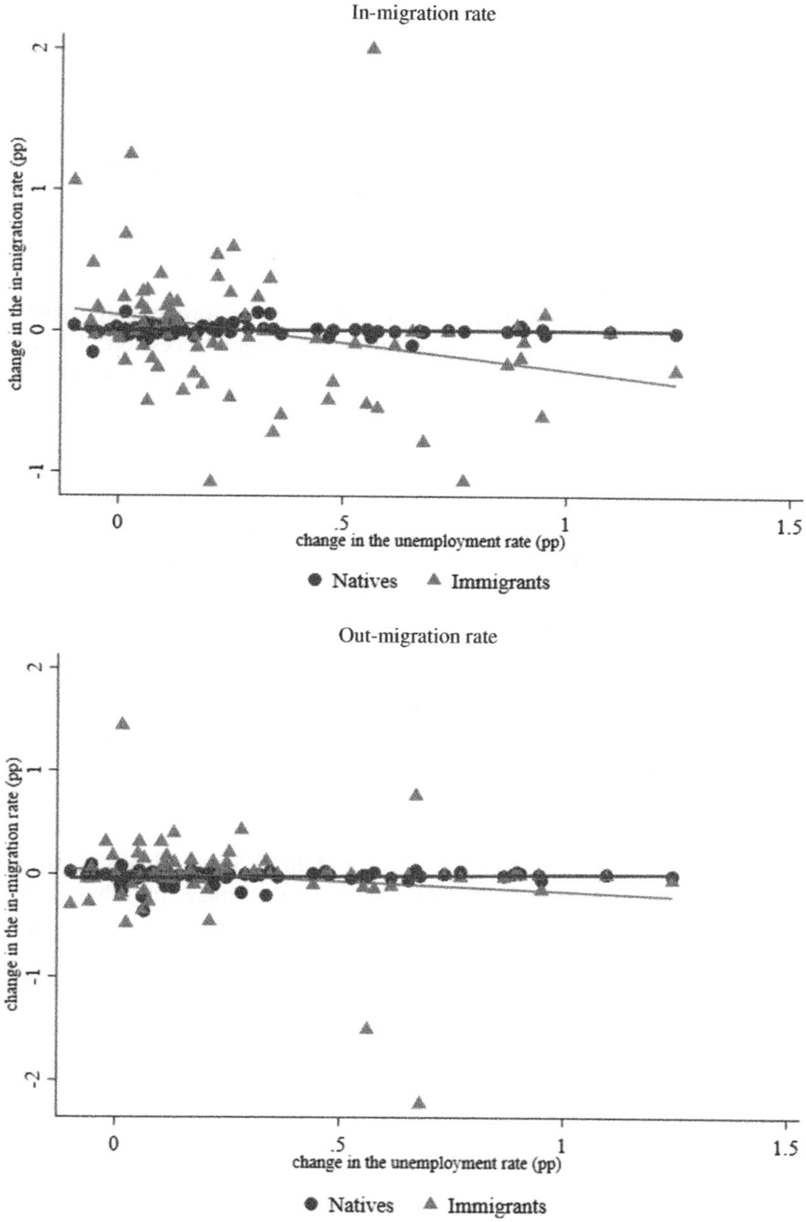

Fig. 3. Correlation Between In- and Out-Migration Rate and Unemployment at the Regional Level. *Source*: EU-LFS (2003–2017), authors' own calculations. *Note:* The in-migration rate to region r at time t is defined as the number of people that live in region r at time t and were living somewhere else at time $t-1$ (within the same country or abroad), divided by the number of people that live in region r in time t. The out-migration rate from a region r at time t is defined as the number of people that were living in region r at time $t-1$ and were living in another region (and in the same country) at time t, again divided by the number of people that live in region r in time t. The scatter diagram correlates the average change of each flow rate and the average change in unemployment for the period 2003–2017. Each point refers to a region. The regression line gives the linear relationship between the two variables. Sample of countries: Belgium, Greece, France, Portugal, Spain, and Sweden.

manufacturing, sectors that are more sensitive to economic downturns, especially in Spain (16%) and Greece (18%), where demand sharply fell during the recession. Similarly, construction and accommodation and food services, closely tied to the tourism sector, were hit hard by the crisis, particularly in Spain and Portugal, where many foreigners worked. The collapse of the housing market and the decline in tourism led to significant job losses in these sectors.[3] These sectoral patterns help explaining why regions with higher foreign employment in vulnerable sectors faced bigger shocks during the Great Recession. Therefore, the responses in the movement of foreigners to the same increase in the unemployment rate may differ from a recession to a boom, as foreigners' labor market outcomes may vary greatly depending on the phase of the economic cycle.

To explore this and exploit the cross-country heterogeneity, we first present the correlations between changes in regional unemployment rates and migration flows from the boom to the bust, separately for each country (Table 2). In most cases, an increase in unemployment is associated with lower inflows of foreigners, consistent with the idea that migrants respond to worsening labor market conditions. However, the magnitude of this negative correlation varies across countries. It is strongest in Spain (−0.48), Belgium (−0.45) and Greece (−0.42), suggesting that in these countries, foreigners' inflows are particularly sensitive to labor market conditions. In contrast, the correlation is weakest in France (0.37) and Sweden, where foreign inflows appear less responsive or even positively correlated with the increase in unemployment.

Foreign outflows also display notable variation across countries. In most cases, the correlation between unemployment and foreign outflows is negative, meaning that as unemployment rises, fewer foreigners leave. This is particularly evident in Portugal (−0.84) and Belgium (−0.60), suggesting that in these countries, foreigners are less likely to leave when labor market conditions worsen, possibly due to constraints or lack of better opportunities elsewhere. In contrast, France (0.29) and Spain (0.08) exhibit positive correlations, reflecting a

Table 2. Correlation Between In- and Out-Migration Rate and Unemployment at the Regional Level by Country.

Country	Inflows		Outflows	
	Foreigners	Natives	Foreigners	Natives
Belgium	−0.45	0.53	−0.60	−0.20
Spain	−0.48	−0.16	0.08	0.30
Greece	−0.42	0.03	−0.24	0.40
Portugal	−0.16	−0.64	−0.84	0.01
Sweden	0.31	0.09	−0.19	0.04
France	0.37	0.14	0.29	0.01

Source: EU-LFS (2003–2017), authors' own calculations.

Note: See notes of Fig. 1 for the definition of migration rates. Each cell correlates the average change of each migration rate and the average change in unemployment from the boom to the bust period.

more mobile foreign-born population. By contrast, native outflows show a much weaker correlation with unemployment across all countries, with coefficients generally close to zero. This suggests that, unlike foreigners, native workers are less responsive to deteriorating labor market conditions in their regions.

To conclude this subsection, we analyze the correlation between yearly changes in the unemployment rate and yearly changes in the in-migration rate of foreign-born workers during the boom-and-bust cycle. In this figure, each dot represents a specific combination of changes in unemployment and inflows for a given year and region. Similar to Fig. 3, this visualization illustrates the relationship between migration and labor market conditions, but here we allow the slope of the correlation to vary between the boom- and bust-periods. As shown in Fig. 4, the average correlation, captured by the slope of the predicted linear relationship, differs across subperiods – displaying a positive correlation during the boom, which contrasts with the negative correlation observed in the bust.

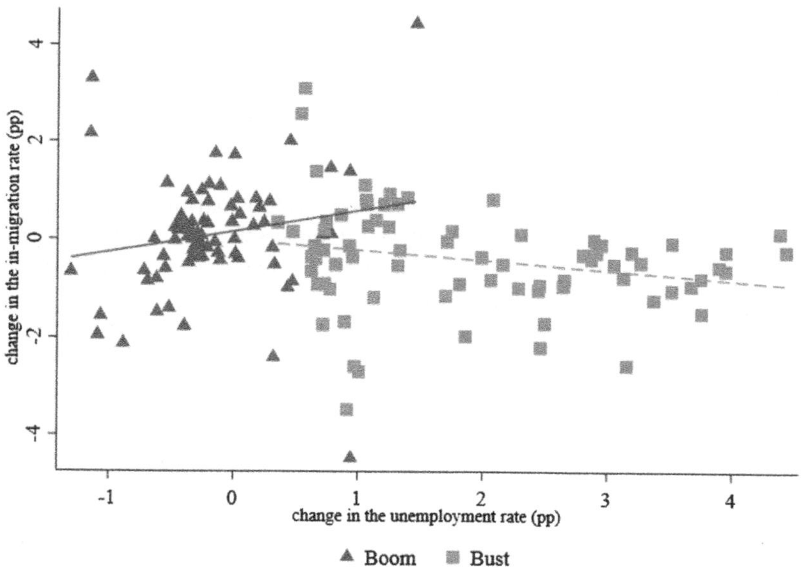

Fig. 4. Correlation Between Foreign In-Migration Rate and Unemployment at the Regional Level. *Source*: EU-LFS (2003–2017), authors' own calculations. *Note:* The in-migration rate to region r at time t is defined as the number of people that live in region r at time t and were living somewhere else at time $t-1$ (within the same country or abroad), divided by the number of people that live in region r in time t. The scatter diagram correlates the average change in inflow rate and the average change in the unemployment rate, for the two subperiods (boom and bust). Each point refers to a region. The regression line gives the linear relationship between the two variables. Sample of countries: Belgium, Greece, France, Portugal, Spain, and Sweden.

3. EMPIRICAL SPECIFICATION AND IDENTIFICATION STRATEGY

Similar to Monras (2021), we use the following equation to estimate the migration response to regional economic shocks:

$$\text{Migration rate}^g_{r,t} = \beta^g \text{ur}_{r,t} + \alpha^g_t + d^g_r + \epsilon^g_{r,t} \tag{2}$$

where α^g_t captures year fixed effects, d^g_r captures region fixed effects, $\epsilon^g_{r,t}$ is the error term, and $\text{ur}^g_{r,t}$ is the regional unemployment rate. The variable $\text{Migration rate}^g_{r,t}$ can be either the in-migration or out-migration rate. The coefficient of interest β^g captures the effect of a change in the regional unemployment rate in the flow rate of that group. The unemployment rate is the standard indicator for labor market shocks; therefore, we use it as the measure of regional economic shocks. Since we construct only one instrument, we use the overall regional unemployment rate as the main regressor instead of group-specific unemployment rates. However, using the overall unemployment rate may overlook potentially uneven effects of business cycles on natives and foreigners (Cadena & Kovak, 2016). To address this concern, a robustness check repeats the main estimation with group-specific unemployment rates, confirming that the results remain robust.

From a methodological point of view, we have to deal with the fact that regional unemployment and migration decisions are likely to be determined jointly: regions with a lower unemployment rate attract more workers. At the same time, an increase in the number of workers, ceteris paribus, would generate upward pressure on the unemployment rate. Conversely, a high-unemployment rate in a region discourages potential inflows and tends to stimulate outflows, while lower inflows or higher outflows can act as a buffer for the recovery of the regional unemployment rate. Consequently, unobservable determinants of migration rates are likely to be correlated with the unemployment rate, which would bias the raw correlation.

To address these concerns, we rely on an IV approach, which aims to isolate the behavior of the unemployment rate that is not caused by the change in migration flows. Following the literature (Basso et al., 2019; Jaeger et al., 2021), we instrument the employment levels of a region r at time t with a proxy of local sector-specific changes in labor demand, as suggested by Bartik (1991). The IV takes the initial distribution of employment by sector in each region at a base year, and it applies the subsequent evolution of the national employment in each sector j over the years, leading to the construction of the following variable for each region:

$$E^{IV}_{r,t} = \sum_j \frac{E_{r,j,2000}}{E_{r,2000}} E_{C,j,t}$$

where the index C indicates the corresponding country and j is an index for each sector of activity identified in the EU-LFS. We choose 2000 as the base year, which is the first year available in the survey.[4] From the instrumented regional employment, we construct the IV unemployment rate as the fraction of unemployed workers predicted by the instrument over the labor force:[5]

$$\mathrm{ur}^{\mathrm{IV}}_{r,t} = \frac{LF_{r,t} - E^{IV}_{r,t}}{LF_{r,t}}$$

Notice that the IV unemployment rate is the same for each group, foreigners and natives, while the endogenous variable is group-specific (Basso et al., 2019). This implies that in the IV estimate, the estimated responses of each group migration rates to the Bartik-type demand shock are different because they are scaled by different first-stage coefficients. The first-stage IV regression can be written as follows:

$$\mathrm{ur}_{r,t} = \alpha_0 + \alpha_1 \mathrm{ur}^{IV}_{r,t} + \alpha^g_t + d^g_r + \mu^g_{r,t}$$

where α^g_t captures year fixed effects, d^g_r captures region fixed effects, $\mu^g_{r,t}$ is the error term, and $\mathrm{ur}^g_{r,t}$ and $\mathrm{ur}^{\mathrm{IV}}_{r,t}$ are the actual and predicted unemployment rates, respectively.

The power and the validity of this instrument depend on its relevance for predicting the unemployment rate in the region (i.e., it depends on the correlation between $\mathrm{ur}_{r,t}$ and $\mathrm{ur}^{\mathrm{IV}}_{r,t}$ and on the assumption about the exclusion restriction (i.e., $\mathrm{Cov}(\mathrm{ur}_{r,t} \times \mathrm{ur}^{\mathrm{IV}}_{r,t}, \mu^g_{r,t} \mid \alpha^g_t, d^g_r, \mu^g_{r,t} = 0))$). The exclusion restriction implies that the Bartik instrument (initial regional shares of employment in each sector interacted with the national employment in each sector over time) does not directly affect the regional unemployment rate, and it does so only through its impact on the regional employment levels. If the initial sectoral composition of employment in a region is correlated with unobserved factors that directly affect the unemployment rate, that would violate the exclusion restriction. To minimize the potential correlation, the ideal approach would be to use the maximum lag periods as the base year for the construction of the instrument. However, due to data limitations, we select the year 2000 as the base, which is the earliest year available in the survey. We ensure that the initial sectoral composition of employment is exogenous to local economic shocks by conducting two robustness checks.

In the first one, we test how much of the initial industry share (i.e. the 2000 shares) is correlated with potential confounders at baseline in each region (Goldsmith-Pinkham et al., 2020). To do so, we run a series of regressions where the dependent variable is the share of a sector in total regional employment at the base year (2000), and the independent variables include regional characteristics such as the share of male workers, the share of college graduates, the share of married individuals, and the share of foreigners. We estimate separate regressions for each of the top sectors in the base year, as well as for the Bartik shares using employment growth rates from 2000 to 2010. The results, presented in Table 3, reveal three key findings. First, the R^2 values in these regressions are below 0.3 for all sectors except the wholesale and retail trade (Column (2)),

Table 3. Relationship Between Industry Shares and Characteristics.

	(1) Manufacturing	(2) Wholesale and Retail Trade	(3) Agriculture, Forestry, and Fishing	(4) Construction	(5) Public Administration; Social Security	(6) Bartik Shares (2000)
Male	−0.294*	0.217***	0.0317	−0.00508	−0.578***	−0.164
	(0.164)	(0.0488)	(0.150)	(0.0678)	(0.170)	(0.203)
College	0.147	−0.0154	−0.324***	−0.125**	0.191	−0.0274
	(0.124)	(0.0370)	(0.113)	(0.0514)	(0.129)	(0.154)
Married	−0.0467	0.0643	0.149	0.0757	0.0893	−0.0404
	(0.160)	(0.0476)	(0.143)	(0.0662)	(0.166)	(0.199)
Foreigners	−0.667***	0.123*	−0.299	0.00301	−0.160	0.423
	(0.247)	(0.0735)	(0.279)	(0.102)	(0.257)	(0.307)
Observations	80	80	78	80	80	80
R-squared	0.139	0.381	0.306	0.206	0.214	0.062

Source: EU-LFS (2003–2017), authors' own calculations.

Notes: Each column reports results of a single regression of a 2000 industry share on 2000 characteristics. The final column is the Bartik instrument constructed using the growth rates from 2000 to 2010. Standard errors in parentheses. Significance levels: $^*p < 0.05$, $^{**}p < 0.01$, and $^{***}p < 0.001$.

suggesting that regional observables explain only a small fraction of the variation in the initial shares. Second, except for manufacturing (Column (1)), the share of foreigners is not statistically significantly correlated with the initial shares. Third, in the regression for the overall Bartik instrument (Column (6)), none of the regional characteristics are statistically significant, reinforcing the assumption that initial industry shares are not strongly influenced by observable regional characteristics and serve as a valid instrument.

In the second robustness check, we use the initial shares as alternative instruments in the first-stage regression (see Table 4). Regarding the relevance of the instrument, Table 4 reports the estimated coefficient α_1 from the first-stage regression for both the baseline instrument (Column 1–3) and two alternative instruments: one in which we also instrument labor force using lagged demographic structure (in Column 3) and based on the initial shares (Column 4). Notice that Columns (1) – (3) use the same instrument as regressor. However, the dependent variable is the group-specific unemployment rates (natives and foreigners unemployment rate in Column (2) and (3), respectively). These coefficients capture the average change in the regional unemployment rate associated with a change in the IV unemployment rate. The estimated coefficients are positive and highly significant, suggesting that the instruments are strongly correlated with the endogenous variable and have substantial explanatory power in predicting regional unemployment rates. The table also presents the F Kleibergen-Paap rank Wald F-statistics for the first-stage regressions. For the Bartik instrument, the values are high, well above the Stock-Yogo critical values, discarding a weak

Table 4. First-Stage Regression Results.

	(1) Bartik Instrument on Overall Unemployment Rate	(2) Bartik Instrument on Natives Unemployment Rate	(3) Bartik Instrument on Foreigners Unemployment Rate	(4) Bartik With Labor Force IV	(5) Initial Shares
$ur_{r,t}^{IV}$	0.749***	0.714***	0.855***	3.256***	2.986*
	(0.0234)	(0.0229)	(0.0631)	(0.375)	(1.534)
First-stage F-statistic	54.20	50.43	55.89	7.00	2.88
Observations	1,091	1,091	1,091	1,091	1,091

Source: EU-LFS (2003–2017), authors' own calculations.

Note: The table reports the first-stage regression results, where the regional unemployment rate is regressed on the instrumental variable (IV) for regional unemployment. Sample of countries: Belgium, Greece, France, Portugal, Spain, and Sweden. Column (1)–(3) presents results using the Bartik instrument. Column (1) uses the overall unemployment rate, as in the baseline estimation (Eq. 2), while Column (2) additionally instrument for the labor force by using lagged demographic structure, and Column (3) uses the initial shares as an alternative instrument. All regressions include region and year fixed effects. The first-stage F-statistic is reported to assess instrument relevance. The sample consists of 1,091 observations. Significance levels: $^*p < 0.05$, $^{**}p < 0.01$, and $^{***}p < 0.001$.

instrument bias (Stock et al., 2002). This holds for both the overall unemployment rate and the group-specific unemployment rates. However, values are low for the two alternative instruments. The low Kleibergen-Paap F-statistic for the share instrument suggests that the initial sectoral composition alone is a weak predictor of regional employment changes, underscoring the importance of the shock component in the Bartik instrument. This result highlights the relevance of using the full Bartik specification, which combines both the initial shares and sectoral shocks to enhance the instrument's predictive power.

4. MAIN RESULTS

The first row of Table 5 displays the responses of native and foreign in-migration rates and out-migration rates to changes in the unemployment rate over the entire sample period. Each column in the table reports the estimated coefficient (β^g) of the variable of interest ($ur_{r,t}$) for each of the migration rate (inflow and outflow for natives and foreigners, respectively. Standard errors, reported in parenthesis, are clustered at the regional level to take into account regional spillovers in neighboring regions. Our preferred specification does not weight by population size,[6] but weighted regressions produce qualitatively similar results in most specifications, as shown in Table A3 in the Appendix. For the in-migration rate (in columns 1 and 2), the estimated coefficient is −0.286 for foreigners, while for natives it is close to zero and not significant. On average, a 1% point increase in a region's unemployment rate decreases the in-migration rate of foreigners by 0.286% points. Given that the average in-migration rate of a region in the sample is around 2.3%, the estimated coefficient implies that an increase in the regional unemployment rate of 1% point leads to a 12% decrease in the foreign-born in-migration rate (0.286/2.3). The magnitude is comparable to that found by Monras (2021) for metropolitan areas in the United States.[7] In Table A5, we show that the results are similar when using group-specific unemployment rates as regressors.

Table 5 also reports the coefficients by subperiods, displayed in rows. It is interesting to see that most of the overall response is driven by a reduction in the foreigners in-migration rate during the recession (third row of Column 2). While for the boom and the recovery, the estimated coefficients are not significant, and for the bust period, the estimated coefficient is around −0.169. For natives (Column 1), the coefficient is not statistically different from zero in any of the subperiods.

These results suggest that foreign-born workers are more mobile than natives, consistent with the literature on labor mobility and adjustment to local economic shocks (Basso et al., 2019; Cadena & Kovak, 2016). Also, the magnitude of the estimated coefficient is in line with those found by Monras (2021) for metropolitan areas in the United States. Similar to what we claimed in the descriptive section, composition effects may be relevant. The fraction of men and workers with low levels of education is higher among foreigners than natives, and it is well known that economic factors are more relevant to migration decisions among this group of workers than women and highly educated workers.

Table 5. Response of In-Migration and Out-Migration Rates to Unemployment Rates.

	(1) In-Migration Natives	(2) In-Migration Foreigners	(3) Out-Migration Natives	(4) Out-Migration Foreigners
All	0.005	−0.286***	0.007***	−0.039
	(0.013)	(0.068)	(0.003)	(0.027)
Boom	−0.022	0.073	0.002	0.093
	(0.018)	(0.188)	(0.022)	(0.125)
Bust	−0.004	−0.169***	0.001	−0.069**
	(0.010)	(0.056)	(0.003)	(0.033)
Recovery	0.006	−0.200	−0.005	0.023
	(0.029)	(0.354)	(0.013)	(0.137)
		Kleibergen–Paap rk Wald F statistic		
All	54.20	54.20	53.83	53.83
Boom	104.5	104.5	102.1	102.1
Bust	45.38	45.38	45.38	45.38
Recovery	34.15	34.15	34.15	34.15

Source: EU-LFS (2003–2017); authors' own calculations.

Note: Regression of the in-migration and out-migration to the unemployment rate, for foreigners and natives respectively. All regressions include region and year fixed effects. Sample of countries: Belgium, Greece, France, Portugal, Spain, and Sweden. The definition of each subperiod can be found in Section 2. All, Boom, Bust, and Recovery use 1,091, 408, 397, and 286 observations, respectively. Significance levels: $^*p < 0.05$, $^{**}p < 0.01$, and $^{***}p < 0.001$.

Next, we focus on the estimation of the out-migration rate. The first row of Columns 2 and 3 provides the average estimates over the entire period. The estimation suggests that changes in the unemployment rate do not significantly affect the internal out-migration rate of foreign workers. The result is robust to restricting the estimation to the boom and recovery periods (second and forth row). However, the point estimate for the crisis, in the third row, is negative and significant. The negative sign of the coefficient is somehow counterintuitive since we would expect higher outflows as a response to a negative regional shock, as has been found for natives. However, several studies on the United States (Kaplan & Schulhofer-Wohl, 2017; Molloy, 2014; Molloy et al., 2011) have shown that internal migration rates are pro-cyclical (i.e., they fall during bad times). For the European Union, Arpaia et al. (2016) document a sizable drop in migration flows after the financial crisis, especially in the most severely hit countries, such as Spain, Greece, and Portugal. Also, in Italy and the United Kingdom, internal flows peaked in the mid-2000s and fell after the crisis.

Several channels may be behind this result. First, emigrating is costly. In the context of recession, where the risk of unemployment and overall uncertainty is high, the decision to migrate is affected (Czaika, 2015). Secondly, notice that our measure of outflows is restricted to internal migration. Several papers have documented that an important fraction of foreign outflows during the crisis were outflows abroad (for Spain, see Gálvez-Iniesta, 2024; Özgüzel, 2021; Prieto-Rosas et al., 2018). Thirdly, the literature has widely agreed on the key role played by networks when it comes to driving foreign flows (Bertoli & Moraga, 2015; Patel & Vella, 2013): networks of foreigners are set up in the regions to which they first migrated, reducing incentives to move to other regions in the same country, especially during an economic downturn.

4.1 The Heterogeneous Responses of Migration Rates

The estimated coefficients from the previous section suggest that the responses of in-migration rates to labor demand shocks are higher for foreigners than for natives. This was especially true during the recession. This section tests the heterogeneous responses of inflows and outflows by worker (sex and education) and household (marital status and number of children) and regional characteristics (degree of urbanization, level of unemployment and size).

Worker characteristics. Table 6 shows the estimated coefficient (β^g) of the variable of interest ($\text{ur}_{r,t}$) for each of the in-migration rate for foreigners (Columns 1–4) and for the in-migration rate of natives (Column 5–8), for each of the demographic groups (male, female, non-college and college, respectively). In rows, Table 8 report the estimated coefficients in each subperiod.

The in-migration rates for foreign-born men and women react very similarly to regional economic shocks, as reported in Columns 1 and 2. For the full period, the coefficient is −0.27 for men and −0.25 for women. However, differences arise when looking at the estimates in each subperiod. In particular, we find a larger (more negative) response of inflows for foreigners' men (−0.179) during the crisis than for foreigner women (−0.101). Also, for both male and

Table 6. Response of In-Migration Rates to Unemployment Rates by Worker Characteristics.

	Foreigners				Native			
Period	Male	Female	Non-College	College	Male	Female	Non-College	College
All	−0.272***	−0.249***	−0.241***	−0.219	0.010	0.005	0.003	0.038**
	(0.08)	(0.07)	(0.06)	(0.14)	(0.01)	(0.01)	(0.01)	(0.01)
Boom	−0.096	0.029	0.057	0.667	−0.006	−0.021	0.019	0.031
	(0.25)	(0.11)	(0.21)	(0.43)	(0.03)	(0.01)	(0.03)	(0.06)
Bust	−0.179*	−0.101	−0.196**	−0.472	0.004	−0.004	0.004	−0.009
	(0.07)	(0.06)	(0.07)	(0.31)	(0.01)	(0.01)	(0.02)	(0.02)
Recovery	−0.505	−0.040	−0.419**	−0.710	0.018	0.008	0.040	0.042
	(0.47)	(0.27)	(0.16)	(0.66)	(0.04)	(0.03)	(0.06)	(0.05)
			Kleibergen–Paap rk Wald F statistic					
All	24.67	28.70	54.03	11.44	24.67	28.70	54.03	11.44
Boom	98.77	52.02	55.99	9.56	98.77	52.02	55.99	9.56
Bust	22.77	21.95	31.97	17.81	22.77	21.95	31.97	17.81
Recovery	22.62	31.00	18.88	7.41	22.62	31.00	18.88	7.41

Source: EU-LFS (2003–2017); authors' own calculations.

Note: Regression of the natives and foreigners in-migration rate of each demographic group (male, female, non-college and college, respectively) to the overall unemployment rate of that demographic group. Sample of countries: Belgium, Greece, France, Portugal, Spain, and Sweden. All regressions include region and year fixed effects. The definition of each subperiod can be found in Section 2. All, Boom, Bust, and Recovery use 1,091, 408, 397, and 286 observations, respectively. Significance levels: $*p < 0.05$, $**p < 0.01$, and $***p < 0.001$.

female foreigners, we cannot reject the hypothesis that in-migration rates did not react to increases in regional unemployment rates during the boom and recovery subperiods (second and forth row in Columns 1 and 2). As before, the Kleibergen-Paap rank Wald F-statistics range is 104–788, signifying that the IV estimation does not suffer from a weak instrument problem.

These results suggest that male foreigners were responsible for most of the labor market adjustment during the recession, and it is consistent with the literature documenting higher mobility and more sensitivity to shocks among male workers (Basso & Peri, 2020). For natives, in-migration flows did not react to changes in the unemployment rate and the result is robust to restricting the estimation separately to the male and female populations (Columns 5 and 6).

Table 7 displays the results of the estimation of the out-migration rates. Regardless of nationality and for both males and females, coefficients are close to zero or close to not being significant. This suggests that most of the net migration adjustment works through reductions in in-migration rates, as opposed to increases in internal out-migration rates. The same result has been recently found in the United States (Monras, 2021).

Foreigners are more concentrated in less-educated groups, and workers with different levels of education exhibit very different labor mobility patterns. To

Table 7. Response of Out-Migration Rates to Unemployment Rates by Worker Characteristics.

	Foreigners				Native			
Period	Male	Female	Non-College	College	Male	Female	Non-College	College
All	−0.080*	0.012	−0.027	−0.079	0.008**	0.006	0.004	0.039***
	(0.04)	(0.03)	(0.02)	(0.07)	(0.00)	(0.00)	(0.00)	(0.01)
Boom	−0.034	0.105	0.067	0.111	0.007	−0.002	0.042	0.003
	(0.20)	(0.09)	(0.09)	(0.28)	(0.02)	(0.02)	(0.02)	(0.05)
Bust	−0.107*	−0.038	−0.092	−0.139	0.003	0.001	0.006	0.037
	(0.05)	(0.03)	(0.05)	(0.14)	(0.00)	(0.00)	(0.01)	(0.03)
Recovery	−0.064	0.193	0.152	0.054	−0.001	−0.013	−0.012	0.055
	(0.16)	(0.12)	(0.12)	(0.20)	(0.01)	(0.02)	(0.02)	(0.04)
			Kleibergen–Paap rk Wald F statistic					
All	24.58	28.56	53.78	11.40	24.58	28.56	53.78	11.40
Boom	95.22	51.22	54.77	8.81	95.22	51.22	54.77	8.81
Bust	22.77	21.95	31.97	17.81	22.77	21.95	31.97	17.81
Recovery	22.62	31.00	18.88	7.41	22.62	31.00	18.88	7.41

Source: EU-LFS (2003–2017); authors' own calculations.

Note: Regression of the natives and foreigners out-migration rate of each demographic group (male, female, non-college and college, respectively) to the overall unemployment rate of that demographic group. Sample of countries: Belgium, Greece, France, Portugal, Spain, and Sweden. All regressions include region and year fixed effects. The definition of each subperiod can be found in Section 2. All, Boom, Bust, and Recovery use 1,091, 408, 397, and 286 observations, respectively. Significance levels: $*p < 0.05$, $**p < 0.01$, and $***p < 0.001$.

examine this further, we split the sample between those who have less than a college degree (non-college) and those who have a college degree or more (college). Table 6 shows the IV results. For the entire period, the point estimator indicates a negative and significant coefficient for the non-college group of foreigners, around −0.241 (Column 3). In contrast, the estimated coefficient is not significant for the foreigners that are college graduates (Column 4). The response of the in-migration rate for foreigners' college graduates remains non-significant in the three subperiods (boom, bust, and recovery (see each row in Column 4). However, the response of the inflows of non-college foreigners to changes in the unemployment rate was particularly strong during the recession and the recovery (the estimated coefficients are −0.20 and −0.42, respectively, as displayed in the last two rows of Column 3), while we find no effect during the economic boom (second row of Column 3). For natives, we find a positive response of inflows to increases in the unemployment rate among college graduates. Two reasons cast doubt on the robustness of this, arguably, counterintuitive result. First, the estimation may suffer from a small sample size. As the fraction of college graduates is small in some regions, the calculated average migration rates could be noisy. Secondly, the significance of the result vanishes when we estimate the coefficient in subperiods, which might indicate that average effects may not be very robust. For college-educated natives, we find responses close to zero and statistically insignificant.

Table 8. Response of In-Migration Rates to Unemployment Rates by Region Size.

	Foreigners		Natives	
Period	Small	Large	Small	Large
All	−0.336***	−0.150*	−0.022***	0.017
	(0.06)	(0.07)	(0.01)	(0.02)
Boom	0.061	0.038	−0.016	−0.009
	(0.20)	(0.27)	(0.04)	(0.02)
Bust	−0.248***	−0.037	−0.030***	0.008
	(0.06)	(0.06)	(0.01)	(0.01)
Recovery	0.690	−0.706**	−0.029	0.012
	(0.38)	(0.27)	(0.03)	(0.03)
	Kleibergen–Paap rk Wald F statistic			
All	141.50	90.31	141.50	90.31
Boom	100.59	104.22	100.59	104.22
Bust	111.01	118.04	111.01	118.04
Recovery	63.19	74.45	63.19	74.45

Source: EU-LFS (2003–2017); authors' own calculations.

Note: Regression of the natives and foreigners in-migration rate to the unemployment rate, splitting the sample according to the region size (below and above the median population size in the sample). Sample of countries: Belgium, Greece, France, Portugal, Spain, and Sweden. All regressions include region and year fixed effects. The definition of each subperiod can be found in Section 2. Small (Large) uses 540 (551), 208 (200), 199 (198), and 133 (153) observations in All, Boom, Bust, and Recovery, respectively. Significance levels: $*p < 0.05$, $**p < 0.01$, and $***p < 0.001$.

Our estimates suggest that college-educated natives and foreign-born individuals did not react to employment changes before, during, or after the Great Recession. The lower levels of mobility and smaller responses to employment shocks seen among natives with lower levels of education were also recently documented in the United States by Ganong and Shoag (2017). They suggest that the rise in housing prices in high-income areas is the main factor that deters the mobility of low-skilled natives. Another factor proposed by the literature is that successful areas enhance local (regional) amenities (i.e., better education, more selective services, etc.) which, in turn, are relatively more valuable for high-skilled workers (Basso & Peri, 2020). This further enhances the cycle, attracting more high-skilled workers, increasing local amenities, and prices, and thereby reducing low-educated natives' incentives to migrate. Why then do low-skilled foreign workers still respond to economic shocks and move toward successful regions? Cadena and Kovak (2016) show that, in the United States, responsive foreigners are those who have recently arrived, and Albert and Monras (2022) hypothesize that foreign workers are less affected by local prices (housing, consumption, etc.) because a higher fraction of their income is used for consumption in their origin country (remittances). Another explanation is the network effect. As explained above, networks largely influence emigration destinations (Bertoli & Moraga, 2015; Card, 2001), i.e., foreigners move to where they know other people. Therefore, prices and other factors may be less important than they are for natives, for whom the enclave theory is less relevant.[8]

In sum, these results reveal that the negative response of foreign inflows (especially during a crisis) works mainly through reductions in the inflow of workers with low levels of education. In contrast, regional economic shocks barely affect the inflow of those with a college degree. This is consistent with Cadena and Kovak (2016), who find that the largest difference in mobility is between less-educated natives and foreigners.

Household characteristics. We now examine two household characteristics: whether the worker is married and whether they have children or not. Table A6 presents the estimated coefficient corresponding to the in-migration rates by household characteristics, categorized by the full period and each of the subperiods (Boom, Bust, and Recovery). The in-migration rates for married foreigners show a more pronounced negative response to regional economic shocks during the bust period, as reflected in Columns 1 and 2. In contrast, we find a bit larger response of in-migration rates of workers with children, suggesting that family responsibility may make them more likely to move during economic downturn. For natives, we did not find statistically significant effects in the in-migration rates for the different groups.

Regional characteristics. We examine how regional migration rates react to economic shocks depending on regional characteristics. We explore three dimensions: degree urbanization, splitting the sample between urban and nonurban areas; economic performance, for which we split regions between low and high unemployment; and size, for which we divide regions between small and large regions.

We start by exploring how regional migration rates react to change in unemployment depending on whether workers live in urban areas or not. Specifically, we create an urbanization index based on the type of area in which the respondents live; the index can take three values: 1 for cities (highly populated areas), 2 for towns and suburbs (medium-density areas), and 3 for rural areas (sparsely populated areas). For each region and year, we compute the average value of the responses and divide the regions depending on whether they are above or below the average value for all regions in the sample.

Table A7 in the Appendix shows the results of the estimation for the sample of regions in the urban category (urban) versus the rest (nonurban). For foreigners, we find a greater response of inflow rates in regions with a lower degree of urbanization (−0.394 vs −0.260). The gap in the coefficient for the entire period is mostly driven by differences during the crisis while for the other two subperiods the coefficient is not significant in any region. For natives, the response of the in-migration rate is not significant in urban or nonurban regions. We can interpret the lower sensitivity of inflows in nonurban areas as a symptom of higher levels of resistance to negative shocks, related to higher sectoral diversification (Brown & Greenbaum, 2017). Higher sectoral diversification may, then, facilitate worker reallocation from the most to the least affected sectors within the same regions. Similarly, these regions, after a negative shock, can keep attracting workers from outside, as their higher diversification might imply that some sectors are still booming, even during a period of recession. In contrast, nonurban regions have arguably less absorbing capacity due to a less diversified economy that is less resilient to local shocks.[9] The greater (more negative) response of inflows to nonurban regions implies that negative economic shocks (especially during recessions) reinforce the clustering of foreigners in highly dense cities.

Table A8, in the Appendix, shows the estimated coefficients for the out-migration rate in urban and nonurban regions. As we expected from the previous sections, we find very similar results for the two samples, with increases in the regional unemployment rate not having significant effects on outflows.

The second relevant dimension of regional heterogeneity that we examine is related to economic performance. For each European region in the sample, we compute the average unemployment rate in 2006 (we take this year as the baseline for pre-Great Recession times). We then categorize as "low-unemployment-rate regions" those exhibiting an unemployment rate below the sample average. We repeat the same estimation as before but we now split the sample based on this categorization. As seen in Table 4, the estimated coefficients indicate that foreign-born inflows reacted more in regions that performed better before the Great Recession (−0.39 and −0.259, for low- and high-unemployment-rate regions, respectively). That is, the detrimental effect of negative regional shocks on the in-migration rate of foreigners was higher in the more dynamic regions, meaning that a similar increase in the unemployment rate (a 1% point increase) may have stronger effects when the unemployment rate is low. In other words, two shocks, that in absolute terms have a similar magnitude, could be perceived differently by agents, depending on the relative state of the economy.

Last, we explore the heterogeneity across regions size. For that, we run a separate regression for regions that are below or below the median population of the sample in 2006. The results for the in-migration rates are reported in Table 8. For foreigners, we observe a stronger negative response to regional unemployment in small regions compared to large regions. Over the full period, the in-migration rate of foreigners in small regions decreases significantly (−0.336) whereas the response in large regions is weaker (−0.150). This suggests that foreigners in smaller regions are more sensitive to economic downturns and are more likely to leave when unemployment rises.

Breaking it down by subperiods, during the Bust period, the response remains significantly negative for foreigners in small regions (−0.248), while it is close to zero and statistically insignificant in large regions (−0.037). This indicates that economic downturns drive migration away from small regions more than from large ones. Interestingly, during the Recovery period, we see a sharp contrast – foreigners' in-migration increases in small regions (0.690) but falls significantly in large regions (−0.706). This may suggest that small regions become more attractive for foreigners during recoveries, potentially due to improved job opportunities or lower living costs.

For natives, the in-migration response to unemployment is much weaker than for foreigners. Over the full period, the coefficient is small and negative in small regions (−0.022), while it is close to zero in large regions (0.017). During the Bust period, native workers in small regions reduce their migration rates slightly (−0.030), while those in large regions show no significant response (0.008). The Recovery period does not exhibit strong effects for natives, with coefficients remaining close to zero.

Overall, these results suggest that foreigners are more responsive to economic conditions than natives, particularly in smaller regions. Small regions experience stronger migration shifts during busts and recoveries, while large regions show more stability.

5. CONCLUSION

This chapter investigates the mobility responses of foreigners and natives to regional economic shocks in a sample of European countries from the period 2003–2017. It decomposes the net migration flows into inflows and outflows and examines the sensitivity of each margin to changes in the regional economic conditions during economic expansion and recession.

Our analysis reveals that foreigners' net migration flows are a key driver for population dynamics in most regions and countries in our sample, especially during booms and recessions. We also find a strong correlation between the rise in unemployment during the Great Recession and the reduction in foreigner in-migration, suggesting that migration flows are sensitive to the economic cycle.

To empirically assess the migration response to regional economic shocks, we exploit the high level of heterogeneity in the magnitude of demand shocks across European regions and estimate an empirical equation using an IV approach. Three main results emerge. First, foreigners are highly reactive to negative regional shocks, while natives do not move. Migration offers promising opportunities to enhance regional development, and it has been noted as a fundamental driver of European economic growth (OECD, 2022). The increased geographic response of foreigner-born flows to local economic shocks highlights an additional benefit of immigration to the local economy; through their higher mobility response, foreigners accelerate the adjustment of labor markets during a recession, therefore contributing to a reduction of spatial inequalities.

Second, these findings contribute to understanding the precise margins of mobility that drive population changes following a local economic shock. Our results show that the decrease in the net foreign-born migration rate after a negative shock is explained by a decline in the in-migration rate rather than an increase in the out-migration rate. The fact that foreigners' mobility responses are entirely driven by a decline in the in-migration rate has implications on the labor market effect of immigration and also on the overall understanding of how local labor markets adjust to demand shocks.

Finally, the results reveal that mobility responses might differ depending on the business cycle. Given the asymmetric mobility responses over economic expansions and recessions, the findings highlight the importance of accounting for cyclicality when studying labor mobility and the adjustment of labor markets.

NOTES

1. We would like to thank Pierre-Philippe Combes and Jesús Fernández-Huertas Moraga for their valuable feedback. The views expressed herein are those of the authors and do not necessarily reflect the views of their institutions. All errors are own.

2. Our sample includes countries that experienced diverse economic shocks during the Great Recession. For example, Spain and Greece, which faced severe credit crunches and housing market disruptions, while countries like Sweden and Belgium were less affected. France and Portugal also experienced significant downturns, with Portugal facing austerity measures and France undergoing a moderate contraction with a focus on labor market disruptions. The variation in unemployment rates across these countries can be attributed to these differing shocks, including credit-related crises affecting firms, households, and the real estate market, as well as changes in total factor productivity (TFP). Given the heterogeneity of these economic shocks and regional differences within countries, we adopt a broad approach that captures the broader migration responses across varied economic contexts.

3. In contrast, public administration, education, and health, sectors that were more stable during the crisis due to steady demand for essential services employ a notable share of foreigners in Belgium, Sweden, and France. These sectors have also grown in recent years in most regions.

4. To the exclusion restriction of the instrument, Jaeger et al. (2021) suggest using a base year that is as far as possible from the period being analyzed. In our case, the baseline year 2000 is far enough away make the exogeneity assumption and close enough to be relevant and have sufficient power (Basso et al., 2019).

5. As a robustness check, we also instrument labor force participation using lagged demographic structure. The main findings are robust, with the coefficient of the in-migration rate of foreigners estimated as the largest (Table A3). However, the Wald test for this alternative instrument is around 7, which is considerably lower than that of the baseline instrument (see Column 4 in Table 4). Also, we believe that, since we do not instrument employment differently for each group, we consider that the labor force participation margin is less relevant.

6. We further examine the role of population size in the next subsection, where we distinguish between large and small regions.

7. In Table A4, we estimate Eq. (2) for the overall regional in- and out-migration rates, pooling both foreigners and natives. The results show that the estimated coefficients are not statistically different from zero, except for the overall out-migration rate, which is negative but small (−0.003, Column 2).

8. If the network hypothesis is correct, we should expect to see a milder reduction in inflows in regions with higher concentrations of specific foreign-born populations. Ideally, in our estimations we could account for the concentration of certain nationalities in each region, and we expect smaller reductions in regions with high presence of these groups. Unfortunately, the variable with the information on the country of birth (or nationality) is aggregated into broad regional categories (e.g., EU-15, North-Africa, Central-America), making it difficult to measure the network effect accurately. Similarity, for sectors, the data are classified at the 1-digit code using the NACE system, which limits the level of detail. We therefore believe that are not able to precisely capture the impact of networks, which could lead to interpreting the findings.

9. The higher sensitivity of inflows in nonurban areas is also consistent with our previous results. In particular, we showed that workers with a low level of education

exhibited higher mobility responses. Given that those workers are more predominant in nonurban regions, the greater response in nonurban regions is not surprising.

REFERENCES

Albert, C., & Monras, J. (2022). Immigration and spatial equilibrium: The role of expenditures in the country of origin. *The American Economic Review*, *112*(11), 3763–3802. https://doi.org/10.1257/aer.20211241

Arpaia, A., Kiss, A., Palvolgyi, B., & Turrini, A. (2016). Labour mobility and labour market adjustment in the EU. *IZA Journal of Migration*, *5*(1). https://doi.org/10.1186/s40176-016-0069-8

Bartik, T. J. (1991). *Economic development policies*. W.E. Upjohn Institute for Employment Research. https://doi.org/10.4135/9781483330006.n10

Basso, G., D'Amuri, F., & Peri, G. (2019). Foreigners, labor market dynamics and adjustment to shocks in the Euro area. *IMF Economic Review*, *67*(3), 528–572. https://doi.org/10.1057/s41308-019-00082-4

Basso, G., & Peri, G. (2020). Internal mobility: The greater responsiveness of foreign-born to economic conditions. *The Journal of Economic Perspectives*, *43*(3), 77–98.

Bertoli, S., & Moraga, J. F.-H. (2015). The size of the cliff at the border. *Regional Science and Urban Economics*, *51*, 1–6. https://doi.org/10.1016/j.regsciurbeco.2014.12.002

Blanchard, O. J., & Katz, L. F. (1992). Regional evolutions. *Brookings Papers on Economic Activity*, *1992*(1), 1–75. https://doi.org/10.2307/2534556

Brown, L., & Greenbaum, R. T. (2017). The role of industrial diversity in economic resilience: An empirical examination across 35 years. *Urban Studies*, *54*(6), 1347–1366. https://doi.org/10.1177/0042098015624870

Cadena, B. C., & Kovak, B. K. (2016). Foreigners equilibrate local labor markets: Evidence from the great recession. *American Economic Journal: Applied Economics*, *8*(1), 257–290. https://doi.org/10.1257/app.20140095

Card, D. (2001). Immigrant inflows, native outflows, and the local labor market impacts of higher immigration. *Journal of Labor Economics*, *19*(1), 22–64. https://doi.org/10.1086/209979

Czaika, M. (2015). Migration and economic prospects. *Journal of Ethnic and Migration Studies*, *41*(1), 58–82. https://doi.org/10.1080/1369183X.2014.924848

Dustmann, C., Glitz, A., & Vogel, T. (2010). Employment, wages, and the economic cycle: Differences between foreigners and natives. *European Economic Review*, *54*(1), 1–17. https://doi.org/10.1016/j.euroecorev.2009.04.004

Edo, A., & Özgüzel, C. (2023). The impact of immigration on the employment dynamics of European regions. *Labour Economics*, *85*, 102433. https://doi.org/10.1016/j.labeco.2023.102433

Gálvez-Iniesta, I. (2024). The role of immigration in a deep recession. *European Economic Review*, *168*, 104814. https://doi.org/10.1016/j.euroecorev.2024.104814

Ganong, P., & Shoag, D. (2017). Why has regional income convergence in the U.S. declined? *Journal of Urban Economics*, *102*, 76–90. https://doi.org/10.1016/j.jue.2017.07.002

Goldsmith-Pinkham, P., Sorkin, I., & Henry, S. (2020). Bartik instruments: What, when, why, and how. *The American Economic Review*, *110*(8), 2586–2624. https://doi.org/10.1257/aer.20181047

Jaeger, D. A., Ruist, J., & Stuhler, J. (2021). Shift-share instruments and the impact of immigration. *SSRN Electronic Journal*. https://doi.org/10.2139/ssrn.3117311

Jauer, J., Liebig, T., Martin, J. P., & Puhani, P. A. (2019). Migration as an adjustment mechanism in the crisis? A comparison of Europe and the United States 2006–2016. *Journal of Population Economics*, *32*(1), 1–22. https://doi.org/10.1007/s00148-018-0716-x

Kaplan, G., & Schulhofer-Wohl, S. (2017). Understanding the long-run decline in interstate migration. *International Economic Review*, *58*(1), 57–94. https://doi.org/10.1111/iere.12209

Lessem, R., & Nakajima, K. (2019). Immigrant wages and recessions: Evidence from undocumented Mexicans. *European Economic Review*, *114*, 92–115. https://doi.org/10.1016/j.euroecorev.2019.02.004

Molloy, R. (2014). Declining migration within the US: The role of the labor market. *SSRN Electronic Journal*. https://doi.org/10.2139/ssrn.2446848

Molloy, R., Smith, C. L., & Wozniak, A. (2011). Internal migration in the United States. *The Journal of Economic Perspectives*, *25*(3), 173–196. https://doi.org/10.1257/jep.25.3.173

Monras, J. (2021). Economic shocks and internal migration. *SSRN Electronic Journal*, 1–71. https://doi.org/10.2139/ssrn.2564973

OECD. (2022). *The contribution of migration to regional development*. https://doi.org/10.1787/57046df4-en

Orrenius, P. M., & Zavodny, M. (2010). Mexican immigrant employment outcomes over the business cycle. *The American Economic Review*, *100*(2), 316–320. https://doi.org/10.1257/aer.100.2.316

Özgüzel, C. (2021). The cushioning effect of immigrant mobility. *SSRN Electronic Journal*. https://doi.org/10.2139/ssrn.3912378

Patel, K., & Vella, F. (2013). Immigrant networks and their implications for occupational choice and wages. *The Review of Economics and Statistics*, *95*(4), 1249–1277. https://doi.org/10.1162/REST_a_00327

Prieto-Rosas, V., Recaño, J., & Quintero-Lesmes, D. C. (2018). Migration responses of foreigners in Spain during the great recession. *Demographic Research*, *38*(1), 1885–1932. https://doi.org/10.4054/DemRes.2018.38.61

Schündeln, M. (2014). Are foreigners more mobile than natives? Evidence from Germany. *Journal of Regional Science*, *54*(1), 70–95. https://doi.org/10.1111/jors.12072

Stock, J. H., Wright, J. H., & Yogo, M. (2002). A survey of weak instruments and weak identification in generalized method of moments. *Journal of Business & Economic Statistics*, *20*(4), 518–529. https://doi.org/10.1198/073500102288618658

Yu, C. (2023). The role of foreigners in the United states labor market and Chinese import competition. *Journal of International Economics*, *144*. https://doi.org/10.1016/j.jinteco.2023.103792

APPENDIX

Table A1. Decomposition of Change in Population Between Natives and Foreigners Inflows and Outflows, All Years.

Rate	Belgium	Spain	France	Greece	Portugal	Sweden
			All periods			
Δ Population	0.294	0.468	−0.025	−0.315	−0.193	0.488
Δ Natives	0.190	−0.056	−0.080	−0.456	−0.204	0.177
Δ Immigrant	0.083	0.427	0.148	0.094	0.005	0.286
Inflow Native	1.846	0.344	0.923	0.205	0.596	2.090
Inflow Immigrant	0.359	0.278	0.145	0.035	0.097	0.151
Outflow Native	1.573	0.226	0.741	0.125	0.415	2.191
Outflow Immigrant	0.133	0.006	0.037	0.000	0.007	0.141
Residual Native	0.021	−0.106	−0.139	−0.581	−0.393	0.203
Residual Immigrant	−0.187	0.241	0.045	0.081	−0.108	0.264

Source: EU-LFS (2003–2017); authors' own calculations.

Note: The change in population (both total, native and immigrant population) is calculated as the difference between the population in region r at year t and the population in region r at year $t-1$. The inflow of natives (foreigners) is measured as the number of natives (foreigners) residing in region r at year t who did not live in region r in year $t-1$. Outflows account only for internal outflows (see the text for details). The residual is determined by subtracting inflows from the observed change in population and adding outflows. Therefore, the residual captures for external outflows, aging affects, and potential data mismeasurement. All components are expressed as percentage of total population.

Table A2. Sectoral Composition of Foreigners.

Sector	Industry	Belgium	Spain	Greece	Portugal	Sweden	France
A, B	Agriculture, forestry, fishing and mining	1.43	3.93	15.98	6.69	2.38	3.07
C	Manufacturing	12.61	13.4	8.99	12.17	12.46	13.12
D, E	Electricity, gas, water and waste management	1.39	1.36	1.64	1.29	1.07	1.61
F	Construction	7.03	6.94	5.46	8.19	7.13	7.1
G	Wholesale, retail trade, and vehicle repair	13.11	16.15	17.9	15.27	11.9	12.95
H	Transportation and storage	5.42	4.64	4.16	3.88	5.05	4.98
I	Accommodation and food services	3.19	6.81	9.63	8.32	3.2	4.0
J	Information and communication	3.23	2.35	1.11	1.86	3.78	1.99
K	Financial and insurance activities	3.83	2.34	1.85	1.9	1.88	2.79
L	Real estate activities	0.62	0.51	0.16	0.68	1.31	1.14
M, N	Professional, scientific and support services	9.79	9.58	6.02	6.75	11.03	10.56
O, P, Q	Public administration, education and health	33.42	26.3	23.62	26.82	33.57	30.78
R, S, T, U	Arts, entertainment and other services	4.91	5.99	3.53	6.18	4.77	5.44

Table A3. Robustness Checks: Response of In-Migration and Out-Migration Rates to Unemployment Rates.

	(1) In-Migration Natives	(2) In-Migration Foreigners	(3) Out-Migration Natives	(4) Out-Migration Foreigners
IV for labor force	−0.024	−0.738***	−0.003	−0.273**
	(0.029)	(0.203)	(0.008)	(0.135)
Weighted regression	0.006	−0.189***	0.000	−0.031**
	(0.008)	(0.057)	(0.002)	(0.013)
	Kleibergen–Paap rk Wald F statistic			
IV for labor force	7.078	7.078	7.004	7.004
Weighting	146.9	146.9	146.7	146.7

Source: EU-LFS (2003–2017); authors' own calculations.

Note: Regression of the in-migration and out-migration to the unemployment rate, for foreigners and natives respectively. Sample of countries: Belgium, Greece, France, Portugal, Spain, and Sweden. The first row uses the IV that instrument for labor force participation. The second row repeat the baseline estimation but weighting for the population at 2006. All regressions include region and year fixed effects. The definition of each subperiod can be found in Section 2. The estimation uses 1,091 observations, respectively. Significance levels: $*p < 0.05$, $**p < 0.01$, and $***p < 0.001$.

Table A4. Response of Overall In-Migration and Out-Migration Rates to Unemployment Rate.

	(1) In-Migration	(2) Out-Migration
All	−0.014	−0.003
	(0.015)	(0.004)
Boom	−0.001	0.010
	(0.018)	(0.025)
Bust	−0.013	−0.004
	(0.011)	(0.004)
Recovery	−0.003	−0.033**
	(0.030)	(0.015)
	Kleibergen–Paap rk Wald F statistic	
	54.20	54.20
	104.5	104.5
	45.38	45.38
	34.15	34.15

Source: EU-LFS (2003–2017); authors' own calculations.

Note: Regression of the overall in-migration and out-migration to the unemployment rate. All regressions include region and year fixed effects. Sample of countries: Belgium, Greece, France, Portugal, Spain, and Sweden. The definition of each subperiod can be found in Section 2. All, Boom, Bust, and Recovery use 1,091, 408, 397 and 286 observations, respectively. Significance levels: $*p < 0.05$, $**p < 0.01$, and $***p < 0.001$.

Table A5. Response of In-Migration and Out-Migration Rates to Group Specific Unemployment Rate.

	(1) In-Migration Natives	(2) In-Migration Foreigners	(3) Out-Migration Natives	(4) Out-Migration Foreigners
All	0.005	−0.251***	0.007***	−0.033
	(0.013)	(0.066)	(0.003)	(0.024)
Boom	−0.022	0.077	0.002	0.099
	(0.018)	(0.195)	(0.023)	(0.139)
Bust	−0.005	−0.140***	0.001	−0.057*
	(0.010)	(0.051)	(0.004)	(0.029)
Recovery	0.006	−0.140	−0.005	0.016
	(0.031)	(0.255)	(0.014)	(0.096)
		Kleibergen–Paap rk Wald F statistic		
All	50.43	55.89	50.10	55.98
Boom	101.8	9.770	99.48	9.539
Bust	37.18	48.06	37.18	48.06
Recovery	31.49	10.51	31.49	10.51

Source: EU-LFS (2003–2017); authors' own calculations.

Note: Regression of the natives and foreigners in-migration and out-migration to the group-specific unemployment rate. Sample of countries: Belgium, Greece, France, Portugal, Spain, and Sweden. All regressions include region and year fixed effects. The definition of each subperiod can be found in Section 2. All, Boom, Bust, and Recovery use 1,091, 408, 397, and 286 observations, respectively. Significance levels: $*p < 0.05$, $**p < 0.01$, and $***p < 0.001$.

Table A6. Response of In-Migration Rates to Unemployment Rates by Household Characteristics.

	Foreigners				Native			
Period	Single	Married	No children	With children	Single	Married	No children	With children
All	0.720	−0.314	−0.650	−0.550	−0.138	0.069	0.078	0.021
	(1.13)	(0.24)	(0.43)	(0.30)	(0.15)	(0.04)	(0.04)	(0.03)
Boom	−0.018	0.277	0.367	0.033	0.097**	−0.006	−0.012	−0.006
	(0.20)	(0.24)	(0.28)	(0.14)	(0.03)	(0.03)	(0.04)	(0.04)
Bust	−0.738*	−0.276	−0.357*	−0.477*	0.011	0.054	0.012	0.015
	(0.34)	(0.21)	(0.17)	(0.22)	(0.02)	(0.03)	(0.02)	(0.03)
Recovery	−0.607	−0.468	−0.691	−0.610*	0.027	0.106	0.047	0.020
	(0.31)	(0.78)	(0.41)	(0.28)	(0.04)	(0.07)	(0.06)	(0.02)
	Kleibergen–Paap rk Wald F statistic							
All	24.58	28.56	53.78	11.40	24.58	28.56	53.78	11.40
Boom	44.56	16.30	48.56	48.96	44.56	16.30	48.56	48.96
Bust	5.40	11.86	17.96	9.75	5.40	11.86	17.96	9.75
Recovery	12.38	21.88	21.95	23.72	12.38	21.88	21.95	23.72

Source: EU-LFS (2003–2017); authors' own calculations.

Note: Regression of the natives and foreigners in-migration rate of group *g* (single, married, no children and with children) to the unemployment rate of group *g*. Sample of countries: Belgium, Greece, France, Portugal, Spain, and Sweden. All regressions include region and year fixed effects. The definition of each subperiod can be found in Section 2. All, Boom, Bust, and Recovery use 1,091, 408, 397, and 286 observations, respectively. Significance levels: $^{*}p < 0.05$, $^{**}p < 0.01$, and $^{***}p < 0.001$.

Table A7. Response of In-Migration Rates to Unemployment Rates by Regional Characteristics.

Period	Foreigners				Native			
	Nonurban	Urban	Low-Unemployment	High- Unemployment	Nonurban	Urban	Low-Unemployment	High-Unemployment
All	−0.394***	−0.260**	−0.392***	−0.259**	−0.006	0.008	−0.000	0.007
	(0.09)	(0.09)	(0.09)	(0.09)	(0.01)	(0.02)	(0.01)	(0.02)
Boom	−0.011	0.227	0.207	−0.031	−0.031	−0.043	−0.025	−0.016
	(0.26)	(0.29)	(0.32)	(0.23)	(0.03)	(0.04)	(0.02)	(0.02)
Bust	−0.175**	−0.164**	−0.194*	−0.192**	−0.006	−0.006	−0.008	−0.000
	(0.08)	(0.08)	(0.09)	(0.07)	(0.01)	(0.01)	(0.01)	(0.01)
Recovery	−0.064	−0.287	0.280	−0.834	0.015	−0.004	−0.024	0.049
	(0.17)	(0.66)	(0.46)	(0.45)	(0.02)	(0.05)	(0.02)	(0.06)
	Kleibergen–Paap rk Wald F statistic							
All	15.54	45.62	35.02	32.83	24.58	28.56	53.78	11.40
Boom	36.30	73.93	49.58	55.71	95.22	51.22	54.77	8.81
Bust	22.77	21.95	31.97	17.81	22.77	21.95	31.97	17.81
Recovery	12.07	20.93	17.00	18.34	22.62	31.00	18.88	7.41

Source: EU-LFS (2003–2017); authors' own calculations.

Note: Regression of the natives and foreigners in-migration rate to the unemployment rate, splitting the sample according to regional characteristics. Sample of countries: Belgium, Greece, France, Portugal, Spain, and Sweden. All regressions include region and year fixed effects. The definition of each subperiod can be found in Section 2. Urban (Nonurban) uses 571 (520), 230 (178), 199 (198), and 142 (144) observations in All, Boom, Bust, and Recovery, respectively. Low-unemployment (High-unemployment) uses 608 (483), 204 (204), 228 (169), and 176 (110) observations in All, Boom, Bust and Recovery, respectively Significance levels: $^{*}p < 0.05$, $^{**}p < 0.01$, and $^{***}p < 0.001$.

Table A8. Response of Out-Migration Rates to Unemployment Rates by Regional Characteristics.

	Foreigners				Native			
Period	Non-urban	Urban	Low-Unemployment	High- Unemployment	Non-urban	Urban	Low-Unemployment	High-Unemployment
All	−0.092	−0.018	−0.075	−0.003	0.010*	0.004	0.005	0.009*
	(0.05)	(0.03)	(0.04)	(0.04)	(0.00)	(0.00)	(0.00)	(0.00)
Boom	0.274	0.002	0.279	0.005	0.018	−0.025	0.030	−0.010
	(0.26)	(0.08)	(0.14)	(0.18)	(0.04)	(0.02)	(0.04)	(0.03)
Bust	−0.087	−0.074	−0.173*	−0.015	0.003	−0.002	−0.006	0.006*
	(0.06)	(0.04)	(0.08)	(0.02)	(0.01)	(0.00)	(0.01)	(0.00)
Recovery	0.202	−0.072	0.102	−0.052	0.009	0.006	−0.015	0.005
	(0.25)	(0.11)	(0.22)	(0.09)	(0.02)	(0.02)	(0.02)	(0.02)
				Kleibergen–Paap rk Wald F statistic				
All	15.54	45.62	35.02	32.83	24.58	28.56	53.78	11.40
Boom	36.30	73.93	49.58	55.71	95.22	51.22	54.77	8.81
Bust	22.77	21.95	31.97	17.81	22.77	21.95	31.97	17.81
Recovery	12.07	20.93	17.00	18.34	22.62	31.00	18.88	7.41

Source: EU-LFS (2003–2017); authors' own calculations.

Note: Regression of the natives and foreigners out-migration rate to the unemployment rate, splitting the sample according to regional characteristics. Sample of countries: Belgium, Greece, France, Portugal, Spain, and Sweden. All regressions include region and year fixed effects. The definition of each subperiod can be found in Section 2. Urban (Nonurban) uses 571 (520), 230 (178), 199 (198), and 142 (144) observations in All, Boom, Bust, and Recovery, respectively. Low-unemployment (High-unemployment) uses 608 (483), 204 (204), 228 (169), and 176 (110) observations in All, Boom, Bust, and Recovery, respectively Significance levels: $*p < 0.05$, $**p < 0.01$, and $***p < 0.001$.

INTERNATIONAL STUDENT MIGRATION: DID BREXIT CLOSE THE DOOR TO EU STUDENTS?

Joanna Clifton-Sprigg[a], Ines Homburg[b], Anneleen Huyghe[b] and Sunčica Vujić[b]

[a]*University of Bath, UK*
[b]*University of Antwerp, Belgium*

ABSTRACT

This chapter examines the effect of the Brexit process on international student migration from the European Union (EU) to the United Kingdom. Using administrative data on higher education students in the United Kingdom, the authors employ a dynamic and a synthetic difference-in-differences (DD) estimator to compare EU to non-EU students. The authors show that the Brexit referendum itself and the introduction of visa requirements did not affect EU student migration. However, the introduction of higher tuition fees led to a large reduction in EU student applications to UK universities and colleges and, subsequently, a decline in place offers, student acceptances, and enrolments. The effect ranges from 48% to 64%. The authors' findings suggest that increased tuition fees acted as a deterrent for EU students wanting to study in the United Kingdom.

Keywords: Brexit; European Union; international student mobility; synthetic difference-in-differences; United Kingdom; higher education

1. INTRODUCTION

On June 23, 2016, the UK population voted to leave the European Union (EU). The result came as a shock and set off a long period of uncertainty. Brexit

Migration, Human Capital and the Labor Market
Research in Labor Economics, Volume 53A, 37–103

Published under exclusive licence by Emerald Publishing Limited
ISSN: 0147-9121/doi:10.1108/S0147-91212026000053A002

represented an unprecedented change in the relationship between the EU and the United Kingdom. Both the referendum and the subsequent exit have had substantial economic, political, and social implications on both sides of the Channel (Ahmad et al., 2023; Born et al., 2019; Breinlich et al., 2020; Carr et al., 2020; Geiger & Güntner, 2023; Oberhofer & Pfaffermayr, 2021). One of the main concerns after the referendum was how Brexit would affect international migration between the EU and the United Kingdom. The United Kingdom lost its appeal as a destination country for EU migrants while some natives and migrants previously settled in the United Kingdom left the country (Auer & Tetlow, 2023; Clifton-Sprigg et al., 2023; Di Iasio & Wahba, 2023; Portes, 2021, 2022).

Besides affecting the long-term migration plans of Europeans, Brexit also disrupted international student mobility. New legal and financial requirements were phased in to equalize the terms of access to UK higher education for EU applicants with those of non-EU applicants. Immediately after the referendum (Phase 1), the future of the right of free movement and residency, which made the United Kingdom a major destination for EU students wishing to study abroad, was unclear. However, no practical changes took place. As of the academic year 2020/21 (Phase 2), EU students were subject to additional administrative requirements since they needed to obtain (pre-)settled status or a student visa. As a final step (Phase 3), in the autumn of 2021, tuition fees were drastically increased (as EU students moved from home to overseas tuition status), and newly enrolling students lost access to the UK loan scheme (see Section 2). As a result, the United Kingdom became a much less attractive destination for EU students. Understanding how Brexit impacted student mobility is crucial. As the second-largest host of international students worldwide (Migration Advisory Committee, 2018), the United Kingdom has long relied on the various positive economic benefits they bring.[1] However, Brexit restricted the United Kingdom's ability to recruit international students and enjoy the associated benefits.

To this end, we examine how the United Kingdom's unexpected decision to leave the EU and the subsequent institutional changes faced by prospective EU students affected the inflow of EU students into the United Kingdom. We consider how the various phases of Brexit—immediately post-referendum (Phase 1), Brexit itself (Phase 2), and the tuition fee increase (Phase 3)—impacted EU student applications to UK higher education institutions (HEIs) and the consequent place offers, acceptances and enrolments. We use data from the Universities and Colleges Admissions Service (UCAS) (academic years 2006/07 to 2022/23) and the Higher Education Statistics Agency (HESA) (academic years 2009/10 to 2022/23). In a dynamic and synthetic difference-in-difference (DD) setting, we compare an array of outcomes for EU students (treated units) and non-EU students from high and upper-middle-income countries (control units) in the United Kingdom. We find no impact on EU students' mobility to the United Kingdom after the referendum or in the first year after Brexit. Only when EU students become subject to higher tuition fees, in 2021/22 and 2022/23, we find that student applications drop sharply (−56%), resulting in a decline in offers (−56%) and acceptances (−64%). The ultimate impact on student enrolments is −48%. Offer rates from HEIs increase slightly and students' acceptance rates decrease. The heterogeneity analysis shows a larger impact on Northern or Central and Eastern European students. We do not find strong differences in other demographic student characteristics or administrative HEI characteristics, such as students' sex, age, or university classification. The impact is larger for students originating from countries with weaker economies and labor markets.

Furthermore, we consider the special case of Croatia, a new EU member starting in 2013. Croatia offers an additional policy discontinuity in terms of student mobility, as we also observe the introduction of free movement and home tuition fees for Croatian students in the United Kingdom. We demonstrate that the introduction of these preferential policies had effects that were opposite but symmetrical to those observed upon their removal, following Brexit. The results are robust to placebo tests, alternative sample specifications, and alternative control group compositions. We ensure that our results are not driven by violations of the parallel trends assumption, using Rambachan and Roth's (2023) approach, or by violations of the Stable Unit Treatment Value Assumption (SUTVA) using alternative counterfactual scenarios. We also perform several checks on the confounding effect of Covid-19, by showing that our results hold when excluding students from countries with strong mobility restrictions (imposed by their own government or by the United Kingdom) or many Covid-19 cases.

Our findings suggest that the uncertainty related to the status of EU students in the United Kingdom and the introduction of EU visa requirements were not considerable enough barriers. Potential students remained motivated to study in the United Kingdom up until tuition fees were increased, illustrating that finances are a primary determinant in students' decision to study abroad. To further illustrate the economic impact of Brexit, we estimate the potential monetary losses associated with the decrease in EU students. We show that the significant loss of tuition fees due to the reduced student inflow can be outweighed by the increased tuition fee for remaining EU students. However, when accounting for students' spending on accommodation and general day-to-day expenditures, we find a large financial loss due to Brexit.

Our study contributes to the growing literature on the implications of Brexit for international student migration. The closest work to ours is that by Amuedo-Dorantes and Romiti (2024), which analyses how the referendum (Phase 1) changed students' willingness to study in the United Kingdom. Using UCAS data from 2013 to 2019 and a DD estimator, they find a 7% reduction in the growth rate of EU applications compared with those from non-EU countries, resulting in a decline in the growth of student enrolments. This result differs from our findings, which can be explained by methodological differences in our approaches. Amuedo-Dorantes and Romiti (2024) have more detailed data on the studied subjects and chosen institutions by applicants while we use more comparable origin countries and a synthetic DD. The impact is larger for students applying for Science, Technology, Engineering or Mathematics subjects, and, similar to us, they find larger responses among students originating from countries with weaker economies and employment prospects. The authors do not examine whether the changing growth rate translates into changing levels of EU students in the United Kingdom. They also do not examine the actual Brexit and its associated introduction of visa requirements (Phase 2) and increased tuition fees (Phase 3). Falkingham et al. (2021) examine the effect of triggering Article 50 (the official start of Brexit negotiations) on international students' return intentions. Using the Survey of Graduating International Students, they distinguish between graduate and postgraduate final-year students from EU and non-EU countries. Using a DD approach, they find that EU students are more likely to plan on leaving the United Kingdom after graduation than non-EU students. However, the decision of students who had already decided to stay did not change. Di Iasio and Wahba (2023) use a similar strategy to estimate the referendum's effect on overall migration flows between the United Kingdom and the EU, using the Long-Term International Migration estimates and Labour Force Survey. They find a large impact on work-motivated migration flows. When focusing particularly on movements motivated by study, they find no significant effect on the flow of EU students entering the United Kingdom or British students leaving their country. Finally, Davies and Specht (2024) predict the long-term impact of Brexit using a structural gravity model. Using aggregate bilateral data on inbound foreign student stocks from 2003 to 2015, they employ a general equilibrium approach. They model different counterfactual scenarios in which Brexit represents an additional cost for students migrating between the EU and the United Kingdom. They do not make the distinction between different potential mechanisms or policy changes. The authors predict a large drop in EU students in the United Kingdom (−20% to −40%) and a decline in British students studying abroad.[2]

In addition, our study relates to the broader literature on the determinants of student mobility (Beine et al., 2014; Kahanec & Králiková, 2011; Rosenzweig, 2008), particularly on the role of policy and institutional factors. Studies on the role of visa regulation and administrative requirements focus mainly on visa restrictions after graduation (i.e., labor market openness) (Kato & Sparber, 2013; Shih, 2015). The literature on the role of credit constraints is richer and relies mainly on tuition and grant reforms (Dwenger et al., 2012; Nielsen et al., 2010; Van der Klaauw, 2002), loan accessibility cut-offs (Solis, 2017), or experimental settings (Burland et al., 2023; Dynarski, 2003). Most studies find that credit constraints play an important role; only a few remain ambiguous on the role of education fees in the decision to study (Beine et al., 2014; Wakeling & Jefferies, 2013). For the United Kingdom, most notably, Dearden et al. (2014) find that the re-introduction of maintenance grants for low-income students had a positive effect on attendance rates at HEIs (a 3.95 percentage points (pp) increase in attendance for a £1,000 increase in aid). Considering a tuition fee reform in England, Sá (2019) finds that the fee increase negatively affected applications (price elasticity of −0.11) and attendance rates (a 0.23 pp increase for a £1,000 increase in tuition). These studies, however, only consider domestic students.

Our contribution is fourfold. First, we study the effect of the complete Brexit process (from the referendum (Phase 1) to the changing visa requirements (Phase 2) and increased tuition fees (Phase 3)) on the inflow of EU students into the United Kingdom. This allows us to consider separately and in conjunction the role that increased legal requirements and tuition fees played in the decline in post-Brexit international students at UK HEIs. We bridge various strands of literature on student mobility, which typically consider one factor at a time. Second, we provide new insights into the determinants of migrants' study choices. By exploiting the various policy changes throughout the Brexit process, we show that tuition fees are a primary determinant of EU student mobility. To our knowledge, we are the first to show that financial constraints rather than visa restrictions are the main drivers of the Brexit effect. Third, using Croatia's accession to the EU prior to Brexit, we show that the effects of lifting and introducing access restrictions to UK HEIs were relatively symmetric. Fourth, we illustrate the importance of international recruitment by estimating the monetary losses associated with the Brexit-induced reduction in international students.

The chapter is structured as follows. Section 2 provides background information on the relevant regulations for international students in the United Kingdom and the policy implications of Brexit. Section 3 presents the data and descriptive statistics. Section 4 discusses the empirical strategy, followed by the empirical results in Section 5. Section 6 shows that our results hold throughout a set of robustness checks, and in Section 7, we calculate the monetary loss due to the decreased inflow of EU students. Section 8 concludes the chapter with a brief discussion.

2. STUDYING IN THE UNITED KINGDOM FOR EU AND NON-EU STUDENTS

2.1 Before the Referendum (Phase 0)

Prior to Brexit, students from the EU, European Economic Area (EEA), and Switzerland (hereinafter referred to as EU students) benefited from freedom of movement and were entitled to study at any UK university or college under the same conditions as home students. Non-EU students, on the other hand, were subject to several additional regulations and requirements. This had several consequences.

First, EU and non-EU students were subject to varying tuition fees, as HEIs differentiated between overseas and home tuition fees. At the undergraduate level, home fees have long been capped. While universities can charge below the tuition fee cap, most of them charge the maximum (Hubble & Bolton, 2018). Caps on home fees for full-time undergraduate courses range between £1,820 and £9,250, depending on the UK country. Additionally, home students in Wales can receive grants to cover their costs and home students in Scotland can have their tuition fees paid for by the Student Award Agency Scotland, resulting in free higher education (Hubble & Bolton, 2018; Lewis, 2023a,b, 2024). Overseas fees for non-EU undergraduate students have never been capped and are determined by providers. Fees vary from £11,400 to £38,000, with an estimated average cost of around £22,200 per year (British Council, 2023). At the postgraduate level, there is no cap and fees vary widely. Home fees are on average around £11,000 per year (UCAS, 2023c) while international tuition fees tend to be higher, with an average estimated around £17,109 per year (British Council, 2023). Further information on UK tuition fees is provided in Appendix A1.1.

Second, as a result of the lower, subsidized tuition fees, HEIs have over time been restricted in the number of home fee (i.e., UK students and pre-Brexit EU students) undergraduate students they could recruit. An admission cap was first introduced in the 1990s in England. Between the academic years 2012/13 and 2014/15, this restriction was relaxed, until the cap was abolished in 2015/16. In the following years, UK universities were free to recruit as many UK and EU-domiciled students as they wanted to. Non-EU students were never under any quota control as they were subject to higher overseas fees (Hillman, 2020). After Brexit, limiting student admissions from both EU and non-EU origin countries became a topic of debate. Admission caps have been proposed with the aim of stabilizing student admissions, dampening competition between universities, or bringing down net migration. However, at the time of writing, no cap has been formally introduced. Further information on UK admission caps is provided in Appendix A1.2.

Finally, EU and non-EU students had differing visa regulations before Brexit. EU students were free to study in the United Kingdom without any passport or visa requirements while non-EU students had to apply for a Tier-4 Student or Tier-5 Short-term Study visa (Gower, 2018). To obtain the study visa, students had to provide a "Confirmation of Acceptance for Studies" from a recognized education institution, hold a valid passport, prove they could support themselves financially, show sufficient knowledge of English, and pay an application fee (UK Home Office, 2023a). Students had restrictions on how long they could stay in the United Kingdom, whether they were allowed to bring dependents, and how much they were permitted to work outside of their studies. Over time, these UK policies on non-EU student mobility have only slightly changed. Only minor adaptations to the Tier-4 student visa were introduced, which generally facilitated the applications. In 2020, at the time of Brexit, the various Visa Tiers were replaced by visa routes. These routes would supposedly simplify the visa regime, and although this included reforms in certain areas, nothing much changed regarding student visas. The only main difference is that now both EU and non-EU citizens fell under the visa regulations (UK Home Office, 2023a). Appendix A2 provides a more detailed summary of relevant policy changes for foreign students in the United Kingdom.

2.2 Brexit Referendum and Brexit Process (Phases 1–3)

The UK referendum on EU membership, i.e., the Brexit referendum, was held in the United Kingdom on June 23, 2016, to determine whether the country should remain an EU member state. The Conservative Party had pledged to hold such a referendum in their 2015 election campaign, and the first plans were made after their victory in the General Election of May 2015. The official campaign period began in February 2016 and highlighted various issues such as sovereignty, immigration, and trade opportunities. The Leave campaign particularly emphasized the need to take control over the United Kingdom's borders and limit free movement within the EU (Joppke, 2020). The referendum had a high turnout (72.2%) and ended with an unexpected result; nearly 52% of voters elected to leave the EU. The Leave campaign won by a margin of approximately 1.3 million votes. In March 2017, the United Kingdom triggered Article 50. This gave formal notification of the United Kingdom's intention to leave the EU and officially initiated the withdrawal process. The long and difficult negotiations began. After postponing the withdrawal deadline several times, a Withdrawal Agreement was finally reached near the end of 2019. The United Kingdom officially left the EU on January 31, 2020, which was followed by a transition period until December 31, 2020 (Walker, 2021).

After the transition period, the freedom of movement between the EU and the United Kingdom ended and entry requirements for EU citizens changed. Fig. 1 provides a schematic overview of the changing requirements faced by EU students in the United Kingdom. We describe each phase of the Brexit process in turn below.

2.2.1 *Phase 1 (Post-referendum)*

The referendum did not change any entry requirements (British Council, 2021; Universities UK, 2021). EU students were able to study in the United Kingdom under the same conditions as UK students. However, the referendum did cause uncertainty about EU students' future in the United Kingdom and may have caused migrants to perceive the United Kingdom as a less welcoming place.

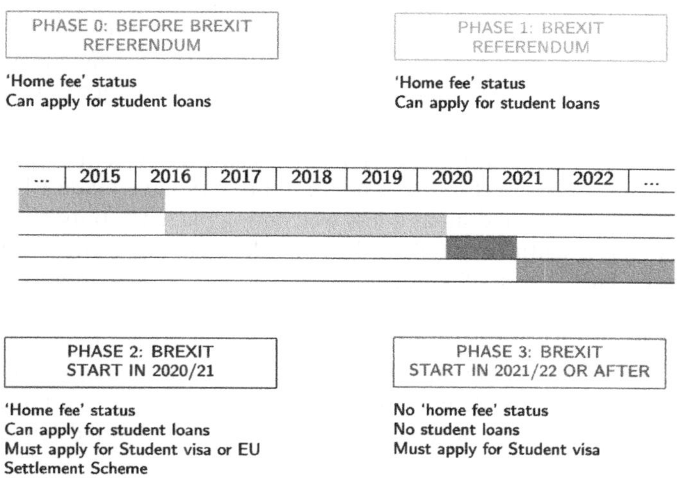

Fig. 1. Changing Requirements for EU Students. *Notes:* Composed by the authors based on British Council (2021); Citizens Information (2021); Universities UK (2021).

2.2.2 Phase 2 (Legal Requirements)

Students who started their degree in the academic year 2020/21 were part of the second phase. During this period, nothing changed concerning tuition fees. EU students could still enjoy the home tuition status and remained eligible for the other benefits. Students of this cohort, however, had additional administrative requirements. Those who arrived in the United Kingdom before December 31, 2020, could apply for the EU Settlement Scheme. The EU Settlement Scheme is a UK government program designed to allow EU citizens and their family members to continue living and working in the United Kingdom after Brexit. Under the Settlement Scheme, eligible EU citizens who were UK residents before the end of the transition period (December 31, 2020) were able to apply for settled or presettled status. The settled status grants the right to stay in the United Kingdom indefinitely, while presettled status allows EU citizens to stay in the United Kingdom for up to five years, after which they can apply for settled status. This means that EU students could stay in the United Kingdom for their studies without the need to apply for a visa after the transition period (Universities UK, 2021). Those that arrived after December 31, 2020, could no longer apply for the EU Settlement Scheme. Similar to non-EU students, they needed to acquire a student visa and were eligible to apply for the Graduate route. This Graduate visa makes it possible for EU and non-EU students to study in the United Kingdom and stay for two years after graduation. If they find employment upon graduation, they can switch to the work route (Universities UK, 2021).

2.2.3 Phase 3 (Higher Tuition Fees)

In the last phase, the favorable requirements for EU students had completely faded. All EU students who started in the academic year of 2021/22 or later were subject to the same higher overseas tuition fees and stricter visa and immigration requirements as non-EU students. Additionally, they were no longer eligible for student loans (British Council, 2021, 2023; Universities UK, 2021).

To summarize, the Brexit process may have affected international student mobility in several ways. First, the referendum may have made EU students perceive the United Kingdom as a less welcoming place to study as a result of both the anti-EU sentiments reflected during the campaigns and the increased uncertainty. The status of students and their families would be insecure during their studies and after graduation. Second, after Brexit, EU students faced increased administrative procedures and legal requirements. Lastly, they suffered negative economic consequences through increased tuition fees and loss of access to student loans (Falkingham et al., 2021). Overall, this likely made EU students more hesitant to study in the United Kingdom.

3. DATA AND DESCRIPTIVE STATISTICS

3.1 Data Description

First, we use publicly available administrative data from UCAS, running from the academic years 2006/07 to 2022/23. As the managing institution of applications to undergraduate courses, the UCAS publishes data on student applications, admissions, and acceptances to HEIs in the United Kingdom. The data provide information on all full-time undergraduate UK and non-UK students in England, Northern Ireland, and Wales. The data focus on first-degree[3] and only some sub-degree courses; most sub-degree courses are not processed by UCAS. For Scotland, applications for colleges providing school-level qualifications, university entrance qualifications, or more vocational courses are not included, which encompasses around one-third of undergraduates. The UCAS data include information on students' personal characteristics (origin country, age, and sex) and time of applying. The data do not include any information on the specific courses or universities (UCAS, 2022, 2023a,d,e). We obtain five outcome variables from this source: international student applications to UK higher education providers, offers to international students, offer rates (share of offers compared to total applications from a given origin country), international students' acceptances, and acceptance rates (share of accepted offers compared to total applicants from a given origin country).[4]

Second, we obtain statistics on enrollment into HEIs from HESA. HESA provides annual data on the registration of non-UK-domiciled students at universities, colleges, and other higher education providers, from the academic years 2009/10 to 2022/23. We do not use data from earlier years, as these have incomplete information on students' origin country. The administrative dataset contains information on students' country of origin, level of study (undergraduate/postgraduate), mode of study (full-time/part-time), and detailed information on the HEIs. Compared to the UCAS data, the enrollment data are more comprehensive in the sense that they also include part-time students, postgraduate students, and students who applied directly to the institutions. The data, however, only include numbers from publicly funded higher education providers (HESA, 2023c, 2024).[5]

3.2 Descriptive Statistics

Table 1 summarizes the composition of international students in the United Kingdom before the referendum. It provides the yearly mean outcome variables, by the various regions of origin of migrant students. It only includes students from origin countries in our specific sample (see Section 4 for further information). Most students come from Asia, with yearly 104,350 applications and 93,807 enrolments on average. Within this group, China is the most frequent origin country. Besides Asia, many international students originate from within the EU, with the majority coming from Southern (yearly 42,885 undergraduate applications and 28,209 total enrolments) and Western Europe (yearly 39,586 undergraduate applications and 25,376 total enrolments). The remaining

Table 1. Descriptive Statistics on Student Outcomes in the United Kingdom by Origin Region.

	(1) Applications	(2) Offers	(3) Offer Rate (%)	(4) Acceptances	(5) Acceptance Rate (%)	(6) Enrolments
	Mean	Mean	Mean	Mean	Mean	Mean
Northern Europe	24,023	13,302	55.5	3,256	59.0	9,486
Central and Eastern Europe	32,820	20,877	62.8	4,835	65.9	15,197
Southern Europe	42,885	24,653	57.0	6,153	66.2	28,209
Western Europe	39,586	22,064	56.0	6,241	63.4	25,376
Other EEA and Schengen	11,008	6,960	62.9	1,703	65.8	5,366
Other Europe and Central Asia	9,833	6,516	66.1	1,354	64.5	7,154
Asia	104,350	69,544	66.8	16,167	71.1	93,807
Oceania and Pacific Islands	1,935	829	43.1	204	39.4	1,614
Middle East and North Africa	13,969	7,462	53.5	1,886	60.0	15,053
Sub-Saharan Africa	4,417	2,548	57.5	569	55.8	2,339
North America	18,653	9,007	48.3	2,398	48.2	15,850
Latin America and Caribbean	5,244	2,687	51.4	630	51.4	5,492

Notes: Authors' estimations based on UCAS (2006/07–2015/16) and HESA (2009/10–2015/16) data. The table shows the yearly mean per origin region for each outcome variable for the pre-referendum period.

students most commonly arrive from North America or the Middle East and North Africa. Interestingly, we find the largest offer rate and consequent acceptance rate for students originating from Asian and other European non-EU countries, likely indicating stronger self-selection from these origins. These summary statistics are in line with the composition of all international students in the United Kingdom (see for example HESA, 2023a).

Next, Table 2 reports summary statistics (yearly mean per origin country) of the outcome variables before the referendum (Phase 0, 2006/07 to 2015/16), in between the referendum and Brexit (Phase 1, 2016/17 to 2019/20), and after Brexit (Phases 2 and 3, 2020/21 to 2022/23). The outcomes are reported separately for EU and non-EU countries. Before the referendum, the majority of higher education applications came from EU students. Consequently, an average EU country accounts for more offers, acceptances, and enrolments. The offer and acceptance rates are also higher for EU students. After the Brexit vote, both EU and non-EU outcomes increased, although only significantly for EU students. This upward trend for both EU and non-EU students has been documented before and is in line with other sources (Migration Observatory, 2022). After Brexit, we observe a clear break in existing trends as EU numbers decrease while numbers for non-EU students remain relatively stable.

Table 2. Descriptive Statistics on EU and Non-EU Student Outcomes in the United Kingdom.

		(1)		(2)		(3)		(4)	(5)
		Before Referendum		Referendum – Brexit		After Brexit		Diff.	Diff.
		Mean	Sd	Mean	Sd	Mean	Sd	(2)-(1)	(3)-(2)
Applications	EU	5,183	4,863	7,264	6,358	4,713	5,107	2,081**	−2,551**
	non-EU	1,864	5,441	2,677	8,409	3,663	14,366	813	986
Offers	EU	3,029	2,949	4,756	4,212	3,082	3,403	1,726***	−1,674**
	non-EU	1,160	3,657	1,749	5,794	2,224	8,957	589	475
Offer rate (%)	EU	55	12	62	13	63	11	7***	1
	non-EU	42	26	48	25	47	24	6***	−1
Acceptances	EU	765	743	1,066	908	649	756	301**	−416***
	non-EU	273	882	353	1,219	457	1,917	80	104
Acceptance rate (%)	EU	57	14	58	13	51	14	1	−8***
	non-EU	32	28	32	26	30	25	−0	−1
Enrolments (undergr.)	EU	2,662	2,412	3,286	2,854	2,893	2,755	624*	−393
	non-EU	1,226	4,444	1,517	5,873	1,722	1,226	4,444	1,517
Enrolments (postgr.)	EU	1,392	1,764	1,360	1,806	1,064	1,383	−32	−295
	non-EU	1,127	4,755	1,396	7,346	1,664	1,127	4,755	1,396

Notes: Authors' estimations based on UCAS (2006/07–2022/23) and HESA (2009/10–2022/23) data. The table shows the yearly mean per origin country and standard deviation of each outcome variable. The table compares the period before the referendum (2006/07–2015/16), between the referendum and Brexit (2016/17–2019/20), and after Brexit (2020/21–2022/23). Differences in means are tested using a t-test for unequal variances, $^{***}p < 0.01$, $^{**}p < 0.05$, and $^{*}p < 0.1$. The mean number of applications and offers is much higher than the acceptances, as students can have up to 5 applications. The mean number of enrolments is higher than the acceptances, as these include postgraduate courses, part-time students, and students who applied directly to institutions.

Fig. 2 visualizes the applications, offers, acceptances, and enrolments over time. The outcomes are normalized to 100 in the first year to account for differences in levels. Before Brexit, both EU and non-EU student numbers were increasing. We observe a small short-lived decline in the EU outcomes after 2012, the year tuition fees for UK and EU students were increased in England (Hubble & Bolton, 2018). Around 2015, non-EU outcomes slowed down slightly, perhaps as a result of the Home Secretary's proposals to toughen student visa rules or due to the introduction of the Immigration Health Surcharge (Cook, 2015; Gil, 2015). For the student applications, offers, and acceptances, these movements over time are rather small and the upward trends are relatively steady. After the referendum, the number of EU students seemed to stabilize slightly. For student enrolments, the EU and non-EU trends are diverging already before the referendum, with non-EU enrolments increasing faster. For all outcomes, Brexit is followed by a noticeable drop. The decrease is especially distinct in the academic year 2021/22, when tuition fees increased.

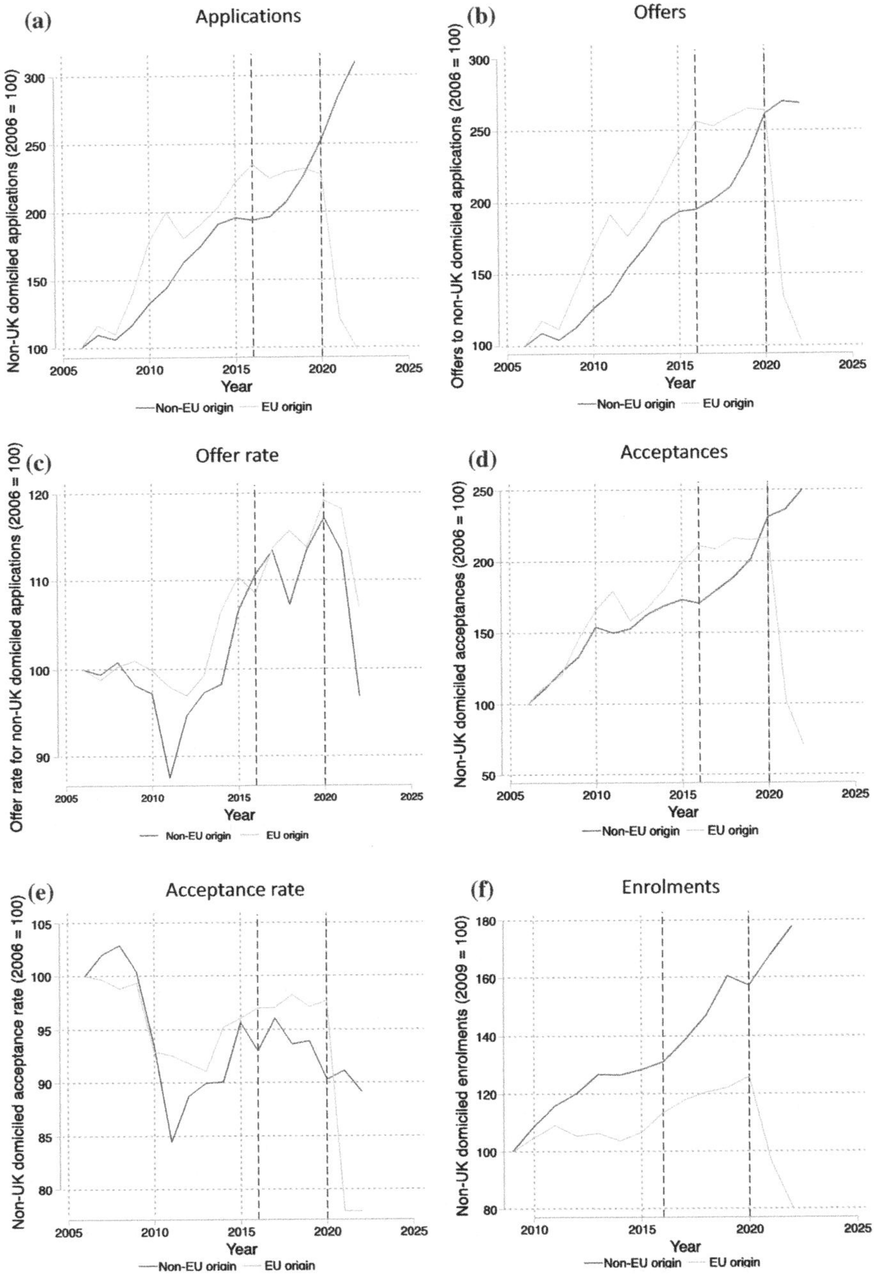

Fig. 2. EU and Non-EU Student Outcomes in the United Kingdom. *Notes:* Authors' estimations based on UCAS (2006/07–2022/23) and HESA (2009/10–2022/23) data. The figure shows the total outcomes of all sample countries over time. The dotted lines indicate the years of the referendum and Brexit. Quarterly outcome variables by origin country were first aggregated by EU and non-EU region.

4. EMPIRICAL STRATEGY

We employ a DD strategy and consider six outcome variables: international student applications to UK HEIs, institutions' offers to international students, offer rate (%), international students' acceptances, acceptance rate (%), and international student enrolments. We use academic years as time units. An academic year usually runs from early September to mid- or late August in the following year. We use the years from 2006/07 or 2009/10 to 2022/23, depending on data availability. The unit of analysis is the origin country of the international students, where we compare EU students (treated units) with non-EU students (control units) in the United Kingdom. By using non-EU origin countries as a control group, we isolate the impact of the Brexit-induced change in regulations for international students. We exclude other possible time-varying confounders, such as the negative economic impact or increased political tensions following the referendum, as we expect both groups to be equally affected by this.

To compare similar types of international students driven by similar confounders, we only include high and upper-middle-income countries[6] as control units. We exclude Ireland and Croatia from the main analysis. Irish students could continue studying in the United Kingdom under the same conditions after Brexit due to the Common Travel Area. Croatia, a new EU member starting in 2013, has an additional policy discontinuity in terms of student mobility, which we examine as a separate case study. Countries that are part of the EEA or Schengen Area experienced the same Brexit-induced change in visa requirements and tuition fees as EU students and are therefore considered as treated. As a result, the treated group consists of 29 EU-origin countries[7] and the control group consists of 85 non-EU-origin countries.[8]

First, we estimate the log-linear dynamic DD model shown in Equation (1):

$$\text{lnStudent}_{it} = \alpha_0 + \sum_{2006}^{2022} \alpha_t \text{EU}_i * \text{YEAR}_t + \delta_i + \gamma_t + \epsilon_{it} \tag{1}$$

The outcome variable lnStudent_{it} captures the logarithmic[9] number of students in the United Kingdom from an origin country i during the academic year t. The dummy variable EU_i indicates the origin countries that were impacted by Brexit. The variable YEAR_t indicates the academic year. We use 2015/16 as the baseline period, the last year before the Brexit referendum. The coefficient α_t captures the average treatment effect on the treated (ATT) of Brexit for each period and models any anticipation toward it. We include origin-fixed effects, represented by δ_i, and year-fixed effects, represented by γ_t. Standard errors are clustered at the origin-country level.

Additionally, we estimate a similar DD model, capturing the main events and policy changes during the Brexit process: the referendum (Phase 1), the introduction of visa restrictions (Phase 2), and the introduction of increased tuition fees (Phase 3). This is captured in Equation (2):

$$\begin{aligned}\text{lnStudent}_{it} = {} & \alpha_0 + \alpha_1 \text{EU}_i * \text{REFERENDUM}_t + \alpha_2 \text{EU}_i * \text{VISA}_t \\ & + \alpha_3 \text{EU}_i * \text{TUITION}_t + \delta_i + \gamma_t + \epsilon_{it}\end{aligned} \tag{2}$$

The dummy variable REFERENDUM_t marks the post-referendum period, starting 2016/17. VISA_t is a dummy variable equal to one starting 2020/21 and TUITION_t is a dummy variable equal to one from 2021/22 onwards. The remainder of the equation is specified similarly as before.

We complement the analysis using a synthetic DD estimator. The synthetic DD re-weights units to align pre-treatment trends. The estimator constructs two types of optimal weights. Unit weights are designed to make the average treated outcome parallel to the weighted average control outcome before the adoption of the treatment while allowing for a constant difference between treated and control units and over time. Unit weights thus aim to make units follow parallel pre-trends, not identical pre-trends. Time weights aim to balance pre- and post-treatment periods by making the average post-treatment outcome differ by a constant from the weighted average pre-treatment outcomes for each control unit. Essentially, this puts more weight on the pre-treatment periods which are more similar to post-treatment periods. In the main analysis, estimates are not conditioned on any covariates. The variance is estimated using a block bootstrap with 200 replications, which offers the best properties for inference with panel data and is suitable as the number of treated units is large enough (Arkhangelsky et al., 2021; Clarke et al., 2023).

We implement the synthetic DD to create event-study-type graphs on the treatment effect of the Brexit referendum. The synthetic DD works slightly differently as it does not estimate treatment effects relative to one chosen baseline period. Instead, the baseline is simply the pre-treatment aggregates, as determined by the optimal pre-treatment time weights. The synthetic event-study coefficients then capture how the differences between treated units and synthetic controls (as re-weighted by the unit weights) have changed when compared to baseline differences (Arkhangelsky et al., 2021; Clarke et al., 2023).

Additionally, we focus on the actual exit in 2020 and summarize the Brexit effect in one coefficient by implementing the synthetic DD on Equation (3):

$$\text{lnStudent}_{it} = \alpha_0 + \alpha_1 \, \text{EU}_i * \text{BREXIT}_t + \delta_i + \gamma_t + \epsilon_{it} \tag{3}$$

The variable EU_i indicates the treated units and the dummy variable BREXIT_t equals one for the academic year in which or after which the transition period has ended (the academic year 2020/21 and onwards). As discussed previously, visa requirements changed in the academic year 2020/21 and tuition fee regulations changed for the academic year 2021/22. The coefficient α_1 captures the ATT, the impact experienced by EU students exposed to the changing requirements due to Brexit. To exclude any potential anticipation effect, the period between the referendum and Brexit (2016/17 to 2019/20) is removed.

By using non-EU origin countries as a control group, we make some important implicit assumptions. First, the condition of parallel trends must be satisfied. We assume that had Brexit not occurred, the difference between the treated and untreated outcome would have been constant over time and EU and non-EU student migration to the United Kingdom would have continued to follow parallel paths. To credibly make this assumption, the requirements for non-EU students, before and after Brexit, cannot have changed. As discussed in Section 2.1 and further elaborated in Appendix A2, there are only a few changes in UK policies on non-EU student mobility over time. Overall, these policy adaptations did not seem to impact the outcome variables for our sample (see descriptive evidence in Section 3.2). Additionally, by re-weighting units with the synthetic DD, we weaken the reliance on this parallel trend assumption. Any remaining concerns are addressed in the robustness checks, where we perform several placebo tests (Section 6.1) and follow Rambachan and Roth's (2023) "credible approach" to parallel trends (Section 6.2).

Second, we assume that non-EU students were unaffected by the change in EU students' behavior following Brexit, i.e., that there were no spillover effects (Stable Unit Treatment Value Assumption or SUTVA). Universities and colleges have generally set firm limits on the number of home fee students (UK students and EU students pre-Brexit) they admit, either independently or due to restrictions from the UK government. Non-EU students, on the other hand, were never subject to any quota control as they were subject to higher overseas fees, unaffected by Brexit. These students have always been actively recruited by institutions to maintain financial stability. Offers are generally made to all applicants who can demonstrate the needed academic potential (Hillman, 2020; Universities UK International & IDP Connect, 2021; University of Bristol, 2011). As a result, changes in the number of EU students should not affect students from outside the EU and we should not expect any substitution. Nonetheless, we perform further checks to evaluate how potential changes in HEIs' recruitment behavior may affect our results (Section 6.3). We replicate our analysis using alternative counterfactual scenarios in which we assume that the non-EU inflow either continued growing at the same rate as before the referendum or experienced zero growth. These results dispel concerns about spillover effects.

Overall, to strengthen the validity of our empirical approach, we perform further robustness checks. We use alternative specifications (i.e., we include origin country control variables, use an inverse hyperbolic sine transformation, or employ the Poisson estimator on the outcome variables in levels) and alternative control group compositions (i.e., we exclude Asian-origin countries or use all available non-EU countries as control units). We also perform several checks on the confounding effect of Covid-19, by showing that our results hold when excluding students from countries with strong mobility restrictions (imposed by their own government or by the United Kingdom) or many Covid-19 cases. The series of robustness checks listed above adds to the credibility of our results.

5. ESTIMATION RESULTS

5.1 Dynamic DD Results

Table 3 reports the results of the dynamic DD specification from Equation 1 for all outcome variables. The corresponding event study plots can be found in Fig. A3.1 in the Appendix. We observe parallel trends before the Brexit referendum, except for EU enrolments, which had been diverging already. We find no

Table 3. Dynamic DD Estimates.

	(1) Applications	(2) Offers	(3) Offer Rate	(4) Acceptances	(5) Acceptance Rate	(6) Enrolments
Pre-referendum (Phase 0)						
2012	0.06	0.01	−0.04	0.00	−0.02	−0.25***
	(0.08)	(0.09)	(0.03)	(0.07)	(0.03)	(0.09)
2013	0.04	0.01	−0.03	0.01	−0.01	−0.28***
	(0.07)	(0.08)	(0.03)	(0.07)	(0.03)	(0.07)
2014	0.02	−0.01	0.01	−0.00	0.04	0.03
	(0.06)	(0.06)	(0.03)	(0.05)	(0.03)	(0.05)
2015						
Referendum (Phase 1)						
2016	−0.09	−0.07	−0.02	0.08*	0.02	0.02
	(0.08)	(0.08)	(0.03)	(0.04)	(0.02)	(0.05)
2017	−0.02	−0.03	−0.03	0.05	0.01	0.04
	(0.06)	(0.07)	(0.03)	(0.05)	(0.02)	(0.07)
2018	0.06	0.03	0.01	0.10	0.03	0.07
	(0.07)	(0.08)	(0.03)	(0.07)	(0.03)	(0.07)
2019	−0.06	−0.02	−0.00	0.05	0.04	0.01
	(0.08)	(0.08)	(0.03)	(0.08)	(0.03)	(0.09)
Settlement scheme/visa requirements (Phase 2)						
2020	−0.04	−0.04	−0.00	0.04	0.03	0.16
	(0.08)	(0.09)	(0.02)	(0.08)	(0.03)	(0.10)
Increased tuition fees (Phase 3)						
2021	−0.71***	−0.69***	0.02	−0.81***	−0.18***	−0.21**
	(0.10)	(0.11)	(0.03)	(0.14)	(0.04)	(0.10)
2022	−1.03***	−1.01***	0.06*	−1.19***	−0.11***	−0.77***
	(0.12)	(0.13)	(0.03)	(0.14)	(0.03)	(0.10)
Observations	1,767	1,725	1,611	1,592	1,350	1,393
R-squared	0.33	0.34	0.17	0.29	0.31	0.16
Origin countries	111	109	103	108	92	112
EU 2015 mean	6,991	4,350	0.61	999.8	0.57	4,182
EU 2019 mean	7,313	4,878	0.62	1,077	0.58	4,787

Notes: Dynamic DD estimations of the log-linear model based on UCAS (2006/07–2022/23) (Columns 1–5) and HESA (2009/10–2022/23) (Column 6) data. Cluster robust standard errors in parentheses. ***$p < 0.01$, **$p < 0.05$ and *$p < 0.1$. The model includes time fixed effects and country fixed effects. The exact percentage changes can be calculated using the following formula: $\exp(\beta) - 1$.

significant changes in the years following the vote. It seems that the Brexit-induced policy uncertainty and the psychological effect of the growing anti-EU sentiments during the referendum did not significantly impact students' behavior. There also does not seem to be any anticipation effect awaiting the changing regulations. In the first year of Brexit, 2020/21, there are no significant changes in any of the outcome variables despite the changing visa requirements for EU students. Only starting the academic year of 2021/22, we observe a significant drop in applications, offers, acceptances, and enrolments from EU students. The decreases become even larger in 2022/23, with around 64.3% fewer applications, 63.6% fewer offers, 69.6% fewer acceptances, and 53.7% fewer enrolments. The offer rate increased slightly and the acceptance rate declined, which means the decrease in students' offers (acceptances) was relatively smaller (larger) than the decrease in total applications.

To capture the different policy changes during the Brexit process, Table 4 reports the results of the DD specification from Equation 2. These results are broadly aligned with those from the year-on-year analysis. In Phase 1, indicating the post-referendum period, we find no effect on applications, offers, acceptances or the offer rate. We find a small positive effect on the acceptance rate and enrolments, likely driven by diverging trends before Brexit. There is no evidence of a change in the outcomes following the introduction of visa requirements (Phase 2), except in the case of enrolments. The increase in enrolments in the last year prior to tuition fee introduction may be a sign of anticipatory behavior on students' behalf. Finally, there is clear evidence of a negative effect of the tuition fee increase on applications (−56.3%), offers (−55.7%), acceptances (−64.5%) and enrolments (−48.3%), as well as an impact on the offer (4%) and acceptance rates (−16%).

Table 4. DD Estimates on Brexit Phases.

	(1) Applications	(2) Offers	(3) Offer Rate	(4) Acceptances	(5) Acceptance Rate	(6) Enrolments
Brexit referendum (Phase 1)	−0.05	−0.01	0.02	0.09	0.06***	0.24***
	(0.08)	(0.09)	(0.02)	(0.09)	(0.02)	(0.09)
Settlement/visa requirements (Phase 2)	−0.01	−0.01	0.01	−0.03	0.01	0.13**
	(0.05)	(0.05)	(0.02)	(0.04)	(0.02)	(0.06)
Tuition fees increased (Phase 3)	−0.83***	−0.81***	0.04*	−1.04***	−0.18***	−0.66***
	(0.10)	(0.10)	(0.02)	(0.10)	(0.02)	(0.07)
Observations	1,767	1,725	1,611	1,592	1,350	1,393
R-squared	0.21	0.23	0.10	0.20	0.17	0.06
Origin countries	111	109	103	108	92	112
Pre-Brexit EU mean	7,313	4,878	0.62	1,077	0.58	4,787
% change (Phase 3)	−56.29	−55.65	4.382	−64.49	−16.07	−48.29

Notes: DD estimations of the log-linear model based on UCAS (2006/07–2022/23) (Columns 1–5) and HESA (2009/10–2022/23) (Column 6) data. Three dummy variables (that stay on) capture the relevant events during the Brexit process. Cluster robust standard errors in parentheses. $^{***}p < 0.01$, $^{**}p < 0.05$, $^{*}p < 0.1$. The model includes time fixed effects and country fixed effects. The exact percentage changes can be calculated using the following formula: $\exp(\beta) - 1$. The table also reports the mean outcome for EU origin countries in 2019 and the exact percentage change for Phase 3 coefficients.

Based on the estimated impact of the tuition fee increase, we estimate price elasticities to assess the degree of responsiveness to the change. Before Brexit, EU students benefited from capped home tuition fees of a maximum of £9,250 in England and even lower in other parts of the United Kingdom. After Brexit, overseas undergraduate degrees cost on average £22,200 per year although overseas fees are set individually by institutions and can vary. EU students thus experienced a price increase of at most +140%, leading to a decrease in applications of −56.3% in the two years of increased fees after Brexit (2021/22–2022/23). This implies a price elasticity of demand of applications (i.e., demand for UK higher education) of −0.40.[10] This is larger than previous estimates on the price elasticity of demand for higher education. Particularly for the United Kingdom, Sá (2019) found a −0.11 price elasticity in applications from domestic English students, affected by the 2012 increase in home tuition fees.[11] On the one hand, this may suggest that foreign students are more price-sensitive toward UK education, as they are highly mobile and have more alternatives available. On the other hand, the tuition increase for EU students after Brexit was, in absolute terms, much large than previous tuition fee reforms in the UK. This potentially led to stronger reactions.

5.2 Synthetic DD Results

To strengthen our conclusions, Fig. 3 plots the coefficients of the synthetic DD. The period before the referendum is the baseline period. The event study figures show the difference between the treated outcomes and re-weighted untreated outcomes. We observe parallel trends before the referendum, indicated by the coefficients very close to zero, for EU applications, offers, acceptances, and enrolments. The impact remains insignificant in the years after the vote, highlighting the absence of a referendum effect or Brexit anticipation effect. In the first year of Brexit (Phase 2), we only observe a small significant increase in EU enrolments, likely in anticipation of the rising tuition fees. Starting 2021/22 (Phase 3), student applications, offers, acceptances, and enrolments are significantly negatively affected by the increased tuition fees.

We find a small significant increase in the offer rate. On the one hand, this may indicate that universities and colleges tried to offset the decline in applications by increasing their offers. As EU students paid full tuition fees after Brexit, HEIs may have had more incentive to recruit them. On the other hand, this may simply reflect that students who continue to apply self-select and show higher potential. We cannot distinguish between the two possibilities. We, again, find a significant decrease in students' acceptance rate, illustrating that some EU students declined offers despite having gone through the entire application process. For both the offer and acceptance rates, our conclusions are more indicative, as we observe that pre-trends are not perfectly parallel.

To summarize the Brexit effect, in Table 5, we perform a synthetic DD with only the Brexit period as treated (see Equation 3). We calculate the overall change in the outcomes due to Brexit (Phase 2 and 3). Unit and time weights are reported in the Appendix, in Figs. A4.1 and A4.2, and Table A4.1. Although we find no significant effect of the Brexit referendum in the previous analysis, we exclude the

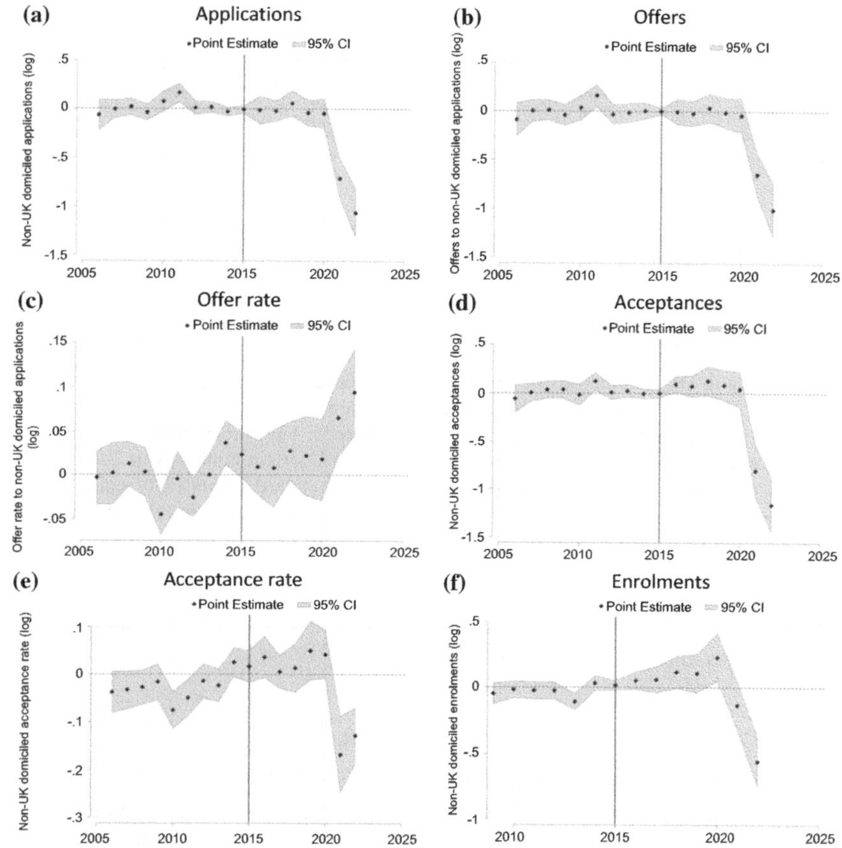

Fig. 3. Synthetic DD, Referendum as Treatment. *Notes:* Synthetic DD estimations based on UCAS (2006/07–2022/23) (figures a–e) and HESA (2009/10–2022/23) (figure f) data. Confidence intervals are calculated using 200 bootstrap replications.

period between the referendum and Brexit to be cautious and exclude any possible anticipation effect. We find that Brexit reduced the number of student applications from an average EU country by 45.6%. Consequently, we find a significant reduction in average university and college offers (43.1%) and students' acceptances (47.8%). The offer rate increased by 6.7% and the acceptance rate decreased by 7.3%. We find a reduction in enrolments of 14.8% due to Brexit. This is smaller than the impact on other outcome variables, partly because the increased enrolments in the first year of Brexit (in anticipation of the higher tuition fees) offset the decrease in 2021/22. Additionally, this may reflect differences in data, as the

Table 5. Synthetic DD, Brexit as Treatment.

	(1) Applications	(2) Offers	(3) Offer Rate	(4) Acceptances	(5) Acceptance Rate	(6) Enrolments
ATT	−0.61***	−0.56***	0.07***	−0.65***	−0.08**	−0.16*
	(0.10)	(0.10)	(0.02)	(0.10)	(0.03)	(0.10)
Observations	1,209	1,170	1,079	1,066	923	890
Origin countries	93	90	83	82	71	89
Pre-Brexit EU mean	7,313	4,878	0.62	1,077	0.58	4,787
% change	−45.61	−43.14	6.72	−47.79	−7.32	−14.78

Notes: Synthetic DD estimations of the log-linear model based on UCAS (2006/07–2022/23) (Columns 1–5) and HESA (2009/10–2022/23) (Column 6) data. The period between the referendum and Brexit (2016/17–2019/20) is excluded. The table reports the average treatment effect on the treated, the mean outcome for EU origin countries in 2019, and the treatment effect as a percentage change. Bootstrapped standard errors (200 replications) in parentheses. $***p < 0.01$, $**p < 0.05$, and $*p < 0.1$. Percentage change is calculated using the following formula: $\exp(\beta) - 1$.

numbers on enrolments are more comprehensive (e.g., the data also include postgraduates and part-time students).

5.3 Heterogeneous Results

To uncover if Brexit affected distinct types of students differently, we separate our outcome variables by students' socio-demographic and origin country characteristics or HEIs' administrative characteristics and employ the same synthetic DD as previously. In the Appendix, Table A5.1 reports the main results for different categories of student applications. The heterogeneity analyses for offers and acceptances are reported in Tables A5.2 and A5.3. Table A5.4 reports the results on various categories of student enrolments. Although the coefficients are generally not significantly different from each other, we observe some interesting distinctions. Event-study figures for each outcome are reported in the Appendix (Figs. A5.1–A5.4) and do not show anything noteworthy unless discussed otherwise below.

5.3.1 Applications

We find that the decrease in applications is relatively stable by age category although slightly larger for students above 30 (Fig. A5.1). We find no differences between female and male students. The impact is slightly larger for applications for the January deadline.[12] When examining students' origin country, we find a larger impact for Northern or Central and Eastern European students. Northern European countries have been increasingly offering English-taught programs (Airey et al., 2017), providing students the opportunity to obtain high-quality degrees in their home country. Students from Central and Eastern Europe likely have a higher sensitivity to tuition fees, the availability of student loans, and uncertainties around post-study work opportunities, likely due to lower income levels in these regions. Despite previously demonstrating strong demand for UK degrees, these students may now choose universities closer to home that offer subsidized degrees (Universities UK International, 2022).

To examine whether origin countries' economy and labor market characteristics played a role, we estimate the impact of Brexit separately for students from countries with above or below median GDP per capita and unemployment rates. We find that the decrease is more pronounced for origin countries with a lower GDP per capita and higher unemployment rate. This suggests that students from countries with lower employment opportunities, thus facing greater credit constraints but with the most to gain from studying in the United Kingdom (higher expected returns), were impacted most by Brexit. Students from countries with stronger economies and tighter labor markets were impacted less by Brexit. This may suggest that the tuition-related income effect is a more important channel than students' concerns about employment prospects or feeling unwelcome in the United Kingdom.

5.3.2 Offers and Acceptances

The impact of Brexit on university and colleges' offers and students' acceptances follows a very similar pattern, except for the age differences. The decrease in acceptances is driven by those aged 19–20, a common higher education enrollment age in many European countries. Older students, likely pursuing a second degree or already holding work experience, seemed to have adapted their behavior earlier in the process compared to younger students (Fig. A5.2 and Fig. A5.3).

5.3.3 Enrolments

For students' enrolments into higher education, the effect is concentrated among first-degree undergraduate and taught postgraduate courses.[13] We find no significant effect for students enrolled in research-oriented postgraduate degrees, possibly because the increase in respective fees was not as substantial and because research students often secure scholarships to pursue their degrees. Therefore, they face different financial constraints. As before, the decrease is most pronounced for Northern European students. We find a decrease for students studying in Scotland and an increase for institutions located in Wales, due to diverging trends before Brexit. We do not find any significant impact when restricting our sample to enrolments into universities,[14] universities belonging to the Russell group,[15] or other education institutions. This suggests that the selectivity of HEIs did not dampen the impact of Brexit.

Finally, the overall decrease in enrolments is slightly more pronounced for students from countries with a high GDP per capita and low unemployment rate. However, the coefficients are weakly significant and may be partially explained by anticipation effects. Specifically, in Fig. A5.4, we see that enrolments of students from countries with a lower GDP and higher unemployment rate increased slightly after the referendum and in the first year of Brexit, in anticipation of the increased tuition fees. After the tuition fee increase, student enrolments among this group dropped sharply. This sharp reaction is offset by the anticipation. Enrolments of students from countries with a high GDP and lower unemployment rate did not experience this anticipation. These results highlight the role that students' home economy and labor market play in educational decisions.

5.4 Case Study on Croatia

As the most recent member of the EU, Croatia lends itself to a natural extension of our research design by offering an additional policy discontinuity in terms of student mobility. The country became an official EU member on July 1, 2013, following a rigorous accession process that spanned several years. Following the accession, member states were allowed to implement transitional arrangements to limit the access of citizens from the new member country to their labor markets. The United Kingdom, along with several other EU countries, chose to exercise this option and imposed a seven-year transitional period during which Croatian nationals faced restrictions when seeking employment in the United Kingdom (UK Home Office, 2012). There were, however, no transitional restrictions related to students in higher education. Croatian students immediately had access to all the benefits associated with being an EU member; they were now subject to lower (capped) tuition fees and were exempt from visa requirements. Croatian students benefited from this preferential treatment for several academic years, up until 2020. After Brexit, freedom of movement was restricted again, and as for all EU nationals, it became more challenging for Croatians to migrate and study in the United Kingdom.

Fig. 4 visualizes the applications, offers, acceptances, and enrolments of Croatian and non-EU students over time. The outcomes are normalized to 100 in the first year. Before 2013, the inflow of Croatian students in the United Kingdom followed a similar trend as the inflow of non-EU students. After Croatia's accession, student numbers increased strongly up until a few years later, when the inflow stabilized again. Between the referendum and Brexit, the number of applications, offers, and acceptances of Croatian and non-EU students seem to follow parallel trends again. For enrolments, this stabilization is less visible although the increase also slowed down. In 2021/22, all Croatian student outcomes declined almost back to pre-2013 levels.

Table 6 implements the synthetic DD estimator, using the same set of non-EU control countries as in the main specification, on the two separate treatments experienced by Croatia: the EU accession (using data from 2006/07 to 2015/16) and Brexit (using data from 2015/16 to 2022/23). After becoming an EU member state, Croatian student applications, offers, and acceptances more than tripled while enrolments more than doubled. After Brexit, the applications, offers, acceptances, and enrolments decreased again by between 35.8% and

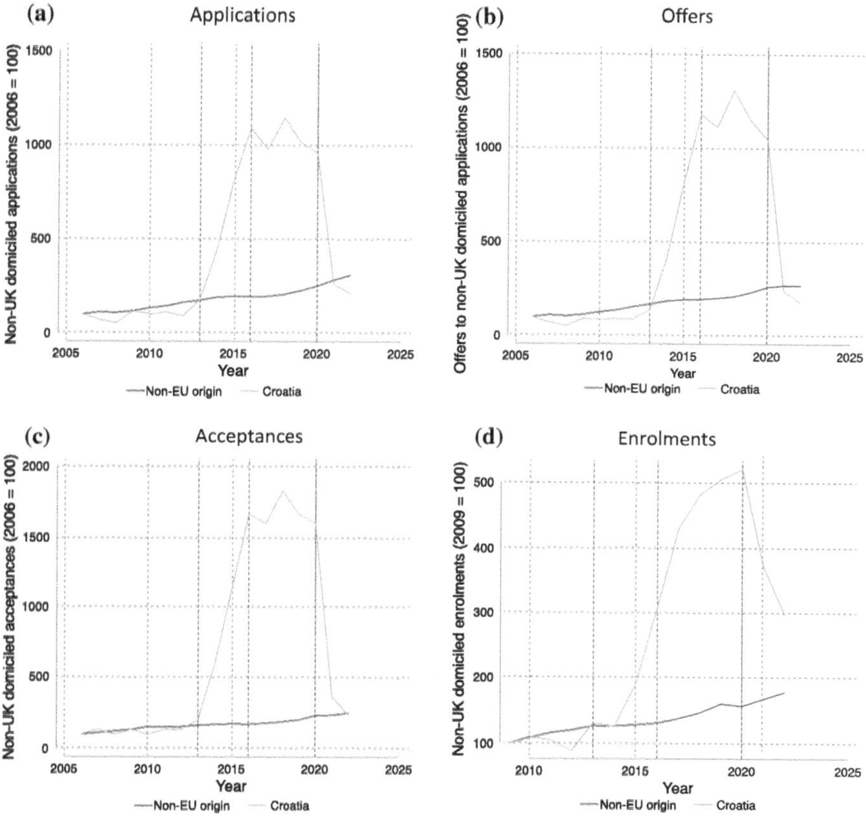

Fig. 4. Croatian and Non-EU Student Outcomes in the United Kingdom. *Notes:* Authors' estimations based on UCAS (2006/07—2022/23) and HESA (2009/10—2022/23) data. The figure shows the total outcomes of Croatia and all non-EU sample countries over time. The dotted lines indicate the years of the Croatian accession, the referendum, and Brexit.

70.1%. This means that outcomes returned almost entirely back to pre-2013 levels.

Besides illustrating the enormous impact that being an EU member has on student mobility, our results also suggest that the effects of entering and leaving the agreement are relatively symmetric. By entering the EU, Croatian students were incentivized to study in the United Kingdom, and as this academic study path became more widespread, awareness of its benefits likely increased. It is possible this allowed the United Kingdom to build a lasting reputation. However, our results indicate that despite having more experience with studying in the United Kingdom, Croatian students were strongly discouraged by the higher tuition fees after Brexit.

Table 6. Synthetic DD, EU Accession and Brexit as Treatment for Croatia.

	Applications		Offers		Acceptances		Enrolments	
	(1)	(2)	(3)	(4)	(5)	(6)	(7)	(8)
Accession	1.24***		1.22***		1.31***		0.76*	
	(0.33)		(0.29)		(0.26)		(0.44)	
Brexit		−1.03***		−1.21***		−1.18***		−0.44*
		(0.26)		(0.24)		(0.22)		(0.23)
Observations	660	511	630	483	570	420	441	434
Origin countries	66	73	63	69	57	60	63	62
2012 value	135		90		20		175	
2019 value		1,530		1,150		250		985
% change	244.9	−64.15	237.7	−70.06	269.7	−69.19	113.7	−35.81

Notes: Synthetic DD estimations of the log-linear model based on UCAS (2006/07–2015/16 for Columns 1, 3, and 5; 2016/17–2022/23 for Columns 2, 4, and 6) and HESA (2009/10–2015/16 for Column 7; 2016/17–2022/23 for Column 8) data. The table reports the average treatment effect on the treated (Croatia), the outcome for Croatia in 2012 and 2019, and the treatment effect as a percentage change. Placebo standard errors (200 replications) in parentheses. $^{***}p < 0.01$, $^{**}p < 0.05$ and $^{*}p < 0.1$. Percentage change is calculated using the following formula: $\exp(\beta) - 1$.

6. ROBUSTNESS CHECKS

6.1 Alternative Specifications and Control Groups

The robustness checks are reported in Appendix A6. Table A6.1 summarizes a series of robustness checks on the synthetic DD results. First, in Panels A and B, we test for the impact of a hypothetical event prior to the referendum. As nothing changed, we should observe no significant changes. We find some significant coefficients for the offer and acceptance rate, and we observe some anticipation in the enrolment of EU students. As mentioned previously, prereferendum trends for these outcomes were not perfectly parallel and results should be interpreted with caution. Apart from this, we find no significant impact of the placebo events.

Panel C includes a set of yearly origin control variables in our main specification: GDP (current US$) unemployment rate, and population. The variables are assigned to academic years based on their start year (e.g., a control variable from 2016 is assigned to the academic year 2016/17) and are thus slightly lagged. The control variables are used following the 'projected' procedure specified by Kranz (2022). The synthetic control is calculated on the residuals of all units after a regression adjustment based on parameters estimated only in control units. These parameters are obtained from a baseline fixed effects regression of the outcomes on the covariates (only for untreated units) and projected on all units. This procedure essentially removes the impact of the covariates on the outcome variables before implementing the synthetic DD. Similar to before, we find a significant negative impact on EU student applications, offers, acceptances, and the acceptance rate. We, again, find a significant positive impact on the offer rate and no significant change in EU enrolments. In Panel D, we show results of the analysis with the same set of yearly control variables but for the United Kingdom instead of students' origin countries. This controls for changes in the UK economy as a whole. These variables affect both EU and non-EU students in the same manner and thus do not affect the estimates.

Next, we exclude Asian-origin countries from the control units, as these students may not be sufficiently comparable to EU students. On the one hand, UK universities have become increasingly reliant on Asian students over the past decades. The majority of non-EU students originate from China (around one-third of newly enrolled students); Malaysia and Hong Kong are popular sending countries as well (Migration Observatory, 2022). Numbers have been increasing for a long time and the United Kingdom's reliance on these students is a frequent topic of discussion in the media (Adams, 2014, 2020). At the same time, these students have been exposed to other confounders over time. In 2020, students may have been discouraged by the increased racial hate crimes against East Asians as a result of Covid-19 (Carr et al., 2022). In early 2021, the recruitment of Hong Kong students was facilitated by the introduction of a new British National (Overseas) Citizen visa (Migration Observatory, 2020). Panel E finds that these origin countries are not driving our results.

In Panel F, we replicate our analysis including all the non-EU countries and independent territories available in the data. This check ensures that the results are not driven by the selected control units. Our conclusions remain the same with this alternative sample.

Next, we restrict the period of analysis further. In Panel G, we estimate the synthetic DD while only including the three years before the referendum as the pre-period. In doing so, we focus on obtaining parallel trends in the more relevant periods, closely before the referendum. In Panel H, we exclude the year 2015/16 (in addition to the anticipation period between the referendum and Brexit). Descriptive evidence shows a one-time decline in non-EU student migration that academic year. The estimates do not change in magnitude and our conclusions stay the same. We only observe a slight increase in the standard errors as the number of observations has been reduced.

Finally, in Panel I, we apply an inverse hyperbolic sine transformation to our outcome variables. This allows for a similar interpretation as the logarithmic outcomes while retaining zero-valued observations. Given the recent concerns on log-like transformations (Chen & Roth, 2023; Mullahy & Norton, 2022), Panel J replicates the analysis using a Poisson estimator on the outcome variables in levels. When outcome variables can equal zero, the Poisson regression offers an alternative approach to obtain unit-free ATTs expressed as a percentage and avoid placing arbitrary weights on the extensive margin (Chen & Roth, 2023). We obtain similar relative treatment effects as in the main analysis.

6.2 Credible Approach to Parallel Trends

The validity of our identification strategy depends on the parallel trend assumption, stating that in the absence of treatment, the difference between the treated and untreated outcome is constant over time. The dynamic DD from above already illustrates the credibility of this condition by inspecting whether trends are parallel pre-referendum. The synthetic DD further weakens the reliance of our results by manufacturing pre-trends to be parallel. In this section, to further inspect the robustness of our results, we perform a sensitivity analysis following Rambachan and Roth's (2023) credible approach to parallel trends.

Rambachan and Roth (2023) exploit the fact that the pre-treatment differences observed in the data are informative about the counterfactual differences in the post-treatment period. They impose that the counterfactual difference in trends cannot be 'too different' from the pre-trend differences. By varying the size of the counterfactual differences, we can create confidence bounds for the treatment effect under different violations of the parallel trend assumption. Thus, instead of assuming a common trend (i.e., a zero difference between counterfactual treated and observed untreated outcomes), we relax this assumption. The approach lends itself naturally to sensitivity analysis. By relaxing the assumption up to a varying degree, we find a cut-off point up to which the treatment effect is still significant.

Rambachan and Roth (2023) specify different types of restrictions that formalize the relationship between the pre- and post-treatment differences. The most suitable approach in our setting is to impose so-called bounds on relative magnitudes, denoted by $\Delta^{RM}(M)$. This restriction allows for differential economic shocks and assumes that shocks after the referendum cannot be much larger in magnitude than those before. In particular, the possible violations of parallel trends are bounded by M times the maximum pre-treatment violation. Imposing bounds of $M = 1$ thus restricts the post-treatment violations to be no larger than the maximal observed pre-treatment violation of parallel trends. Likewise, imposing bounds of $M = 2$ implies that the post-treatment violation cannot be larger than twice the maximal violation in the pre-period.

As our dynamic DD estimator finds large significant coefficients for the academic years 2021/22 and 2022/23, we implement the credible approach to parallel trends on the average of these two ATTs. We restrict violations relative to the maximal violation observed in the six years before the referendum. The resulting bounds for the treatment effect of each outcome variable are shown in Fig. A6.1 (a) to (f). For the negative treatment effect on applications, offers, and acceptances, we find cut-off values around $M = 2$ or higher. This means that we can reject a null effect even when allowing for violations of parallel trends up to twice the magnitude of the maximum pre-treatment violation. This illustrates that the results are insensitive to violations in parallel trends, reassuring the robustness of our findings. The positive impact on the offer rate was insignificant in the dynamic DD. The negative impact on the acceptance rate was relatively small and we find a cut-off point at $M = 0.8$. The treatment effect on student enrolments was small, leading to a cut-off value $M = 0.8$. As soon as we allow for rather small violations of the parallel trends assumption, we are unable to reject a null effect anymore, indicating this result is sensitive to the parallel trends assumption.

6.3 Addressing Potential Spillover Effects

To exclude that our results are driven by a violation of the SUTVA, we use alternative counterfactual scenarios. We follow the same approach as Di Iasio and Wahba (2023) and Amuedo-Dorantes and Romiti (2024) when analyzing the impact of the referendum on labor migration and student migration, respectively. Table A6.2 shows the results for our baseline synthetic DD (Panel A) and the results using two alternative counterfactual scenarios for the (control) non-EU student inflow. In the first scenario (Panel B), we assume that in the absence of Brexit, the inflow of non-EU students would have continued to evolve at the same growth rate as before the referendum. We thus assume that the inflow from non-EU countries between 2016/17–2022/23 continues at the same trajectory as the country's pre-referendum growth rate. If spillover effects had occurred (i.e., if non-EU students applied and enrolled more due to the reduced number of EU students), our baseline estimates would be larger than this scenario and overstate the Brexit impact. In the second scenario (Panel C), we assume that the inflow of non-EU students experienced no growth and remained stable at its pre-referendum value, as measured in 2015/16. Results for this scenario can be interpreted as a lower bound of the true effect, as it is unlikely that non-EU inflow completely stopped growing in the true counterfactual. We find that our baseline estimates lie in between both scenarios. This suggests that we find conservative estimates of the Brexit effect, likely close to the true impact, and that spillover effects were limited.

6.4 Coincidence With Covid-19

Finally, we inspect how the Covid-19 crisis coincided with Brexit. The pandemic decreased international student mobility and shifted mobility flows. Our identification strategy only partly controls for this, as the pandemic was distributed unevenly across the world and thus affected student flows differently (Mok et al., 2021). Generally, we expect mobility to be more constrained for students from outside of Europe and therefore, if anything, we underestimate the Brexit impact. To further ensure that the Covid-19 crisis is not driving our findings, this section excludes countries from our sample that had the strongest travel restrictions or were hit hardest.

6.4.1 Covid-19 in the United Kingdom

The Covid-19 virus arrived in Europe in March 2020, and similar to other countries, the United Kingdom was hit hard. In the first months, the British Government immediately implemented strict regulations, including a first lockdown ordering people to stay home. By the summer, restrictions were slowly eased up until September 2020, when a second wave hit Europe. New restrictions were implemented, including a curfew and region-specific lockdowns. In

December 2020, however, the Covid-19 vaccination program in the United Kingdom was set up for priority groups. Starting in spring, the situation improved, the vaccination program was accelerated, and restrictions were slowly lifted. By July 2021, most restrictions were removed. In December, the Omicron variant caused some rules to be re-introduced (e.g., face masks indoors, NHS COVID pass, etc.) (Institute for Government, 2022). By March 2022, all restrictions were again lifted in the United Kingdom (UK Health Security Agency, 2022). Specifically, in terms of higher education, this meant that the 2020/21 academic year took place under strict restrictions with remote teaching. In 2021/22, universities and colleges phased back in. While some teaching continued to be online, much face-to-face teaching and in-person exams returned (HESA, 2023b).

The unpredictable nature of the Covid-19 pandemic in the United Kingdom likely deterred international students from applying. Generally, government policies applied equally to all, and everyone was forced to adhere to the same regulations, regardless of their origin country. Following this reasoning, the use of non-EU students as the control group should capture any confounding impact of Covid-19, with one exception. In early 2021, the United Kingdom introduced stronger travel restrictions for non-UK nationals traveling from a ‘red list’ of countries and territories, mostly from outside the EU. Restrictions varied over time and, at some point, consisted of a full travel ban (Department of Health and Social Care, 2021, 2023), which may have discouraged students. To ensure that we do not underestimate the Brexit impact, Panel A of Table A6.3 excludes the ‘red list’ countries from the synthetic DD analysis and shows that this does not affect our estimates. Table A6.4 lists the excluded countries.

6.4.2 Covid-19 Across the World

The circumstances in the students’ origin country may also affect their motivation to study abroad. Those from countries with many cases or strict regulations may find it difficult to travel or, to the contrary, may be encouraged to leave. To consider these behavioral responses, we use the Oxford COVID-19 Government Response Tracker from Hale et al. (2021). This dataset collected information on when and which pandemic response measures were enacted by governments from 2020 to 2022. The data reflect the extent of government action and aggregates recorded policies into policy indices. We implement our synthetic DD analysis on a group of 50 countries hit least hard by Covid-19, according to different indices and records provided by the Government Response Tracker. In Panel B of Table A6.3, we use the mean government response index, which summarizes all policy responses (containment/closure, economic, health, or vaccination) into one index. We specify this further by using the average stringency index (in Panel C), which summarizes all policies on containments/closure and health-related public information. Finally, we also use the number of confirmed cases (Panel D) and deaths (Panel E) relative to the origin population to capture the severity of Covid-19 across countries. Table A6.4 in the Appendix lists the 50 included countries for each measure. The selected countries are quite different per measure, showing the variety of possible reactions to the crisis.

We find that the decrease in applications, offers, and acceptances remains large and significant in most specifications. The increased offer rate and decreased acceptance rate remain significant as well. The impact on student enrolments is again insignificant, except when focusing on countries with the lowest number of Covid-19 deaths. Overall, we find relatively similar coefficients as in the main analysis. The small differences across specifications more likely highlight that Brexit impacted various EU countries differently rather than invalidating our results. The results suggest that the Covid-19 crisis is not driving our results.

7. BACK-OF-THE-ENVELOPE CALCULATIONS ON ECONOMIC IMPACT

Our results indicate that UK HEIs attract fewer EU students due to Brexit, and particularly due to the increased tuition fees. To illustrate the importance of this impact, this section estimates the potential monetary loss due to the decreased number of EU students.

In Table A7.1 in the Appendix, we estimate the number of students "lost" due to Brexit. Using estimates from a DD analysis on the Brexit phases (see Section 5 and Equation 2 in Section 3), we calculate the counterfactual post-Brexit EU mean and compare this with the observed numbers. We do so for two scenarios. In the first scenario, we assume that all students accepting offers also eventually enroll. Given the decrease in student acceptances of 64.5%, we estimate that around 22,712 undergraduate EU students per year were lost. In the second scenario, we estimate the decrease in student enrolments. Because the enrolment data are more comprehensive, this second scenario allows us to differentiate between undergraduate and postgraduate enrolments. We estimate a yearly decrease of 44.0% and 47.1%, respectively, resulting in a loss of 57,383 and 24,486 students.

In Table 7, we use these estimates to calculate the potential financial implications due to Brexit. We estimate how the reduction in EU students translates into monetary losses, given the change in tuition fees and students' average main expenditures in the United Kingdom that are now not being made. We find that universities and colleges miss out on large amounts of tuition fees (ranging from –£181.1 to –£457.5million/year depending on the scenario). However, interestingly, this loss is partly or entirely compensated by the increased tuition fees (i.e., the change from home fee to international fee) for the remaining EU students in the United Kingdom (ranging from +£177.9 to +£1,040.1million/year). When accounting for spending on accommodation (ranging from –£94.9 to –£239.9million/year) and other day-to-day expenditures (groceries, clothes, study material, etc.) (ranging from –£194.0 to –£490.1million/year), the potential monetary losses of Brexit become apparent for all scenarios. Based on acceptances, we find that on average, a minimum of 292 million pounds per year is lost.

Table 7. Potential Monetary Losses due to Brexit (Back-of-The-Envelope).

	Estimated value/cost of education per student	Estimated yearly loss (in million) due to Brexit		
		[1]	[2]	
		Acceptances	Student enrolments	
		Undergrad	Undergrad	Postgrad
Tuition fees for EU students				
Average tuition fee per student lost by Brexit	Undergraduate £7,973 per year[a] Postgraduate £11,000 per year[b]	−181.09	−457.51	−269.34
Average increased tuition fee per remaining student[c]	Undergraduate £22,000 vs. £7,973 Postgraduate £17,109 vs. £11,000	177.91	1,040.14	167.88
Average other expenditure[d]				
Rent for accommodation	£4,180 per year (10 months)	−94.94	−239.86	−102.35
Remaining day-to-day expenses	£8,541 per year (39-week academic year)	−193.99	−490.10	−209.13
Total		**−£292.11m**	**−£147.34m**	**−£412.95m**

[a]The average home undergraduate tuition fee varies by nation and has been calculated as the weighted average of each tuition fee based on the distribution of enrolments across nations (£9,250 in England, £9,000 in Wales, £3,145 in Northern Ireland, and no tuition fees in Scotland (Hubble & Bolton, 2018; Lewis, 2023a, 2023b, 2024)), with weights based on nations' share of EU students in the year before Brexit, 2019/20.

[b]Home postgraduate tuition fees vary from £4,900 a year to over £30,000, with an average of around £11,000 per year (UCAS, 2023c).

[c]International undergraduate tuition fees vary from £11,400 to £38,000. The average cost is estimated to be around £22,200 per year. International postgraduate tuition fees vary from £9,000 to £30,000. The average cost is estimated to be around £17,109 per year (British Council, 2023).

[d]The Save The Student's National Money Survey 2023 found that the average monthly rent for 2023 was £418 and the UCAS's Student Lifestyle Report found that students are on average spending £219 in a typical week, excluding rent (UCAS, 2023b). For a 39-week academic year, this equals £4,180 of rent and £8,541 of remaining expenditures (groceries, clothes, study material, etc.). These numbers are for UK students and are likely higher for foreign visiting students. For instance, Conlon et al. (2011) estimate that undergraduate and postgraduate international students spent, respectively, £10,003 and £13,337 in 2007/08 for accommodation and other day-to-day expenses. These expenses equal £14,473 and £19,296 when inflated forward to 2022/23 using the Consumer Price Index. The more recent (lower-bound) estimates were preferred for the above calculations.

The estimated losses based on enrolment data reach 147 and 413 million pounds per year, for undergraduate and postgraduate students respectively.

Naturally, these back-of-the-envelope calculations do not cover all financial changes. We ignore that part-time students have lower tuition fees and expenditures that may partly be funded from income generated within the United Kingdom through part-time work (Conlon et al., 2011). We do not consider possible changes in the expenditure patterns of the remaining EU students (e.g., post-Brexit students likely self-select and have more funds available or, to the contrary, have more constraints due to the increased fees). We ignore other benefits arising from international students. As illustrated by Conlon et al. (2011), income from overseas sources can also originate from consultancy contracts, research grants, charitable donations from overseas alumni, the licensing of intellectual property and new technologies, or selling shares in spin-off companies derived from HEIs. In addition, the UK economy also benefits from recent international graduates entering employment, for instance, through their fiscal contributions (Vickers & Bekhradnia, 2007). Finally, we do not include the potential costs that international students may bring. These costs may include scholarships, subsidized loans, or administrative costs (Vickers & Bekhradnia, 2007). These costs are, however, likely smaller than the numerous benefits associated with international students in the United Kingdom. Despite these omissions listed above, our simplified analysis illustrates the magnitude of the potential financial impact of Brexit.

8. DISCUSSION AND CONCLUSION

By voting to leave the EU, the United Kingdom created a more challenging environment for prospective EU students. Visa requirements changed, tuition fees increased, uncertainty about the long-term status of EU students was introduced, and EU migrants may have felt unwelcome. This chapter provides causal evidence on how this impacted international student mobility. By implementing dynamic and synthetic DD estimators on UCAS and HESA data, we compare the evolution in the number of EU students in the United Kingdom with the number of students from unaffected high-income and upper-middle-income non-EU economies. We find that EU students were discouraged from studying in the United Kingdom due to Brexit.

We find no significant impact after the referendum or in anticipation of the exit. In the first year after Brexit, 2020/21, we observe no effect despite changes in the visa requirements. Only starting in 2021/22, when EU students became subject to higher tuition fees, we observe a significant impact on EU students. In the two years of increased tuition fees (2021/22–2022/23), we find a large decline in student applications to HEIs of around −56%, which translates into a price elasticity of −0.40. Naturally, this results in a reduction in university and colleges' place offers (−56%), students' acceptances (−64%), and enrolments (−48%). The overall impact of Brexit (2020/21–2022/23) is also significantly negative for all these outcome variables. Our results indicate that the offer rate increased, suggesting that HEIs received applications of better quality or that they had more incentive to recruit EU students as a result of the increased tuition fees. Students' acceptance rate decreased, indicating that students with the intention to study in the United Kingdom canceled their plans relatively late in the process. These results on the offer and acceptance rates are, however, sensitive to the specification and empirical assumptions made. The observed reductions in applications, offers, and acceptances are relatively constant across age groups, sex, and application types, but are driven by students from Northern or Central and Eastern Europe. For enrolments, the reduction is concentrated among first-degree undergraduate and taught postgraduate courses, Northern European students, and students studying in Scotland. For all outcomes, we find evidence that the decline is most pronounced for students from countries with weaker economies and lower employment opportunities, highlighting the importance of credit constraints. Our results are robust to a large set of specification checks, and we illustrate that these results are not driven by the coincidence with the Covid-19 crisis.

Our findings reveal that the initial uncertainty on the status of EU students in the United Kingdom and the introduction of visa requirements for EU citizens in the United Kingdom had no apparent impact. This highlights that students are willing to incur these increased administrative and time costs. They do not necessarily form a barrier and individuals remain motivated to study in the United Kingdom. The large increase in tuition fees, however, had a great impact on students' behavior, illustrating that this is an important deterrent. Our results indicate a price elasticity of demand for UK higher education of −40, which is higher than previous estimates (e.g., Sá (2019) found a much lower elasticity (−0.11) among domestic English students after the 2012 tuition fee increase). This suggests that foreign students may be more price-sensitive, likely due to their greater mobility and access to alternative options, coupled with the substantially larger tuition fee increase faced by EU students post-Brexit. Although previous literature is ambiguous on the significance of tuition fees in students' decision to study abroad (Beine et al., 2014; Dwenger et al., 2012; Wakeling & Jefferies, 2013), our results are as expected. For European students, there is an abundance of cheaper alternative English-taught programs available within the EU (Mayhew, 2022).

These results reveal one of the broader consequences of Brexit. International students generally generate several positive externalities that are now lost for the United Kingdom. They foster innovation and generate important revenues for local economies and institutions (Bound et al., 2020; Gu & Li, 2023; Stuen et al., 2012). In addition, they promote international collaboration in higher education and research, and international graduates generally form an important source of skilled workers (Hou et al., 2022; She & Wotherspoon, 2013). As such, the reduced inflow of EU students may significantly affect the United Kingdom's economy and higher education quality. Our study highlights this indirect impact of Brexit by illustrating the large potential monetary losses in a brief back-of-the-envelope calculation.

Although our results are specific to the United Kingdom, they are relevant too for other countries considering implementing barriers to limit international enrollment growth (e.g., the Netherlands (ICEF monitor, 2023a,b) or Canada (ICEF monitor, 2023c)). For policymakers wishing to curb international students after reflecting on the wider consequences, our results suggest that raising tuition fees may be the most effective way. In the following years, it is essential for the United Kingdom to ensure student inflows and retain their positive externalities. The limited number of initial initiatives and bilateral agreements (see Highman et al. (2023) or UK Home Office (2023b)) have proven insufficient and recent changes to the United Kingdom's visa policy (UK Home Office, 2024) have further restricted access to UK higher education for international students. Therefore, available scholarships and financial aid offers can be expanded and should be listed with their associated eligibility criteria and requirements. Both higher education and government institutions can further promote educational programs and raise awareness of the benefits of studying in the United Kingdom. Brexit can be considered as a nudge to forge new educational markets. British higher education providers should consider setting up new collaborations nationally and internationally and should actively pursue new initiatives and opportunities.

ACKNOWLEDGMENTS

We thank the editors Ben Elsner and Sol Polachek, three anonymous referees, Elsa Leromain, and the participants at the University of Antwerp seminar and 2024 LESE conference for their valuable comments and discussions. We gratefully acknowledge the financial support from the Fund for Scientific Research (FWO-Flanders) (Project Number 11C8923N).

NOTES

1. Previous research highlights that the strong recruitment of international students in the UK resulted in various positive economic benefits, including creative spillovers and innovation, as well as cross-subsidizing the education of domestic students (Migration Advisory Committee, 2018) and generating important revenues for local economies and public universities (Bound et al. 2020; Vickers & Bekhradnia, 2007).

2. Other survey-based research has also shown how changes in visa requirements or tuition fees impacted students' decisions to study in the UK after Brexit (Acar et al., 2018). There also exists further descriptive discussion on the repercussions of Brexit on student mobility (Corbett & Hantrais, 2023; Dias Lopes et al., 2024; Fowler et al., 2018; Mayhew, 2017, 2022). Some authors have focused on specific topics, such as the consequences on the Erasmus program (Brooks & Waters, 2023; Cardwell, 2021).

3. First-degrees are more commonly known as bachelor's degrees and take three years to complete. Non-first-degree (sub-degree) courses are usually shorter courses that can stand alone as qualifications. This includes foundation degrees, higher national diplomas, certificates of higher education, national vocational qualifications, institutional undergraduate credit, and other higher education qualifications of less than degree standard. This type of degree is much less common (HESA, 2023a).

4. Students can submit up to five applications and may thus receive up to five offers. After receiving applications, universities and colleges can make a conditional or unconditional offer to students they wish to admit. Students can then accept one offer. In case of a conditional offer, they may also accept an 'insurance' offer (UCAS, 2023a). When accepting an offer, students agree to a contract with their chosen institution. Students can still attempt to change their accepted offer through a detailed administrative process or withdraw their entire application when deciding not to attend any undergraduate programs that year (UCAS, 2023a).

5. Private higher education in the UK is subject to little regulation and its student body remains largely unknown. However, estimates suggest around 800 providers, with around half principally offering programs at sub-degree level (Hunt & Boliver, 2023). Most

privately funded HE providers cater only for a small number of students; the majority has less than 250 registered students (Hughes et al., 2013).

6. We limit the control group to non-EU high and upper-middle-income countries, following the World Bank's classification of 2016. Countries that were re-classified as lower-middle-income economies (Mongolia, Algeria, and Iran), became unclassified (Venezuela), or were in conflict (Iraq) between the referendum and Brexit are excluded (The World Bank, 2023). As a robustness check, we also consider all non-EU countries available in the data as control units.

7. Northern Europe: Denmark, Estonia, Finland, Latvia, Lithuania, Norway, Iceland, Sweden. Central and Eastern Europe: Bulgaria, Czech Republic, Hungary, Poland, Romania, Slovakia, Slovenia. Southern Europe: Cyprus, Greece, Italy, Malta, Portugal, Spain. Western Europe: Austria, Belgium, France, Germany, Liechtenstein, Luxembourg, Netherlands, Switzerland.

8. Other Europe and Central Asia: Albania, Azerbaijan, Belarus, Bosnia and Herzegovina, Kazakhstan, Macedonia, Montenegro, Russia, Serbia, Turkey, Turkmenistan. Asia: Brunei, China, Hong Kong, Japan, Malaysia, Maldives, Singapore, South Korea, Taiwan, Thailand. Oceania and Pacific Islands: American Samoa, Australia, Fiji, French Polynesia, Guam, Marshall Islands, Nauru, New Caledonia, New Zealand, Northern Mariana Islands, Palau, Tonga, Tuvalu. Latin America and Caribbean: Antigua and Barbuda, Argentina, Aruba, the Bahamas, Barbados, Belize, Brazil, British Virgin Islands, Cayman Islands, Chile, Colombia, Costa Rica, Cuba, Curacao, Dominica, Dominican Republic, Ecuador, Grenada, Guyana, Jamaica, Mexico, Panama, Paraguay, Peru, Puerto Rico, St. Kitts and Nevis, St. Lucia, St. Vincent and The Grenadines, Suriname, Trinidad and Tobago, Turks and Caicos Islands, Uruguay, US Virgin Islands. Middle East and North Africa: Bahrain, Kuwait, Lebanon, Libya, Oman, Qatar, Saudi Arabia, United Arab Emirates. Sub-Saharan Africa: Botswana, Equatorial Guinea, Gabon, Mauritius, Namibia, Seychelles, South Africa. North America: Bermuda, Canada, United States.

9. By using logarithmic outcome variables, we lose origin countries with zero values. This is not an issue, as these origin countries experienced little variation over time and are not very informative. Additionally, Table A6.1 reports a regression using inverse hyperbolic sine transformed outcome variables and a Poisson regression using untransformed outcome variables. This does not change our results.

10. We estimate the elasticity of applications, as this is commonly referred to in the literature. The elasticities can also be estimated for the other outcome variables. We find elasticities of −0.40 (offers), −0.46 (acceptances), and −0.34 (enrolments).

11. Sá (2019) finds a demand elasticity of −0.36, for domestic students in England and Scotland using a log-log regression over the period from 1998 to 2015. When focusing on the 2012 reform in English tuition fees and comparing English applications to untreated Scottish applications in a DD setting (offering a causal interpretation), the estimated elasticity equals −0.11.

12. Generally, the deadline to apply is at the end of January of the year when the course starts. Students can still apply after this date until June of the same year, but applications are not guaranteed to be considered. After June, all applications received are entered into Clearing, the specific process by which universities and colleges fill any remaining places after the normal application window. The application deadline may be earlier. For Oxford, Cambridge and most programs in medicine, dentistry, and veterinary science, applications should arrive by October, one year before classes begin.

13. We also observe a decrease in non-first-degree courses. This decrease is the direct result of the diverging trends from before Brexit. Therefore, we do not attach much importance to this result.

14. HEIs with the right to use the university title can be found for each jurisdiction at https://www.officeforstudents.org.uk/advice-and-guidance/the-register/the-ofs-register/#/, https://www.economy-ni.gov.uk/articles/higher-education-policy, https://www.gov.scot/policies/universities/, and https://www.gov.uk/check-university-award-degree/recognised-bodies-wales. Universities are recognized educational organizations, required to meet

certain education qualities, that provide study programs for (first-degree) undergraduate and postgraduate degrees. Colleges offer further education courses, often more vocational, leading to specific degrees or qualifications (UCAS, 2023d).

15. The Russell Group is an organization of 24 universities that have a shared focus on research and a reputation for academic achievement. Universities of the Russell Group can be found at https://www.theuniguide.co.uk/advice/choosing-a-course/what-is-the-russell-group.

REFERENCES

Acar, I., Courtois, A., Gibson, A. J., Hazelkorn, E., Horvath, A., Jungblut, J., Kilin, E., Maassen, P., Madsen, M., & Magalhães, A. (2018). *Higher education and Brexit: Current European perspectives*. Working Papers on University Reform no. 28.

Adams, R. (2014). Almost a quarter of postgrad students at English universities are Chinese. *The Guardian*. https://www.theguardian.com/education/2014/apr/02/quarter-postgrad-student-english-universities-chinese

Adams, R. (2020). Universities face £460m loss from expected drop in east Asian students. *The Guardian*. https://www.theguardian.com/education/2020/jun/08/universities-face-460m-loss-from-expected-drop-in-east-asian-students-coronavirus

Ahmad, S., Limão, N., Oliver, S., & Shikher, S. (2023). Brexit uncertainty and its (dis) service effects. *American Economic Journal: Economic Policy*, *15*(4), 459–485.

Airey, J., Lauridsen, K. M., Räsänen, A., Salö, L., & Schwach, V. (2017). The expansion of English-medium instruction in the Nordic countries: Can top-down university language policies encourage bottom-up disciplinary literacy goals? *Higher Education*, *73*, 561–576.

Allegretti, A., & Adams, R. (2023). Sunak to force English universities to cap numbers of students on 'low-value' degrees. *The Guardian*. https://www.theguardian.com/education/2023/jul/14/rishi-sunak-force-english-universities-cap-low-value-degrees

Amuedo-Dorantes, C., & Romiti, A. (2024). International student applications in the UK after Brexit. *Journal of Economic Geography*, *24*(5), 637–662. https://doi.org/10.1093/jeg/lbae019

Arkhangelsky, D., Athey, S., Hirshberg, D. A., Imbens, G. W., & Wager, S. (2021). Synthetic difference-in-differences. *The American Economic Review*, *111*(12), 4088–4118.

Auer, D., & Tetlow, D. (2023). Brexit, uncertainty, and migration decisions. *International Migration*, *61*(4), 88–103.

Beine, M., Noël, R., & Ragot, L. (2014). Determinants of the international mobility of students. *Economics of Education Review*, *41*, 40–54.

Bolton, P. (2014). *HE in England from 2012: Student numbers*. House of Commons Library. https://commonslibrary.parliament.uk/research-briefings/sn06205/

Bolton, P. (2023). *Higher education student numbers*. House of Commons Library. https://commonslibrary.parliament.uk/research-briefings/cbp-7857/

Born, B., Müller, G. J., Schularick, M., & Sedláček, P. (2019). The costs of economic nationalism: Evidence from the brexit experiment. *The Economic Journal*, *129*(623), 2722–2744. https://doi.org/10.1093/ej/uez020

Bound, J., Braga, B., Khanna, G., & Turner, S. (2020). A passage to America: University funding and international students. *American Economic Journal: Economic Policy*, *12*(1), 97–126.

Breinlich, H., Leromain, E., Novy, D., & Sampson, T. (2020). Voting with their money: Brexit and outward investment by UK firms. *European Economic Review*, *124*, 103400.

British Council. (2021). *EU students in the UK*. https://www.britishcouncil.bg/en/study-uk/eu-students

British Council. (2023). *Cost of studying and living in the UK*. https://study-uk.britishcouncil.org/moving-uk/cost-studying#

Brooks, R., & Waters, J. (2023). An analysis of the UK's Turing scheme as a response to socio-economic and geo-political challenges. *Higher Education*, 1–19.

Burgess, A., Senior, C., & Moores, E. (2018). A 10-year case study on the changing determinants of university student satisfaction in the UK. *PLoS One*, *13*(2), e0192976.

Burland, E., Dynarski, S., Michelmore, K., Owen, S., & Raghuraman, S. (2023). The power of certainty: Experimental evidence on the effective design of free tuition programs. *The American Economic Review: Insights*, *5*(3), 293–310.

Cardwell, P. J. (2021). Erasmus and the Turing scheme: A metaphor for Brexit? *The Parliament Magazine*, *528*, 38–39. https://www.theparliamentmagazine.eu/news/article/erasmus-and-the-turing-scheme-a-metaphor-for-brexit

Carr, J., Clifton-Sprigg, J., James, J., & Vujić, S. (2020). *Love thy neighbour? Brexit and hate crime*. IZA Discussion Paper No. 13902. https://doi.org/10.2139/ssrn.3738844

Carr, J., James, J., Clifton-Sprigg, J., & Vujić, S. (2022). *Hate in the time of COVID-19: Racial crimes against East Asians*. IZA Discussion Paper No. 15718.

Chen, J., & Roth, J. (2023). Logs with zeros? Some problems and solutions. *Quarterly Journal of Economics*, *139*(2), 891–936.

Citizens Information. (2021). Studying in the UK including Northern Ireland. https://www.citizensinformation.ie/en/education/third_level_education/studying_abroad/studying_in_the_uk_including_northern_ireland.html. Accessed on February 2, 2023

Clarke, D., Pailañir, D., Athey, S., & Imbens, G. (2023). Synthetic difference in differences estimation. *arXiv preprint arXiv:2301.11859*.

Clifton-Sprigg, J., Homburg, I., James, J., & Vujić, S. (2023). *A bad break-up? Assessing the effects of the 2016 brexit referendum on migration*. IZA Discussion Paper No. 16468.

Conlon, G., Litchfield, A., & Sadlier, G. (2011). *Estimating the value to the UK of education exports*. BIS research paper, no. 46. https://www.gov.uk/government/uploads/system/uploads/attachment_data/file/32395/11-980-estimating-value-of-education-exports.pdf

Cook, C. (2015). Home secretary proposes tougher rules for student visas. https://www.bbc.com/news/uk-politics-33561040

Corbett, A., & Hantrais, L. (2023). Higher education and research in the Brexit policy process. *Journal of European Public Policy*, 1–24. https://doi.org/10.1080/13501763.2023.2181854

Davies, R. B., & Specht, L. S. (2024). Brexit and foreign students in gravity. *Review of International Economics*.

Dearden, L., Fitzsimons, E., & Wyness, G. (2014). Money for nothing: Estimating the impact of student aid on participation in higher education. *Economics of Education Review*, *43*, 66–78.

Department of Health and Social Care. (2021). *Travel Update: 47 countries and territories removed from red list*. UK Home Office. https://www.gov.uk/government/news/travel-update-47-countries-and-territories-removed-from-red-list

Department of Health and Social Care. (2023). *Travel to England from another country – COVID-19 rules*. UK Home Office. https://www.gov.uk/guidance/travel-to-england-from-another-country-during-coronavirus-covid-19#full-publication-update-history

Di Iasio, V., & Wahba, J. (2023). Expecting Brexit and UK migration: Should I go? *European Economic Review*, *157*, 104484.

Dias Lopes, A., Mateos-Gonzalez, J. L., & Wakeling, P. (2024). How do tuition fee increases affect international mobility? The case of European Union students in England. *European Journal of Education*, *59*(1), e12592.

Dwenger, N., Storck, J., & Wrohlich, K. (2012). Do tuition fees affect the mobility of university applicants? Evidence from a natural experiment. *Economics of Education Review*, *31*(1), 155–167.

Dynarski, S. M. (2003). Does aid matter? Measuring the effect of student aid on college attendance and completion. *The American Economic Review*, *93*(1), 279–288.

Falkingham, J., Giulietti, C., Wahba, J., & Wang, C. (2021). The impact of Brexit on international students' return intentions. *The Manchester School*, *89*(2), 139–171. https://doi.org/10.1111/manc.12356

Fowler, S., Direito, I., Rich, J., & Mitchell, J. (2018). Initial impact of Brexit on European students and academic staff in UK's engineering higher education. In *46th SEFI Annual Conference 2018*.

Geiger, M., & Güntner, J. (2023). The chronology of Brexit and UK monetary policy. *Journal of Monetary Economics*, *142*, 103516.

Gil, N. (2015). A guide to the government's new rules for international students. *The Guardian*. https://www.theguardian.com/education/2015/jul/29/a-guide-to-the-governments-new-rules-for-international-students

Gower, M. (2018). *The UK's points-based system for immigration*. House of Commons Library. https://commonslibrary.parliament.uk/research-briefings/cbp-7662/

Gu, Y., & Li, S. (2023). International student inflow and city innovation: Evidence from China. *Regional Science Policy & Practice*, *15*(9), 1907–1926.

Hale, T., Angrist, N., Goldszmidt, R., Kira, B., Petherick, A., Phillips, T., Webster, S., Cameron-Blake, E., Hallas, L., & Majumdar, S. (2021). A global panel database of pandemic policies (Oxford COVID-19 Government response tracker). *Nature Human Behaviour*, *5*(4), 529–538. https://doi.org/10.1038/s41562-021-01079-8

HESA. (2023a, September 14). *Higher education student statistics: UK, 2021/22 - Where students come from and go to study*. https://www.hesa.ac.uk/news/19-01-2023/sb265-higher-education-student-statistics/location

HESA. (2023b, September 14). *The impact of the COVID-19 pandemic on 2021/22 Student data*. https://www.hesa.ac.uk/insight/19-01-2023/impact-covid-19-2022-student-data

HESA. (2023c, August 5). *Rounding and suppression to anonymise statistics*. https://www.hesa.ac.uk/about/regulation/data-protection/rounding-and-suppression-anonymise-statistics

HESA. (2024, August 5). *Where do HE students come from? HE student enrolments by domicile*. https://www.hesa.ac.uk/data-and-analysis/students/where-from

Highman, L., Marginson, S., & Papatsiba, V. (2023). Strategic European partnerships for UK universities post-Brexit: Navigating a globally contested field of world-class universities. *Tertiary Education and Management*, *29*(3), 295–314. https://doi.org/10.1007/s11233-023-09123-0

Hillman, N. (2014). *A guide to the removal of student number controls*. Higher Education Policy Institute. https://www.hepi.ac.uk/wp-content/uploads/2014/09/Clean-copy-of-SNC-paper1.pdf

Hillman, N. (2020). *Universities and Brexit: Past, present and future*. UK in a Changing Europe. https://ukandeu.ac.uk/long-read/universities-and-brexit-past-present-and-future/

Hou, C., Fan, P., Du, D., Gui, Q., & Duan, D. (2022). Does international student mobility foster scientific collaboration? Evidence from a network analysis. *Compare: A Journal of Comparative and International Education*, *52*(2), 327–344.

Hubble, S., & Bolton, P. (2018). *Higher education tuition fees in England*. House of Commons Library. https://commonslibrary.parliament.uk/research-briefings/cbp-8151/

Hughes, T., Porter, A., Jones, S., & Sheen, J. (2013). *Privately funded providers of higher education in the UK*. BIS RESEARCH PAPER. NO. 111. https://assets.publishing.service.gov.uk/government/uploads/system/uploads/attachment_data/file/207128/bis-13-900-privately-funded-providers-of-higher-education-in-the-UK.pdf

Hunt, S. A., & Boliver, V. (2023). The private higher education provider landscape in the UK. *Studies in Higher Education*, *48*(9), 1346–1360. https://doi.org/10.1080/03075079.2023.2199317

ICEF monitor. (2023a). *Dutch government asks universities to suspend active international recruitment amid capacity concerns*. ICEF GmbH.

ICEF monitor. (2023b). *Netherlands takes another step toward limiting international enrolment growth*. ICEF GmbH. https://monitor.icef.com/2023/04/netherlands-takes-another-step-toward-limiting-international-enrolment-growth/

ICEF monitor. (2023c). *What if there is no room? The link between student housing and enrolment capacity*. ICEF GmbH. https://monitor.icef.com/2022/07/what-if-there-is-no-room-the-link-between-student-housing-and-enrolment-capacity/

Institute for Government. (2022). *Timeline of UK government coronavirus lockdowns and restrictions*. Institute for Government. https://www.instituteforgovernment.org.uk/data-visualisation/timeline-coronavirus-lockdowns

Joppke, C. (2020). Immigration in the populist crucible: Comparing Brexit and Trump. *Comparative Migration Studies*, *8*(1), 1–18.

Kahanec, M., & Králiková, R. (2011). *Pulls of international student mobility*. IZA Discussion Paper No. 6233. https://doi.org/10.2139/ssrn.1977819

Kato, T., & Sparber, C. (2013). Quotas and quality: The effect of H-1B visa restrictions on the pool of prospective undergraduate students from abroad. *The Review of Economics and Statistics*, *95*(1), 109–126. https://doi.org/10.1162/rest_a_00245

Kranz, S. (2022). *Synthetic difference-in-differences with Time- varying covariates*. https://github.com/skranz/xsynthdid/blob/main/paper/synthdid_with_covariates.pdf

Lewis, J. (2023a). *Eligibility for home fee status and student support in Scotland*. House of Commons Library. https://commonslibrary.parliament.uk/eligibility-for-home-fee-status-and-student-support-in-scotland/#:~:text=Undergraduate%20home%20fees%20are%20capped,on%20the%20course%20and%20institution

Lewis, J. (2023b). *Eligibility for home fee status and student support in Wales*. House of Commons Library. https://commonslibrary.parliament.uk/eligibility-for-home-fee-status-and-student-support-in-wales/

Lewis, J. (2024). *Eligibility for home fee status and student support in Northern Ireland*. House of Commons Library. https://commonslibrary.parliament.uk/eligibility-for-home-fee-status-and-student-support-in-northern-ireland/#:~:text=For%20the%202023%2F24%20academic,live%20elsewhere%20in%20the%20UK

Mayhew, K. (2017). UK higher education and Brexit. *Oxford Review of Economic Policy*, *33*(suppl_1), S155–S161. https://doi.org/10.1093/oxrep/grx012

Mayhew, K. (2022). Brexit and UK higher education. *Oxford Review of Economic Policy*, *38*(1), 179–187. https://doi.org/10.1093/oxrep/grab043

Migration Advisory Committee. (2018). *Impact of international students in the UK*. Migration Advisory Committee. https://assets.publishing.service.gov.uk/government/uploads/system/uploads/attachment_data/file/739089/Impact_intl_students_report_published_v1.1.pdf

Migration Observatory. (2020). *The new Hong Kong British National (Overseas) visa*. https://migrationobservatory.ox.ac.uk/resources/commentaries/qa-the-new-route-to-citizenship-for-some-hong-kong-residents/

Migration Observatory. (2022). *Student migration to the UK*. The Migration Observatory. https://migrationobservatory.ox.ac.uk/resources/briefings/student-migration-to-the-uk/

Mok, K. H., Xiong, W., Ke, G., & Cheung, J. O. W. (2021). Impact of COVID-19 pandemic on international higher education and student mobility: Student perspectives from mainland China and Hong Kong. *International Journal of Educational Research*, *105*, 101718. https://doi.org/10.1016/j.ijer.2020.101718

Mullahy, J., & Norton, E. C. (2022). *Why transform Y? A critical assessment of dependent-variable transformations in regression models for skewed and sometimes-zero outcomes*. NBER Working Paper Series. No. 30735.

Nielsen, H. S., Sørensen, T., & Taber, C. (2010). Estimating the effect of student aid on college enrollment: Evidence from a government grant policy reform. *American Economic Journal: Economic Policy*, *2*(2), 185–215.

Oberhofer, H., & Pfaffermayr, M. (2021). Estimating the trade and welfare effects of Brexit: A panel data structural gravity model. *Canadian Journal of Economics/Revue canadienne d'économique*, *54*(1), 338–375.

PA media. (2022). Cap on foreign student numbers could send UK universities 'over the edge'. *The Guardian*. https://www.theguardian.com/education/2022/nov/25/cap-on-foreign-student-numbers-could-send-uk-universities-over-the-edge

Portes, J. (2021). *Between the lines: Immigration to the UK between the referendum and brexit*. Brexit Institute. WP N.12 - 2020. https://doi.org/10.2139/ssrn.3759590

Portes, J. (2022). Immigration and the UK economy after Brexit. *Oxford Review of Economic Policy*, *38*(1), 82–96. https://doi.org/10.1093/oxrep/grab045

Rambachan, A., & Roth, J. (2023). A more credible approach to parallel trends. *The Review of Economic Studies*, *90*(5), 2555–2591.

Rosenzweig, M. R. (2008). *Higher education and international migration in Asia: Brain circulation*. Annual World Bank conference on development economics.

Sá, F. (2019). The effect of university fees on applications, attendance and course choice: Evidence from a natural experiment in the UK. *Economica*, *86*(343), 607–634.

She, Q., & Wotherspoon, T. (2013). International student mobility and highly skilled migration: A comparative study of Canada, the United States, and the United Kingdom. *SpringerPlus*, *2*(1), 1–14.

Shih, K. (2015). Labor market opennes, H-1B visa policy, and the scale of international student enrollment in the United States. *Economic Inquiry*, *54*(1), 121–138. https://doi.org/10.1111/ecin.12250

Solis, A. (2017). Credit access and college enrollment. *Journal of Political Economy*, *125*(2), 562–622.

Stuen, E. T., Mobarak, A. M., & Maskus, K. E. (2012). Skilled immigration and innovation: Evidence from enrolment fluctuations in US doctoral programmes. *The Economic Journal*, *122*(565), 1143–1176.

The World Bank. (2023, January 26). World Bank Country and Lending Groups. https://datahelpdesk.worldbank.org/knowledgebase/articles/906519-world-bank-country-and-lending-groups

UCAS. (2022). *Statistical Releases – Daily Clearing Analysis 2022*.

UCAS. (2023a). *After you apply*. https://www.ucas.com/undergraduate/after-you-apply

UCAS. (2023b). *How much does uni or college cost?* https://www.ucas.com/discover/support-cost-living/how-much-does-uni-or-college-cost#:~:text=Outside%20of%20tuition%20fees%2C%20which,a%20typical%20week%2C%20excluding%20rent

UCAS. (2023c). *Postgraduate fees and funding*. https://www.ucas.com/postgraduate/postgraduate-fees-and-funding

UCAS. (2023d). *Studying at a higher education college*. https://www.ucas.com/applying/you-apply/what-and-where-study/study-options/studying-higher-education-college

UCAS. (2023e). *What is UCAS?* https://www.ucas.com/about-us/who-we-are

UK Health Security Agency. (2022). *Public reminded to stay safe as COVID-19 England restrictions lift*. UK Home Office. https://www.gov.uk/government/news/public-reminded-to-stay-safe-as-covid-19-england-restrictions-lift

UK Home Office. (2012). *Statement of intent: Accession of Croatia to the EU*. https://assets.publishing.service.gov.uk/media/5a7b4cabed915d3ed90637c4/statement-of-intent.pdf

UK Home Office. (2023a). *Study in the UK on a student visa*. https://www.gov.uk/study-uk-student-visa

UK Home Office. (2023b). *The UK and Spain sign an agreement on education cooperation*. https://www.gov.uk/government/news/the-uk-and-spain-sign-an-agreement-on-education-cooperation

UK Home Office. (2024). *Tough government action on student visas comes into effect*. https://www.gov.uk/government/news/tough-government-action-on-student-visas-comes-into-effect

Universities, UK. (2021). Changes for EU students in the UK: FAQs on fees, immigration, Erasmus+. https://www.universitiesuk.ac.uk/topics/international/changes-eu-students-uk-faqs-fees

Universities UK International. (2022). *International student recruitment from Europe: The road to recovery*. Universities UK International. https://www.universitiesuk.ac.uk/sites/default/files/field/downloads/2022-11/UUKi%20Studyportals%20International%20student%20recruitment%20from%20Europe.pdf

Universities UK International & IDP Connect. (2021). *International student recruitment: Why aren't we second? Universities UK*. IDP Connect. https://www.universitiesuk.ac.uk/sites/default/files/field/downloads/2021-09/WAWS_2_Final.pdf

University of Bristol. (2011). *Undergraduate admissions principles and procedures (overseas) 2011*. https://www.bristol.ac.uk/media-library/sites/university/migrated/documents/ugappoverseas2011.pdf

Van der Klaauw, W. (2002). Estimating the effect of financial aid offers on college enrollment: A regression–discontinuity approach. *International Economic Review*, *43*(4), 1249–1287.

Vickers, P., & Bekhradnia, B. (2007). The economic costs and benefits of international students. *Higher Education Policy Institute*. https://www.hepi.ac.uk/wp-content/uploads/2014/02/32Economiceffectsofinternationalstudents.pdf

Wakeling, P., & Jefferies, K. (2013). The effect of tuition fees on student mobility: The UK and Ireland as a natural experiment. *British Educational Research Journal*, *39*(3), 491–513.

Walker, N. (2021). *Brexit timeline: Events leading to the UK's exit from the European Union*. House of Commons Library. https://researchbriefings.files.parliament.uk/documents/CBP-7960/CBP-7960.pdf

APPENDIX: SUPPLEMENTARY MATERIAL

A1. HIGHER EDUCATION IN THE UK

A1.1 Tuition Fees

After having free higher education for several decades, the UK government introduced tuition fees of £1,000 per year for full-time graduate courses across the UK in 1998. Given that education is a devolved power, the constituent parts of the UK could implement their own requirements and as such, over the years, tuition fees have diverged.

Starting in 2006, universities in England were allowed to charge variable fees of up to £3,000 a year for full-time graduate courses. In 2006 and 2007, the same maximum fee was introduced in Ireland and Wales, respectively. In the following years, this cap on tuition fees gradually rose with inflation up to £3,145 (Burgess et al., 2018). In England, tuition fees were drastically raised to £9,000 per year starting the academic year 2012/13. Most ongoing direct public funding for tuition was cut, and loan repayment terms were changed. Five years later, the cap was further increased to £9,250 a year (Hubble & Bolton, 2018). Northern Ireland increased its tuition fees in the same manner to £9,250 per year, but only for students living in the UK outside of Northern Ireland. Residents of Northern Ireland remained under the previous cap, adjusted for inflation (Lewis, 2024). In Wales, the cap on tuition fees for full-time undergraduate courses was increased to £9,000 per year and remains at this level to date. UK students from outside of Wales must pay their tuition fees in full while Welsh students receive grants from almost half the cap to help cover their costs (Lewis, 2023b).

Scotland followed a different path. Several years after the higher education tuition fees of £1,000 were introduced, the Scottish government abolished the upfront tuition fees in 2000. They were replaced with a mandatory student contribution made after completing a degree-level course, initially set at £2,000. This one-off endowment fee was scraped in 2008. Tuition fees were re-introduced and are, at this date, capped at £1,820 for Scottish students and £9,250 for students who live elsewhere in the UK or Ireland. Home students can, however, if they meet the requirements, have their tuition fees paid for by the Student Award Agency Scotland, resulting in free higher education for these students (Burgess et al., 2018; Lewis, 2023a).

While UK universities can charge below the tuition fee cap, most of them charge the maximum. Fees for international (or 'overseas') students have never been capped and are determined by providers. They can be much higher depending on the course and the institution. Fees vary from £11,400 to £38,000, with an estimated average cost of around £22,200 per year (British Council, 2023).

At the postgraduate level, there is generally no fee cap. Tuition fees vary but still tend to be significantly lower for home students than for international students (Hubble & Bolton, 2018). Home postgraduate tuition fees range from

£4,900 a year to over £30,000, with an average of around £11,000 per year (UCAS, 2023c). International postgraduate tuition fees vary from £9,000 - £30,000, with an average estimated around £17,109 per year (British Council, 2023).

A1.2 Admission Caps

HEIs in the UK must adhere to a series of regulations that often vary over time. These regulations include, among others, restrictions on the number of students that universities and colleges can recruit.

Starting in the 1990s, each higher education institution in England could only recruit a maximum number of home-fee undergraduate students (i.e., UK students and pre-Brexit EU students). In 2012/13, this regulation was relaxed, and universities were allowed to accept as many students as they liked who had at least two A grades and a B grade at A-level or equivalent. Other students remained under the cap. In 2013/14, this exemption was expanded to also include those with one A grade and two B grades. In December 2013, the UK government further announced its plans to end student number controls altogether. The cap was first relaxed in 2014/15 by providing an additional 30,000 student places. In 2015/16, the cap on the number of UK and EU-domiciled undergraduates was abolished. The government estimated this to result in an additional 60,000 students a year (Bolton, 2014; Hillman, 2014). In the following years, all UK universities were free to recruit as many students as they wanted to. In 2020, the government debated introducing a temporary cap on student numbers in 2020/21. The cap was intended to stabilize student admissions and dampen the heightened competition between universities for UK students. This heightened competition was a result of the (expected) loss of international students due to the Covid-19 pandemic. However, before the academic year could start, the cap was already lifted (Bolton, 2023).

Limiting student admissions continues to be a topic of debate. For instance, starting in 2022, the UK government discussed the introduction of a cap to limit the number of students taking "low-value" degrees in the UK, particularly with a focus on foreign students as an attempt to bring down net migration (e.g., Allegretti & Adams (2023) and PA media (2022) in the Guardian). At the time of writing, no actual cap has been formally introduced.

A2. FOREIGN STUDENTS IN THE UNITED KINGDOM: VISA REQUIREMENTS AND OTHERS

Non-EU migration in the United Kingdom is governed by a points-based system of immigration that admits migrants based on their qualifications and potential benefit to the United Kingdom. At the time of Brexit in 2020, the system categorized migrants into 5 Tiers: highly skilled workers (1), sponsored skilled workers (2), low skilled workers (3), students (4), and special categories of temporary migrants (short-term or voluntary visas) (5). International non-EU students usually apply for the Tier-4 student visa or, in some cases, for the Tier-5 short-term study visa (Gower, 2018).

Generally, before applying for a student visa, international students must have been accepted by a recognized education institution in the UK and must be able to provide a 'Confirmation of Acceptance for Studies'. During the visa application process, students must have a current passport and pay an application fee. They must also prove they can support themselves financially during their studies, show a sufficient knowledge of English, and pay a healthcare surcharge (£470 for students in 2020). Once arrived in the UK, students must collect their Residence Permit and must comply with the terms and conditions of the student visa (e.g., not working more hours than allowed) (UK Home Office, 2023a).

Most students apply for a Tier-4 student visa, which costs almost £400. How long students can stay in the UK depends on their studies. Usually, they can stay for up to five years for courses at degree level and up to two years for courses below degree level. The visa allows students to bring dependents (i.e., a partner and children) and permits them to work outside of their studies. Students can easily extend their visas if they wish to continue their studies in the UK. Students can also switch to another visa in the months prior to the expiry of their current visa if they wish to stay in the UK after graduation. Students can switch to a Tier-2 category (e.g. Skilled Worker visa) or, since 2021, to a Graduate visa. The Graduate visa allows you to stay in the UK for at least two years after successfully completing your studies. It is not tied to a specific job or skill level and has no salary or sponsorship requirements (UK Home Office, 2023a).

Since the introduction of the point-based immigration system in 2008, there have been made several changes to the regulations and requirements for migrants. Table A2.1 summarizes the evolution of all relevant policy changes.

Table A2.1. Changes in British Migration Regulations.

Feb-2008	Points-based immigration system launched through successive Statements of Changes to Immigration Rules. The visa system with 5 Tiers is now in place
Jan-2010	Target of reducing total net migration < 100,000 introduced. Although target includes international students, this did not translate into immediate relevant policy changes
Apr-2011	Small adaptations in Tier-4 regulations: restrictions on permission to work, restrictions on the entitlement to bring dependents, and tightened English language requirements
Apr-2012	Tier-1 (Post-study work) route which allowed non-EU students to stay in the UK and work at any skill level up to two years after graduation, is closed
Apr-2013	Introduction of doctorate extension scheme, allowing students 1 year in the UK after completing a PhD
Jan-2014	Transitional restrictions on Bulgarians and Romanians (joined EU in 2012) lifted
Nov-2014	Tier 4 permitted refusal rate is reduced from 20% to 10%: if 10% of sponsor's prospective students are refused, they lose ability to recruit international students
Apr-2015	(Extended) student visitor routes re-branded into new routes for short-term study (Tier 5)
Apr-2015	Immigration health surcharge to gain access to NHS introduced for non-Europeans in UK for +6 months. Surcharge set at £200/year and £150/year for students
Jun-2016	**Brexit referendum**
Jan-2018	Certain part-time studies removed from short-term study route and included in Tier 4
Jan-2018	Small adaptations in Tier-4 regulations: permission to apply within UK for leave to complete work placement/study abroad and dependents' work rights remain valid when applying to same course
Jan-2018	Small adaptations in Tier-5 regulations: Minimum age requirement short-term study route reduced from 18 to 16, students permitted to remain in UK up to 30 days after their study, and students permitted to complete electives in certain scenarios
Jun-2018	Transitional restrictions on Croatians (joined EU in 2013) lifted
Jul-2018	Small adaptations in Tier-4 regulations: Minimum length postgraduate course needed to be eligible for bring dependents reduced, documentary requirements for applications reduced for 11 countries, and all students allowed to participate in study abroad program
Dec-2018	Immigration health surcharge increased to £400/year and £300/year for students
Jul-2019	Target of reducing total net migration < 100,000 scrapped. This again did not translate into immediate relevant policy changes
Aug-2019	Higher Education Reform changes to Tier 4: full privileges are extended to Higher Education Providers with a track record of compliance
Oct-2020	Immigration health surcharge increased to £624/year and £470/year for students
Dec-2020	Tiers are revised, simplified, and replaced by routes: Student routes replace Tier 4 (General), skilled Worker route replace Tier 2 (General), Intra-company routes replace Tier 2 (Intra-Company Transfer/Graduate Trainee), etc.
Dec-2020	**Brexit: Free movement between the UK and EEA/Switzerland ended. EEA/Swiss students are now subject to same visa requirements, tuition fees, etc. as non-EEA/Swiss students**
Jul-2021	Graduate route introduced, allowing international students to stay in the UK after graduation and work, or look for work, at any skill level for 2 or years. Discontinuation of Doctorate Extension scheme for PhD students who can now apply for Graduate route

Notes: More detailed changes and updates in British migration policy or legislation are provided by the UK Home Office, https://www.gov.uk/government/publications/policy-and-legislative-changes-affecting-migration-to-the-uk-timeline.

A3. EVENT STUDY FIGURES

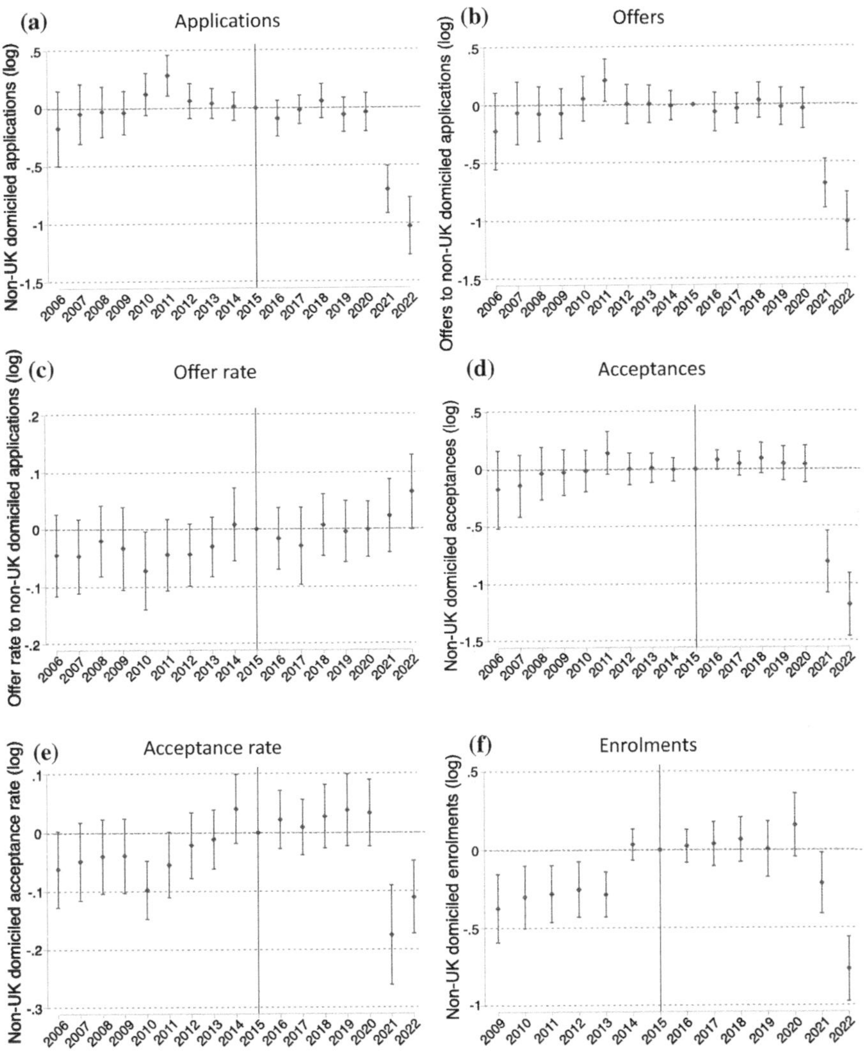

Fig. A3.1. Dynamic DD, Referendum as Treatment. *Notes:* Dynamic DD estimations of the log-linear model based on UCAS (2006/07–2022/23) (figures a–e) and HESA (2009/10–2022/23) (figure f) data. Confidence intervals based on cluster robust standard errors.

A4. SYNTHETIC DD WEIGHTS

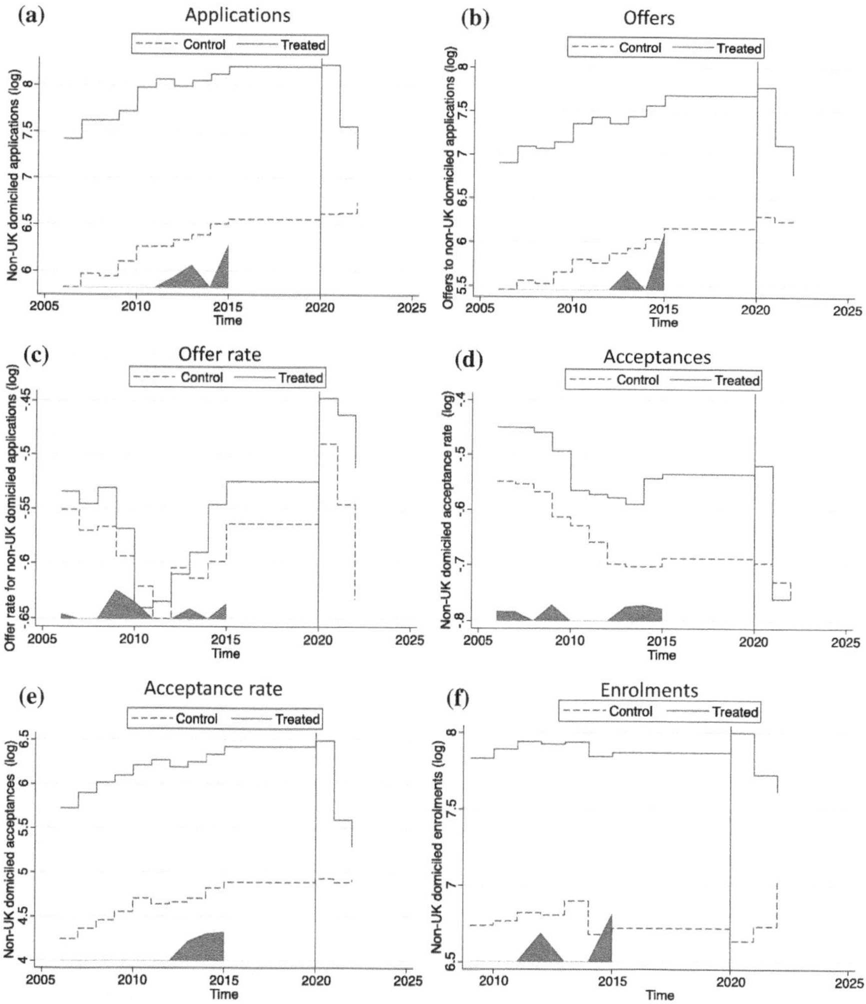

Fig. A4.1. Time Weights, Synthetic DD. *Notes:* Treatment and synthetic control outcome trends and their time-specific weights. Estimations based on UCAS (2006/07–2022/23) and HESA (2009/10–2022/23) data. The period between the referendum and Brexit (2016/17–2019/20) is excluded, which is reflected in the long horizontal line between those periods.

(a)

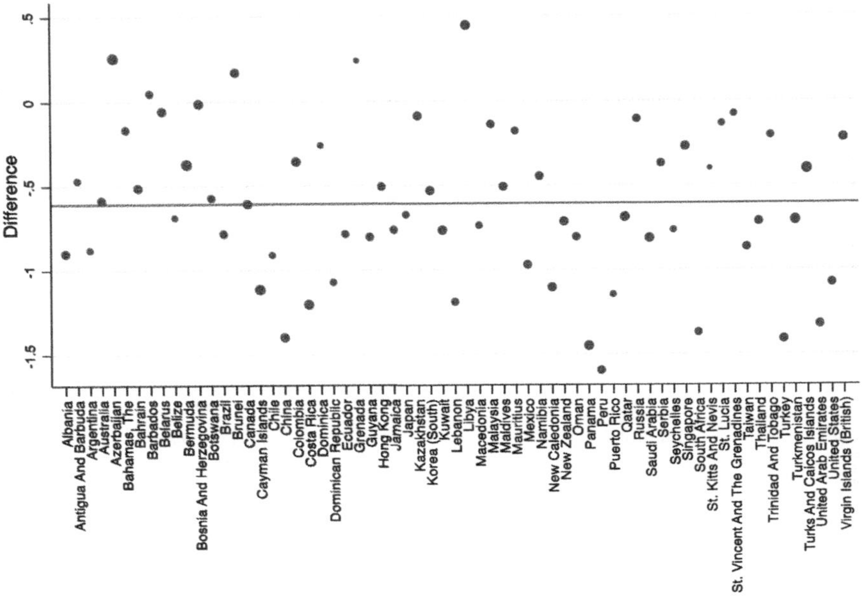

(b)

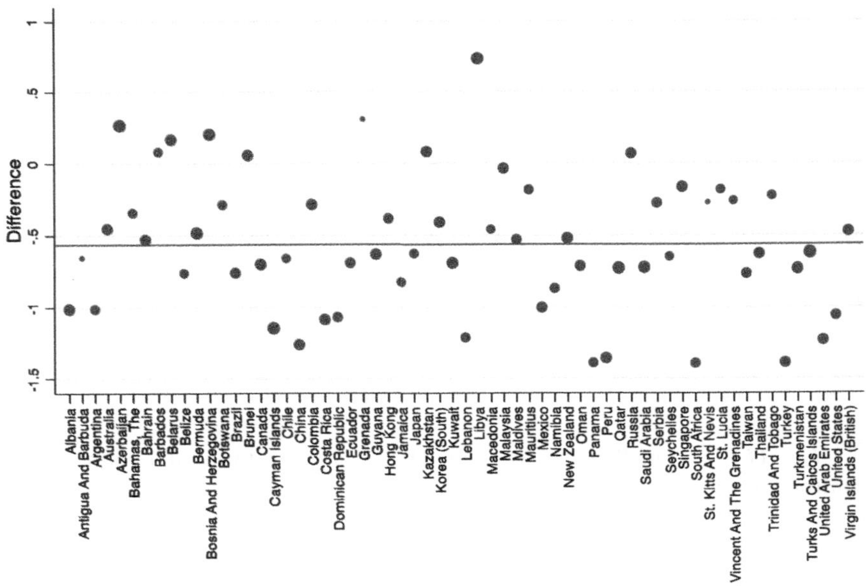

Fig. A4.2. Unit Weights, Synthetic DD. *Notes:* Unit-specific weights for synthetic DD estimator. Estimations based on UCAS (2006/07–2022/23) and HESA (2009/10–2022/23) data.

(c)

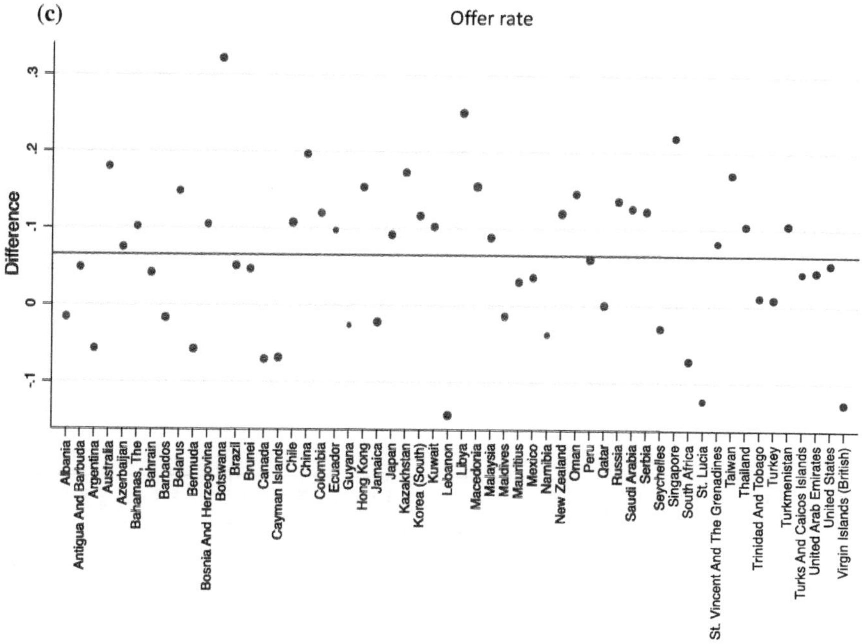

(d)

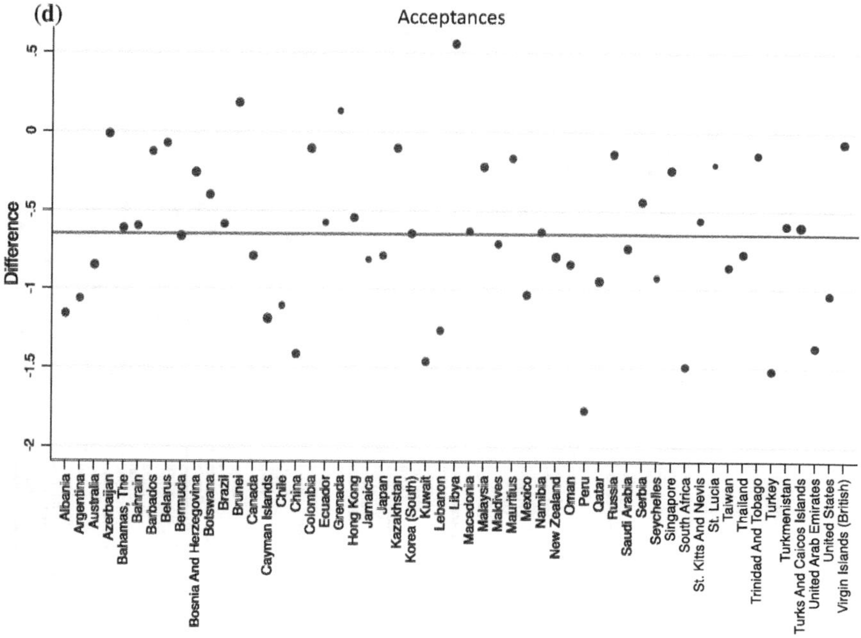

Fig. A4.2. **(Continued)**

(e)

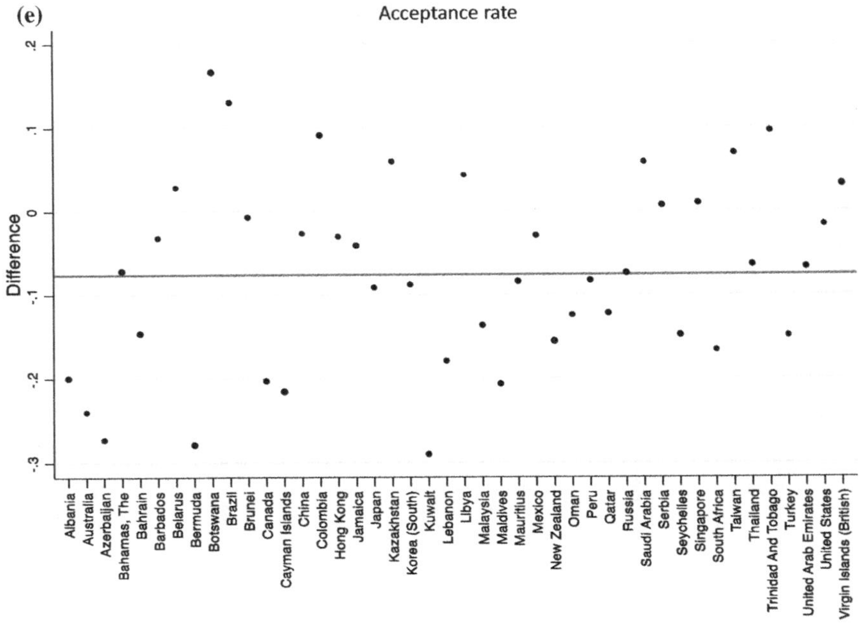

(f)

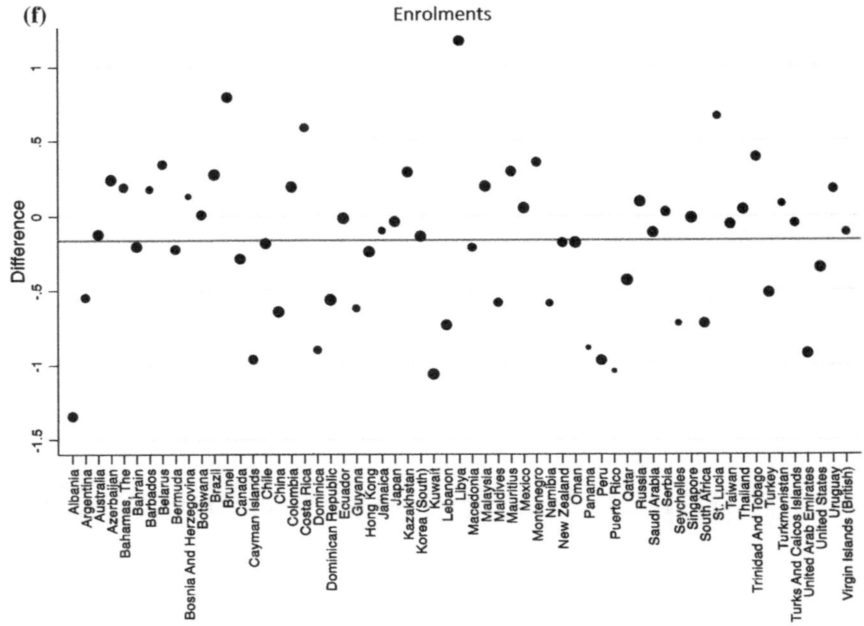

Fig. A4.2. **(Continued)**

Table A4.1 Unit Weights Top 15 Countries, Synthetic DD.

Applications		Offers		Offer Rate	
Turks & Caicos Islands	0.0267	Turks & Caicos Islands	0.0244	Macedonia	0.0243
Bermuda	0.0261	Azerbaijan	0.0242	Chile	0.0232
Azerbaijan	0.0256	Cayman Islands	0.0240	Jamaica	0.0223
Turkmenistan	0.0250	Libya	0.0236	Lebanon	0.0221
Cayman Islands	0.0241	Qatar	0.0224	Libya	0.0220
Costa Rica	0.0223	Bermuda	0.0217	Peru	0.0220
Libya	0.0216	Bosnia & Herzegovina	0.0215	New Zealand	0.0214
Panama	0.0215	Saudi Arabia	0.0209	Cayman Islands	0.0206
Qatar	0.0208	Kuwait	0.0204	Barbados	0.0206
Saudi Arabia	0.0202	Turkmenistan	0.0203	Botswana	0.0205
Colombia	0.0201	Belarus	0.0198	Japan	0.0204
Bosnia & Herzegovina	0.0199	Peru	0.0193	Turkey	0.0204
Kuwait	0.0195	Albania	0.0192	Turkmenistan	0.0201
Singapore	0.0188	Costa Rica	0.0192	Bermuda	0.0201
Virgin Islands (UK)	0.0186	New Zealand	0.0192	South Africa	0.0198

Acceptances		Acceptance rate		Enrolments	
Turks & Caicos Islands	0.0280	Cayman Islands	0.0320	Dominican Republic	0.0235
Cayman Islands	0.0254	Virgin Islands (UK)	0.0307	Qatar	0.0235
New Zealand	0.0240	New Zealand	0.0295	Kuwait	0.0234
Bermuda	0.0239	Botswana	0.0270	Oman	0.0234
Bosnia & Herzegovina	0.0236	Bermuda	0.0268	Ecuador	0.0225
Qatar	0.0226	Russia	0.0265	Singapore	0.0224
Colombia	0.0223	The Bahamas	0.0264	Hong Kong	0.0223
Australia	0.0220	Bahrain	0.0258	Mexico	0.0221
Virgin Islands (UK)	0.0219	Albania	0.0258	China	0.0218
Azerbaijan	0.0214	Colombia	0.0257	Azerbaijan	0.0216
Brunei	0.0214	Jamaica	0.0255	Brazil	0.0213
Singapore	0.0214	Seychelles	0.0252	United Arab Emirates	0.0212
Turkmenistan	0.0210	Turkmenistan	0.0251	United States	0.0211
Canada	0.0209	Mauritius	0.0249	Russia	0.0210
China	0.0204	Cayman Islands	0.0320	Ecuador	0.0225

Notes: Unit-specific weights from the top 15 control countries for synthetic DD estimator. Estimations based on UCAS (2006/07—2022/23) and HESA (2009/10—2022/23) data. Weights lie very close to each other and no countries receive zero weight.

A5. SYNTHETIC EVENT-STUDY, HETEROGENEOUS RESULTS

Table A5.1. Synthetic DD Estimates by Student Characteristics, Applications.

	Age				
	Below 18	18	19	20	21–24
	(1)	(2)	(3)	(4)	(5)
ATT	−0.42***	−0.58***	−0.58***	−0.63***	−0.55***
	(0.15)	(0.11)	(0.14)	(0.13)	(0.12)
Observations	715	1,040	1,040	936	949
Pre-mean	652	2,760	2,321	778	646

	Age		Sex	
	25 to 29	30 and over	Female	Male
	(6)	(7)	(8)	(9)
ATT	−0.72***	−0.83***	−0.62***	−0.57***
	(0.19)	(0.20)	(0.11)	(0.09)
Observations	676	546	1,157	1,118
Pre-mean	111	45	4,310	3,002

	Application deadline		
	October	January	June
	(10)	(11)	(12)
ATT	−0.53***	−0.69***	−0.49***
	(0.11)	(0.11)	(0.13)
Observations	728	1,001	871
Pre-mean	221	1,212	245

	EU origin region			
	North	East	South	West
	(13)	(14)	(15)	(16)
ATT	−0.85***	−0.83***	−0.29*	−0.35***
	(0.18)	(0.19)	(0.16)	(0.09)
Observations	884	871	845	884
Pre-mean	3,904	8,333	11,454	6,901

	EU origin's economy strength			
	GDP pc.		Unemployment rate	
	Below median	Above median	Below median	Above median
	(17)	(18)	(19)	(20)
ATT	−0.91***	−0.50***	−0.56***	−0.75***
	(0.26)	(0.10)	(0.13)	(0.16)
Observations	546	624	546	494
Pre-mean	12,032	6,717	4,748	10,407

Notes: Log-linear synthetic DD estimations based on UCAS (2006/07–2022/23) data. The period between the referendum and Brexit (2016/17–2019/20) is excluded. The table reports the average treatment effect on the treated and the mean outcome for EU origin countries in 2019. Bootstrapped standard errors (200 replications) in parentheses. $^{***}p < 0.01$, $^{**}p < 0.05$, and $^{*}p < 0.1$.

Table A5.2. Synthetic DD Estimates by Student Characteristics, Offers.

	Age				
	Below 18	18	19	20	21–24
	(1)	(2)	(3)	(4)	(5)
ATT	−0.32*	−0.51***	−0.63***	−0.50***	−0.47***
	(0.16)	(0.11)	(0.12)	(0.13)	(0.13)
Observations	637	962	936	793	845
Pre-mean	438	1,934	1,601	479	352
	Age		Sex		
	25–29	30 and over	Female	Male	
	(6)	(7)	(8)	(9)	
ATT	−0.55***	−0.64**	−0.56***	−0.54***	
	(0.19)	(0.28)	(0.11)	(0.10)	
Observations	572	351	1,131	1,066	
Pre-mean	55	18	2,871	2,006	
	EU origin region				
	North	East	South	West	
	(10)	(11)	(12)	(13)	
ATT	−0.75***	−0.78***	−0.23	−0.35***	
	(0.16)	(0.18)	(0.15)	(0.09)	
Observations	845	832	806	845	
Pre-mean	2,523	6,081	7,742	4,121	
	EU origin's economy strength				
	GDP pc.		Unemployment		
	Below median	Above median	Below median	Above median	
	(14)	(15)	(16)	(17)	
ATT	−0.80***	−0.48***	−0.48***	−0.70***	
	(0.27)	(0.11)	(0.13)	(0.21)	
Observations	533	598	546	468	
Pre-mean	8,840	4,333	3,029	7,080	

Notes: Log-linear synthetic DD estimations based on UCAS (2006/07–2022/23) data. Period between referendum and Brexit (2016/17–2019/20) is excluded. The table reports the average treatment effect on the treated, the mean outcome for EU origin countries in 2019. Bootstrapped standard errors (200 replications) in parentheses. $^{***}p < 0.01$, $^{**}p < 0.05$, and $^{*}p < 0.1$.

Table A5.3. Synthetic DD Estimates by Student Characteristics, Acceptances.

	Age				
	Below 18 (1)	18 (2)	19 (3)	20 (4)	21–24 (5)
ATT	−0.52***	−0.74***	−0.92***	−0.97***	−0.61***
	(0.17)	(0.11)	(0.14)	(0.14)	(0.15)
Observations	429	793	793	676	702
Pre-mean	85	378	332	126	119

	Age		Sex	
	25–29 (6)	30 and over (7)	Female (8)	Male (9)
ATT	−0.61**	−0.23	−0.66***	−0.68***
	(0.24)	(0.31)	(0.12)	(0.13)
Observations	390	169	962	949
Pre-mean	25	12	628	450

	EU origin region			
	North (10)	East (11)	South (12)	West (13)
ATT	−0.87***	−0.91***	−0.25	−0.43***
	(0.18)	(0.15)	(0.21)	(0.10)
Observations	754	741	715	741
Pre-mean	534	1,248	1,824	1,054

	EU origin's economy strength			
	GDP pc.		Unemployment	
	Below median (14)	Above median (15)	Below median (16)	Above median (17)
ATT	−0.84***	−0.64***	−0.63***	−0.77***
	(0.24)	(0.12)	(0.14)	(0.23)
Observations	455	572	520	416
Pre-mean	1,804	984	702	1,536

Notes: Log-linear synthetic DD estimations based on UCAS (2006/07–2022/23) data. Period between referendum and Brexit (2016/17–2019/20) is excluded. The table reports the average treatment effect on the treated, the mean outcome for EU origin countries in 2019. Bootstrapped standard errors (200 replications) in parentheses. $^{***}p < 0.01$, $^{**}p < 0.05$, and $^{*}p < 0.1$.

Table A5.4. Synthetic DD Estimates by Student Characteristics, Enrolments.

	Education level				Study type
		Other	Postgraduate		
	First degree	undergraduate	(research)	(taught)	Full-time
	(1)	(2)	(3)	(4)	(5)
ATT	−0.25***	−0.91***	−0.12	−0.23**	−0.21**
	(0.10)	(0.18)	(0.10)	(0.09)	(0.08)
Observations	820	480	620	800	440
Pre-mean	3,408	75	384	920	4,502

	Study type	EU origin region			
	Part-time	North	East	South	West
	(6)	(7)	(8)	(9)	(10)
ATT	−0.16	−0.36***	0.07	0.01	−0.12
	(0.12)	(0.09)	(0.13)	(0.21)	(0.09)
Observations	330	630	620	610	620
Pre-mean	285	1,992	4,654	8,462	5,644

	UK region			
	England	Wales	Scotland	Northern Ireland
	(11)	(12)	(13)	(14)
ATT	−0.14	0.39***	−0.42***	−0.49
	(0.10)	(0.13)	(0.10)	(0.33)
Observations	890	580	710	230
Pre-mean	3,944	183	650	10

	Higher educ. classification		University classification	
	University	Other	Russel	Other
	(15)	(16)	(17)	(18)
ATT	−0.01	−0.05	−0.18	0.03
	(0.09)	(0.12)	(0.11)	(0.09)
Observations	356	264	308	352
Pre-mean	4,247	539	573	4,214

	EU origin's economy strength			
	GDP pc.		Unemployment	
	Below median	Above median	Below median	Above median
	(19)	(20)	(21)	(22)
ATT	0.08	−0.20*	−0.13	−0.06
	(0.23)	(0.11)	(0.11)	(0.19)
Observations	400	460	420	380
Pre-mean	6,955	4,574	3,457	6,494

Notes: Log-linear synthetic DD estimations based on HESA (2009/10–2022/23) data. Information on study type is only available for 2014/15–2022/23. Information on higher education classification and university classification is only available for 2014/15–2021/22. The period between the referendum and Brexit (2016/17–2019/20) is excluded. The table reports the average treatment effect on the treated, the mean outcome for EU origin countries in 2019. Bootstrapped standard errors (200 replications) in parentheses. ***$p < 0.01$, **$p < 0.05$, and *$p < 0.1$.

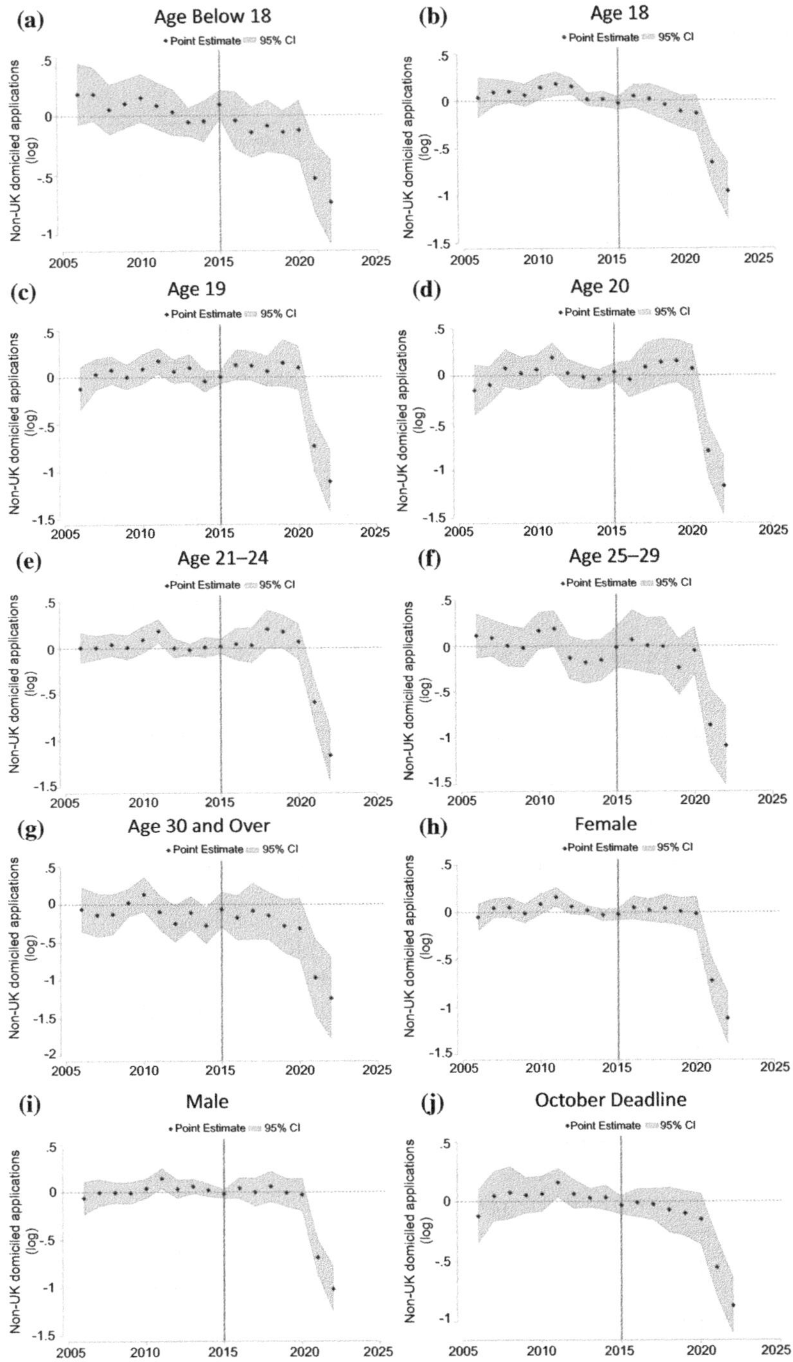

Fig. A5.1. Synthetic DD by Student Characteristics. *Notes:* Synthetic DD estimations based on UCAS data (2006/07—2022/23). Confidence intervals are calculated using 200 bootstrap replications.

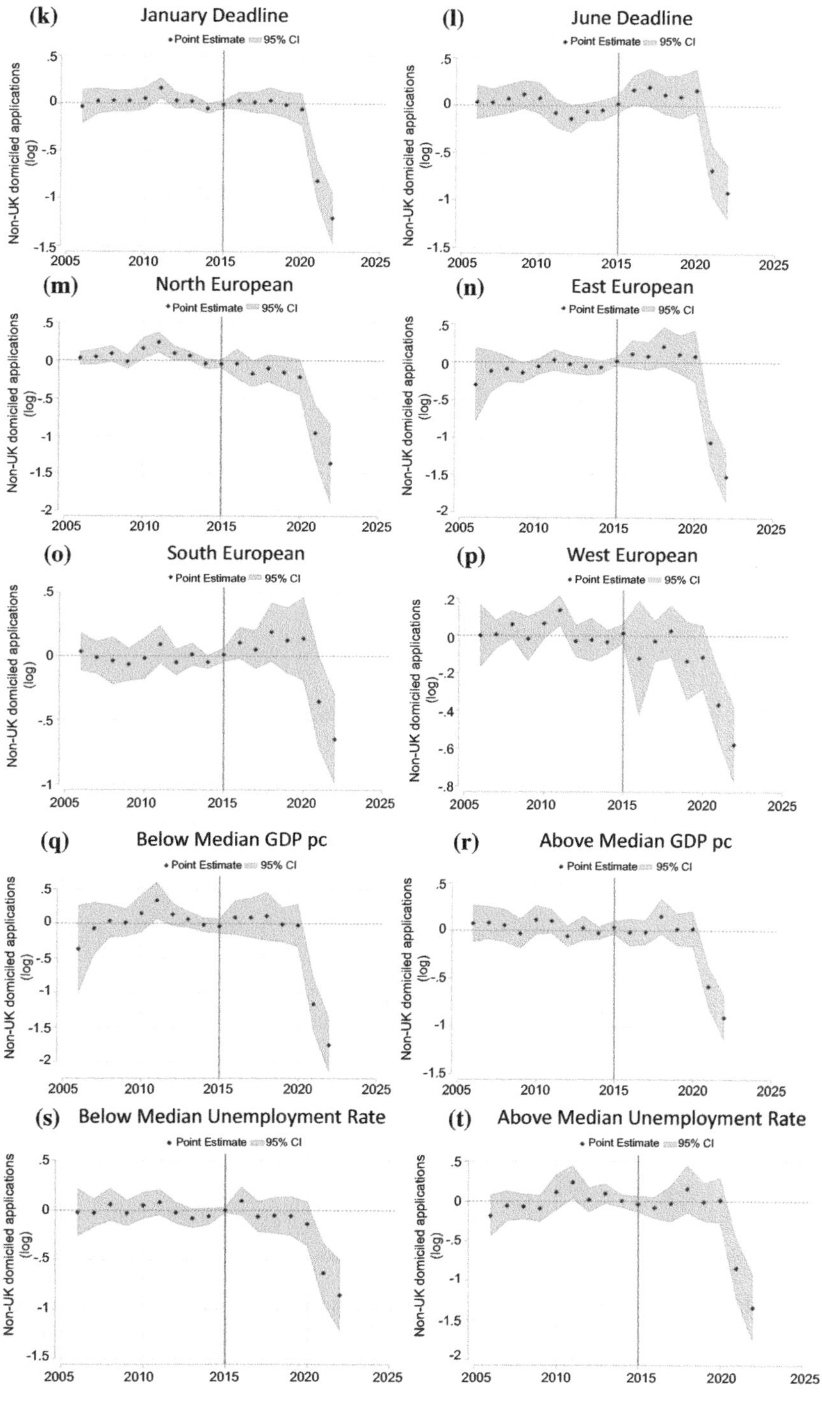

Fig. A5.1. **(Continued)**

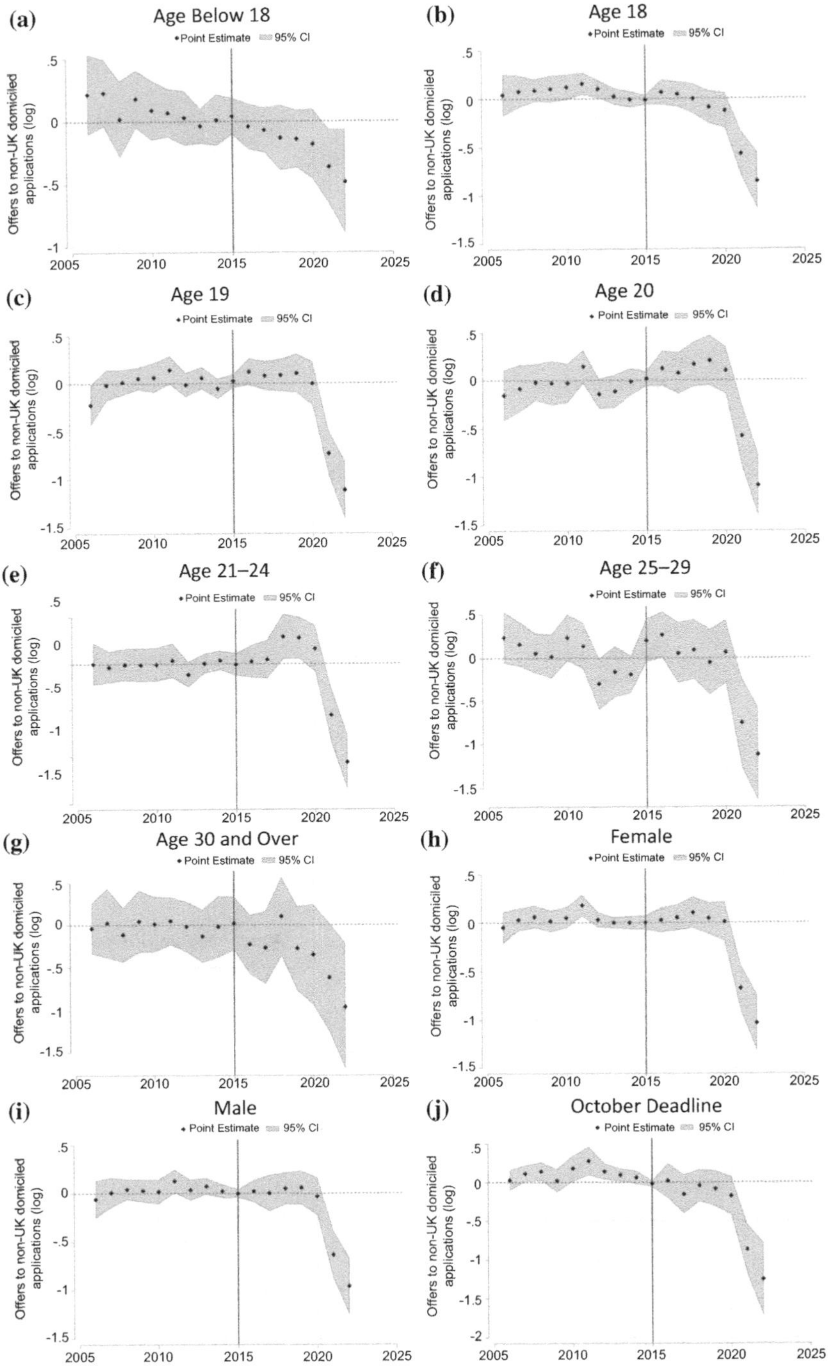

Fig. A5.2. Synthetic DD by Student Characteristics, offers. *Notes:* Synthetic DD estimations based on UCAS data (2006/07–2022/23). Confidence intervals are calculated using 200 bootstrap replications.

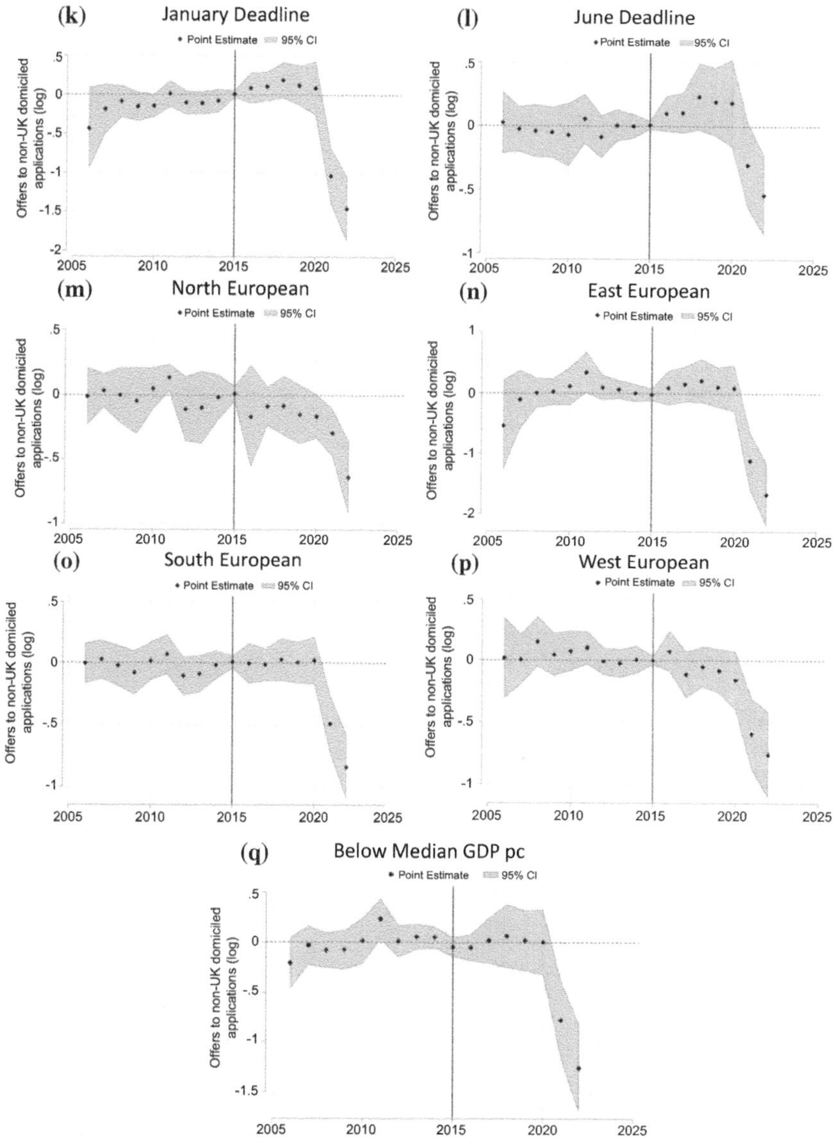

Fig. A5.2. **(Continued)**

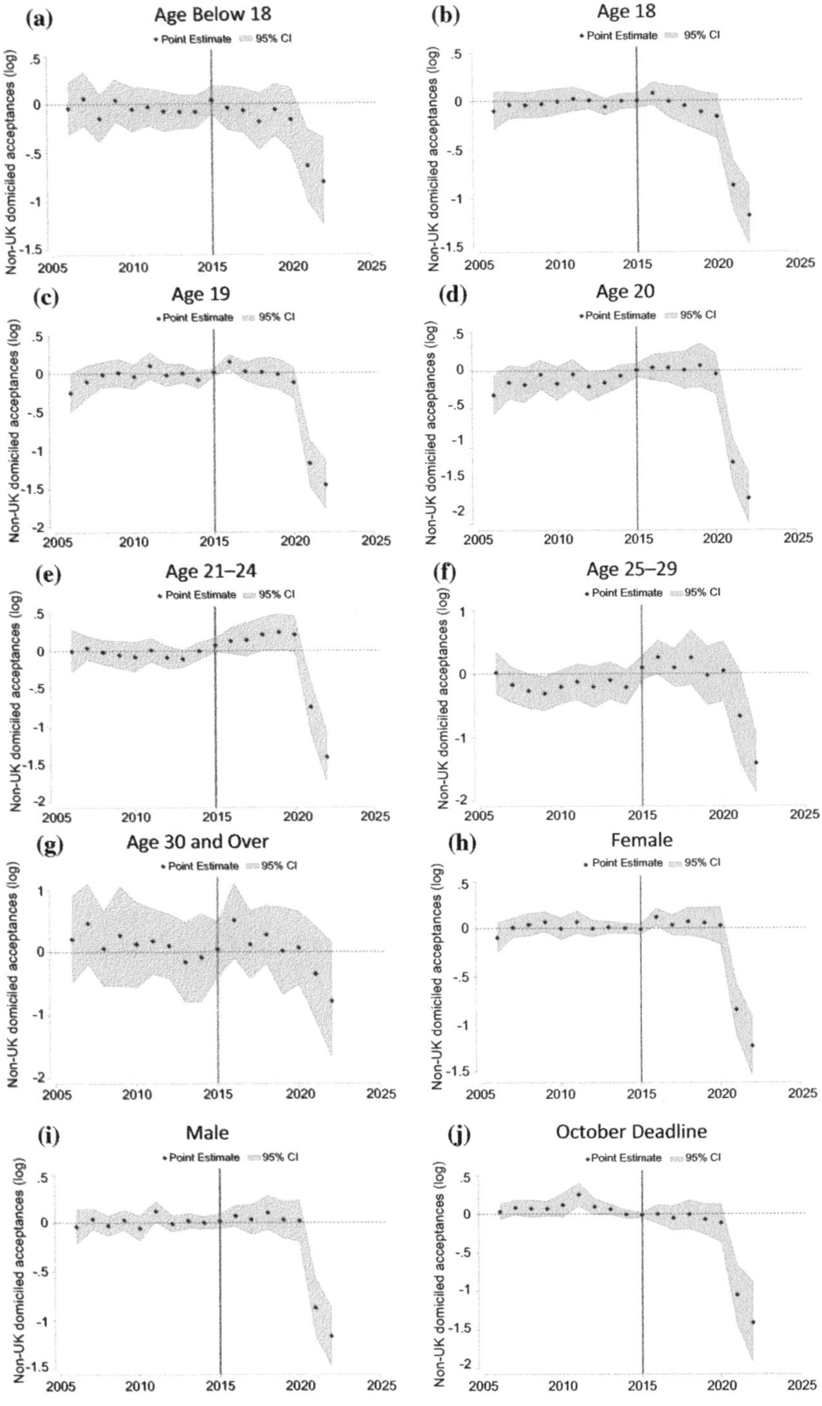

Fig. A5.3. Synthetic DD by Student Characteristics, Acceptances. *Notes:* Synthetic DD estimations based on UCAS data (2006/07–2022/23). Confidence intervals are calculated using 200 bootstrap replications.

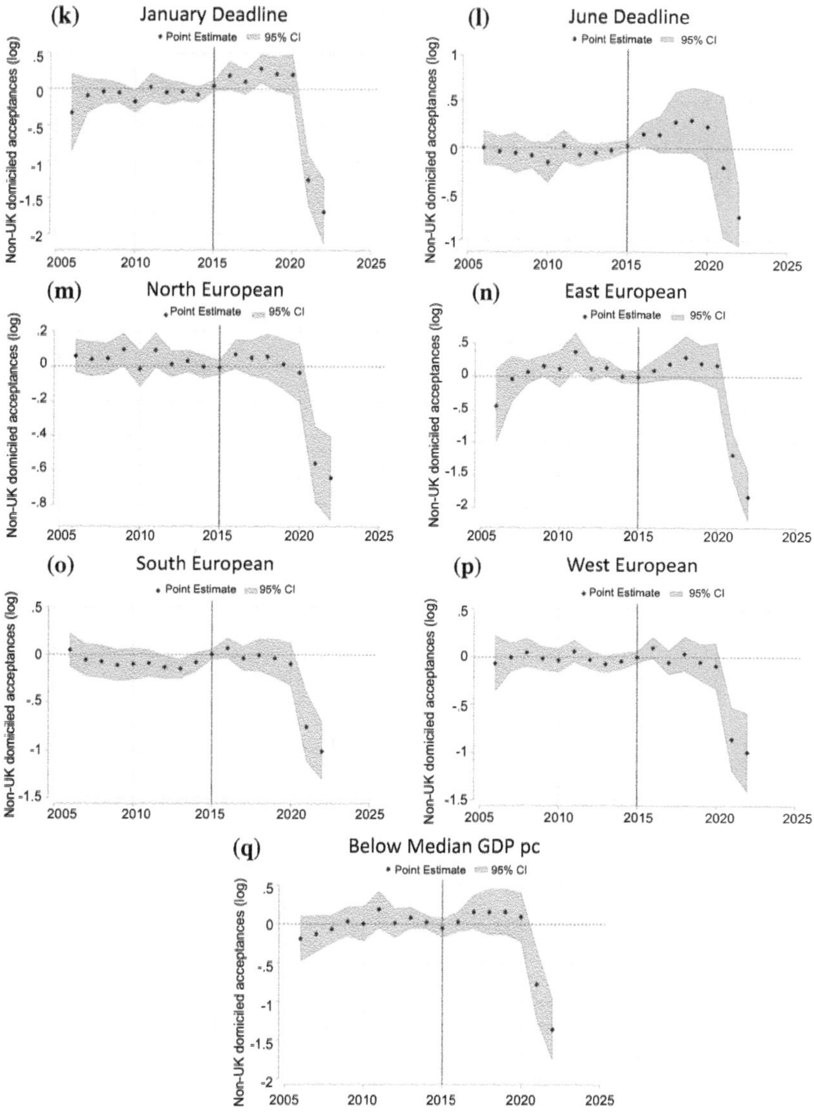

Fig. A5.3. **(Continued)**

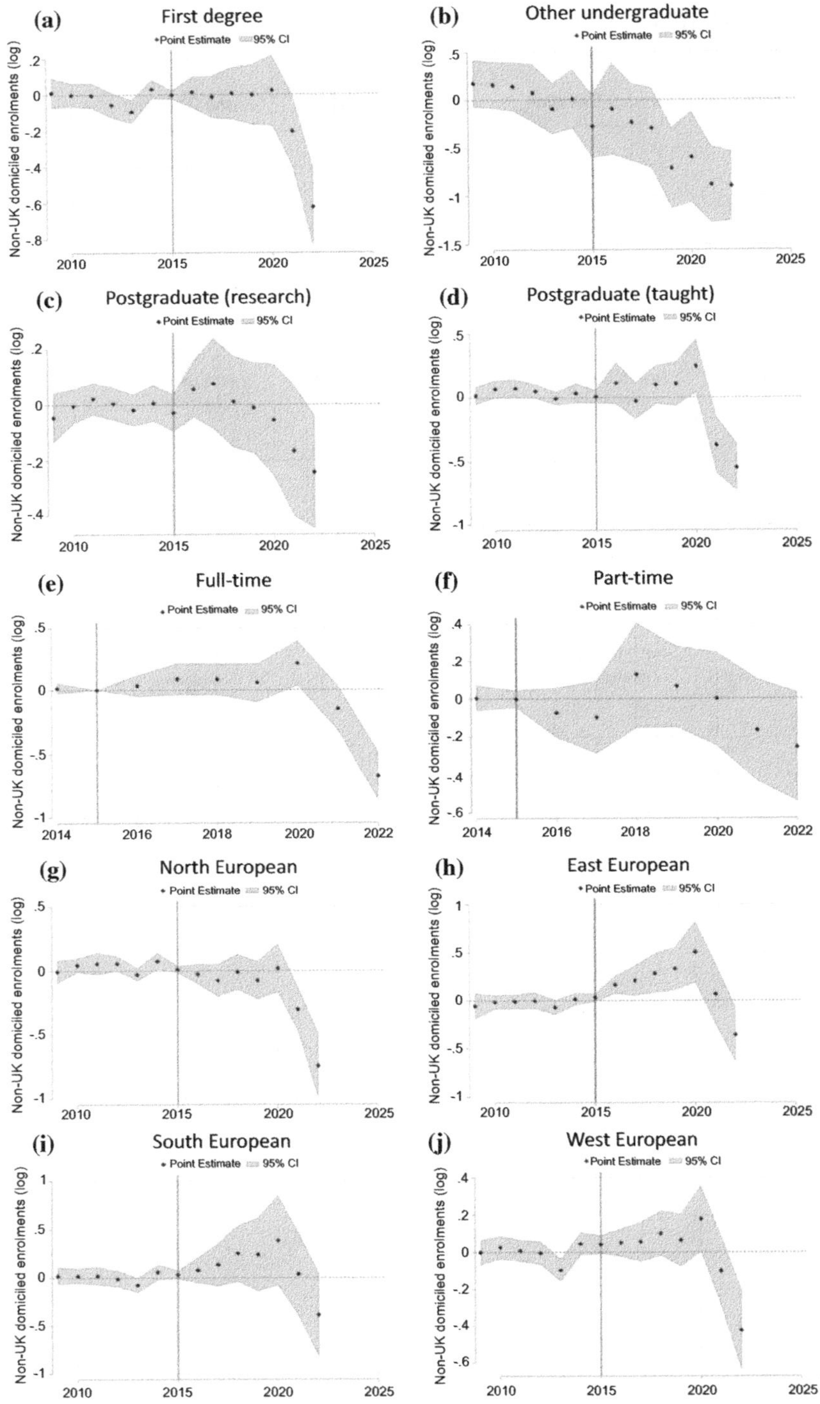

Fig. A5.4. Synthetic DD by Student Characteristics, Enrolments. *Notes:* Synthetic DD estimations based on HESA data (2009/10–2022/23). Confidence intervals are calculated using 200 bootstrap replications.

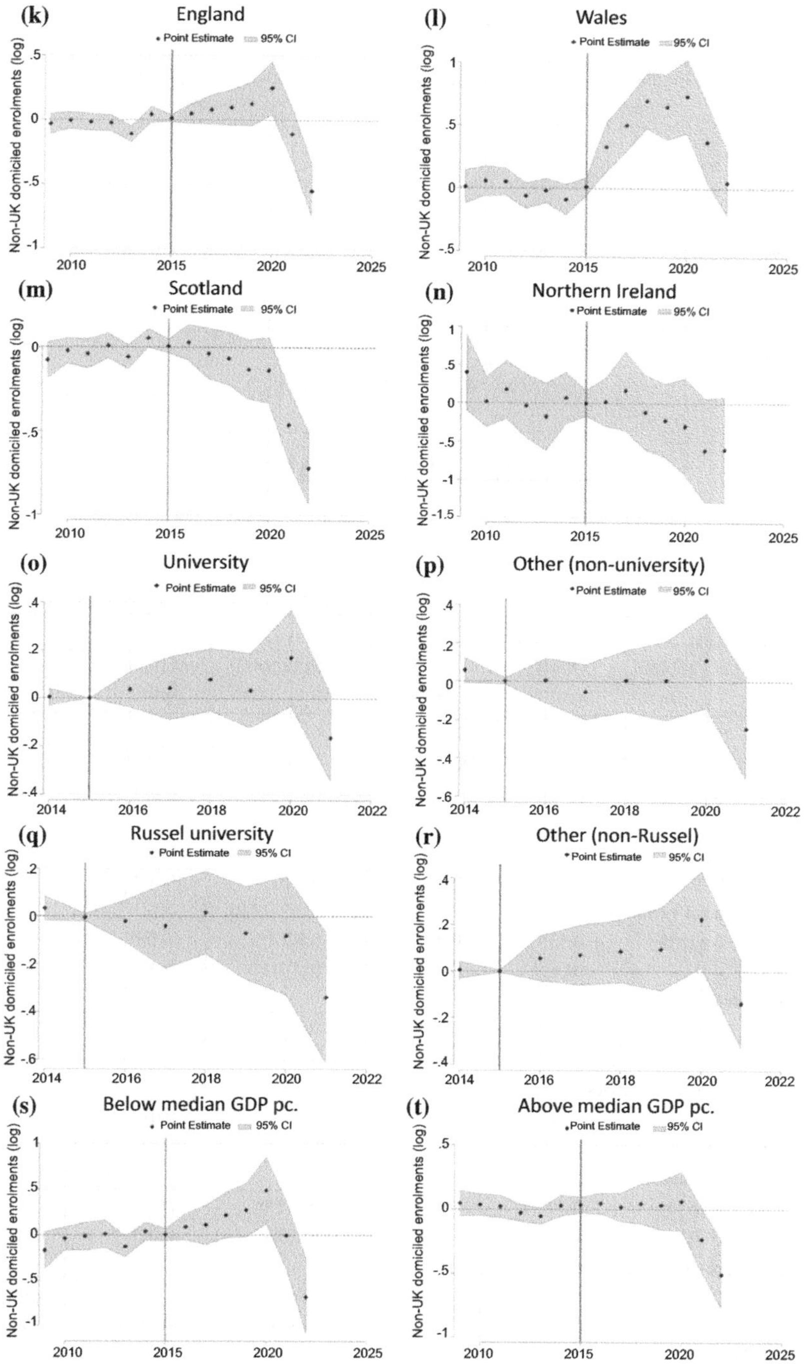

Fig. A5.4. **(Continued)**

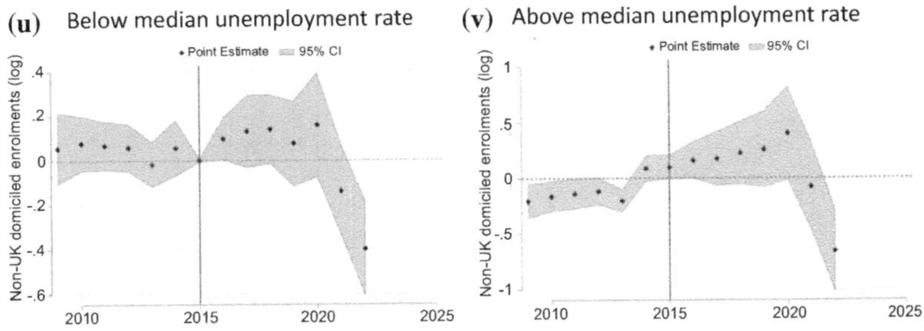

Fig. A5.4. **(Continued)**

A6. ROBUSTNESS CHECKS

Table A6.1. Robustness Checks, Alternative Specifications of the Synthetic DD.

	(1) Applications	(2) Offers	(3) Offer Rate	(4) Acceptances	(5) Acceptance Rate	(6) Enrolments
A. Placebo 2013						
ATT	−0.08	0.01	0.05***	0.00	0.05***	0.14**
	(0.06)	(0.06)	(0.02)	(0.05)	(0.01)	(0.06)
B. Placebo 2015						
ATT	0.02	0.02	0.02	0.03	0.08***	0.03
	(0.05)	(0.07)	(0.02)	(0.06)	(0.03)	(0.03)
C. Origin control variables						
ATT	−0.61***	−0.53***	0.09***	−0.67***	−0.08*	−0.05
	(0.11)	(0.12)	(0.03)	(0.14)	(0.04)	(0.11)
D. UK control variables						
ATT	−0.61***	−0.56***	0.07***	−0.65***	−0.08**	−0.16*
	(0.10)	(0.10)	(0.02)	(0.11)	(0.03)	(0.10)
E. Excluding Asian countries						
ATT	−0.63***	−0.59***	0.05**	−0.66***	−0.08**	−0.18*
	(0.11)	(0.11)	(0.02)	(0.12)	(0.04)	(0.10)
F. All non-EU countries						
ATT	−0.65***	−0.59***	0.07***	−0.71***	−0.07***	−0.27***
	(0.09)	(0.09)	(0.02)	(0.10)	(0.02)	(0.09)
G. Shorter pre-period (3 years)						
ATT	−0.60***	−0.58***	0.03	−0.66***	−0.10***	−0.11
	(0.09)	(0.10)	(0.02)	(0.10)	(0.03)	(0.09)
H. Excluding 2015						
ATT	−0.61***	−0.55***	0.07***	−0.64***	−0.07**	−0.07
	(0.11)	(0.12)	(0.02)	(0.11)	(0.03)	(0.12)

Table A6.1. *(Continued)*

	(1) Applications	(2) Offers	(3) Offer Rate	(4) Acceptances	(5) Acceptance Rate	(6) Enrolments
I. Inverse hyperbolic sine						
ATT	−0.60***	−0.57***	0.02	−0.58***	−0.05***	−0.14*
	(0.11)	(0.11)	(0.01)	(0.12)	(0.01)	(0.08)
J. Poisson regression						
ATT	−0.77***	−0.63***	0.02	−0.68***	−0.08	−0.39**
	(0.21)	(0.20)	(0.03)	(0.20)	(0.05)	(0.17)

Notes: Log-linear synthetic DD regressions with alternative samples or specifications, inverse hyperbolic sine transformed synthetic DD regression, and Poisson regression, based on UCAS and HESA data. Bootstrapped standard errors (200 replications) or clustered standard errors in parentheses. *** $p < 0.01$, ** $p < 0.05$, and * $p < 0.1$.

Table A6.2. Addressing Potential Spillovers With Counterfactual Scenarios.

	(1) Applications	(2) Offers	(3) Offer rate	(4) Acceptances	(5) Acceptance rate	(6) Enrolments
A. Original SDID						
ATT	−0.61***	−0.56***	0.07***	−0.65***	−0.08**	−0.16*
	(0.10)	(0.10)	(0.02)	(0.10)	(0.03)	(0.10)
B. Counterfactual Scenario 1						
ATT	−0.98***	−0.90***	0.05***	−1.05***	−0.10***	−0.16**
	(0.13)	(0.11)	(0.02)	(0.13)	(0.02)	(0.06)
C. Counterfactual Scenario 2						
ATT	−0.50***	−0.46***	0.05***	−0.63***	−0.14***	−0.09
	(0.07)	(0.08)	(0.02)	(0.09)	(0.02)	(0.06)
Observations	1,209	1,170	1,079	1,079	923	890
Origin countries	93	90	83	83	71	89
% change (sc. 1)	−62.62	−59.29	5.12	−64.97	−9.54	−14.55
% change (sc. 2)	−39.46	−36.94	5.27	−46.81	−13.13	−8.50

Note: Synthetic DD estimations of the log-linear model based on UCAS (2006/07–2022/23) (columns 1–5) and HESA (2009/10–2022/23) (Column 6) data. The period between the referendum and Brexit (2016/17–2019/20) is excluded. The table reports the average treatment effect on the treated for the baseline estimation (Panel A) and two alternative counterfactual scenarios. Panel A is based on counterfactual non-EU inflows that followed the same growth rate post-referendum as prereferendum. Panel B is based on counterfactual non-EU inflows that remained constant post-referendum. Bootstrapped standard errors (200 replications) in parentheses. ***$p < 0.01$, **$p < 0.05$, and *$p < 0.1$. Percentage change is calculated using the following formula: $\exp(\beta) - 1$.

Table A6.3. Robustness Check, Covid-19 Coincidence.

	(1) Applications	(2) Offers	(3) Offer rate	(4) Acceptances	(5) Acceptance rate	(6) Enrolments
A. Excluding countries on Covid-19 Red list						
ATT	−0.49***	−0.42***	0.06**	−0.57***	−0.10***	−0.11
	(0.11)	(0.14)	(0.02)	(0.12)	(0.04)	(0.11)
B. Lowest overall government response						
ATT	−0.69***	−0.61***	0.09**	−0.78***	−0.07	−0.15
	(0.15)	(0.14)	(0.04)	(0.19)	(0.04)	(0.14)
C. Lowest stringency						
ATT	−0.57***	−0.52***	0.08**	−0.65***	−0.09**	−0.08
	(0.13)	(0.13)	(0.03)	(0.15)	(0.04)	(0.12)
D. Lowest relative cases						
ATT	−0.87***	−0.79***	0.03	−0.94***	−0.12**	−0.27
	(0.20)	(0.23)	(0.04)	(0.20)	(0.05)	(0.17)
E. Lowest relative deaths						
ATT	−0.56***	−0.50***	0.04	−0.62***	−0.13**	−0.37***
	(0.19)	(0.17)	(0.02)	(0.21)	(0.05)	(0.11)

Notes: Synthetic DD estimations with alternative samples, based on UCAS (2006/07–2022/23) and HESA (2009/10–2022/23) data. The period between the referendum and Brexit (2016/17–2019/20) is excluded. Bootstrapped standard errors (200 replications) in parentheses. $^{***}p < 0.01$, $^{**}p < 0.05$, and $^{*}p < 0.1$. Countries included in the sample are listed in Appendix Table A6.4.

Table A6.4. Sample Countries for Robustness Check, Covid-19 Coincidence.

A. Excluding countries on Covid-19 Red list
Excluded: Argentina, Bahrain, Botswana, Brazil, Chile, Colombia, Costa Rica, Dominican Republic, Ecuador, Guyana, Maldives, Namibia, Oman, Panama, Paraguay, Peru, Qatar, Seychelles, South Africa, Surinam, Trinidad and Tobago, United Arab Emirates, Uruguay
B. Lowest overall government response
Included: Albania, Aruba, Belarus, Bermuda, Bosnia And Herzegovina, Botswana, Brazil, Brunei, Bulgaria, Costa Rica, Denmark, Dominica, Dominican Republic, Estonia, Finland, France, Gabon, Guam, Hungary, Iceland, Kazakhstan, Kuwait, Latvia, Libya, Liechtenstein, Lithuania, Luxembourg, Mauritius, Mexico, Namibia, New Zealand, Norway, Oman, Paraguay, Poland, Puerto Rico, Russia, Serbia, Seychelles, Slovenia, Sweden, Switzerland, Taiwan, Thailand, Tonga, Turkey, Turkmenistan, United States, Uruguay, Virgin Islands (US)
C. Lowest stringency
Included: Albania, Aruba, Bahrain, Belarus, Belgium, Bermuda, Bosnia and Herzegovina, Botswana, Brunei, Bulgaria, Costa Rica, Czech Republic, Denmark, Dominica, Estonia, Finland, France, Guam, Hungary, Iceland, Ireland, Japan, Latvia, Liechtenstein, Lithuania, Luxembourg, Malta, Mauritius, Namibia, Netherlands, New Zealand, Norway, Paraguay, Poland, Portugal, Puerto Rico, Russia, Serbia, Singapore, Slovakia, Slovenia, South Africa, South Korea, Sweden, Switzerland, Taiwan, Thailand, Turkey, United States, Uruguay, Virgin Islands (US)

Table A6.4. (*Continued*)

D. Lowest relative cases

Included: Albania, Azerbaijan, Bahamas, Belarus, Belize, Bosnia and Herzegovina, Botswana, Bulgaria, Canada, China, Colombia, Costa Rica, Cuba, Dominica, Dominican Republic, Ecuador, Fiji, Finland, Gabon, Guyana, Hong Kong, Jamaica, Japan, Kazakhstan, Kuwait, Libya, Malaysia, Malta, Mauritius, Mexico, Namibia, New Zealand, Norway, Oman, Paraguay, Peru, Poland, Puerto Rico, Qatar, Romania, Russia, Saudi Arabia, South Africa, Surinam, Thailand, Tonga, Trinidad and Tobago, Turkey, United Arab Emirates, Virgin Islands (US)

E. Lowest relative deaths

Included: Albania, Australia, Azerbaijan, Bahrain, Barbados, Belarus, Belize, Bermuda, Botswana, Brunei, China, Costa Rica, Cuba, Cyprus, Denmark, Dominica, Dominican Republic, Estonia, Fiji, Finland, Gabon, Germany, Guyana, Hong Kong, Iceland, Ireland, Jamaica, Japan, Kazakhstan, Kuwait, Libya, Malaysia, Malta, Mauritius, Namibia, Netherlands, New Zealand, Norway, Oman, Puerto Rico, Qatar, Saudi Arabia, Seychelles, Singapore, South Korea, Thailand, Tonga, Turkey, United Arab Emirates, Virgin Islands (US)

Notes: Panel A lists the countries on the Covid-19 Red list, which were excluded from the analysis. Panels B to E list the countries hit the least by Covid-10 according to different measures, which were included in the analysis.

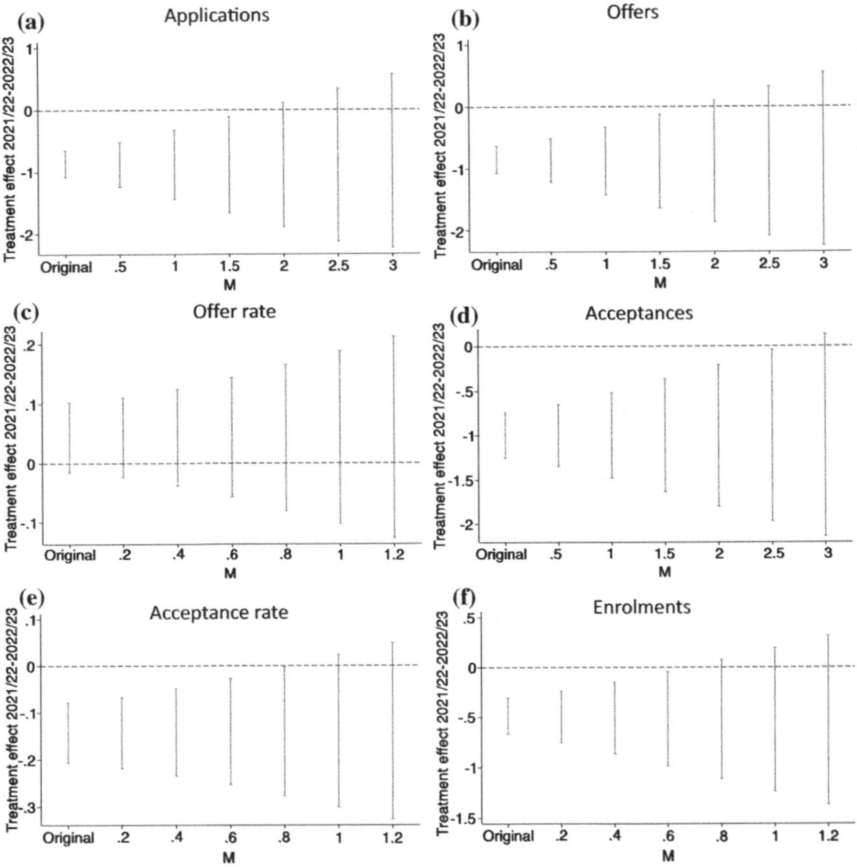

Fig. A6.1. Credible Approach to DD Parallel Trends Assumption. *Notes:* Credible approach to parallel trends implemented on the dynamic DD estimations based on UCAS (2006/07–2022/23) and HESA (2009/10–2022/23) data. The sensitivity analysis is performed on the significant treatment effects after Brexit, 2021/22–2022/23 (figures a to f). Confidence bounds are based on relative magnitude restrictions that allow for M times the max. common trends violation in 2010/11–2015/16.

A7. BACK OF THE ENVELOPE CALCULATIONS

Table A7.1 Estimated Counterfactual of EU Student Numbers in the UK, 2021/22–2022/23.

	[1]	[2]	
	Acceptances	Student enrolments	
	Undergrad	Undergrad	Postgrad
Observed summary statistics			
Observed pre-referendum yearly mean (per EU origin)	765.1	2,661.9	1,391.6
Observed pre-referendum yearly mean (total)	22,186.5	54,037.5	28,249.5
Observed post-Brexit yearly mean (per EU origin)	431.2	2,521.0	947.6
Observed post-Brexit yearly mean (total)	12,505.0	73,110.0	27,480.0
Estimated % change	**−64.5**	**−44.0**	**−47.1**
Estimated counterfactuals			
Counterfactual post-Brexit yearly mean (per EU origin)	1,214.4	4,499.7	1,791.9
Counterfactual post-Brexit yearly mean (total)	35,217.6	130,492.5	51,965.7
Yearly absolute loss due to Brexit (per EU origin)	−783.2	−1,978.7	−844.3
Yearly absolute loss due to Brexit (total)	−22,712.6	−57,382.5	−24,485.7

Notes: Authors' calculations based on summary statistics and DD estimations of the Brexit phases using a log-linear model. Pre-referendum statistics are estimated for the years 2006/07 to 2015/16. Post-Brexit statistics are estimated for the years 2021/22 to 2022/23. We estimate the counterfactual post-referendum mean based on the estimated effect of increased tuition fees (2021/22 to 2022/23) (Phase 3) (see Equation 2), stating that the observed post-referendum mean is between 44.0 to 64.5% lower than the counterfactual, depending on the outcome. The yearly absolute loss is calculated as the difference between the observed and the counterfactual post-referendum mean.

SECTION II

IMMIGRANT INTEGRATION AND SUCCESS

INTEGRATING REFUGEES BY ADDRESSING LABOR SHORTAGES? A POLICY EVALUATION

Mette Foged[a], Janis Kreuder[a] and Giovanni Peri[b]

[a]*University of Copenhagen, Denmark*
[b]*UC Davis, USA*

ABSTRACT

The authors evaluate how a policy introduced in Denmark in 2013, matching refugees to occupations experiencing local labor shortages, affected their employment after arrival. Leveraging the differential exposure to the policy across different cohorts of arrivals and municipalities, the authors find that the policy increased employment probability of refugees by 5–6% points one year after arrival and 10% points two years after. The policy was especially effective for male refugees and refugees with some secondary education. Additionally, the policy did not have any significant displacement effect on other immigrants' employment.

Keywords: Immigrants integration; refugees; labor shortages; active labor market policies; difference in difference

1. INTRODUCTION

Technological and demographic changes continue to modify the demand for and supply of labor across occupations in developed countries (Autor, 2015, 2019; Autor & Dorn, 2009).[1] Notably, a large set of manual, low-paid jobs that are hard to mechanize and offshore in sectors such as retail, personal, safety, food, and housekeeping services have experienced continued employment growth in developed countries (Goos et al., 2014). Traditionally, relatively young and less educated individuals supplied labor for these jobs; however, their number and their willingness to do these jobs at current wages in rich countries have been declining. Newly arrived immigrants could be a group helping to alleviate these

Migration, Human Capital and the Labor Market
Research in Labor Economics, Volume 53A, 107–128

ISSN: 0147-9121/doi:10.1108/S0147-91212026000053A003

shortages, by providing workers willing to perform those jobs. Policies designed to facilitate their matching with the relevant employers would facilitate this process.[2]

The quick and efficient matching of new immigrants to those jobs would have two main effects. First, faster employment would reduce the fiscal/economic initial burden of immigrants, especially on local communities, by promptly making them contributors to local production. Second, employment in jobs experiencing a high level of unfilled vacancies would minimize competition effects for natives and increase immigrants' complementarity with them, as their entry into the labor market would fill needs not met by natives and could even support employment of other natives in related jobs (as shown in Peri & Sparber, 2009). While both those effects are desirable, a potential downside of this policy is to prioritize immediate employment to general human capital accumulation and hence potentially place immigrants on lower earnings trajectories relative to policy regimes that emphasize investments in human capital, such as language training (Arendt, 2022; Foged, Hasager, & Peri, 2024a).

Several countries have suggested that their immigration system, when allowing foreigners for working reasons, should prioritize based on a list of occupations in high demand and short supply according to various labor market indicators.[3] However, these lists have mostly targeted jobs that require relatively sophisticated skills and are not thought of as ways to improve the supply-demand matching for low-paying jobs. At the same time, many countries have faced difficulties in integrating and employing newly arrived refugees and less skilled and educated immigrants.

Eleven years ago, Denmark introduced a policy aimed at addressing, jointly, the two issues of labor shortages in some low-wage occupations and immigrant integration. The way was to match local labor demand in those occupations with labor supply coming from recently arrived refugees. One third of municipalities in Denmark adopted this policy, called "Industry Packages," between 2013 and 2018. The policy was conceived not as an admission tool, regulating the number and type of skills of immigrants allowed into the country, but rather as an integration policy for the refugees who were already entering the country. It identified area-specific labor needs, helped connecting employers and newly settled refugees, and provided refugees with a minimum of the specific skills needed for those jobs.

Such a policy could potentially increase employment of newly arrived refugees and be desirable to the host country as it addresses labor market needs. It may also increase the perception of refugees as "helpful" to the receiving economy. However, by targeting prompt employment in relatively low-paying jobs, the policy also entails a risk of lowering the longer-run earnings trajectories of refugees, relative to a policy investing more up-front in general skill and general human capital upgrading. Additionally, part of the spending on the program indirectly subsidizes firms, which benefit from higher productivity of workers in the occupations selected to be part of the program. This chapter evaluates the effect of such a policy on the employment probability of refugees in Denmark.

In a previous study (Foged et al., 2024a), which evaluated comprehensively a large set of policies for the integration of refugees in Denmark, two of us and Linea Hasager performed a simple analysis of the effectiveness of this policy. Here, we analyze a larger set of results, performing robustness and validity checks, considering a longer period and a more detailed heterogeneity analysis.

To identify the effects of the policy, we use its roll-out across municipalities in Denmark and we compare outcomes across cohorts of refugees who arrived in a municipality when the program was available with those who arrived in a municipality when it was not. The crucial quasi-random variation identifying the causal effects in the empirical strategy is the month a refugee was placed in the municipality relative to the month of initial roll-out (implementation) of the policy. We show that the characteristics and number of newly arrived refugees did not change around the time of implementation in the municipality, suggesting that such timing was uncorrelated with the size and composition of the inflow, hence providing a quasi-experimental setting for our analysis.

We show that the outcomes of newly arrived refugees evolved in a similar way in early and late adopting municipalities, prior to implementation, which is consistent with the hypothesis that changes in the months following the implementation are produced by the policy rather than by pre-existing economic or political factors in the municipalities. Additionally, we perform a placebo exercise using immigrants from Eastern Europe and other immigrants with similar characteristics but who did not qualify for the program and arrived at the same time as the refugees. The findings of no significant effect on their labor market outcomes, after the adoption of the policy, constitute an important check that unobservable variables affecting the local labor market conditions for immigrants in low-skilled jobs are not responsible for a spurious correlation.

As we do not have exact information on refugees who actually attended the program, our key estimated parameter is the average intention to treat (ITT) effect of the policy, namely the program's impact on the eligible population of refugees. However, for the population we consider, the participation in the program was likely close to 100%, so the average treatment effect on the treated (ATT) was likely very similar to the ITT. In our analysis, we show evidence consistent with constant treatment effects across municipalities (with different dates of implementation) and over the first years since implementation. These conditions are consistent with the validity of the standard two-way fixed effect estimation of the difference-in-difference model.[4]

Our study has three main findings. First, we find a significant average ITT effect of the "Industry Packages" policy on the employment probability of refugees equal to 5–6% points one year after the arrival in the municipality and equal to 10% points two years after.[5] Second, the effects are similar but slightly smaller in magnitude using employment criteria that exclude subsidized jobs or require at least 80 hours of employment per month. This implies that the increased probability of employment does not occur because of being hired in a marginal or temporary job. Third, we find that the effect is concentrated on males with secondary education, i.e., those individuals who were already likely to be "on the boundary" of employment and are ready to take advantage of the matching with jobs and training. Notice that young individuals (below 25 years old) and individuals with a university degree were not targeted by the policy, as for them pursuing higher education or more professional jobs was considered a priority. We do not observe any significant effect on women or on those with no primary schooling. Their skills, more limited working experience, and cultural attitudes toward working women could make them less likely to participate and less ready to benefit from such a policy. An important caveat is that we cannot look at longer-run effects to check whether these good initial outcomes were attenuated by a higher probability of careers in lower-paying jobs.

Our results are important, qualitatively and quantitatively, in the light of the literature pointing out the significant employment gap and the slow and incomplete economic assimilation of refugees. Dustmann et al. (2017) and Brell et al. (2020) recently summarized the size of the initial gap and the lack of convergence in employment rates of refugees across developed countries. In most European countries, refugees start with an employment rate as low 10–20% points during the early years after arrival and an employment rate gap with other immigrants ranging from 20 to 60% points. Hence, an improvement of 5–10% points during the first years, as we find in this chapter, represents an increase by more than 50% relative to the baseline (the employment rate in our sample is 9% after one year in the country).

Recent review articles (Arendt et al., 2022; Bahar et al., 2024; Foged et al., 2024a; Fouka, 2024) point out that the evidence on the effectiveness of active labor market policies (ALMP) on employment and earnings of refugees depend on several implementation details, and characteristics of refugees may be important for their outcomes. Hence, both the need for better outcomes in the economic integration of refugees and the limited existing evidence on evaluating labor market programs make this chapter an important contribution in this area.

Three recent studies evaluate policies and are related to the one we study here. The "Industry Packages" policy was deemed a success early on, and in general, the idea of prioritizing employment for refugees has become more prominent in the recent years (e.g. Arendt, 2022). Eleven additional municipalities in Denmark implemented policies inspired by the same approach and supported by state subsidies for refugees arriving after the Syrian crisis. These are mostly different municipalities from those that we study in this chapter, and they largely implemented this program after the period of our analysis.[6]

Based on a matching strategy, Thuesen and Rotger (2023) estimate that a related version of the Industry Package policy increased employment. This positive effect is consistent with our finding; however, they find a stronger effect on women than men while we find the opposite. This is likely due the fact that their analysis and the later adopting municipalities they consider include a broader group of Non-Western immigrants, especially those who have been in the country longer and are still unemployed. Dahlberg et al. (2023, 2024) conducted a randomized control trial in the city of Goteborg in Sweden where 140 newly arrived, low-educated refugees were assigned to an intense training program in collaboration with a large local employer (the largest real estate company in Goteborg). The program was an intensive training program with a language training component and is related to the policy we study in its focus on labor demand and collaboration with local employers. They find that program participation increased earnings by 15% points (roughly 50% of baseline) within one year. They also find that the control group catches up four years after program participation, suggesting only temporary effects.

At a broader level, our chapter is relevant to the literature analyzing the effects of labor market integration policies for unemployed individuals. Our main estimated effects are in line with the large literature evaluating ALMP and recently summarized in Card et al. (2018). They show that, on average, ALMP have a 1–3% point effect on the employment probability less than one year post program and a 3–5% point effect 1–2 years post program. Our point estimates are somewhat larger but comparable to that. Card et al. (2018), however, never focus on immigrants, who may be a group benefiting more intensely from training in targeted industries and connection to employers especially in the first year after arrival.

Our estimates are also economically significant when compared to studies of the impact of policies targeted to the economic integration of immigrants and refugees. Heller and Mumma (2023); Lochmann et al. (2019); Sarvimäki and Hämäläinen (2016) and Foged et al. (2024b) evaluate the impact of language training finding positive effects on either employment or earnings or on both. Foged et al. (2024b) find a permanent, positive effect of increasing language training on the employment rate between 5 and 6% points and an increase by $3,000 in earnings. These effects are persistent in the long run (18 years after arrival). The other studies analyze a shorter time horizon and were unable to detect significant effects on employment. Sarvimäki and Hämäläinen (2016) and Heller and Mumma (2023), however, find significant positive earnings effects. Relative to these estimates, the impact of an up to 6(10)% point increase within one (two) year(s) of arrival, as we find in this chapter, is economically very significant.

Finally, we can compare our analysis to the findings of a series of papers that have analyzed the impact of local economic conditions on the labor market integration of immigrants (Aksoy et al., 2023; Azlor et al., 2020; Åslund & Rooth, 2007; Damm & Rosholm, 2010; Godøy, 2017). They identify the impact of being placed in municipalities with more or less favorable employment conditions. These papers exploit Spatial Dispersal Policies in Denmark, Norway, Sweden, and Germany that allocate refugees quasi-randomly. On average, they find that strong initial labor market conditions, say a higher employment rate by one standard deviation in a location, is associated to 1–2% points higher employment probability of recently arrived refugees in the first 1–5 years after arrival. Hence, our estimates are quite large even relatively to those effects. Our findings, as the papers cited, speak to the importance of early employment opportunities, but rather than the general labor market conditions, we evaluate the role of improved matching of refugees with vacant jobs and basic training for those.

2. BACKGROUND AND POLICY DESCRIPTION

The policy we evaluate targeted refugees and family members reunified to refugees (for brevity we refer to all as refugees). Refugees were assigned to an initial municipality, which was in charge of the integration and employment support provided under the Danish Integration Program.[7] All refugees were offered language training, job-search support and general training upon arrival in their assigned municipality. The "Industry Packages," which falls under the Danish Integration Program, has gained popularity in the past decade (Simic et al., 2018; Thomassen, 2019; Thuesen & Rotger, 2023).

The policy was developed in 2013 in the municipality of Vejle in collaboration with a consultancy firm (LG insight) and local employers. The idea behind the policy arose from the observation that while some low-wage, mainly manual, jobs in Denmark experienced shortages and postings for these jobs remained open for long periods, recently arrived refugees were unemployed, underemployed, or had a hard time to find employment. The goal of the new policy was to provide to refugees who were willing, the fastest avenue to a job in one of the industries with labor shortages. A program of training that was specific to each of the identified industries was carefully crafted.

The different training programs were termed "Industry Packages" for their industry specificity. The policy worked as follows. Refugees with no university degree and no job (representing the large majority of new arrivals) were presented with the job options in the target industries soon after their first placement in a municipality. After a short introduction course of typically eight weeks, they had to choose an "Industry Package" to attend. The following training varied depending on the progress of the participant. Some completed all steps within three months while other took up to a year.

The industry-specific training was offered directly by the businesses operating in the selected industry. It was kept short and focused on the necessary skills and knowledge for employment in the industry. For instance, within the "Cleaning Package" participants were taught which equipment and products to use for cleaning specific materials and are provided training on safety issues and on the correct postures to minimize injuries. They were also taught soft skills, such as interacting with customers and colleagues on-the-job. As they progressed, participants were introduced to more advanced cleaning equipment and materials. While differing in specific training, all "Industry Packages" had a similar structure and a clear progression toward the competence requirements of the targeted industry. The competencies of the refugees were measured relative to these requirements to identify needs for additional training. The consultants we interviewed stressed that the clear structure, goal and progression were important and created a sense of meaning, purpose and motivation for the individual refugee.

Between 2013 and 2018, the policy was adopted in several other municipalities, after initial anecdotal evidence of its success in the municipality of Vejle and possibly also in response to the national increase in the number of refugees.[8] Most municipalities had the program implemented by one of the two consultancy firms, LG Insight, and Foreningen Nydansker. We were able to get the starting date of the first training and details about implementation of the program from the digital archives of the two firms. As information about the program became available, some municipalities adopted the policy without involving those consulting firms. We ran a nationwide survey to identify municipalities who had ever adopted the policy and a follow-up survey about details relative to their implementation of the policy.[9]

In the wake of the increase in refugee arrivals especially from Syria, between 2014 and 2016, the Danish government took two types of measures. On the one hand, a series of tightening of asylum rules tried to slow the flow. On the other hand, in order to accelerate integration in the labor market it introduced requirements that all refugees actively search for a job and participate in on-the-job training immediately upon arrival (Arendt, 2020). In addition, a paid internship program became available for newcomers aged 18–40. These policies were enacted at the same time by all municipalities in 2016, and, therefore, they do not interfere with the identification of the impact of the "Industry Packages" as general time trends are controlled for in our analysis, as long as their effect was homogeneous across municipalities.

3. EMPIRICAL STRATEGY

3.1 Exposure to Treatment Across Arrival Cohorts

To identify the effect of the policy, we exploit the differential exposure to the policy for different cohorts of arrivals of refugees across 30 Danish municipalities, which we know eventually adopted the policy.[10] These municipalities include half of the Danish working age population and are representative of the whole country in terms of their average immigrant shares, employment rates, immigrant employment rates, and income.

The identifying variation in our analysis is across different cohorts of arrival of refugees, across municipalities. Hence, the event time for a refugee i placed in municipality m is the month of placement, t, relative to the month of first implementation of the policy in that municipality, E_m. Our design is similar to a difference in differences estimate across adopting municipalities. Namely, we compare the outcome one year after arrival for refugee cohorts that arrived after the start of the policy, and were fully exposed to it, with those arriving before and were not exposed (or only partially exposed) to it.

Fig. 1 shows the mean employment of refugees *one year after arrival* plotted against event time, $K_{t,m} = t - E_m$, binned in half-year (6 months) intervals. The plotted coefficients are obtained from a regression including the same control variables as our baseline specification (see Section 3.2). The first month of the Interval 0 is the initial month of policy implementation. Refugees arriving at Interval 0 or later are fully exposed to the policy. Those arriving at -1 or -2 can be treated for at most 11 and 5 months and hence partially treated. The group arriving at -3 is the latest cohort arriving at least one year prior to implementation and not treated at all one year after arrival, when we measure the employment outcome. The employment rate one year after arrival of this last untreated arrival cohort is standardized to 0.[11]

The figure provides the first piece of evidence that the policy had a significant effect on the employment rate of refugees. Three features are visible and relevant. First, the graph shows no evidence of trends in employment outcomes for cohorts arrived prior to the implementation of the policy. This is a check that underlying trends in refugee integration are not affecting our results. The F-test statistic for zero pretrend in Fig. 1 is 1.99 (P-value 0.084).[12]

Second, the graph indicates that there is a higher employment rate for partially treated cohorts of refugees (those arrived in periods −1 and −2) shown between the vertical continuous and dashed line. The cohort treated for at least 6 months (−2) shows a significant 5% higher employment rate than the last untreated cohort. Finally, for the cohorts that were fully treated, to the right of the solid vertical line, the estimates employment rate one year after arrival is between 5 and 7% points higher than for the last untreated cohort. The effect of treatment one year after arrival is reasonably constant across cohorts 0, 1, and 2, which is one of the conditions under which the standard two-way fixed effects with binary treatment provide unbiased estimates of the ITT effect.

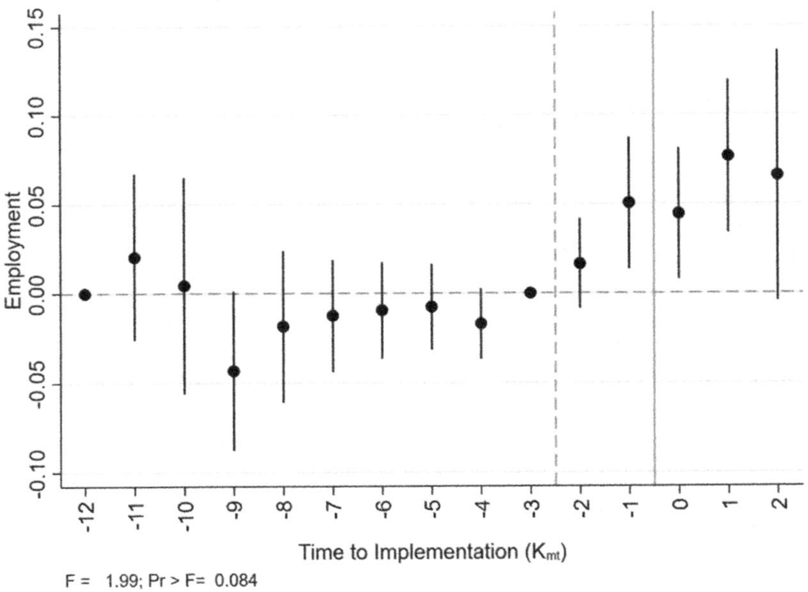

Fig. 1. Refugees' Employment Rate One Year After Arrival By Event Time. *Notes:* The plotted estimates are the conditional mean employment of refugees one year after placement, grouped in cohorts of arrival by half-year bins of event time and relative to event time −3. The estimated values are obtained from a specification similar (1) in the text. We report 95% confidence intervals for the coefficients.

3.2 Estimating Equation, Identification, and Validity

The estimating equation estimates the average ITT effect of the policy on the policy-exposed relative to the nonexposed cohorts:

$$Y_{i,t+T,m} = \alpha f_i(K_{t,m}) + X_i'\beta + \gamma_t + \sigma_m + \epsilon_{i,t,m}. \tag{1}$$

The variable $Y_{i,t+T,m}$ measures the outcome in period $t + T$ for refugee i, who arrived in municipality m at time t. f is a function of event time, $K_{t,m}$, which captures exposure to the policy (hence exposure to treatment). The coefficient α is the parameter of interest. We estimate three versions of Eq. (1) to investigate the robustness of the results to different ways of capturing policy exposure during the early period (T) after arrival, which is our treatment variable.

In our first specification, the function f associates to refugees who arrived in event-month $K_{t,m}$, the share of the first year after arrival for which the policy was active, and hence the share of year they were potentially exposed to the treatment. Hence, this variable is equal to zero for cohorts that arrived more than one year before implementation and are not treated, it is one for cohorts that arrived at or after implementation and are fully treated, and it is a fraction between 0 and 1 for those who arrived from one year before, up to the initial month of implementation (i.e. between the two vertical lines in Fig. 1).

In a second specification, the function f consists of three dummies. One that equals one for the arrival cohorts experiencing start of the policy in the second semester since arrival ($K_{m,t} = -2$) and is 0 for any other cohort. One equal to one for the cohort for which the policy was started within the first semester after arrival ($K_{m,t} = -1$) and 0 for the other cohorts. And the third dummy equal to one for all cohorts arriving in or after the month of when the policy was started ($K_{m,t} \geq 0$) and 0 for the others.

In the third specification, we drop the partially treated cohorts arriving in $K_{m,t} = -2$ and $K_{m,t} = -1$, and we only compare fully exposed to the nonexposed cohorts using only one dummy, $1(K_{m,t} \geq 0)$. We use the simpler third version of Eq. (1) to estimate the impact on outcomes measured after 12, 18, and 24 months to obtain evidence on the persistence of the effect. In this implementation, we exclude one additional event time interval for each half year that we expand the time horizon so that we always compare cohorts that are fully treated with those untreated at the time we measure the outcome.

Our main outcome variable, $Y_{i,t+T,m}$, is an indicator equal to one if refugee, i, who arrived in municipality, m, in month, t, is employed at least four hours in month $T + t$ where $T = 12$, 18, and 24 months after the initial month of placement, t. Our alternative employment indicators exclude subsidized employment or consider probability of employment for at least 80 hours in the month, corresponding to roughly half to full-time employment. We also measure employment in a more continuous way, as a fraction of full-time employment. Finally, we estimate the impact on the probability of being unemployed.

The control variables—which were included also in producing Fig. 1—are as follows. The term X_i includes the following individual characteristics: a quadratic function of age, a dummy variable to control for gender, country of origin dummies, one for asylum versus family reunified, one capturing the initial reported level of education of the refugee, and dummies for having children under ages 3 or 6. The variable $empl\_rate_{t,m}$ is municipal employment rate in month t, γ_t is a set of alternative period fixed effects; σ_m is a set of municipality fixed effects, and $\epsilon_{i,t,m}$ is an idiosyncratic zero-mean error term.

Almost all municipalities in our sample receive refugees every year during the sample period. The number of new refugees arriving in municipalities, however, is low early and late in the period and highest around the peak of the Syrian refugee crisis. Not all the municipalities receive at least one new refugee every month (see online Appendix Fig. 1). Our data are, therefore, too thin to estimate a model that is fully saturated with month fixed effects, and we proceed with alternative period fixed effects in the main specification, and we perform tests of the stability of our estimated effects across municipalities and time of implementation in the robustness checks (Section 5.2).

We selected only the municipalities that implemented the policy in a very similar and coordinated way (most of them with the same two consultancy firms), and we test for potential heterogeneous effects across institutional setting. These show no evidence of heterogeneous effects across important dimensions, giving us confidence that the more restrictive model we implement, which assumes some homogeneity in the ITT, is reasonable.[13]

4. DATA

The month and year of implementation of the "Industry Packages" in each municipality, crucial to determine exactly the beginning of the treatment exposure in a municipality, were made available to us by the consultancy firms that implemented the policy in 21 out of the 30 adopting municipalities. For the remaining 9 municipalities, we collected the starting dates and additional information about the adoption of the program through a survey.[14] The other important piece of information is the date of first placement of the refugee in a municipality, which we sometimes refer to as the "arrival date." This is available from Danish administrative registers.

The population included in the analysis (from the administrative registry) are individuals who were granted refugee status (79%) or members of the family who were reunified to a refugee (21%). We only include those who were legally settled in a Danish municipality from January 2008 to April 2019, and we further restrict the sample to individuals targeted by the policy in all municipalities, namely the newly arrived refugees aged 25–64 at arrival and without a university degree.[15] The majority in the sample are men (63%) who fled the conflict in Syria (58%) and had only basic education at arrival (70%). All of them were targeted by the program, and they are indeed the typical participants as described by those running the first Introductory course of the "Industry Packages" in 21 out of the 30 municipalities. Hence, while technically our estimate is the ITT effect of the policy, participation was close to one; thus, our estimate is very close to the average treatment effect (ATT).

The primary data source for our outcomes is the monthly employer-reported tax returns, which contain information on the hours, earnings, and industry of employment of each individual. We supplement this with weekly information on unemployment status of the individual. The detailed tax return data allow us to produce several employment measures. Our main employment variable follows ILO definition of employment, which requires at least one hour of employment in the reference week, which we translate into at least four hours in the considered month.[16]

5. RESULTS

5.1 Main Results

Table 1 shows the main estimated effect of the "industry package" policy on employment probability of refugees one year after arrival. In particular, the coefficients in the table represent the average intent to treat (ITT) effects of the policy using different ways of capturing the exposure to it. As previously mentioned, we believe our ITT estimates are very close to the ATT due to how we constructed the sample.

Table 1. The Effect On Employment One Year After Placement.

	Main, 4 Hours (1)	Excl. Wage Subsidies (2)	80 Hours (3)	Share of Fulltime (4)	Unemployment (5)
Share of first year	0.053**	0.036**	0.030*	0.031**	−0.047*
	(0.020)	(0.017)	(0.015)	(0.014)	(0.023)
$1(K_{m,t} = -2)$	0.023*	0.015	0.003	0.009	−0.019
	(0.012)	(0.011)	(0.009)	(0.009)	(0.014)
$1(K_{m,t} = -1)$	0.055***	0.034**	0.030**	0.033**	−0.054***
	(0.017)	(0.016)	(0.013)	(0.012)	(0.014)
$1(K_{m,t} \geq 0)$	0.056***	0.041***	0.034*	0.037**	−0.058**
	(0.019)	(0.013)	(0.017)	(0.016)	(0.026)
Mean (Dep.)	0.09	0.07	0.06	0.06	0.88
Observations	8,205	8,205	8,205	8,205	8,205
Individual controls	X	X	X	X	X
Municipality FE	X	X	X	X	X
Year FE	X	X	X	X	X
Employed-to-population	X	X	X	X	X

Notes: $*p < 0.10$, $**p < 0.05$, $***p < 0.01$. Each column contains two separate regressions based on Eq. (1) and shows the parameter(s) of interest (α) and the standard error(s) in parentheses. Each column shows a different employment measure or unemployment.

In the first row of Table 1, we show the parameter estimates on the variable measuring the share of the first 12 months since arrival during which the policy was active in the municipality where the refugee was placed. This variable ranges from 0 for those arrived at least one year before the policy started to 1 for those arrived in the month when the policy was started or after that, with fractional values for those arrived in between.

The coefficients on the treatment variable show a significant positive impact of the policy on the employment rate of refugees one year after arrival (Columns 1–4) as well as significant negative effect on the probability of unemployment (Column 5). The estimate implies 5.3% points higher employment rate—with at least 4 hours of work per month—(Column 1), one year after arrival, for the cohorts exposed to the policy for the full year relative to the nonexposed. The employment effect is slightly smaller in magnitude when we exclude subsidized employment in Column 2 (3.6% points) or when we define employment as probability of at least half of full-time employment, namely 80 hours per month (Column 3) or as a share of full-time equivalent (Column 4). In each case, the exposure to a full year of policy increases employment probability one year after arrival by around 3% points. Exposure to the policy reduced the probability of being unemployed by 4.7% points as shown in Column 5.

In the next three rows of the table, we split the treatment into full first-year exposure ($K_{m,t} \geq 0$), exposure between 6 and 11 months ($K_{m,t} = -1$), and exposure between 1 and 5 months ($K_{m,t} = -2$). For those with at least 6 months exposure, we find evidence of a positive significant effect on the employment rate between 3.0 and 5.6% points, depending on the definition used for employment. The higher probability of employment corresponds to a similar and opposite decrease in probability of unemployment (−5.4 to −5.8% points), suggesting that the effect stems from a higher rate of job finding rather than from a change in labor force participation.

Notice that the estimated effect of 6–11 months of treatment ($K_{m,t} = -1$) are not very different from the estimates for one full year ($K_{m,t} \leq 0$). However, the effect from less than 6 months of potential exposure is estimated to be much smaller and often nonsignificant. This is very reasonable as the "Industry Packages" typically imply from three–four months to one year of training depending on the progression of the participant. Hence, most participants would not be able to complete the required training and apply for jobs within 6 months. Overall, these results indicate that the program was effective in connecting refugees and jobs and increasing their probability of being employed by the first year of residence in Denmark.

5.2 Robustness and Placebo Tests

Our results are unbiased estimates of the impact of the policy under three conditions. The robustness and placebo tests in Fig. 2 address each of them and sensitivity to changes in the sample used for estimation. The top panel (a) in this figure shows the estimates for the main ITT effect on employment probability (from Row 1, Column 1 of Table 1) introducing several variations.

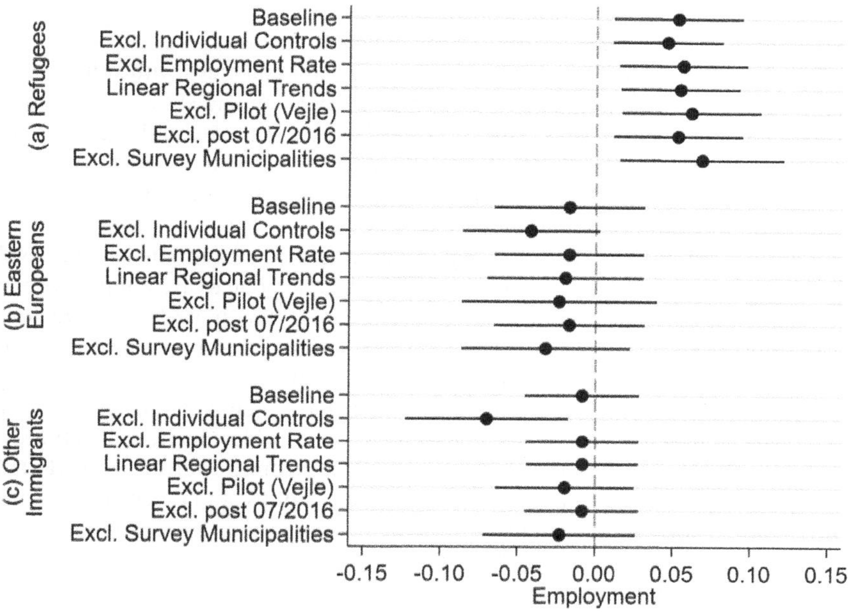

Fig. 2. Robustness and Placebo Tests. *Notes:* The figure shows estimates of α and 95% confidence intervals based on the share specification of Eq. (1).

First, implementation of the policy must be uncorrelated with the characteristics of refugees placed in the municipality. In particular, a change in characteristics of refugees before and after the policy introduction would be a worrisome sign of potential unobservable confounders. In Fig. 2, the comparison between the baseline and the second estimate, excluding individual controls, shows that the coefficient of interest is unaffected by the inclusion/exclusion of those. This indicates that the exposure to the policy is uncorrelated with refugees' characteristics, which may affect the outcome, and it serves as a test of a balanced sample between treated and untreated cohorts.

Second, macro-trends in refugee outcomes must be sufficiently controlled for because uncontrolled macro-trends correlated with the timing of the policy would lead to bias. The municipality and year fixed effects are crucial and included in all our specifications. They control for structural differences across municipalities and national trends in refugee integration. To assuage concerns that national trends could still contaminate the parameter of interest, we exclude municipalities adopting the policy after the notable shift in Danish integration policy toward a job-first approach in July 2016 (sixth estimate in Fig. 2 Panel (a)).

Half of the municipalities adopted after this date, but the parameter of interest is remarkably robust to this exercise. One reason is that the number of new refugees drops sharply in year 2017 and 2018. Hence, the latest adopting municipalities carry little weight in the individual-level regressions because few refugees got placed there close to the implementation time.[17]

Third, the estimates are biased if implementation coincides with other labor market changes in the municipalities such as a labor demand shock. We include the local employment rate as control in our baseline estimate and exclude it in the third estimate in Fig. 2. The two-point estimates are almost identical, suggesting that differences in employment opportunities over time within municipalities are unlikely to drive our results.[18]

Finally, as Denmark has five regions as intermediate administrative level between the country and the municipalities and some policies are adopted at the regional level, the fourth estimate includes a separate time trend for each region. The estimates are, once more, very stable and robust and do not change much.

Panels (b) and (c) of Fig. 2 show a set of placebo tests, aimed at checking further that our results are not driven by local labor demand shocks, possibly specific to immigrants. In these specifications, we consider, instead of refugees, who were eligible for the policy, immigrants either from Eastern Europe (Panel b) or from other source countries (Panel c). These groups, and especially Eastern Europeans, tended to be employed in similar occupations as the refugees but were not eligible for the policy.[19]

The small, negative, and mostly not statistically significant effects estimated for immigrants from Eastern Europe and from other source countries, arriving at the same time as refugees but not eligible to the program, suggest that higher demand for immigrant labor was unlikely to drive the positive employment effects observed for refugees (Panel b and c of Fig. 2). Additionally, this analysis on other immigrants shows also that the "industry package" policy did not produce significant negative spillover effects on that potentially competing group as that group did not experience significant employment effects in response to the policy. The fact that the policy focused on industries and occupations experiencing shortages of workers, to employ refugees, likely minimized any crowding-out of other potential workers, both natives and immigrants.

5.3 Heterogeneity

Fig. 3 shows heterogeneity of the estimates along two important dimensions. We split the employment effect by the level of human capital at arrival (Panel a) and by gender (Panel b) of the refugees. Human capital at arrival is measured either based on the initial assignment to a Danish language training track after an assessment of language teachers (indicated with squares in Fig. 3, Panel a) or using the self-assessed level of schooling at arrival by the refugee (indicated with triangles in Fig. 3 Panel a).

The group denoted as "Low" are individuals with elementary schooling or no schooling at all. The group denoted as "High" are either those assigned to the fast-learner language track (intended for people with some postsecondary education from abroad) or those reporting postsecondary education. The group denoted as "Medium" includes people assigned to the intermediate language

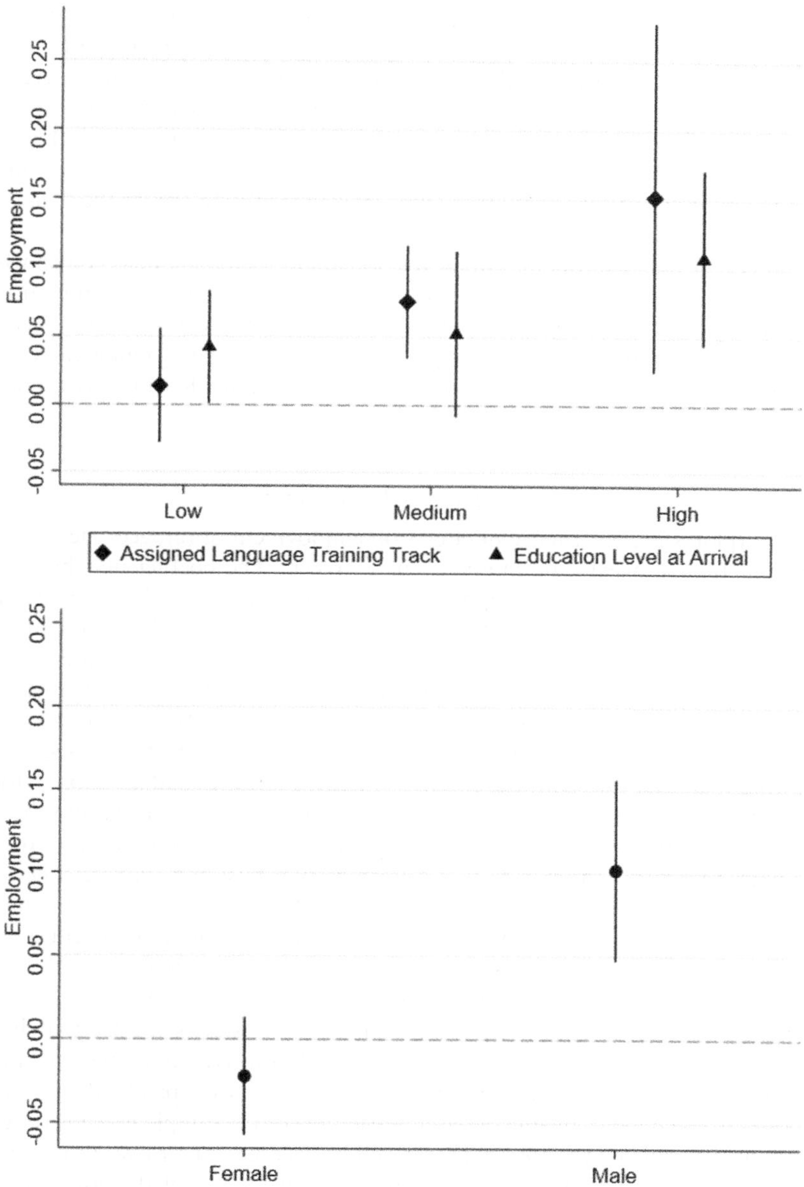

Fig. 3. Heterogeneous Effects. *Notes:* The figure shows estimates of α and 95% confidence intervals based on the share-specification of Eq. (1). Initial human capital is categorized into low, medium, or high based on assignment to Danish language training track 1, 2, or 3 and level of education from abroad. Danish 1 is intended for individuals with only basic schooling (and those who do not know the Latin alphabet). Basic schooling is the lowest education category. Danish 3 is the fast learner track, and Danish 2 is the intermediate track. Danish 3 is intended for individuals with postsecondary education, which corresponds to the highest education level.

training track or reporting secondary education. The graph shows that the employment effect of the policy is strongest for group with the highest level of education among those eligible for the policy (university graduates were not included in the policy and therefore are not in the analysis). We find no significant (or only borderline significant) effects for the low human capital group. This indicates that the policy was more likely to help individuals who were more "ready" in finding a job, likely those with higher schooling and at the "margin" of achieving employment.

Panel b of Fig. 3 shows that the whole impact of the policy was on men while women did not experience any significant effect. Due to cultural/historical reasons, refugee women (mostly from the Middle East and Muslim) were likely to have less labor market experience and were farther from being employable than refugee men. Those factors may have constituted a hurdle hard to overcome by the policy.[20]

5.4 Longer-Run Effects

Fig. 4 explores the persistence of effects on employment of refugees measured at different (and longer) time intervals since arrival. The coefficients shown are based on estimates implementing the third version of Eq. (1), where we compare cohorts who could participate from arrival (fully treated) to cohorts that arrived too early to participate at all in the program when the employment outcome was measured (nontreated). The coefficients show the effects on employment rate 12 months (Panel a), 18 months (Panel b), and 24 months (Panel c) after arrival. The estimates in Panel (a) confirm the results presented in the previous sections, showing that after one year, the cohorts of treated refugees had an improvement 5–6% points in their probability of employment (and lower probability by 5% points of unemployment) relative to nontreated. The different version of the estimates (mirroring those in Fig. 2) confirm very robust and stable coefficients.

The estimates of Panel (b), relative to the effect after 18 months, show similar coefficients as after 12 months, possibly a bit more sensitive to specifications. Most of those effects are still significant and around 5–6% points.

Finally, Panel (c) shows larger and statistically significant effects around 10% points after 2 years (baseline estimate in Panel c). Exposure to the program had a significant impact, lasting at least up to 2 years. As the average employment rate of refugees is also growing with time since arrival (independently of being exposed to the policy), the impact as a percentage of the sample mean is roughly constant. So while we cannot say that the effect becomes larger over time, we can say that the estimates of panel (c) suggest the persistence of the effects of the policy. Fig. 3 in Section 4.4 of the Online Appendix extends the estimates of the effects up to 36 months after arrival. While the coefficients are quite imprecisely estimated due to loss of observations, the point estimates after 2 years continue to be large and significantly positive.

Some caution is needed when interpreting the estimated impact beyond the first year. Since the number of observations is smaller, as we need to drop a larger number of "partially treated" and those who are not observed, e.g. 2 years

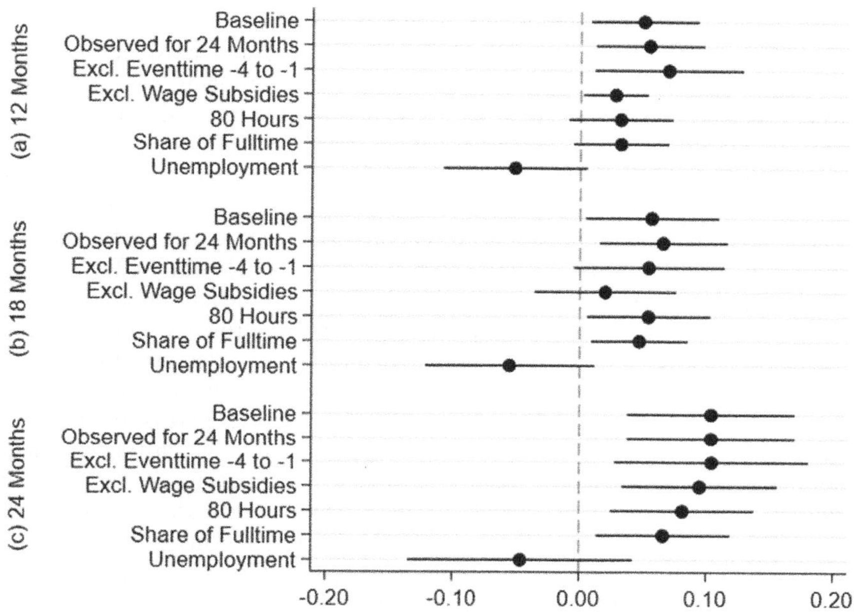

Fig. 4. Impact Over Time. *Notes:* The figure shows estimates of α and 95% confidence intervals based on the dummy-specification of Eq. (1) excluding cohorts who could not be treated from arrival. Hence, event time $K_{m,t} = -2$ and $K_{m,t} = -1$ are excluded when the outcome is measured after 12 months, and one additional event-time parameter is excluded for each additional semester the time horizon is extended. The regressions after 2 years (24 months), therefore, exclude observations toward the end of the sample period that cannot be observed for 24 months because the panel ends and observations with event times $t = \{-4,-3,-2,-1\}$.

after arrival, part of the difference in estimates between different time horizons can be due to the different samples.

Looking at some specific coefficients, we notice that in Panel b of Fig. 4 the employment effect appears to be smaller and more noisy 12–18 months after arrival when we exclude subsidized employment (the fourth estimates from in each panel). However, Panel (c) shows a significant effect on this variable after 24 months. The fifth to seventh estimate of Panel b and c show a significant effect on the share who worked at least 80 hours in the past month and a significant increase in employment measured in full-time equivalents. Finally, the effect on unemployment (last estimate in each panel) is generally more imprecisely estimated, but the point estimates are similar to negative of the employment effect and to what reported in Table 1. Taken together, these findings suggest that the policy helped refugee find employment, including substantial employment for more than 80 hours per month, and such an effect lasted for at least 2 years after arrival.

5.5 Additional Extension and Robustness Checks

We performed some additional checks and extension, and most of these are reported in the Online Appendix. Three are worth mentioning here. First, we checked whether the gain in employment occurred in the targeted industries (see Table A2 in Section 1 of the Online Appendix for a list of such industries in each municipality). The estimate of the impact of the policy on employment in a targeted industry was approximately half of the overall employment effect.[21] Due to the imprecision of the estimates, however, this effect is not significant, and the confidence interval includes the point estimates overall employment effect. As the lists of targeted industries is from the time of first implementation, it is possible that targeted industries changed for cohorts further away from the cutoff, leading to bias toward zero in the estimate of employment in "targeted" industries.

Additionally, we test whether the "Industry Packages" diverted refugees from taking the language classes, which were offered to them as part of the Integration Program. As two of us found extremely beneficial and long-lasting effects of additional language training on employment and income of refugees in Denmark (see Foged et al., 2024b), a displacement from those could have negative implications for employment in the long run. This policy of basic training could complement or substitute language training and language proficiency; hence, crowding out is not necessarily the expected outcome. The estimated association between being exposed to "Industry Packages" and progressing in language training (shown in Table A9 of the Online Appendix) is quantitatively very small and usually not statistically significant. This suggests that the policy did not crowd out the ability of refugees to get language training during the first years of residence in Denmark.

As final check of our results, we apply the recent estimation methods (Borusyak et al., 2024; Sun & Abraham, 2021) to the event study approach with discrete treatment (0–1). The homogeneity of the treatment effect across municipalities and over time suggests that the potential bias in the canonical estimates should be small. Additionally, the limited number of observations per month indicates that these methods may be too demanding in terms of fixed effects.

The results of these estimations are shown in Table A9 of the Online Appendix. While the coefficient estimates before the event are rather noisy, none is significantly different from 0, consistently with no pre-event trend. Most of the estimates after the event, especially when using the Borusyak et al. (2024) estimator, are positive and significant and close to an effect of 5–6% points, confirming our previous findings.

6. CONCLUDING REMARKS

This chapter provides evidence that an integration policy helping to match refugees with jobs experiencing shortages of workers can raise their employment probability within one year of arrival. Such effect persists up to 2 years after arrival and results in substantial employment for individuals (more than 80 hours per month) and shortened and reduced unemployment.

The policy, implemented starting in 2013, on refugees arriving in Denmark was particularly effective in increasing the probability of employment for male refugees and refugees with intermediate levels of education. Possibly, this is because such a group was ready to take advantage of these opportunities and/or was less constrained by cultural and gender barriers linked to traditions in countries of origin.

Additionally, we find evidence consistent with the notion that increased opportunities for refugees did not come at the expense of other immigrants' employment probability. When analyzing the impact of the policy on the employment of other immigrants, in fact, we find no significant effect.

Finally, we show that the availability of the "Industry Package" program and the improved employment opportunity did not crowd out total time and attendance to the language training courses for the participating refugees. Those were also offered to the refugees, and in previous research, two of us (Foged et al., 2024b) showed that they were important for long-run employment outcomes.

Two caveats need to be mentioned. First, as we do not analyze the effect of the policy past the third year after treatment, we cannot rule out that in the longer run, relative to a policy investing in more general skills, such as language and general education, this policy may put workers on a career trajectory characterized by lower wages, preventing more substantial upward mobility. Second, part of the funding of the policy benefited firms, which could employ more productive workers, rather than directly refugees, implying some transfer to them. Nevertheless, the preponderance of evidence so far from the policy is positive. The intervention helped fill labor market shortages, improved refugees' employment outcomes, and had no negative spillovers on other immigrants.

ACKNOWLEDGEMENTS

This project received funding from the Economic Assimilation Research Network (EARN) generously financed by the Innovation Fund Denmark (grant no. 6149-00024B) and the Economic Policy Research Network (grant no. 118986). The project benefited from discussions with Pascual Restrepo, Jacob Nielsen Arendt, Jakob Søgaard, and participants at the 11th OECD-CEPII-LISER Annual Immigration Conference.

NOTES

1. Occupation mismatches could also be worsened by pervasive events changing domestic labor supply such as the Covid-19 crisis (Peri & Zaiour, 2022).

2. Immigration could be one of a set of solutions for projected labor shortages due to population aging (Johansson et al., 2012). Other potential solutions include technologies and automation (Acemoglu and Restrepo, 2017, 2022). Clemens et al. (2018) provide evidence that immigrants and technology adoption are in fact close substitutes when domestic labor is scarce.

3. See the discussion in Martin and Ruhs (2011) for the United States and in Sumption (2011) for the United Kingdom.

4. We provide in the Online Appendix, Section 4 robustness checks using the more recent approaches to event study analysis.

5. As the baseline employment rate of refugees in the host country is very low, the estimated effects after one and two years represent roughly a 50% increase in the baseline employment probability relative to that year.

6. We only include municipalities that strictly adhered to the initial concept.

7. Azlor et al. (2020) provide information about the dispersal policy, and Foged et al. (2024b) describe the Danish Integration Program in place since 1999.

8. Table A1 of the Online Appendix shows the month of initial implementation of the policy in each municipality.

9. See Sections 1 and 2 of the Online Appendix about the data we collected on the roll-out and implementation of the policy as well as detailed information about the policy and how it was implemented. We only include municipalities that followed the original concept.

10. We exclude the remaining municipalities as they could have adopted the policy without our knowledge or related policies (such as those analyzed in Thuesen & Rotger, 2023).

11. Note that this is somewhat different from the typical difference in differences and event estimators where treatment switches from 0 to 1 between two periods. Here, we allow for partial treatment (between 0 and 1) of intermediate cohorts.

12. This is a joint test that all the coefficients −12 to −3 are equal to zero. This cannot be a rejected with a *P*-value of 0.084. Notice that the dynamic specification is under-identified, and we follow Borusyak et al. (2024) and exclude one additional event-time parameter (the earliest event-time parameter where we observe all municipalities).

13. The recent difference-in-differences estimators allow for arbitrary heterogeneity of effects across units of potential treatment and over time. In Eq. (1), however, we assume constant effects across municipalities and time except for period −1 and −2 where we allow a gradual onset of the effect, which we argue are reasonable in our setting. The recent estimators are better suited for a binary treatment, introduced discretely, while we have a window of gradual increase in treatment exposure in the municipality which model with the functional form of *f*, and we estimate in a more canonical framework.

14. We show that the results are robust to excluding the municipalities where information about the program is based on the survey (Fig. A2). Sections 1 and 2 in the Online Appendix provide detailed information about the data collection, and Table A1 in the Online Appendix shows the start dates for the program in each municipality.

15. Highly educated refugees typically received support to access occupations where they could use their qualifications. Those who are 18–24 years old are directed to take some form of education in Denmark.

16. Section 1 and 2 of the Online Appendix describe the data sources and the sample, show more details on the variable definitions, and provide descriptive statistics.

17. We did a few additional checks that specific municipalities are not driving our results: The seventh estimate shows our results are robust to excluding the self-adopting municipalities ("Survey Municipalities"). The fifth estimate shows robustness to excluding the pilot municipality.

18. The employment rate in the municipality of initial settlement may also affect directly employment probability of refugees, as the literature on the impact of initial local conditions (Azlor et al., 2020; Åslund & Rooth, 2007; Damm & Rosholm, 2010 and Godoy, 2017) show.

19. In Table A4, Section 3 of the Online Appendix we show that Eastern European immigrants and refugees worked in similar industries and received a similar hourly pay. Nonrefugee immigrants from other source countries are a more heterogeneous group, and we find that their placebo impact estimates are more sensitive to the inclusion of control variables, suggesting that their composition could change over time in adopting municipalities.

20. Since we estimate an ITT effect, it is possible that the lack of an effect for women and individuals with little human capital at arrival is partly or completely due to lower participation in the program for these groups.
21. These estimates are shown in Column (2) of Table A8 of the online appendix.

REFERENCES

Acemoglu, D., & Restrepo, P. (2017, May). Secular stagnation? The effect of aging on economic growth in the age of automation. *The American Economic Review*, *107*(5), 174–179. https://www.aeaweb.org/articles?id=10.1257/aer.p20171101

Acemoglu, D., & Restrepo, P. (2022, January). Demographics and automation. *The Review of Economic Studies*, *89*, 1–44.

Aksoy, C. G., Poutvaara, P., & Schikora, F. (2023). First time around: Local conditions and multi-dimensional integration of refugees. *Journal of Urban Economics*, *137*, 103588. https://doi.org/10.1016/j.jue.2023.103588

Arendt, J. N. (2020). Labor market effects of a work-first policy for refugees. *Journal of Population Economics*, *35*, 169–196. https://doi.org/10.1007/s00148-020-00808-z

Arendt, J. N. (2022, January). Labor market effects of a work-first policy for refugees. *Journal of Population Economics*, *35*(1), 169–196. https://doi.org/10.1007/s00148-020-00808-z

Arendt, J. N., Dustmann, C., & Ku, H. (2022). Refugee migration and the labour market: Lessons from 40 years of post-arrival policies in Denmark. *Oxford Review of Economic Policy*, *38*(3), 531–556.

Åslund, O., & Rooth, D. (2007, April). Do when and where matter? Initial labour market conditions and immigrant earnings. *The Economic Journal*, *117*(518), 422–448. https://doi.org/10.1111/j.1468-0297.2007.02024.x

Autor, D. H. (2015, September). Why are there still so many jobs? The history and future of workplace automation. *The Journal of Economic Perspectives*, *29*(3), 3–30. https://www.aeaweb.org/articles?id=10.1257/jep.29.3.3

Autor, D. H. (2019, May). Work of the past, work of the future. *AEA Papers and Proceedings*, *109*, 1–32. https://www.aeaweb.org/articles?id=10.1257/pandp.20191110

Autor, D., & Dorn, D. (2009, May). This job is "getting old": Measuring changes in job opportunities using occupational age structure. *The American Economic Review*, *99*(2), 45–51. https://www.aeaweb.org/articles?id=10.1257/aer.99.2.45

Azlor, L., Damm, A. P., & Schultz-Nielsen, M. L. (2020). Local labor demand and immigrant employment. *Labour Economics*, *63*(101808).

Bahar, D., Brough, R. J., & Peri, G. (2024, March). *Forced migration and refugees: Policies for successful economic and social integration* (Working Paper No. 32266). National Bureau of Economic Research. http://www.nber.org/papers/w32266

Borusyak, K., Jaravel, X., & Spiess, J. (2024). Revisiting event-study designs: Robust and efficient estimation. *The Review of Economic Studies*, *91*(6), 3253–3285. https://doi.org/10.1093/restud/rdae007

Brell, C., Dustmann, C., & Preston, I. (2020). The labor market integration of refugee migrants in high-income countries. *The Journal of Economic Perspectives*, *34*(1), 94–121.

Card, D., Kluve, J., & Weber, A. (2018). Active labor market program evaluations: A meta-analysis. *The Economic Journal*, *120*(November), 894–931.

Clemens, M. A., Lewis, E. G., & Postel, H. M. (2018, June). Immigration restrictions as active labor market policy: Evidence from the Mexican bracero exclusion. *The American Economic Review*, *108*(6), 1468–1487. https://www.aeaweb.org/articles?id=10.1257/aer.20170765

Dahlberg, M., Egebark, J., & Vikman, U. (2023). *Long-run integration of refugees: Rct evidence from a Swedish early intervention program* (Vol. 23). IFAU Working Paper.

Dahlberg, M., Egebark, J., Vikman, U., & Özcan, G. (2024). Labor market integration of refugees: Rct evidence from an early intervention program in Sweden. *Journal of Economic Behavior & Organization*, *217*, 614–630.

Damm, A. P., & Rosholm, M. (2010). Employment effects of spatial dispersal of refugees. *Review of Economics of the Household, 8*(1), 105–146.

Dustmann, C., Fasani, F., Frattini, T., Minale, L., & Schönberg, U. (2017). On the economics and politics of refugee migration. *Economic Policy, 32*(91), 497–550.

Foged, M., Hasager, L., & Peri, G. (2024). Comparing the effects of policies for the labor market integration of refugees. *Journal of Labor Economics, 42*(S1).

Foged, M., Hasager, L., Peri, G., Arendt, J. N., & Bolvig, I. (2024). Language training and refugees' integration. *The Review of Economics and Statistics, 106*(4), 1157–1166.

Fouka, V. (2024). State policy and immigrant integration. *Annual Review of Political Science, 27*.

Godøy, A. (2017). Local labor markets and earnings of refugee immigrants. *Empirical Economics, 52*(1), 31–58.

Goos, M., Manning, A., & Salomons, A. (2014, August). Explaining job polarization: Routine-biased technological change and offshoring. *The American Economic Review, 104*(8), 2509–2526. https://www.aeaweb.org/articles?id=10.1257/aer.104.8.2509

Heller, B., & Mumma, K. S. (2023). Immigrant integration in the United States: The role of adult English language training. *American Economic Journal: Economic Policy, 15*(3).

Johansson, Å., Guillemette, Y., Murtin, F., Turner, D., Nicoletti, G., de la Maisonneuve, C., Bousquet, G., & Spinelli, F. (2012). *Looking to 2060: Long-term global growth prospects: A going for growth report*. OECD Economic Policy Papers, No. 3. OECD Publishing, Paris.

Lochmann, A., Rapoport, H., & Speciale, B. (2019). The effect of language training on immigrants' economic integration: Empirical evidence from France. *European Economic Review, 113*, 165–296.

Martin, P., & Ruhs, M. (2011). Labor shortages and U.S. immigration reform: Promises and perils of an independent commission. *International Migration Review, 45*(1), 174–187. http://www.jstor.org/stable/23016193

Peri, G., & Sparber, C. (2009). Task specialization, immigration and wages. *American Economic Journal: Applied Economics, 1*(3), 135–169.

Peri, G., & Zaiour, R. (2022). *Labor shortages and the immigration shortfall*. https://econofact.org/labor-shortages-and-the-immigration-shortfall. Accessed on October 6, 2022.

Sarvimäki, M., & Hämäläinen, K. (2016). Integrating immigrants: The impact of restructuring active labor market programs. *Journal of Labor Economics, 34*(2), 479–508.

Simic, N., Marklund, K., Jönsson, A., Lagercrantz, H., Lagercrantz, C., Erichsen, D., & Ólafsdóttir, A. (2018). *New in the nordic countries: Labour market inclusion of migrants*. Nordic Council of Ministers.

Sumption, M. (2011). *Filling labor shortages through immigration: An overview of shortage lists and their implications*. The Online Journal of the Migration Policy Institute. https://www.migrationpolicy.org/article/filling-labor-shortages-through-immigration-overview-shortage-lists-and-their-implications. Accessed on February 23, 2011.

Sun, L., & Abraham, S. (2021). Estimating dynamic treatment effects in event studies with heterogeneous treatment effects. *Journal of Econometrics, 225*(2), 175–199. https://www.sciencedirect.com/science/article/pii/S030440762030378X (Themed Issue: Treatment Effect 1). https://doi.org/10.1016/j.jeconom.2020.09.006

Thomassen, H. (2019). *The integration of refugees in Denmark. Study for the committee on Employment and Social Affairs, Policy Department for Economic, scientific and quality of life policies, European Parliament, Luxembourg*. https://www.europarl.europa.eu/RegData/etudes/STUD/2019/638397/IPOL STU(2019)638397(ANN02)EN.pdf. Accessed on 6 June, 2021.

Thuesen, F., & Rotger, G. P. (2023). *Assessing the effectiveness of the industry packages programme for non-western immigrants*. VIVE Rapport.

THE LABOR MARKET ATTAINMENT OF IMMIGRANTS IN THE ANTEBELLUM UNITED STATES

Barry R. Chiswick and RaeAnn Halenda Robinson

George Washington University, USA

ABSTRACT

This chapter analyzes the occupational status of adult White foreign-born men in the antebellum United States, compared to White native-born men, and among the foreign born by country of origin. Hypotheses are developed regarding the effects on occupational status of human capital, demographic, and immigrant-related variables. The hypotheses are tested using the digitized microdata for the 100% sample (full count) from the 1850 Census of Population, the first census to ask for the male respondent's occupation, as well as the linked 1850–1860 Census data. Two quantitative measures of occupational status serve as the dependent variables—the Occupational Income Score (OccInc) and the Ducan Socioeconomic Index (SEI). The hypotheses are found to be consistent with the data. Moreover, other variables are the same, while there is a large gap in occupational status between the foreign and native born just after the former arrive, this gap narrows very quickly, and, other variables the same, White male immigrants reached occupational-income parity with their native-born counterparts at about 8.4 years after immigration.

Keywords: 1850 Census of Population; antebellum United States; Duncan socioeconomic index; immigrants; longitudinal analysis (1850–1860); labor market analysis; Occupational Income Score; occupational status

1. INTRODUCTION

The United States has viewed itself as a country of immigrants, with ebbs and flows over time in the share of the population that is foreign born, as well as their countries of origin.[1] There have also been ebbs and flows in the research interest

Migration, Human Capital and the Labor Market
Research in Labor Economics, Volume 53A, 129–168

ISSN: 0147-9121/doi:10.1108/S0147-91212026000053A004

in the relative economic achievements of immigrants compared to the native-born population.[2] In large part due to limitations on the availability of quantitative data on the immigrant experience in the United States in the antebellum period, there has been relatively little research on this period.[3]

The purpose of this chapter is to do the first systematic quantitative nationwide analysis of the occupational attainment of White foreign-born adult males compared to their White native-born counterparts in the antebellum period. This will be done using the recently released full count (100% sample) microdata file from the 1850 Census of Population, Schedule 1, on the free population of the United States (Minnesota Population Center, 2020).[4] The methodology is a quantitative analysis using the economic approach to the study of immigrant labor market attainment developed for the late 20th century. The measure of immigrants labor market attainment will be based on their detailed occupations as reported in the 1850 Census. Reported occupations are a categorical variable that are converted into a continuous quantitative variable by using two measures, the Occupational Income Score (OccInc) and the Duncan Socioeconomic Index (SEI) (Duncan, 1961; Hauser and Warren, 1997; IPUMS-USA, n.d.-c; Warren, Sheridan, & Hauser, 1998). The full count 1850 Census of Population microdata file, with these two quantitative measures of occupational status for all free adult men, has been made available by the Minnesota Population Center (MPC) (2020).

We hypothesize that among adult male immigrants and the native-born free people, occupational attainment is higher among those with greater labor market experience, who are literate, who are married, who live in an urban area, and among the foreign born, with longer duration in the United States. These hypotheses are consistent with the data. While the foreign born at arrival have a lower occupational attainment than the native born, the gap narrows with duration in the United States and closes by the end of the first decade in the country. Differences by country of origin among the foreign born are also explored.

Section II, The Background, sets the stage for the analysis by providing a brief historical context of the foreign-born population in 1850. Section III describes the 1850 Census of Population, with a particular focus on the variables that are of central concern in the statistical analysis. The statistical model and the central hypotheses to be tested are presented in Section IV. This is followed in Section V by the econometric analysis of adult White male immigrant occupational status in 1850 compared to the White native-born adult men, and among the foreign born by country of origin. Section VI is a longitudinal econometric analysis using the linked data from the 1850 and 1860 Censuses of Population. The Summary and Conclusions are reported in Section VII.

2. THE BACKGROUND

Immigration to the United States was first recorded on a large scale in 1820 for entry at seaports due to a 1819 law that required every ship carrying passengers that arrived from a foreign port to file with the US port authorities a list of passengers on the ship (Cohn, 2017). The volume of immigration was low during the 1820s (128,502 during the decade compared to a total population of about 12.9 million in 1830), increasing in the 1830s (538,381 arrivals compared to a total population of 17.1 million in 1840), and—because of famines and revolutions in western and central Europe—increased further in the 1840s (1,427,337 arrivals compared to a total population of 23.2 million in 1850) (U.S. Department of Homeland Security, Office of Immigration Statistics, 2014, Table 2; and De Bow, 1853, Table 1). The crossings of land borders with Canada and Mexico were not systematically recorded in those years.[5]

While the volume of immigration to the United States varied over time, the 1840s and early 1850s can be considered one of the waves of mass migration, and in fact, the period from 1847 to 1854 saw the highest rate of immigration in US history. Further, this marked an increase in the diversity of immigrants coming to the United States. In colonial times and at the turn of the 19th century, most immigrants were English-speaking Protestants, primarily arriving from Britain. However, in the 1830s and 1840s, more rapid population growth in Europe, as well as the impact of the potato famine on not only Ireland but also other parts

Table 1 Country of Birth of White Males, Age 20 and Over, 1850 Census of Population (%).[a]

Country of Birth	All	Foreign Born
The United States	80.18	–
Germany	5.42	27.36
Ireland[b]	8.43	42.52
Great Britain[c]	3.58	18.06
Other Europe	1.18	5.93
Canada	0.97	4.91
Mexico	0.15	0.76
Other Americas	0.06	0.29
Africa	0.00	0.02
Asia	0.02	0.08
Other[d]	0.01	0.07
Total[e]	100.00	100.00
Sample size	4,793,809	950,176[f]

Source: Minnesota Population Center (2020).

[a]Original 1850 reporting of "place of birth" recoded by MPC.

[b]Includes Northern Ireland.

[c]Includes England, Channel Islands, Guernsey, Jersey, Isle of Man, Scotland, Wales, and UK-not specified.

[d]Other includes Oceania, At Sea, Other Countries Not Specified, and Unknown.

[e]Detail may not add to total due to rounding.

[f]There were 1,991 free foreign-born males, age 20 and over, who were not reported as White (0.2 %).

Table 2 Occupational Distribution of White Males, Age 20 and Over, by Country of Birth, 1850 (%).

Occupation	Native Born	Foreign Born						
		All	Ireland	Germany	Great Britain	Canada	Mexico	Other Countries
PTK	3.5	2.0	1.2	2.0	2.9	1.6	1.2	4.8
Farmers	52.2	18.5	12.5	22.5	23.6	25.0	8.1	22.9
Managers	5.3	5.8	4.3	6.7	6.7	3.4	5.0	11.9
Clerical	0.3	0.2	0.2	0.1	0.5	0.2	0.0	0.4
Sales	1.7	2.2	1.8	2.7	2.3	1.5	0.5	3.7
Craft	16.0	20.4	15.0	26.2	25.1	21.1	4.7	19.1
Operatives	9.0	16.9	14.1	15.8	23.4	13.9	53.6	19.2
Service	0.5	1.6	1.9	1.6	1.0	0.5	1.9	3.1
Farm laborers	3.0	4.0	5.1	3.2	2.6	5.8	5.8	2.5
Non-farm laborers	8.6	28.5	44.1	19.3	12.0	27.1	19.2	12.5
Total	100.0	100.0	100.0	100.0	100.0	100.0	100.0	100.0
Sample size	3,843,633	950,176	404,015	259,955	171,625	46,642	7,244	60,695

Source: Minnesota Population Center (2020).

Notes: Free men who reported an occupation. PTK is Professional, Technical and Kindred occupations, Farmers include farm owners, farm tenants, and farm managers, Managers is limited to non-farm managers. All apprentices are included as operatives. Detail may not add to total due to rounding.

of Northwestern Europe, in addition to revolution and civil unrest in Western and Central Europe, resulted in an increased rate of immigration, particularly from Ireland and Germany, in addition to those from Britain (Cohn, 2017).[6] The accelerating industrialization of the United States and the opening up of new farmlands made immigration to the United States more attractive. Additionally, improvements in shipping, such as the use of steamships to cross the Atlantic starting in the 1840s, not only dramatically decreased the voyage duration but also increased its comfort and safety for passengers, thus encouraging an increase in the volume of immigration.

This was a period with virtually no restriction on immigration into the United States, a policy which was challenged during a nativist outbreak in the 1850s (Cohn, 2017). The anti-immigrant sentiment arose, in part, due to the fact that more of the recent arrivals in the 1840s were "Catholic and unskilled," in contrast to commercial workers, mainly merchants, and other skilled workers, who made up a higher proportion of immigrants in the 1820s–1830s (Cohn, 2017; U.S. Department of Commerce, 1976). In the first half of the 19th century, farmers comprised a significant portion of immigrants arriving to the United States though their relative proportion declined over time. Laborers began replacing the farmers in the 1840s and early 1850s; these unskilled workers would have had an easier time finding work in the United States during that period when the economy was strong relative to their European origins (Cohn, 2017).

In fact, the average skill level of immigrants decreased over the period 1820–1850, with less than 40% among the least skilled groups during the 1820s, a proportion which increased to 76% by the 1847–1854 period (Cohn, 2017). However, many of these immigrants experienced upward mobility in the US job market. During the antebellum period of high migration, the majority of immigrants from Britain and Germany generally improved their occupational status over time (Ferrie, 1999). Ferrie found that over three-quarters of British and German immigrants reporting low-skilled jobs on the arriving passengers lists moved into higher skilled occupations over time. In contrast, immigrants from Ireland were less likely to increase in job skill level (only 40%) and more likely to move into low-skilled jobs (over 50%) (Cohn, 2017; Ferrie, 1999).

Ferrie's (1997) analysis also provides insight into the temporal pattern of immigrant occupational mobility. He found that while most immigrants took an unskilled job immediately upon arrival, their occupational mobility (movement into more skilled occupations) in subsequent years varied by nativity. The majority of British and Germans who reported white-collar, skilled, or semi-skilled jobs in the passenger arrival lists "had returned to these jobs or entered farming within a year of entering the United States" (Ferrie, 1997, p. 311). The same pattern holds for the Irish immigrants but at a lower level, with only 40% moving up from unskilled work.

Nativity differences arise, however, in the impact of an additional year in the United States based on the immigrants' reported skill level upon arrival: Germans and Irish had a higher probability of moving from unskilled work if they reported unskilled or farm labor occupations upon arrival (as opposed to white collar, skilled, or semi-skilled), while the opposite was true for the British (Ferrie, 1997, p. 312). Reasons for these differences among the European immigrants include the differential skill levels of arrival cohorts. Causes of immigration should be considered. Ferrie (1997) found no difference in skill levels of British immigrants throughout the 1840s, but there were differences among the Germans and Irish. After the German Revolutions in 1848, the German immigrants to the United States were of a "higher quality", i.e., more skilled, than those arriving earlier in the 19th century. In contrast, Irish immigrants in the late 1840s were fleeing the famine (1846–1850) and were potentially of a "lower quality" than previous Irish immigrants. In addition, anti-immigrant sentiment increased in the United States in the late 1840s and was particularly directed at Irish immigrants.

Overall, the gender and age breakdown of immigrant arrivals was fairly consistent through the 19th century, based on data from the passenger lists. About 60% of immigrants were male (Cohn, 2017; US Department of Commerce, 1976). Generally, about 2,090 were children, 70% were adults up to age 44, and the remaining 1,090 were older adults (Cohn, 2017; US Department of Commerce, 1976). The data gathered from the passenger lists provides much insight into the characteristics of immigrants from 1820 forward and is a useful complement to the data from the 1850 Census when analyzing the occupational attainment of immigrants on a nationwide scale in the antebellum period.

According to the 1850 Census, the White male population of the United States age 20 and over with a gainful occupation numbered nearly five million, of whom just under one million were foreign born (Table 1). Of the foreign born, 88% were coded by the MPC as having been born in one of three countries: Ireland (42.5% of the immigrants), Germany (27.4%), or Great Britain (18.1%).[7] Other parts of Europe contributed 5.9% of the foreign born, Canada 4.9%, and Mexico 0.8%, with about 0.5% of the adult White men having been born elsewhere in the world (Table 1).

Table 2 reports the frequency distribution of occupation, for the ten major categories, by nativity, first for the native born White men and then the foreign born White men by country of birth. Most striking is the difference in the proportion who are farmers (owners, tenants, and managers): 52% among the native born compared to only 19% among the foreign born. Even among the foreign born there are important differences in the proportion who are farmers by specific country of birth, very low for the Mexicans (8%) and Irish (13%) and higher for all other origins (ranging from 23% to 25%), but still less than half of the proportion among the native born. Another large disparity is among non-farm laborers, one of the low-skilled occupations in which newly arrived immigrants often engaged, with only 9% of the native born in this occupational category, compared to 29% of the foreign born. Over four in ten of the Irish-born men (44%) were non-farm laborers in contrast to only 12% for the British, 19% for the Germans, and 27% for the Canadians. The immigrants were more likely to be operatives (which includes all apprentices), 17% compared to the 9% for the native born. Operatives were most prevalent among the British (23%) and especially the Mexicans (54%). The immigrants were also somewhat more likely to be craft workers (20% compared to 16% for the native born), with craftwork most common among the British and German men, and less so among the Irish and Mexicans.

Thus, among White men age 20 and over who reported an occupation, the native born were more likely to be farmers, while the foreign born were more likely to be in urban occupations, such as non-farm laborers, craft, and operative workers, with the Irish appearing to be the least skilled among the major immigrant groups.

Professionals, such as doctors, lawyers, teachers, etc., were relatively few in number in 1850, with a higher frequency for the native born (3.5%) than the immigrants (2.0%) (Table 2). Among the immigrants, professionals were most common among the British (3%) and least frequent among the Irish and Mexicans (about 1% for each). However, the type of professional occupation varied by immigrant nativity: Germans were far more likely to be musicians and music teachers (20.8% of German professionals) and physicians (24.0% of German professionals), while those from Ireland were more likely to be clergymen (19.5% of Irish professionals, of whom over a third were listed as Catholic) and school teachers (23.7%), and British professionals were most commonly clergymen (22.5% of professionals from Britain, who were primarily listed as Baptist,

Methodist, and Episcopalian with very few Catholics) and physicians (19.5%). Medicine has a higher level of skill transferability across countries (as opposed to many other professions, such as law). More state occupational licensing laws were enacted earlier in the 19th century in the legal profession than in medicine (National Council of State Governments, 1952).

Table 2 data report a disparity among the occupations of the native born and the foreign born. By themselves, the data do not indicate whether the native born or the foreign born are of a higher occupational status nor do they shed light on the determinants of occupational status. These issues are addressed in the econometric analysis.

3. THE 1850 CENSUS OF POPULATION

The 1850 Census of Population has been referred to as the first modern census. The census had been taken in every decade since 1790, as mandated by the US Constitution; however, up through 1840, the unit of observation was the household. Since 1850, the unit of observation has been the individual. The 1850 Census Schedule 1 was the first to inquire into the personal characteristics of free people (US Bureau of the Census, 1979, p. 22). There were thirteen questions on Schedule 1, which included recording for each individual their location (and thereby identifying county and rural/urban location), name, age, sex, "color," literacy, place of birth, and, for males, occupation. It is, therefore, the earliest nationwide data that can be used to study the labor market adjustment of immigrants in the United States.

The instructions for the marshals conducting the enumeration were to "ask the place of birth of each individual in the family" and, for those not born in a US state or territory, to list "the name of the government or country" in which they were born (US Office of the Census, 1850).[8] This has been re-coded by the MPC into modern country listings. Unfortunately, the 1850 Census did not ask the foreign born when they came to the United States or their duration in this country. This issue will be addressed below.

The 1850 Census was the first to record individuals' occupations but only for males over 15 years of age. Schedule 1 asked for the "profession, occupation, or trade of each person over 15 years of age" though the instructions to enumerators further clarified that the marshal should record for "each male the specific profession, occupation, or trade which the said person is known and reputed to follow in the place where he resides - as clergyman, physician, lawyer, shoemaker, student, farmer, carpenter, laborer, tailor, boatman, sailor, or otherwise, as the fact may be" (US Office of the Census, 1850).[9] For a clergyman, the initials of the denomination were to be identified. And, "[w]hen a person follows several professions or occupations, the name of the principal one only is to be given" (US Office of the Census, 1850). Finally, if "a person follows no particular occupation, the space is to be filled with the word "none"" (US Office of the Census, 1850).

The MPC digitized microdata file used for this study provides not only the original string data for occupation, that is, the transcription of each individual's occupation as it was recorded by the census enumerator, but also a separate variable in which the occupations were coded into a consistent classification scheme by the MPC. This allows for a more nuanced analysis of the occupations of men in 1850, as it enables analysis that is consistent across the United States as a whole, regardless of variations in spelling or word choice between enumerators (e.g., "farmer" vs "planter"), as well as more detailed analysis when necessary (such as the breakdown by religious order of clergymen).

The respondents were also asked their age, their sex, and if they were "married during the year previous to the 1st of June, whether male or female" (US Office of the Census, 1850). Marital status was not recorded beyond this, and the low frequency of affirmative responses indicates that recent marriages were relatively few. However, there were specific instructions for the enumerators to follow as to the order in which individuals within each household were listed. Therefore, using that information along with names, ages, and sex of each respondent, the MPC was able to create a number of imputed variables for family interrelationships, which allow us to infer the marital status of each individual.[10] Specifically, this is used to infer whether the person was "married, spouse present in the household" or a different marital status, though it is not possible to distinguish among those never married, widowed, divorced, or married with an absent spouse.

The marshals were also instructed to indicate each person "over 20 years of age who cannot read and write... If the person can read and write a foreign language, he is to be considered as able to read and write" (US Office of the Census, 1850). Persons who could read but not write were considered illiterate. There is, however, no information on what constitutes the ability to "read and write." It is not clear if merely being able to read and write one's own name would constitute literacy, nor an indication whether the individual was literate in English or another language.

The 1850 Census, Schedule 1, on Free People instructed the marshals to record each respondent's "color," based on the enumerators' observations. Specifically, "in all cases where the person is white, leave the space blank; in all cases where the person is black, insert the letter B; if mulatto, insert M. It is very desirable that these particulars be carefully regarded" (US Office of the Census, 1850). Among the native-born free males age 20 and over with a recorded occupation in the 1850 Census, 97.96% were implicitly coded as White, 1.44% were coded as Black, and 0.59% as "Mulatto." Among the foreign born, the proportions were 99.79% White, 0.12% Black, and 0.08% "Mulatto." To avoid confounding the analysis with the small proportion of non-White immigrants, the analysis in this study will be limited to White men.[11]

The 1850 Census did not ask foreign-born individuals any questions regarding when they arrived in the United States. One cannot directly incorporate the immigrants' years since migration (YSM) into the model. However, YSM is an important component of the analysis of occupational attainment for immigrants, as it provides a proxy variable for characteristics acquired after migration that would be valuable in the destination labor market, such as language proficiency, cultural adaptation, formation of local networks, etc.[12] However, for this analysis, we can utilize other existing data to create for the first time an estimated years since arrival variable. This constitutes a methodological contribution of this chapter.

There are immigrant flow data covering the years 1820–1850 for the distribution of foreign-born passengers' arrival to the United States by nationality (Willcox, 1929, pp. 370–383, Table I). These data are used to create a frequency distribution of arrivals for the major countries of origin during this time period—Great Britain, Ireland, and Germany—as well as a category for immigrants from all other countries of origin (See Appendix Table A4). Furthermore, immigration statistics from 1820 to 1850 include a distribution of the total number of passengers arriving to the United States by year categorized into three age brackets: under 15 years old, 15–40 years, and over 40 years (see Appendix Table A5). There are, therefore, two distinct probability distributions that can be utilized to estimate YSM: the probability of a foreign-born individual arriving to the United States in a given year based on their nativity and the probability of an individual arriving to the United States in a given year based on their age group. Combining these, and knowing the respondent's age and country of birth from the 1850 Census data, it is possible to calculate an expected value for the individual's duration in the United States (see Appendix A).

Among the country groups considered here, the estimated YSM would be subject to the least measurement error for immigrants from Britain, Germany, and Ireland, due to the magnitude of immigration and method of arrival into the United States. This technique would result in substantial and not necessarily random measurement error for immigrants from Canada and Mexico because of the non-systematic underreporting of land crossings during this period. For this reason, a country-specific YSM value is calculated for individuals from Britain, Germany, and Ireland, while the estimated YSM for all other immigrants uses the combined immigrant flow data for all other countries. The values of estimated YSM for all other countries (other than the big three) are used for Mexico and Canada when the analysis is for all countries but are not included when the regressions are computed for Mexico and Canada individually.

The MPC added to the 1850 data file two quantitative continuous measures of occupational status, which are described in more detail in Appendix A. One is the OccInc and the other is the Duncan SEI (Duncan, 1961; Hauser & Warren, 1997; IPUMS-USA, n.d.-c; Warren, Sheridan, & Hauser, 1998). The OccInc is based on the median income of individuals in the occupation derived from the 1950 Census data. The SEI is based on predicted occupational prestige scores from a regression of survey-based prestige ratings of the occupation on the male median income and educational level of the occupation from the 1950 Census data. While the two measures are closely related (see Table A2 for their correlations), the SEI gives greater weight to the role of level of educational attainment in assessment of the occupational status. Because of the positive skewness of both measures of occupational status, the natural logarithms of these measures are used in the econometric analysis.

See Appendix A for more detail on the variables used in the statistical analysis.

4. THE MODEL AND HYPOTHESES

The model and hypotheses reported here are based on the literature regarding the labor market attainment of adult White men, whether native born or foreign born.

In the econometric analysis, the *natural logarithm of the two quantitative occupational status scores* for White males age 20 and over with a reported gainful occupation is regressed on a set of human capital and demographic variables, as well as immigration variables for the foreign born.

In mathematical terms:

$$\ln Occ = b_0 + \sum_{i=1}^{n} b_i X_i + c_i \sum_{i=n}^{m} FB_i \qquad (1)$$

where *Occ* is our occupational attainment dependent variable, X_i is a set of human capital and demographic variables common to the immigrants and the native born, and FB_i are dichotomous variables for foreign country of birth in the pooled native- and foreign-born equations and the estimated country-specific YSM variable.

There is no information on years of schooling or educational attainment in the 1850 Census, but the data on literacy are utilized, where it is hypothesized that the *literate* men have a higher occupational score than their illiterate counterparts.

There are no explicit data on years of labor market experience, but it will be assumed that labor market experience, if any, prior to age 15 has little or no relevance for adult male occupational attainment. It is also assumed that investment in on-the-job training or labor market experience is greatest in the early years in the adult labor market and declines with duration in the labor force. A quadratic experience variable will be used, that is, *EXP* = *Age-15* and $EXPSQ=(Age\text{-}15)^2$.

It is also hypothesized that men who are married and living with their spouse (*married*) will have a higher occupational status than men who were never married, are divorced/separated, or are widowers. This hypothesis arises, in part, from married men, spouse present, experiencing a greater division of labor between household and labor market activities, and a greater incentive to have higher income (higher occupational status) if one is responsible for supporting a wife.[13] Moreover, high occupational status men would be more attractive in the marriage (and remarriage) market, whether they are among the young, not-yet-married men or among the formerly married (divorced or widowed) men, and hence more likely to become married.

The association between father's occupational status and the number of children in the family (*children*) may be ambiguous. Higher occupational status families may have more children through an income effect. On the other hand, there is a substitution (or price) effect, namely, the children of lower income families are more likely to begin working at a younger age, contributing to household finances and thereby lowering the cost of extra children, and inducing the parents to have more children.[14]

Other relevant demographic variables refer to place of residence. It is hypothesized that because of the low occupational status score of farmers (owners, managers, tenants, and laborers), occupational scores will be higher for men living in *urban* areas.

It is also hypothesized that among White men, whether native-born or foreign-born, other variables the same, occupational status scores will be higher in the *South* as enslaved labor would be engaged in the lowest-skilled jobs in the Southern slave-holding states.

There are two sets of immigration variables in the analysis. One is country of birth, with the *foreign-born* dichotomous variable. It is hypothesized that the foreign-born variable is associated with a lower occupational attainment among men, especially among men who are not farmers. This would be a consequence of the less than perfect transferability of skills of the immigrants—including language skills, knowledge of labor markets and local information networks, and knowledge of technology that may be specific to the US economy—and the recency of their arrival. These deficiencies are likely to be the greatest for the immigrants from Germany and least severe for those from Great Britain, with the Irish in-between.

The other immigration-specific variable is the estimated duration in the United States, *estimated YSM*. It is hypothesized that immigrants would make large investments in skills relevant for the US labor market shortly after arrival and that these new investments would decline with duration as the most profitable investments would have already been made, as well as the increase in the value of their time. That is, an immigrant population that has been in the United States longer would have experienced a greater adjustment to the US economic environment and have greater English proficiency and, hence, a higher occupational status than more recently arrived immigrants. The impact on occupational attainment of immigrant assimilation into the United States would be strongest in the early years after an individual arrives; therefore, this variable is entered as a quadratic, *YSM* and YSM^2, where the hypothesized signs are plus and minus, respectively.

The population under study and the variables used in the econometric analysis are explained in greater detail in Appendix A.

5. THE EMPIRICAL ESTIMATION

The econometric analysis uses the full count (100%) microdata on native-born and foreign-born White men, age 20 and over, with a reported gainful occupation from the 1850 Census of Population, Schedule 1 (Minnesota Population Center, 2020).

The means and standard deviations of the variables used in the analysis are reported in Table 3. The mean OccInc in Table 3 is 20.2 for the native born (the equivalent of shoemakers and landlords), while it is higher (22.1) among the foreign born (the equivalent of bookkeepers and hackney or coach drivers). On the other hand, the mean SEI is higher for the native born (20.7—for example, farm foremen and constables) than the foreign born (19.1—for example, carpenters). The fundamental difference in the construction of the two measures is the weight given to the median level of schooling of men in the occupation in the 1950 Census (see Statistical Appendix) for the SEI, which plays no direct role in the OccInc. The implication is that the immigrants in 1850 were more concentrated than the native born in lower skilled occupations, that is, occupations which (a century later) required a lower level of schooling.

The foreign-born White men in 1850 were on average two years younger than the native born (age 35 compared to age 37), less likely to be living with a wife (54% married compared to 65%), much more likely to live in an urban area (42% compared to 11%), but less likely to live in the South (16% compared to 33%) (Table 3). The immigrant men on average also had fewer of their own children

Table 3 Descriptive Statistics of the Variables Used in the Regression Analysis, Free White Males Age 20 and Over, By Nativity, 1850 Census of Population.

		Foreign Born						
	Native Born	All	Ireland	Germany	Great Britain	Canada	Mexico	Other Countries
Dependent variables:								
OccInc	20.23	22.10	21.33	22.46	23.09	20.77	22.52	23.81
	(10.62)	(8.510)	(7.469)	(8.873)	(9.272)	(8.260)	(7.046)	(10.59)
SEI	20.66	19.07	16.05	20.85	21.92	17.27	14.70	25.49
	(17.75)	(16.90)	(15.13)	(16.98)	(18.10)	(14.64)	(14.64)	(21.29)
Explanatory variables:								
EXP	21.92	19.97	19.18	19.89	22.09	18.29	17.66	21.18
	(13.93)	(11.93)	(11.61)	(11.63)	(12.70)	(12.06)	(10.85)	(12.16)
EXPSQ	674.50	541.18	502.62	530.91	649.23	479.91	429.57	596.69
	(830.6)	(670.8)	(648.7)	(641.2)	(744.9)	(660.7)	(571.6)	(698.3)
Literate	0.93	0.91	0.86	0.98	0.97	0.79	0.49	0.95
	(0.260)	(0.287)	(0.350)	(0.148)	(0.184)	(0.406)	(0.500)	(0.223)
Married	0.65	0.54	0.49	0.59	0.60	0.55	0.21	0.48
	(0.478)	(0.499)	(0.500)	(0.493)	(0.490)	(0.498)	(0.406)	(0.500)
Number of children	2.05	1.39	1.27	1.42	1.66	1.65	0.50	1.22
	(2.388)	(1.985)	(1.933)	(1.920)	(2.131)	(2.247)	(1.337)	(1.896)
Urban	0.11	0.42	0.44	0.48	0.35	0.20	0.05	0.42
	(0.310)	(0.494)	(0.497)	(0.500)	(0.477)	(0.398)	(0.225)	(0.494)
South	0.33	0.16	0.14	0.23	0.11	0.04	0.29	0.31
	(0.469)	(0.371)	(0.343)	(0.420)	(0.312)	(0.185)	(0.452)	(0.464)
Estimated YSM		7.77	7.08	7.19	8.47	NE	NE	NE
		(2.783)	(2.452)	(1.909)	(3.104)			
Sample size	3,843,633	950,176	404,015	259,955	171,625	46,642	7,244	60,695

Source: Minnesota Population Center (2020).

Notes: Means and Standard Deviations (in parentheses) for free White males age 20 and over who reported an occupation and have an occupational score, whether native born or foreign born. NE: Not estimated.

living at home, on average. Indeed, immigrants from each of the major origins in Table 3 were more likely than the native born to be younger, unmarried, and urban Northerners. The Mexican-born men, on the other hand, were far less urban (only 5%) and tended to live in the Southwestern part of the United States (California and Texas).[15]

On average, the immigrant men were slightly less likely to be literate (91% compared to 93% for the native born), but we do not know their level of literacy or proficiency in English. Literacy was greatest among the British, German, and Other Countries (primarily European) immigrants (95–98%), lower among the Irish (86%) and Canadian (primarily from Quebec, 79%) immigrants, and lowest among the Mexican-born (only 49%).[16] While both the British and German immigrants have very high rates of literacy (97 and 98%, respectively), the literacy in English is likely to be lower for the Germans than among the British.

Also, on average, the expected duration in the United States for the foreign born is just under 8 years (7.8 years). Of the three countries that supplied the overwhelming majority of immigrants, the British had the longest expected tenure in the United States (8.5 years), followed by the Germans (7.2 years) and the Irish (7.1 years). The expected duration for Mexicans, Canadians, and all other immigrants is longer on average though recall that these data on arrivals are subject to more measurement error.

Tables 4 and 5 report the reduced form regression analysis of the OccInc and the SEI, respectively, for the native born (Column (1)), the foreign born (Columns (2)–(4)), and the pooled sample (Columns (5)–(8)) of White males age 20 and over with a reported occupation. Nearly all of the explanatory variables are highly statistically significant. Further, the partial effects are all largely unchanged even when including additional immigration-specific controls (country of birth and expected YSM) for the foreign born, implying robust findings.

An older age, that is, greater labor market experience, raises both occupational scores, at a decreasing rate, but by much less for the immigrants. This is consistent with at least some of the immigrants' labor market experience acquired abroad not being fully transferable to the American labor market.

Literacy, which is a proxy measure for educational attainment, has a positive effect on occupational status for both nativity groups, but depending on the outcome measure, the relative effects for immigrants and natives differ. Literacy has a larger positive effect for the native born when the measure is the occupational income score, which is based solely on the relation between occupation and income. On the other hand, using the socioeconomic index, which incorporates the relation between occupational attainment and both income and level of schooling, literacy (in any language) has a larger positive impact among the foreign born. This suggests that while overall immigrants were more concentrated than the native born in lower skilled occupations, controlling for other variables, the immigrants are more concentrated in occupations that in 1950 involve more formal education, consistent with the above results for OccInc and SEI averages.

Table 4 Analysis of Occupational Income Score (OccInc) of Native-Born and Foreign-Born White Men, Age 20 and Over, By Nativity, 1850.

	Native Born	Foreign Born			Native and Foreign Born			
	(1)	(2)	(3)	(4)	(5)	(6)	(7)	(8)
EXP	0.009182***	0.004413***	0.004088***	−0.0003005*	0.008675***	0.008598***	0.008471***	0.008106***
	(158.21)	(40.96)	(38.06)	(−1.99)	(169.36)	(167.96)	(159.25)	(153.14)
EXP^2	−0.000174***	−0.0000954***	−0.0000929***	−0.000042***	−0.000166***	−0.000165***	−0.000163***	−0.000159***
	(−188.18)	(−52.07)	(−50.89)	(−19.40)	(−201.06)	(−200.21)	(−193.78)	(−189.04)
Literate	0.1142***	0.06843***	0.06215***	0.06822***	0.1079***	0.1070***	0.1070***	0.1080***
	(152.99)	(57.91)	(51.20)	(57.77)	(169.01)	(166.47)	(166.48)	(169.23)
Married	0.02646***	0.05137***	0.05089***	0.05281***	0.02928***	0.02943***	0.02929***	0.02932***
	(53.66)	(60.26)	(59.77)	(61.71)	(68.19)	(68.54)	(68.19)	(68.25)
Number of children	−0.01877***	−0.008495***	−0.008475***	−0.008961***	−0.01785***	−0.01782***	−0.01778***	−0.01771***
	(−177.89)	(−38.10)	(−38.17)	(−40.13)	(−187.41)	(−187.32)	(−186.66)	(−185.83)
Urban	0.4217***	0.2535***	0.2605***	0.2557***	0.3598***	0.3633***	0.3634***	0.3607***
	(680.83)	(363.35)	(372.14)	(365.86)	(756.81)	(762.07)	(761.96)	(758.00)
South	−0.03394***	0.05426***	0.05313***	0.05360***	−0.02910***	−0.02906***	−0.02909***	−0.02925***
	(−81.72)	(58.73)	(57.01)	(58.06)	(−77.42)	(−77.17)	(−77.26)	(−77.83)
Foreign born					−0.01141***			−0.1238***
					(−25.30)			(−32.44)
Born in Ireland			−0.08212***			−0.04236***	−0.08998***	
			(−85.27)			(−66.80)	(−23.37)	
Born in Germany			−0.06915***			−0.02851***	−0.07773***	
			(−67.04)			(−37.41)	(−19.45)	
Born in Great Britain						0.04557***	−0.003682	
						(49.96)	(−0.91)	
Born in Canada			−0.04464***			0.02228***	−0.02883***	
			(−25.70)			(13.04)	(−6.47)	

	Native Born	Foreign Born			Native and Foreign Born			
	(1)	(2)	(3)	(4)	(5)	(6)	(7)	(8)
Born in Mexico			0.09893***			0.1959***	0.1442***	
			(24.73)			(45.49)	(24.09)	
Born all other countries			−0.01099***			0.03849***	−0.01195**	
			(−7.02)			(25.60)	(−2.75)	
Estimated YSM				0.03942***			0.01095***	0.02179***
				(38.95)			(12.52)	(25.37)
Estimated YSM²				−0.001564***			−0.000534***	−0.000840***
				(−33.84)			(−12.14)	(−19.33)
Constant	2.7105***	2.8010***	2.8652***	2.6659***	2.7233***	2.7247***	2.7263***	2.7306***
	(2836.08)	(1728.45)	(1534.73)	(677.19)	(3270.29)	(3251.73)	(3177.45)	(3210.82)
Sample size	3,843,633	950,176	950,176	950,176	4,793,809	4,793,809	4,793,809	4,793,809
R^2	0.144	0.149	0.158	0.151	0.150	0.152	0.152	0.150

Source: Minnesota Population Center (2020).

Notes: OLS regressions in which the dependent variable is a natural logarithm of the measure of occupational attainment (OccInc). t-ratios in parentheses. For Columns (3) and (4), the benchmark country of birth is Great Britain.

$^{\#}p < 0.10$, $^{*}p < 0.05$, $^{**}p < 0.01$, and $^{***}p < 0.001$.

Table 5 Analysis of Socioeconomic Index (SEI) of Native-Born and Foreign-Born White Men, Age 20 and Over, By Nativity, 1850.

	Native Born	Foreign Born			Native and Foreign Born			
	(1)	(2)	(3)	(4)	(5)	(6)	(7)	(8)
EXP	0.01237***	0.002629***	0.001597***	−0.01802***	0.01108***	0.01087***	0.01042***	0.009088***
	(143.04)	(12.75)	(7.91)	(−62.53)	(138.10)	(136.22)	(125.70)	(109.67)
EXPSQ	−0.000199***	−0.00000886*	−0.000001691	0.0002191***	−0.0001741***	−0.0001722***	−0.00017***	−0.00015***
	(−144.48)	(−2.52)	(−0.49)	(52.65)	(−134.92)	(−134.23)	(−127.27)	(−114.35)
Literate	0.2526***	0.3746***	0.2958***	0.3751***	0.2876***	0.2677***	0.2679***	0.2882***
	(227.23)	(165.59)	(129.58)	(166.68)	(287.53)	(267.24)	(267.49)	(288.46)
Married	0.06082***	0.07551***	0.05779***	0.08478***	0.06116***	0.05741***	0.05764***	0.06175***
	(82.80)	(46.27)	(36.10)	(51.98)	(90.93)	(85.80)	(86.09)	(91.82)
Number of children	−0.01629***	0.007944***	0.008419***	0.005464***	−0.01314***	−0.01294***	−0.01286***	−0.01270***
	(−103.67)	(18.61)	(20.17)	(12.84)	(−88.10)	(−87.28)	(−86.63)	(−85.13)
Urban	0.5486***	0.2950***	0.3120***	0.3050***	0.4527***	0.4592***	0.4596***	0.4561***
	(594.75)	(220.84)	(237.04)	(228.98)	(607.88)	(618.14)	(618.52)	(612.39)
South	0.05582***	0.1491***	0.1225***	0.1465***	0.06148***	0.05668***	0.05663***	0.06102***
	(90.24)	(84.31)	(69.89)	(83.29)	(104.42)	(96.59)	(96.50)	(103.73)
Foreign born					−0.2528***			−0.5848***
					(−357.79)			(−97.88)
Born in Ireland			−0.3062***			−0.4172***	−0.4671***	
			(−169.12)			(−422.14)	(−77.85)	
Born in Germany			−0.08741***			−0.1925***	−0.2433***	
			(−45.07)			(−162.06)	(−39.07)	
Born in Great Britain						−0.08974***	−0.1468***	
						(−63.12)	(−23.30)	
Born in Canada			−0.09161***			−0.1622***	−0.2288***	
			(−28.05)			(−60.89)	(−32.96)	

	Native Born	Foreign Born			Native and Foreign Born			
	(1)	(2)	(3)	(4)	(5)	(6)	(7)	(8)
Born in Mexico			−0.1259***			−0.1948***	−0.2602***	
			(−16.74)			(−29.02)	(−27.89)	
Born all other countries			0.08642***			−0.01094***	−0.08023***	
			(29.38)			(−4.67)	(−11.85)	
Estimated YSM				0.1492***			0.008134***	0.06039***
				(77.33)			(5.97)	(44.92)
Estimated YSM²				−0.005490***			−0.0001435*	−0.002035***
				(−62.33)			(−2.10)	(−29.91)
Constant	2.3580***	2.1012***	2.3497***	1.5997***	2.3389***	2.3636***	2.3693***	2.3644***
	(1656.54)	(677.29)	(669.43)	(213.20)	(1792.82)	(1810.05)	(1771.98)	(1776.07)
Sample size	3,843,633	950,176	950,176	950,176	4,793,809	4,793,809	4,793,809	4,793,809
R^2	0.109	0.096	0.137	0.106	0.104	0.116	0.116	0.106

Source: Minnesota Population Center (2020).

Notes: OLS regressions in which the dependent variable is a natural logarithm of the measure of occupational attainment (SEI). t-ratios in parentheses. For Columns (3) and (4), the benchmark country of birth is Great Britain.

$^{\#}p < 0.10$, $^{*}p < 0.05$, $^{**}p < 0.01$, and $^{***}p < 0.001$.

Married men (living with their wives) have a higher occupational status than men in other marital situations, and the gap is larger for the occupational income score than for the socioeconomic index. Further, the positive relationship between being married and the occupational income score is greater (twofold) for immigrant than native-born men. This may arise from immigrant men who have a low occupational income score being less attractive in the marriage market for native-born women, and the relative scarcity of immigrant women as marriage partners because adult immigrants were disproportionately male in this time period.

Urban residence has a smaller positive effect on occupational status for the immigrants under both measures. While living in the South is consistently associated with a higher occupational score for the immigrants, presumably because the least skilled immigrants avoid the South due to competition with enslaved workers, there is a mixed picture among the native born. Among the native born, who as adults live primarily in the region in which they were born, the occupational income score is lower in the South, but the socioeconomic index is higher. This presumably reflects the higher level of the educational attainment in the South relative to the lower income occupations, particularly farming, that predominate among native-born men in the South.

In the pooled native-foreign regressions, other variables the same, the immigrants overall have a significantly lower occupational status (Tables 4 and 5, Column (5)), but this varies in magnitude across countries of origin and occupational status measure (Column (6)). All of the immigrant countries of origin display a lower socioeconomic index (SEI—Table 5) than the native born, other variables the same, with the gap largest for the Irish and smallest for the British and for the heterogeneous "All Other Countries" category. On the other hand, a mixed country-of-origin picture emerges when the occupational income score is used as the dependent variable (Table 4, Column (6)): the coefficient in the OccInc equation is most negative for the Irish, smaller negative for the Germans, but significantly positive for the British, Canadians, Mexicans, and other countries of origin. This difference in outcomes reflects the pattern for Irish immigrants, and to a lesser extent German immigrants, to be in occupations that are associated with a lower level of formal schooling, and for the British and Canadian immigrants to be more highly concentrated in occupations associated with a higher level of formal education, yet in occupations with lower incomes (e.g., teachers).

The relationship between an immigrant's estimated duration in the United States and their occupational attainment is shown through the partial effects of *Estimated YSM* and *Estimated* YSM^2 in Tables 4 and 5, Columns (4) for immigrants only, and (7) and (8) for the pooled native—foreign-born sample. *Estimated YSM* is positive and statistically significant, while its square is negative and statistically significant. This indicates that immigrants experience an increase in occupational attainment the longer they live in the United States, an effect which is greatest shortly after arrival and diminishes with the passage of time.

The inclusion of estimated YSM and its square results in little change in the other regression results in the pooled sample (Tables 4 and 5, Columns (5) versus (8) and Columns (6) versus (7)), except for country of origin.[17] The significant positive coefficients in Column (6) of these tables for immigrants from Britain, Canada, and Other Countries now become negative, and remain negative for Germany and Ireland. That is, the immigrant groups show a lower occupational level (OccInc and SEI) than the native born when their duration in the United States is evaluated at zero, with the only exception the occupational income score (significant positive) for Mexican immigrants. This is consistent with newly arrived immigrants entering the lowest-skilled and lowest-earning occupations immediately upon arrival.

For OccInc (Table 4), the partial effect of the initial year in the United States increases immigrants' expected occupational score by about half the effect of being literate, holding all else constant (Column 4). From Column (8), the pooled native-foreign born equation, the impact of each additional year in the United States among the immigrants is slightly smaller though still positive and highly significant. This is due to the interaction between being foreign born and some of the other explanatory variables. For example, the partial effect of literacy on occupational status is much smaller in magnitude among the foreign born than the native born, among whom literacy is more likely to be in English, while the partial effect of being married, spouse present, is larger in magnitude among the foreign born than among the native born. Overall, we would expect a foreign-born male to reach occupational income score parity with his native-born counterpart approximately 8.4 years after arrival, all else constant.

The results of duration in the United States on occupational attainment are largely similar for SEI (Table 5). The partial effect of the initial year in the United States increases immigrants' expected SEI score among the foreign born by roughly the equivalent of living in the South (Column (4)). Among the pooled sample (Column (8)), the partial effect of *Estimated YSM* is smaller than among the foreign-born only sample, again due to interactions with other variables. Foreign-born men as a group would not be expected to reach SEI parity with their native-born counterparts although the gap between the two is smallest about 15 years after the immigrants' arrival.

For both dependent variables, the large increase in occupational advancement in the first few years in the United States sharply narrows the occupational gap with the native born, but the impact of additional US experience becomes very small. These results are consistent with Ferrie's (1997, 1999) findings among selected counties in the United States that, while most immigrants entered low-skilled occupations immediately upon arrival the majority of British and German immigrants quickly moved into higher skilled occupations, while only some of the Irish immigrants did. This, combined with the partial effects for nativity on socioeconomic status (Columns (3), (6), and (7) of Tables 4 and 5), suggests that the "higher quality" of German immigrants outweigh the deficiencies of their expected lower transferability of skills compared to the Irish. That is, of the three main immigrant countries of origin, the lack of skill transferability and local networks appears to have negatively impacted the

British the least, followed by the Germans, and finally with the Irish experiencing the strongest negative effect on occupational attainment of the three groups. This could also be related to labor market discrimination that the Irish faced more so than immigrants from other countries of origin.

Tables 6 and 7 repeat the regression equations separately for the six countries of origin groups.[18] The basic explanatory variables have the hypothesized effects for the OccInc in Table 6: occupational status increases at a decreasing rate with total labor market experience, and increases with literacy, being married, having fewer children at home, living in urban areas and in the South. The score increases (at a decreasing rate) with the estimated duration in the United States for immigrants from Britain, Germany, and Ireland.

The pattern is much more mixed in the analysis on the SEI for individual countries of origin (Table 7). The SEI is higher among immigrants for the literate, married, urban and Southern men, except for being lower for the Southern (mainly from Texas) Mexican men. Unlike the OccInc, the SEI increases with number of children, suggesting the income effect outweighs the substitution effect in this case. The estimated partial effects of labor market experience (EXP) and its square are as hypothesized for Britain and Germany, but are both statistically insignificant for Ireland.

In many ways, the analysis for the Mexican immigrants is the anomaly. They are overwhelmingly rural (95%), highly Southern (29%, mainly in Texas), are the least married living in the same household as their wife (21%), and have the smallest number of children living with them (mean of 0.5 children) (Table 3). They have a very high proportion employed as operatives (53.6%, compared to 16.9% for other immigrants) (Table 2). Their employment as operatives is disproportionately in the mining sector (84% of Mexican operatives). Compared to immigrants from other countries, they have a relatively high occupational income score (22.5 compared to 22.1 for all immigrants) and a very low socioeconomic index (14.7 compared to 19.1 for all immigrants) (Table 3).[19]

Although direct information is not available in the 1850 Census, these characteristics of the Mexican immigrants suggest that they may have been temporary workers or sojourners hoping to make their fortunes in the California gold rush, many of whom left their family members back in Mexico while they worked as operatives in a difficult job in the United States (higher occupational income scores) that required little formal schooling or labor market experience (flat experience-earnings profile and low socioeconomic index). Historical context suggests that this was, in fact, the case. Thousands of Mexican mining workers, known as "Sonorans" from the provinces in Northern Mexico, were temporary residents in California in 1850 during the gold rush (Morefield, 1956; Nostrand, 1975). These Sonorans were "for the most part, young males who had come to mine gold...most of them returned [to the Mexican state from whence they came] after the first mining season [in 1848], but repeated the migration in annual pulsations over the next half dozen years" (Nostrand, 1975, p. 384).

Table 6 Analysis of Occupational Income Score (OccInc) of Foreign-Born White Men, Age 20 and Over, By Foreign Origin, 1850.

	Ireland		Germany		Great Britain	
	(1)	(2)	(3)	(4)	(5)	(6)
EXP	0.003883***	0.001569***	0.002583***	−0.002291***	0.005050***	0.003484***
	(25.25)	(3.46)	(11.79)	(−3.64)	(19.67)	(4.90)
EXPSQ	−0.0000811***	−0.0000531***	−0.00007999***	−0.00001650*	−0.0001151***	−0.00009319***
	(−30.75)	(−9.60)	(−21.19)	(−2.01)	(−27.25)	(−10.91)
Literate	0.05620***	0.05631***	0.08865***	0.08803***	0.07232***	0.07230***
	(40.01)	(40.09)	(20.30)	(20.18)	(16.05)	(16.06)
Married	0.06790***	0.06661***	0.04438***	0.03904***	0.05010***	0.04683***
	(54.27)	(52.84)	(27.31)	(23.77)	(24.29)	(22.59)
Number of children	−0.005173***	−0.004931***	−0.01065***	−0.009679***	−0.008911***	−0.008812***
	(−15.38)	(−14.59)	(−24.52)	(−22.16)	(−18.14)	(−17.93)
Urban	0.2107***	0.2107***	0.3074***	0.3066***	0.2860***	0.2856***
	(210.98)	(211.02)	(232.02)	(231.53)	(163.49)	(163.35)
South	0.04608***	0.04575***	0.03443***	0.03373***	0.08172***	0.08074***
	(32.03)	(31.80)	(22.16)	(21.72)	(30.74)	(30.38)
Estimated YSM		0.03412***		0.1128***		0.04311***
		(7.20)		(13.52)		(7.22)
Estimated YSM^2		−0.001745***		−0.006288***		−0.002171***
		(−7.67)		(−14.77)		(−8.52)
Constant	2.7967***	2.6837***	2.7820***	2.3854***	2.8377***	2.6717***
	(1309.92)	(173.95)	(564.34)	(81.47)	(534.91)	(125.44)
Samp. Size	404,015	404,015	259,955	259,955	171,625	171,625
R^2	0.126	0.126	0.203	0.204	0.162	0.163

(Continued)

Table 6 *(Continued)*

	Canada (7)	Mexico (8)	All Other Countries (9)
EXP	0.005157***	0.001141	0.008049***
	(10.33)	(1.05)	(17.32)
EXPSQ	−0.0001022***	−0.00005664**	−0.0001409***
	(-12.00)	(-2.79)	(−18.02)
Literate	0.02863***	0.1052***	0.1289***
	(7.27)	(13.56)	(19.19)
Married	0.07746***	−0.04787***	0.0008591
	(19.20)	(-3.92)	(0.23)
Number of children	−0.01321***	−0.01610***	−0.01262***
	(−13.73)	(−4.58)	(−12.41)
Urban	0.2916***	0.1303***	0.2757***
	(73.65)	(7.79)	(87.77)
South	0.1058***	−0.2040***	0.1222***
	(12.54)	(-20.85)	(36.45)
Constant	2.8172***	3.0845***	2.7367***
	(474.38)	(246.30)	(325.39)
Samp. Size	46,642	7,244	60,695
R^2	0.127	0.174	0.175

Source: Minnesota Population Center (2020).

Notes: All Other Countries excludes Great Britain, Germany, Ireland, Mexico, and Canada. OLS regressions in which the dependent variable is a natural logarithm of the measure of occupational attainment (OccInc). t-ratios in parentheses.

$^{\#}p < 0.10$, $^{*}p < 0.05$, $^{**}p < 0.01$, and $^{***}p < 0.001$.

Table 7 Analysis of Socioeconomic Index (SEI) of Foreign-Born White Men, Age 20 and Over, By Foreign Origin, 1850.

	Ireland		Germany		Great Britain	
	(1)	(2)	(3)	(4)	(5)	(6)
EXP	−0.0005570#	−0.001936*	−0.001191**	−0.006949***	0.005642***	0.006076***
	(−1.85)	(−2.18)	(−2.90)	(−5.88)	(12.01)	(4.67)
EXPSQ	0.00006818***	0.00008101***	−0.00001208#	0.00006257***	−0.00006938***	−0.00007118***
	(13.22)	(7.49)	(−1.70)	(4.05)	(−8.98)	(−4.55)
Literate	0.2903***	0.2900***	0.2616***	0.2609***	0.3176***	0.3176***
	(105.64)	(105.51)	(31.90)	(31.82)	(38.53)	(38.54)
Married	0.06086***	0.06282***	0.04190***	0.03612***	0.08603***	0.08366***
	(24.86)	(25.47)	(13.73)	(11.71)	(22.80)	(22.05)
Number of children	0.01667***	0.01623***	0.007575***	0.008608***	0.002055*	0.002181*
	(25.33)	(24.55)	(9.29)	(10.49)	(2.29)	(2.42)
Urban	0.2394***	0.2394***	0.3209***	0.3201***	0.4045***	0.4042***
	(122.52)	(122.52)	(128.97)	(128.61)	(126.40)	(126.31)
South	0.1166***	0.1171***	0.05652***	0.05576***	0.1879***	0.1872***
	(41.43)	(41.58)	(19.37)	(19.11)	(38.63)	(38.48)
Estimated YSM		−0.002015		0.1279***		0.01698
		(-0.22)		(8.16)		(1.56)
Estimated YSM²		0.0003625		−0.007086***		−0.0009755*
		(0.81)		(-8.86)		(−2.09)
Constant	2.0754***	2.0891***	2.3780***	1.9287***	2.2372***	2.1657***
	(496.82)	(69.21)	(256.85)	(35.05)	(230.54)	(55.55)
Samp. Size	404,015	404,015	259,955	259,955	171,625	171,625
R^2	0.081	0.081	0.074	0.075	0.113	0.113

(Continued)

Table 7 *(Continued)*

	Canada (7)	Mexico (8)	All Other Countries (9)
EXP	0.008980***	−0.00006874	0.01052***
	(10.75)	(-0.04)	(12.64)
EXPSQ	−0.0001375***	0.00001723	−0.0001329***
	(−9.66)	(0.50)	(−9.49)
Literate	0.2988***	0.2738***	0.3032***
	(45.36)	(20.97)	(25.20)
Married	0.1218***	0.06886***	0.04723***
	(18.06)	(3.35)	(7.04)
Number of children	−0.01394***	0.02894***	0.001420
	(-8.67)	(4.90)	(0.78)
Urban	0.3964***	0.4436***	0.4206***
	(59.86)	(15.76)	(74.76)
South	0.3337***	−0.1922***	0.2614***
	(23.66)	(−11.67)	(43.55)
Constant	2.1635***	2.3260***	2.2423***
	(217.85)	(110.40)	(148.88)
Samp. Size	46,642	7,244	60,695
R^2	0.143	0.116	0.150

Source: Minnesota Population Center (2020).

Notes: All Other Countries excludes Great Britain, Germany, Ireland, Mexico, and Canada. OLS regressions in which the dependent variable is a natural logarithm of the measure of occupational attainment (SEI). t-ratios in parentheses.

$^{\#}p < 0.10$, $^{*}p < 0.05$, $^{**}p < 0.01$, and $^{***}p < 0.001$.

6. LONGITUDINAL ANALYSIS

Thus far, the analysis has focused on a single cross-sectional data file, the 1850 Census of Population. To what extent, however, is the finding of a positive quadratic effect of estimated duration in the United States (YSM) due to more recent immigrants having lower innate ability rather than initially less human capital investment relevant for the destination labor market? If there is no difference over time in US-specific investment in human capital by immigrants compared to natives but more recent immigrant cohorts were innately lower quality workers, in a single cross-section one could observe that those in the destination longer would have greater labor market attainment. To obtain the positive quadratic effect of duration, one would need to assume that the decline in immigrant quality was more rapid or more intense in later years.[20]

Ideally, to resolve this issue, it would be best to have nationwide longitudinal data on both the foreign born and the native born.[21] While no such nationwide longitudinal data exist for the antebellum period, this can, in principle, be proxied by using the linked 1850 Census-1860 Census file on individuals constructed by the MPC. Using microdata from the full count census on a set of individual, household, and contextual characteristics, the MPC linked individuals from the 1850 Census to themselves as reported in the 1860 Census.[22]

This linkage is subject to two types of error. One is not being able to match a person in the 1850 Census to the 1860 Census. This failure may arise from several factors: death, name changes (including spelling changes or errors beyond those that would be captured by the Jaro-Winkler algorithm for first and last name similarity used by the MPC), other mismatches between the critical characteristics used for matching individuals, either through errors in recording of the data by census enumerators or changes in reporting of their personal information by the individuals, and the return migration to the country of origin (or a third country) among the foreign born.[23] The second error, which may be less likely, is an incorrect match: the "John Smith" identified as a match may be two different men.

There were 4.8 million White males, age 20 and over, with a reported occupation in the 1850 Census. Of those, slightly over 3.8 million were native born, and the MPC matching to native-born White males, age 30 and over, with a reported occupation in 1860 was completed for almost 1.1 million, a match rate of only 27.7%. Among the nearly one million foreign-born White males, age 20 and over, with a reported occupation in 1850, just over 100 thousand were matched in 1860, a match rate of only 10.8%. These are very low match rates. The lower match rate for immigrants may be due to return migration, more name changes, greater internal mobility, or some combination of these and other factors. The missing matches may not be random with respect to occupational mobility over the decade or between the foreign born and the native born.

Table 8 reports the mean values of the two occupational attainment scores for the matched (linked) 1850–1860 sample for the native born and the foreign born. For reasons that are unclear, the OccInc score declined for both groups, but the decline is smaller for the foreign born. The SEI increased for both nativity groups, with the increase greater for the immigrants. Under both measures, the immigrants in the linked sample improved their relative occupational attainment compared to the native-born men over the decade.

Using the occupation data available in the linked sample, less than one-third (29.8%) of native-born adult men changed occupations over the decade and just over one-third (35.8%) of foreign-born adult men did. Among the native born, there was a shift in aggregate terms from being craft workers and non-farm laborers into farm laborers, managers, and to a lesser extent farmer owners. Among the foreign born, there was aggregate movement away from non-farm laborers, craft, and operative positions into managers and proprietors as well as farm owners. However, this does not account for income or status increasing within the same broad occupational category.[24]

As an additional test, the changes in the two measures of occupational attainment from 1850 to 1860 were regressed on the estimated YSM, as well as the changes in the other explanatory variables.[25] When this is done in the native—foreign regression, the regression for all of the foreign born pooled, and separately for the three primary source countries, the coefficient on the estimated YSM variable is consistently negative and statistically significant, except for the negative insignificant coefficient for Britain in the OccInc analysis. That is, the longer an immigrant cohort has been in the United States, the smaller is the marginal effect of additional time on their occupational attainment. The negative but statistically insignificant coefficient for Britain is consistent with the much higher degree of skill transferability (including English language skills) for British than for other immigrant groups. These findings are consistent with the quadratic effect of duration on the occupational status of immigrants found in the single cross-sectional data.

Table 8 Change in Mean Occupational Attainment Among the Native-Born and Foreign-Born Adult White Men in the Linked 1850–1860 Sample.

	Native Born			Foreign Born		
	1850	1860	Change	1850	1860	Change
OccInc	19.51	19.38	−0.21	21.77	21.75	−0.14
	(10.17)	(10.73)	(8.37)	(8.95)	(9.88)	(7.89)
SEI	19.87	20.63	0.76	20.04	21.78	1.74
	(16.60)	(17.77)	(14.93)	(17.04)	(18.64)	(16.24)
Sample size		1,066,572			103,091	

Source: Minnesota Population Center (2021, 2023).

Notes: Standard deviations in parentheses.

7. SUMMARY AND CONCLUSIONS

This chapter uses the full count (100% sample) 1850 Census of Population microdata for adult White men to study the determinants of the occupational status in the mid-19th century of foreign-born men among themselves and compared to the native born. The 1850 Census is the first US census to record the personal characteristics of individuals, including the occupation of men. Occupational attainment is measured using two indices: the OccInc and the Duncan SEI. Hypotheses are developed based on the human capital, demographic, and immigrant characteristics of the respondents.

In general, it is found that, among White male immigrants and the native born, occupational status increases (at a decreasing rate) with labor market experience and is higher for the literate, married, urban, and (among immigrants) Southern men. Immigrant occupational status also increases (at a decreasing rate) with their estimated duration in the United States.

Differences that emerge between the two measures of occupational status and among the immigrants by country of origin are highlighted.

Although immigrants initially have a lower occupational status than the native born, when other variables are the same, by around 8.4 years in the US immigrants' occupational income score equals and then exceeds that of the native born. However, the SEI of immigrants as a group does not equal that of their native-born counterparts though the gap is smallest approximately 15 years after the immigrant's arrival. This suggests that while overall immigrants initially were more concentrated than the native born in lower skilled occupations, controlling for other variables, the immigrants reached occupational "parity" based on occupational income in the first decade after their arrival in spite of their tendency to be in occupations that involved a lower level of formal schooling.

Immigrants from Mexico display characteristics that differentiate them from European arrivals. They are more likely than other immigrants to be rural residents in California and Texas, working as operatives in the mining sector with demographic characteristics suggesting a higher degree of temporary or sojourner worker migration, consistent with the "Sonoran" phenomenon of annual migration for gold mining. This is consistent with 20th century sojourner Mexican migration patterns.

Overall, it appears that the hypotheses developed in the 20th century regarding the human capital, demographic, and immigrant determinants of immigrant adjustment are consistent with the antebellum immigrant labor market experience in the United States. Moreover, other measured explanatory variables the same, the White male immigrants reached occupational-income parity with their native-born counterparts within a decade of living in the United States, after which they had a higher level on average. These findings are consistent with findings for analyses of contemporary immigrants in the United States (Chiswick, 1978a, 1978b, 1986; Duleep et al., 2022).

ACKNOWLEDGMENTS

The authors would like to thank the IPUMS team at the Minnesota Population Center, University of Minnesota for their assistance in understanding the 1850 Census data file. We appreciate the comments received on an earlier draft of this chapter from Carmel U. Chiswick, the participants at WALES (Washington Area Labor Economics Symposium) April 2024, and the co-editors and two referees at *Research in Labor Economics*.
* Department of Economics, George Washington University Email: Barry R. Chiswick, brchis@gwu.edu, RaeAnn Halenda Robinson, rhalenda@gwu.edu.

NOTES

1. The foreign-born proportion of the population in 1850 was about 10%, increased to about 15% in 1920, then declined to below 5% in 1970, and then has increased to around 14% today (Carter et al., 2006; Migration Policy Institute Data Hub, 2023).

2. For the early 20th century, these studies include Carpenter (1927), Douglas (1919), and US Immigration Commission (1911), commonly known as the Dillingham Commission Report. With the post-WWII increase in immigration, greater availability of data and the ease of analyzing these data, starting with Chiswick (1978a, b), there has been a sharp growth in research on immigrant economic adjustment in the United States and other countries.

3. A notable exception is Ferrie (1999), which tracked the progress of German, Irish, and British immigrants in selected counties from their shipboard arrival in the 1840s to the 1860 Census. For frequency distributions of the occupational attainment of free males in the United States in 1850, but not by country of birth, see the contemporaneous Census analyses in De Bow (1853, 1854). Far more research has been conducted on the immigrants who arrived during the age of mass migration, the four decades from 1880 to 1924. See, for example, Abramitzky et al. (2020 and 2014), Chiswick (2020, Chapters three–5), Douglas (1919), and Duleep et al. (2022). Adjustment patterns for these immigrants mirror those of the late 20th century immigrants.

4. Of note, these data do not include enslaved persons (of whom there were approximately 3.2 million in the United States in 1850, and were enumerated on Schedule 2 of the census) or the majority of Native American tribes (described as “Indians not taxed” in the 1850 Census report, whom were largely not enumerated at all) (De Bow, 1853, p. liv).

5. In the 1850 Census, country of birth data for free males age 20 and over, Canada contributed about 5% of the foreign born, but by the recorded immigration data for 1820 to 1849, Canada provided about 2% of the foreign born (approximately 56 thousand out of 2.4 million), while for Mexico the 0.8% of the foreign born from the Census contrasts with the less than one-half of one percent among recorded immigrants. The sharp difference in the share of immigrants from Canada and Mexico as reported in the Census and as reported in the immigrant arrivals data is consistent with the underreporting of land crossings (U.S. Department of Homeland Security, Office of Immigration Statistics, 2014, Table 2; Minnesota Population Center, 2020, microdata file).

6. See also Thomas (1954), Hatton and Williamson (1998), and Massey (1999). For a history of the two-way border crossings between the United States and Canada in the first half of the 19th century, see Hansen (1940, Chapters 4–6).

7. Great Britain includes England, Channel Islands, Guernsey, Jersey, Isle of Man, Scotland, Wales, and UK-not specified. Ireland consists of what is now the Republic of Ireland and Northern Ireland.

8. The nativity of some Mexican immigrants in 1850 may be misreported because these were primarily individuals living in California and Texas, which were part of Mexico at the time of their birth. Texas gained independence from Mexico in 1836, and was annexed as the 28th state in 1845. California was ceded to the United States in 1848 as a result of the Mexican–American War and became the 31st state on September 9, 1850. While the instructions to enumerators indicate that those born in areas that were part of Mexico at their birth were supposed to report what had subsequently become the US state as their birthplace, it is not clear how many failed to do so. See Nostrand (1975) for further discussion of the Mexican American population in the mid-19th century, including factors that contributed to inaccurately low estimates of its size.

9. Occupation was not asked for free women until the 1860 Census, where only 16% of free women were reported as having a gainful occupation (Chiswick and Robinson, 2021).

10. The census instructions to marshals specified that within each household, "the names are to be written beginning with the father and mother; or, if either, or both, be dead, begin with some other ostensible head of the family; to be followed, as far as practicable, with the name of the oldest child residing at home, then the next oldest, and so on to the youngest, then the other inmates (sic), lodgers and boarders, laborers, domestics, and servants" (IPUMS-USA, n.d.-a).

11. The instructions for the question on "color" made no allowance for men who might have been coded as of Asian or Native American ("Indian") origin. However, enumerators occasionally entered responses outside the prescribed options. In the 1850 full count microdata file, there were 374 males, age 20 and over with a gainful occupation, who were recorded as being of other races, the majority of whom were classified as "American Indian," which equates to less than 0.01% of the sample.

12. Years Since Migration (YSM) generally has a positive relationship, but at a decreasing rate, to immigrant earnings and occupational attainment. See, for example, Chiswick (1978a, 1978b) for a discussion of the relationship between immigrants' duration in the destination, the international transferability of skills, and labor market outcomes.

13. In the mid-19th century, it was not common for married women to work outside the home. Their work was generally unreported but in support of their husband's or father's farm or other business (Chiswick and Robinson, 2021).

14. Becker and Lewis (1973) develop this analysis of the income and substitution effects of family incomes on fertility. Chiswick and Robinson (2025) find a negative association of children and father's occupational status in 1850 Census data, suggesting that the substitution effect was stronger than the income effect on fertility at this time.

15. Among the White adult male Mexican immigrants, 63.9% lived in California and 26.0% in Texas, compared with 1.9% and 0.8% in California and Texas, respectively, among all White adult male immigrants.

16. While there is no information on the respondent's religion, the country-of-origin data suggest that it may reflect greater literacy among Protestant than among Catholic immigrants. Additionally, if there were a language barrier, the enumerator may not have accurately recorded an individual's literacy in their native language (for example, if the respondent spoke French or Spanish but the enumerator only spoke English).

17. Although the estimated YSM is constructed using immigrant flows by grouped age data, the computed regression equations do not show evidence of multicollinearity (e.g., the standard errors do not become very large).

18. Because the estimated duration variable is measured so poorly due to incomplete records of land crossings and inconsistent immigration flows for Canada, Mexico, and All Other Countries, it is not included in these regressions.

19. Note that from Table A3 "mine operatives and laborers" have an OccInc score (24) comparable to that of clergymen, but a very low SEI (10), comparable to that of laborers not elsewhere classified. This may reflect miners relatively high income given their low level of educational attainment.

20. Several studies that have addressed the hypothesis of a decline in immigrant quality during the period of mass immigration and during the second half of the 20th century have rejected the hypothesis. See, for example, Abramitzky et al. (2014, 2020), Douglas (1919), Chiswick (1986), and Duleep et al. (2022).

21. Ferrie (1999) traces a sample of White male immigrants in selected counties identified in shipboard records in the 1840s to the 1850 and 1860 Censuses. He finds that from the 1850 Census to the 1860 Census, the immigrants experienced a steeper improvement in their occupational status than did the native-born White men. Chiswick (1978b) uses information in the 1970 Census microdata on occupational status in 1965 and 1970 to study longitudinal changes in occupation as a function of duration of residence in 1970. He finds that among White male immigrants the increase in occupational status over this five-year period is smaller the longer a cohort has been in the United States. This is consistent with a quadratic effect of duration on occupational status found in single cross-sectional analysis.

22. For additional information on the Multigenerational Longitudinal Panel (MLP) project by MPC and the linking method used, see IPUMS-USA (n.d.-d). For the linked data, see Minnesota Population Center (2021, 2023).

23. A study of the changes in surnames among Jewish immigrants in the late 19th and 20th centuries found that most did not occur at immigration but after some time in the United States (see Fermaglich, 2018). This may have also been the experience of other immigrant groups in the mid-19th century.

24. One drawback of the 1850–1860 linked file is that the occupational string data are not available for this sample. The occupation data are all coded by MPC into the occupation, 1950 basis, categories, which loses some of the nuance available in the string data. For example, in 1860, the census enumerators were instructed to differentiate between self-employed business owners (e.g., master carpenter) and those employed by others (e.g., carpenter). In the occupation, 1950 basis, both individuals would be categorized as "carpenters," without the detail of their rank within the occupation.

25. The regressions are reported in Appendix B, available upon request.

26. There were 2,385 individuals who had a recorded gainful occupation in both censuses and otherwise met the criteria for inclusion in this study, but the MPC data file had the OccInc coded as "00." As their occupation, 1950 basis, in 1860 was known, the corresponding OccInc scores for 1860 were manually entered.

REFERENCES

Abramitzky, R., Boustan, L., & Eriksson, K. (2014). A nation of immigrants: Assimilation and economic outcomes in the age of mass immigration. *Journal of Political Economy*, *122*(3), 467–506.

Abramitzky, R., Boustan, L., & Eriksson, K. (2020). Do immigrants assimilate more slowly today than in the past? *The American Economic Review: Insights*, *2*(1), 125.

Becker, G. S., & Lewis, H. G. (1973). On the interactions between quantity and quality of children. *Journal of Political Economy*, *81*(2 Part 2), S279–S288.

Carpenter, N. (1927). *Immigrants and their children, census monographs VII*. United States Government Printing Office.

Carter, S. B., et al. (2006). *Historical statistics of the United States, millennial edition*. Cambridge University Press.

Chiswick, B. R. (1978a). The effect of Americanization on the earnings of foreign-born men. *Journal of Political Economy*, *86*, 897–921.

Chiswick, B. R. (1978b). A longitudinal analysis of the occupational mobility of immigrants. In *Proceedings of the thirtieth annual meeting of the industrial relations research association.* December 28-30, 1977, Madison, Wisconsin. IRRA.

Chiswick, B. R. (1986). Is the new immigration less skilled than the old? *Journal of Labor Economics*, *4* (2), 168–192.

Chiswick, B. R. (2020). *Jews at work: Their economic progress in the American labor market*. Cham, Springer.

Chiswick, B. R., & Robinson, R. H. (2021). Women at work in the United States since 1860: An analysis of unreported family workers. *Explorations in Economic History*, *82*(October).

Chiswick, B. R., & Robinson, R. H. (2025). Jewish occupational attainment in the antebellum USA: Filling a gap in the literature. *Social Science History*, *49*(3), 670–696.

Cohn, R. L. (2017). Immigration to the United States. In R. Whaples (Ed.). *EH.Net Encyclopedia*. https://eh.net/encyclopedia/immigration-to-the-united-states/. Accessed 10 2, 2024.

De Bow, J. D. B. (1853). *Seventh Census of population, 1850, an appendix, US Census Office*. Robert Armstrong, Public Printer.

De Bow, J. D. B. (1854). *Statistical view of the United States: Compendium of the seventh Census, US Census Office*. Beverly Tucker, Senate Printer.

Douglas, P. H. (1919, June). Is the new immigration more unskilled than the old? *Journal of the American Statistical Association*, 393–403.

Duleep, H., Liu, X., & Regets, M. (2022). How the earnings growth of US immigrants was underestimated. *Journal of Population Economics*, *35*, 381–407.

Duncan, O. D., et al. (1961). A socioeconomic index for all occupations. In A. Reiss (Ed.), *Occupations and social status*. Free Press.

Fermaglich, K. (2018). *A Rosenberg by any other name*. New York University Press.

Ferrie, J. P. (1997). The entry into the U.S. labor market of antebellum european immigrants, 1840-1860. *Explorations in Economic History*, *34*, 295–330.

Ferrie, J. P. (1999). *Yankeys now: Immigration in the antebellum United States, 1840-1860*. Oxford University Press.

Hansen, M. L. (1940). *The mingling of the Canadian and American peoples, volume I, historical*. Yale University Press.

Hatton, T. J., & Williamson, J. G. (1998). *The age of mass migration: Causes and economic impact*. Oxford University Press.

Hauser, R., & Warren, J. R. (1997). Socioeconomic indexes of occupational status: A review, update, and critique. *Sociological Methodology*, *27*(1), 177–298.

IPUMS-USA (n.d.-a). *Family interrelationships*. IPUMS user guide, Minnesota Population Center, University of Minnesota. https://usa.ipums.org/usa/chapter5/chapter5.shtml, Accessed 7/11/2022.

IPUMS-USA. (n.d.-b). *Frequently asked questions*. IPUMS user guide, Minnesota Population Center, University of Minnesota. https://usa.ipums.org/usa-action/faq. Accessed 11 7, 2022.

IPUMS-USA. (n.d.-c). *Occupation codes and income scores*. IPUMS user guide, Minnesota Population Center, University of Minnesota. https://usa.ipums.org/usa/chapter4/chapter4.shtml. Accessed 16 8, 2023.

IPUMS-USA. (n.d.-d). *MLP linking method, multigenerational longitudinal panel (MLP) project*. Minnesota Population Center, University of Minnesota. https://usa.ipums.org/usa/mlp/mlp_linking_method.shtml. Accessed 7 6, 2024.

Massey, D. S. (1999). Why does immigration occur? A theoretical synthesis. In C. Hirschman, P. Kasinitz, & J. DeWind (Eds.), *The handbook of international migration: The American experience* (pp. 34–52). Russell Sage Foundation.

Migration Policy Institute Data Hub. (2023). *US immigrant population and share over time, 1850-present*. https://www.migrationpolicy.org/programs/data-hub/charts/immigrant-population-over-time. Accessed on June 12, 2023.

Minnesota Population Center. (2020). *1850 census of population, full count data. integrated public use microdata series (IPUMS), international: Version 7.3*. IPUMS. https://doi.org/10.18128/D020.V7.3

Minnesota Population Center. (2021). *1850 and 1860 censuses of population, IPUMS ancestry full count data: Version 3.0,* By Ruggles, S., Fitch, C. A., Goeken, R., David Hacker, J., Nelson, M. A., Roberts, E., Schouweiler, M., & Sobek, M. IPUMS. https://doi.org/10.18128/D014.V3.0.

Minnesota Population Center. (2023). *1850 and 1860 linked censuses of population, IPUMS multigenerational longitudinal panel: Version 1.1*. By Helgertz, J., Ruggles, S., Robert Warren, J., Fitch, C. A., David Hacker, J., Nelson, M. A., Price, J. P., Roberts, E., & Sobek, M. IPUMS. https://doi.org/10.18128/D016.V1.1, 2024.

Morefield, R. H. (1956). Mexicans in the California mines, 1848-53. *California Historical Society Quarterly*, *35*(1), 37–46.

National Council of State Governments. (1952). *Occupational licensing legislation in the states*. Council of State Governments.

Nostrand, R. L. (1975). Mexican Americans circa 1850. *Annals of the Association of American Geographers*, *65*(3), 378–390.

Thomas, B. (1954). *Migration and economic growth: A study of Great Britain and the Atlantic economy*. Cambridge University Press.

U.S. Bureau of the Census. (1979). *Twenty censuses: Population and housing questions, 1790-1980*. U.S. Government Printing Office.

U.S. Department of Commerce. (1976). *Historical statistics of the United States*. US Government Printing Office.

U.S. Department of Homeland Security, Office of Immigration Statistics. (2014). *2013 yearbook of immigration statistics*.

U.S. Immigration Commission. (1911). *Reports of the immigration commission* (Vol. 1–41). United States Government Printing Office (Better known as the Dillingham Commission Report).

U.S. Office of the Census (1850) *Instructions to U.S. marshalls, seventh census of population, 1850*. Government Printing Office. https://www.census.gov/programs-surveys/decennial-census/technical-documentation/questionnaires/1850/1850-instructions.html.

Warren, J. R., Sheridan, J., & Hauser, R. (1998). Choosing a measure of occupational standing: How useful are composite measures in analyses of gender inequality in occupational attainment? *Sociological Methods & Research*, *27*(1), 3–76.

Willcox, W. F. (1929). *International migrations, volume 1: Statistics, statistics of migrations, national tables, United States, Table I* (370–383). National Bureau of Economic Research (NBER). http://www.nber.org/chapters/c5134

APPENDIX A: STATISTICAL APPENDIX—DEFINITIONS OF VARIABLES USED IN THE REGRESSION ANALYSIS OF THE 1850 CENSUS OF POPULATION AND THE LINKED 1850–1860 CENSUS DATA

(A) 1850 CENSUS DATA

Sample

- Primary Data Source: 1850 Census of Population, Schedule 1, Public Use Microdata Sample, full count free people sample, Version 7.3, IPUMS International, Minnesota Population Center (MPC), University of Minnesota, Accessed October 15, 2023.
- Definition of population: Free White males, age 20 and older, with a gainful occupation according to the 1850 Census. Individuals with a non-gainful occupation recorded (e.g., unknown, attending school, invalid, and retired) are not included in the sample. Where the person is employed in multiple occupations, the principal one is listed.

Dependent Variables

- Occupational Income Score (OccInc): This is a measure constructed by the Minnesota Population Center (MPC) that assigns a score to each occupation using the 1950 occupational classification scheme. According to the IPUMS codebook, OccInc assigns each occupation a value representing the median total annual income (in hundreds of 1950 dollars) of a sample of individuals (both male and female) with that particular occupation in 1950 (IPUMS-USA, n.d.-c). That is, it provides a continuous quantitative measure of occupations according to the economic rewards enjoyed by people working at them in 1950. See Appendix Table A1 for a list of selected occupations with their OccInc values. The range of OccInc is from a low of three for Newsboys to a high of 80 for Physicians and Surgeons.
- Duncan Socioeconomic Index (SEI): This is a measure constructed by the MPC that assigns an SEI score to each occupation using the 1950 occupational classification scheme (Duncan, 1961). The SEI is a measure of occupational status based on the occupation's prestige predicted from a regression of the prestige score on the male median annual income level and years of schooling associated with each occupation in 1950. The occupational prestige ratings are from a 1947 National Opinion Research Study, and only considered male occupational incumbents. The SEI variable is constructed using the individual responses to occupation, 1950 basis, from the 1850 Census data (IPUMS-USA, n.d.-c). See Appendix Table A1 for a list of selected occupations with their SEI values. The range of the SEI is from a low of four for Lumbermen and Woodchoppers and Porters to a high of 96 for Dentists.

The two measures are interrelated as they both include 1950 occupational income in their construction. The correlations between the two measures for the White men studied are high, but far from perfect—85% for all men, 86% for native-born men, and 81% for the foreign born (Table A2). The difference in the scores reflects the divergence between income level and educational level across occupations (Table A3). The OccInc score tends to be higher than the SEI for occupations that require very little schooling (e.g., laborers), while the opposite is the case for lower income occupations for which higher levels of education are required (e.g., teachers).

Both measures are based on relative occupational incomes in 1950, which may differ from the unknown relative occupational incomes in 1850. In particular, the relative occupational income standing of some occupations may have increased over the century, while others (perhaps farming) may have decreased. We know of no better quantitative measures of occupational (labor market) attainment for the antebellum period.

In the regression analysis, because of the positive skewness in the OccInc and SEI distributions, the natural logarithm of these indices are the dependent variables.

Explanatory Variables

- Potential Labor Market Experience: This is the respondent's age minus 15 years. Age is the self-reported age of the respondent in years as of his last birthday.
- Literate: This is a dichotomous variable that takes the value of 0 if the individual is recorded as "cannot read and write" in any language (English or their native language), and one otherwise (i.e., the individual can read and write). However, the degree of literacy was not defined; therefore, it is unknown whether being able to read/write one's own name qualified them as literate. Individuals who could read but not write were classified as illiterate.
- Married: This is a dichotomous variable that indicates (=1) if the individual is presumed to be married with their spouse present (in the same household). Marital status was not asked in the 1850 Census. Therefore, this variable is constructed using the IPUMS pointer variable for spouse, which identifies the imputed relationships between household members with an estimated 99% accuracy rate (IPUMS-USA, n.d.-a, n.d.-b)
- Children: This is equal to the number of the respondent's own children (of any age or marital status) that are residing in their household. It includes step-children and adopted children as well as biological children.
- Foreign Born: The instructions for the census marshals regarding "Place of Birth" stated that "The marshals should ask the place of birth of each person in the family. If born in the State or Territory where they reside insert the name or initials of the State or Territory, or the name of the government or country if without the United States. The names of the several states may be abbreviated. Where place of birth is unknown, state 'unknown'" (US Bureau of the Census, 1979, p. 22). Based on this information, the MPC defined the county of birth of the foreign born. The implication is that those born in States or Territories that were part of Mexico at their time of birth are coded as what became their US state (native born). Foreign born is a dichotomous variable that distinguishes those with a birthplace outside the United States (=1) from individuals born in a state or territory of the United States (=0). Countries of birth identified for this analysis are: Ireland (including Northern Ireland), Britain, Germany, Canada, Mexico, and All Other foreign countries of birth.
- Estimated Years since Migration (YSM): Since there was no question in the 1850 Census on when foreign-born individuals came to the US, this variable is constructed using immigrant flow data from 1820-1850 by nativity (see Table A4) and by age group (see Table A5). These data are used to create a probability distribution of year of arrival by age and country of origin for the three main countries of origin (Great Britain, Germany, and Ireland) and a fourth group of immigrants from All Other Countries (which includes the small number of recorded arrivals from Mexico and Canada).

The expected YSM value was calculated as a function of immigration flow data based on age (i) and nativity (j) using $E(x_{i,j}) = \sum xP(x_{i,j})$, where x is the

YSM for the year 1820 (YSM = 31, i.e., arrival up to 31 years previously) through 1850 (YSM = 1, i.e., arrival less than 1 year previously). The likelihood of an immigrant arriving in any given year between 1820-1850 is estimated based on their age group in that year (whether they fall into the young (under 15 years old), middle aged (ages 15–40), or older (above 40 years old) age group), and their nativity. The probability distribution function is re-weighted based on age so that in all cases, the sum of the foreign-born individual's probability of arriving is equal to one. The result is that all individuals with the same age and same birth country will be assigned the same estimated YSM, but that estimated YSM varies by age among immigrants with the same nativity and varies by nativity among immigrants of the same age. The computation of estimated YSM takes into account not only the immigrant's age and nativity, but also the rate of immigration over time. This procedure does, by construction, result in some inevitable loss of variability among immigrants; however, without additional individual-level data about their arrival, this is the best that can be estimated using the available data as there is no way to systematically determine which individuals immigrated as children versus young adults versus older adults.

In the regression analysis, YSM and its square are coded as zero (=0) for the native born.

- Urban: This is a dichotomous variable that distinguishes individuals living in an urban household from a rural household. The "urban" definition was applied ex-post by the 1940 Census Bureau, in which cities and incorporated places in 1850 of 2,500 inhabitants or more and townships or other subdivisions having a total population of 10,000 or more as well as a population density of 1,000 or more per square mile were coded as "urban"; all other areas were considered rural.
- South: This is a dichotomous variable that distinguishes all slave-holding states in 1850 from all other states: Delaware, Missouri, Virginia (includes West Virginia), Alabama, Arkansas, Florida, Georgia, Louisiana, Mississippi, North Carolina, South Carolina, Texas, Kentucky, Maryland, Tennessee, and the District of Columbia.
- Occupational Category: This variable was constructed based on the occupation data, 1950 basis. The occupational categories are: PTK (Professional, Technical, and Kindred); Farmers (owners, tenants, and managers); Managers (non-farm); Clerical; Sales; Craft (including military and apprentices); Operatives; Service; Farm Workers for wages and farm laborers and fishermen; Laborers (non-farm); No Occupation; and, Not Applicable. Any laborer with no specified industry living in a household with a farmer is recoded as a farm laborer.

(B) 1850–1860 LINKED CENSUS DATA

Sample

- Data Source for Longitudinal Analysis: 1850 and 1860 Linked Census of Population extract, Public Use Microdata Sample, from full count free people sample from each census year, IPUMS Multigenerational Longitudinal Panel: Version 1.1 and IPUMS Ancestry Full Count Data: Version 3.0, IPUMS, Minnesota Population Center (MPC), University of Minnesota, Accessed June 4, 2024.
- Definition of population: Free White males, age 20 and older in 1850, with a gainful occupation in both the 1850 and 1860 Censuses. Individuals with a non-gainful occupation recorded (e.g., unknown, attending school, invalid, and retired) in either census are not included in the sample. Where the person is employed in multiple occupations, the principal one is listed. The sample is restricted to individuals that could be linked between the 1850 and 1860 Censuses by MPC through the IPUMS Multigenerational Longitudinal Panel (MLP) project. Only about 30% of all individuals in the 1850 Census, Schedule 1, were able to be linked to the 1860 Census. For this study, observations with inconsistencies that are relevant to this analysis were dropped from the sample, e.g., individuals who were listed as native born in one census and foreign born in the other.[26]

Variables Used in the Analyses

- Estimated YSM for 1860 is the individuals estimated YSM from 1850 plus 10 years.
- All other variables for this sample are defined as they were in the 1850 data.

Table A1. Occupational Income Scores (OccInc) and Socioeconomic Index (SEI) Scores for Selected Occupations.

Occupation[a]	SEI	Ln SEI	OccInc	Ln OccInc
PTK				
Physicians & surgeons (075)	92	4.52	80	4.38
Lawyers & judges (055)	93	4.53	62	4.13
Clergymen (009)	52	3.95	24	3.18
Farmers				
Farmers (owners & tenants) (100)	14	2.64	14	2.64
Managers				
Landlords (230)	32	3.47	20	3.00
Officers, ships (240)	54	3.99	42	3.74
Officers & administrators (nec), public administration (250)	66	4.19	36	3.58
Postmasters (270)	60	4.09	29	3.37
Clerical				
Bank tellers (305)	52	3.95	26	3.26
Bookkeepers (310)	51	3.93	22	3.09
Clerical & kindred workers (nec) (390)	44	3.78	25	3.22
Sales				
Hucksters & peddlers (430)	8	2.08	13	2.56
Real estate agents (470)	62	4.13	35	3.56
Salesmen & sales clerks (nec) (490)	47	3.85	24	3.18
Craft				
Bakers (500)	22	3.09	28	3.33
Carpenters (510)	19	2.94	24	3.18
Jewelers, watchmakers (534)	36	3.58	27	3.30
Plumbers & pipe fitters (574)	34	3.53	33	3.50
Shoemakers & repairers (except factory) (582)	12	2.48	20	3.00
Tailors (590)	23	3.14	26	3.26
Operatives				
Sailors & deck hands (673)	16	2.77	23	3.24
Boatmen, canalmen, & lock keepers (623)	24	3.18	30	3.40
Deliverymen & routemen (632)	32	3.47	27	3.30
Switchmen, railroad (681)	44	3.78	36	3.58
Taxicab (hackney) drivers & chauffeurs (682)	10	2.30	22	3.09
Furnacemen (641)	18	2.89	29	3.37
Services				
Bartenders (750)	19	2.94	25	3.22
Janitors & sextons (770)	9	2.20	19	2.94
Marshalls & constables (771)	21	3.04	24	3.18
Cooks (except private household) (754)	15	2.71	16	2.77
Laborers (farm)				
Farm foremen (810)	20	3.00	23	3.14
Farm laborers (wage workers) (820)	6	1.79	9	2.20

(Continued)

Table A1. *(Continued)*

Occupation[(a)]	SEI	Ln SEI	OccInc	Ln OccInc
Laborers (non-farm)				
Gardeners, except farm and groundskeepers (930)	11	2.40	17	2.83
Longshoremen & stevedores (940)	11	2.40	25	3.22
Laborers (nec) (970)	8	2.08	20	3.00
Range:				
Highest SEI: Dentists (032)	96	4.56	63	4.14
Lowest SEI: Lumbermen, raftsmen, & woodchoppers (950)	4	1.39	12	2.48
Porters (780)			18	2.89
Highest OccInc: Physicians and surgeons (075)	92	4.52	80	4.38
Lowest OccInc: Newsboys (460)	27	3.30	3	1.10

Source: Minnesota Population Center (2020).

(a)nec means not elsewhere classified. Occupation code number in parentheses.

Table A2. Correlation of OccInc and SEI for White Men, Age 20 and Older, With a Reported Occupation, by Nativity, 1850.

Variables	All	Native Born	Foreign Born
OccInc and SEI	0.8496	0.8654	0.8107
lnOccInc and lnSEI	0.7380	0.7799	0.6742
Sample size	4,793,809	3,843,633	950,176

Source: Minnesota Population Center (2020).

Table A3. The "Mismatching" of Scores for Selected Occupations for OccInc and SEI Among White Men, Age 20 and Over, With a Reported Occupation, 1850.

Occupation	OccInc	SEI	Difference
Weavers, textiles	23	6	17
Mine operatives and laborers	24	10	14
Laborers (nec)	22	10	12
Porters	18	4	14
Teachers (nec)	27	72	−45
Pharmacists	40	82	−42
Musicians and music teachers	15	56	−41
Clergymen	24	52	−28

Source: Minnesota Population Center (2020).

Notes: nec means "not elsewhere classified".

Table A4. Frequency Distribution of Recorded Immigration by Country of Birth, 1820–1850.

Year of Arrival	Ireland	Germany	Great Britain	All Other Countries	All Foreign Born
1820	0.36	0.17	0.67	0.31	0.35
1821	0.15	0.07	0.89	0.89	0.38
1822	0.22	0.03	0.34	0.72	0.29
1823	0.19	0.03	0.30	0.70	0.26
1824	0.23	0.04	0.35	0.90	0.33
1825	0.48	0.08	0.58	0.61	0.42
1826	0.53	0.09	0.64	0.58	0.45
1827	0.96	0.07	1.16	0.99	0.79
1828	1.23	0.32	1.48	1.70	1.14
1829	0.73	0.10	0.88	2.51	0.94
1830	0.27	0.34	0.32	3.87	0.97
1831	0.57	0.42	0.69	2.65	0.94
1832	1.23	1.76	1.48	7.20	2.52
1833	0.85	1.21	1.36	8.43	2.44
1834	2.42	3.05	2.91	2.81	2.72
1835	2.07	1.44	2.49	1.59	1.89
1836	3.02	3.58	3.63	2.62	3.17
1837	2.82	4.10	3.39	3.29	3.30
1838	1.25	2.02	1.50	2.03	1.62
1839	2.37	3.63	2.85	2.83	2.83
1840	3.90	5.13	0.72	2.73	3.50
1841	3.73	2.64	4.48	2.44	3.34
1842	5.07	3.52	6.10	2.40	4.35
1843	1.94	2.49	2.34	2.20	2.18
1844	3.31	3.58	3.98	2.22	3.27
1845	4.43	5.93	5.32	3.54	4.76
1846	5.11	9.94	6.15	5.07	6.42
1847	10.43	12.83	6.46	7.05	9.77
1848	11.16	10.10	9.74	4.42	9.42
1849	15.75	10.40	15.27	4.93	12.35
1850	13.22	10.91	11.55	15.78	12.89
Total	100.00	100.00	100.00	100.00	100.00
Sample size	1,012,240	579,095	360,937	451,951	2,404,224

Source: Willcox, 1929, pp. 370–383, Table I.

Notes: Year indicates the fiscal year. For 1820-1831, the fiscal year ended September 30; for 1832-1842, the fiscal year ended December 31; and, for 1843-1850, it again ended September 30. Therefore, the data for 1832 covers a 15-month period (October 1, 1831-December 31, 1832) and the data for 1843 covers a 9-month period (January 1, 1943-September 30, 1943).Great Britain includes England, Scotland, Wales, and United Kingdom-not specified. Ireland includes Northern Ireland. Data was not delineated by gender.

Table A5. Distribution of Total Number of Passengers Arrived in the United States by Age, 1820–1850, as a Proportion of the Annual Number of Arrivals.

Year	Under 15 Years	Age 15 to 40	Over 40Years	Sample Size
1820	0.1960	0.6568	0.1472	8,384
1821	0.1448	0.7354	0.1199	9,127
1822	0.1295	0.7587	0.1118	6,911
1823	0.1200	0.7609	0.1191	6,354
1824	0.1073	0.7779	0.1149	7,912
1825	0.1610	0.7495	0.0895	10,199
1826	0.1748	0.7331	0.0921	10,837
1827	0.2169	0.6845	0.0986	18,875
1828	0.2794	0.6200	0.1006	27,382
1829	0.3025	0.6255	0.0720	22,520
1830	0.4066	0.5462	0.0472	23,322
1831	0.3237	0.5983	0.0780	22,633
1832	0.3288	0.5950	0.0762	60,482
1833	0.3128	0.6061	0.0810	58,640
1834	0.2480	0.6517	0.1003	65,365
1835	0.2207	0.6678	0.1115	45,374
1826	0.2146	0.6848	0.1005	76,242
1837	0.2250	0.6758	0.0991	79,340
1838	0.2161	0.6566	0.1273	38,914
1839	0.2114	0.6922	0.0964	68,069
1840	0.2381	0.6799	0.0819	84,066
1841	0.2283	0.6739	0.0978	80,289
1842	0.2356	0.6769	0.0875	104,565
1843	0.2800	0.6281	0.0919	52,496
1844	0.2435	0.6544	0.1021	78,615
1845	0.2276	0.6718	0.1006	114,371
1846	0.2367	0.6551	0.1082	154,416
1847	0.2489	0.6642	0.0869	234,968
1848	0.2364	0.6631	0.1005	226,527
1849	0.2260	0.6717	0.1024	297,024
1850	0.2701	0.6472	0.0827	310,004
Average	0.2440	0.6611	0.0950	–
Sample size	588,112	1,588,127	227,984	2,404,223

Sources: Willcox, 1929, pp. 370–383, Table VII, and authors' calculations.

Notes: Year indicates the fiscal year. For 1820-1831, the fiscal year ended September 30; for 1832-1842, the fiscal year ended December 31; and, for 1843-1850, it again ended September 30. Therefore, the data for 1832 covers a 15-month period (October 1, 1831-December 31, 1832) and the data for 1843 covers a 9-month period (January 1, 1943-September 30, 1943). Source data included a fourth category, age not stated, which was split evenly between those under 15 and age 15 to 40, for consistency with other data sources (see, for example, Cohn, 2017, Table 2). Data was not delineated by gender.

A HISTORICAL NOTE ON THE ASSIMILATION RATES OF FOREIGN-BORN MEN AND WOMEN IN THE UNITED STATES

Harriet Duleep[a], Robert Gesumaria[b], Mark Regets[c], Xingfei Liu[d] and Dan Dowhan[b]

[a]*College of William and Mary, USA*
[b]*U.S. Office of Research, USA*
[c]*National Foundation for American Policy, USA*
[d]*University of Alberta, Canada*

ABSTRACT

The 1924 Immigration Act excluded immigrants from economically developing countries to the point of their near total exclusion. Forty years later, the 1965 Immigration and Nationality Act eliminated most discriminatory county-of-origin barriers. America's doors opened and immigration from economically developing countries soared. Fueling debates about the "quality" of immigrants from economically developing countries, empirical studies based on a well-respected methodology conclude that post-1965 immigrant men have low initial earnings and sluggish earnings growth. This methodology is based on flawed assumptions. Removing these assumptions reveals high earnings growth for post-1965 immigrant men in accordance with the Immigrant Human Capital Investment (IHCI) model. A similar story emerges for immigrant women, contradicting the Family Investment Hypothesis (FIH) first put forth by Long and Duleep and Sanders. It appears a pre-1965/post-1965 transition occurred in the earnings profiles of US immigrants, from earnings resembling those of US natives to low initial earnings but much higher earnings growth than their US-born statistical twins. The transition

Migration, Human Capital and the Labor Market
Research in Labor Economics, Volume 53A, 169–191

ISSN: 0147-9121/doi:10.1108/S0147-91212026000053A005

underlies the overtime success story of immigrant families from economically developing countries; the high earnings growth reflects human capital investment that invigorates the economy.

Keywords: Immigrant earning growth; human capital investment; skill transferability; immigrant quality; sample restrictions; family investment hypothesis; nonparametric estimation

1. INTRODUCTION

Much attention has focused on the decline in immigrant entry earnings in the United States following 1965. Some scholars interpret this as a decline in immigrant quality, a conclusion buttressed by findings of low earnings growth for the post-1965 immigrants. Yet, the findings of low earning growth stem from severely flawed methodologies. Removing problematic assumptions we show for both immigrant men and women that post-1965 immigrants in America had high earnings growth. A decline in immigrant entry earnings accompanied by an increase in earnings growth suggests an entirely different scenario. Following traditional human capital investment theory and empirical results, it suggests high human capital investment.

2. BACKGROUND

The US 1924 Immigration Act favored immigrants from Western Europe and discriminated against immigrants from economically developing countries (Reimers, 2023).[1] Forty years later, the 1965 Immigration and Nationality Act abolished the 1924 country-of-origin preferences and emphasized family reunification while also adding an employment-based admission policy. Immigration from economically developing countries soared (Fig. 1), and the education- and age-adjusted entry earnings of immigrant men, relative to US natives, plummeted. Table 1 and Fig. 2 contrast the entry earnings of immigrants from economically developing versus developed countries.

Among economists, the most famous hypothesis for the post-1965 decline in immigrant entry earnings for men is that immigrant "quality" declined. Published in the *American Economic Review*, Borjas (1987) notes that accompanying the change in immigrant admissions, more US immigration came from countries with high levels of income inequality. Theoretically, individuals at the bottom of their home country's age and education-adjusted income distribution, hence "quality" spectrum, have the most to gain by migrating to the United States; with the increased income inequality, the quality of US immigrants should have decreased. Measuring quality by the difference between immigrants' initial earnings and the earnings of US natives of similar age and education, Borjas (1987, 1992, 2015) documents a profound post-1965 decrease in immigrant

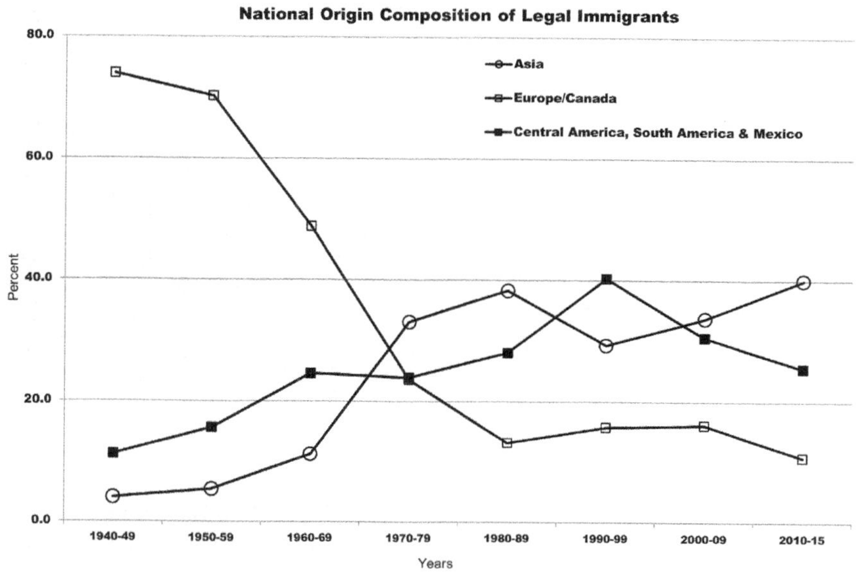

Fig. 1. Over Time National Origin Composition of Legal Immigrants.

Table 1. Median Entry Earnings in 1989 of Immigrant Men, Aged 25–54, Who Entered the United States Between 1985 and 1990 as a Percent of the Earnings of US-Born Men, by Immigrant Region of Origin.

	All	25–39 Years Old; 1–12 Years of School	25–39 Years Old; More Than 12 Years of School	40–54 Years Old; 1–12 Years of School	40–54 Years Old; More Than 12 Years of School
All immigrants	41%	53	48	38	50
Asia	44	59	43	32	44
Central/South America	36	51	45	38	40
Western Europe	101	115	93	84	137

Source: Estimates based on a 6% microdata sample created by combining and reweighting the 1990 Census of Population 5% and 1% Public Use samples. Native born are persons born in the United States; foreign born are defined as persons born outside of the United States excluding those with US parents. The sample includes everyone including students, the self-employed, and persons with zero earnings.

quality, worsening with time, and accompanied by low earnings growth for immigrant men.

Chiswick (1978, 1979) proposes an alternative hypothesis: The post-1965 decline in immigrant entry earnings reflects the lower transferability to the

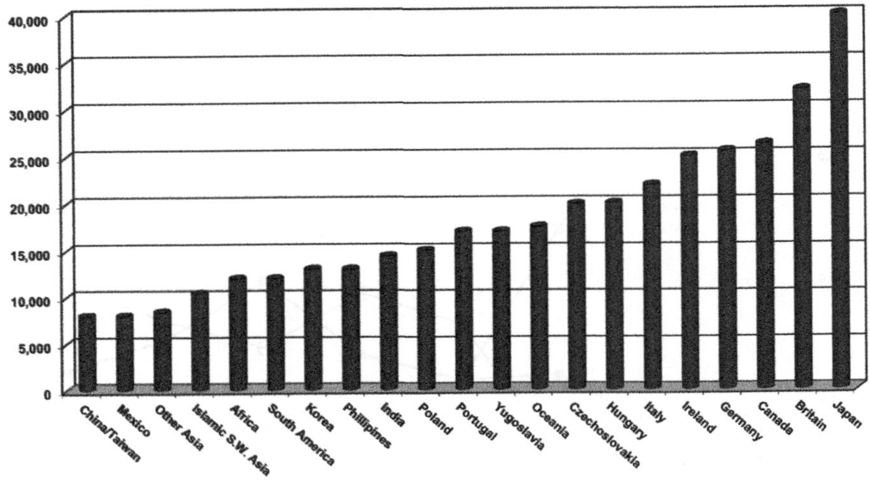

Fig. 2. Median 1989 US Earnings of Men 25–54 Who Immigrated in 1985–1990. *Source:* Estimates based on the 1990 Census of Population 5% and 1% public-use samples.

Notes: The foreign born are defined as persons born outside of the United States excluding those with US parents.

United States of the skills learned growing up and working in economically developing countries. In numerous papers, Chiswick also emphasizes the importance of English proficiency to skill transferability.

Yet, skills learned in developing countries may easily transfer to the United States. Mathematical skills acquired at *given* levels of schooling in developing countries can exceed those acquired in US schools (Rivera-Batiz & Sechzer, 1991). Moreover, immigrants from some economically developing countries with low initial earnings in the United States are more English proficient than immigrants from some West European countries with high initial earnings. Japanese immigrants have low English proficiency but high initial earnings (Duleep et al., 2021).

Building on Chiswick's insights and analyses, we propose a more general hypothesis for the post-1965 decline in immigrant entry earnings that accommodates these disparities and explains why immigrants from economically developing countries (and refugees) have lower skill transferability, hence lower initial earnings, than immigrants from economically developed countries. In countries with opportunities and conditions resembling those in the United States, few will migrate if it involves initial earnings loss and the need for substantial investment in new human capital. In contrast, people who face constraints in their home countries will migrate even if it requires pursuing new training and education, changing careers or, in a word, starting all over. Compared with people in developed countries, individuals in developing countries face more constraints such as war, gang violence, repressive governments, discrimination, limited professional opportunities, less capitalized businesses and research facilities, inflexible labor markets, restricted or nonexistent opportunities for adult education or for changing professions, rigid social structures, and limited opportunities for their children. With such constraints, people in developing countries face not just lower earnings than statistically similar individuals in economically developed countries but fewer opportunities for growth.

According to the Immigrant Human Capital Investment (IHCI) model developed by Duleep and Regets (1992, 1999, 2002), lower skill transferability creates a lower opportunity cost for human capital investment and a higher return to such investment. The higher return to new human capital investment stems from both the utility of otherwise untransferable human capital in learning new skills and the complementarity of new human capital with these older skills. To the extent that immigrants from economically developing countries have lower initial skill transferability, the IHCI model predicts low entry earnings and high earnings growth.[2]

These three hypotheses—differences in immigrant quality, skill transferability, and the IHCI model—were developed to explain the earnings of immigrant men. A fourth hypothesis—the Family Investment Hypothesis (FIH)—seeks to illuminate the earnings of immigrant women.

As first articulated by Long (1980) and Duleep and Sanders (1993), the FIH suggests that immigrant women finance the human capital investment of husbands who lack transferable skills to their new country. Initially, when their husbands' US-specific skills are lowest and their human capital investment most intense, immigrant women are more likely to work, work more hours, and forego human capital investment in favor of jobs with higher wages. As their husbands' host-country human capital grows, the propensity of immigrant women to work decreases. Relative to US natives of similar age and education, their initial earnings are higher than would otherwise be the case, and their earnings growth (by foregoing human capital investment and eventually working less) is lower. The FIH model predicts immigrant women will have low earnings growth (vs US-born women) when immigrant men have high earnings growth (vs. US-born men).

Keeping in mind the various predictions about immigrant earnings growth, we explore historical trends with data described in Part III. In contrast to the typical regression approach for measuring immigrant earnings growth, we pursue a nonparametric methodology, described in Part IV. With this methodology, Parts V and VI estimate historical trends in the earnings growth of immigrant men and women, respectively. Part VII cites issues for further research and two natural experiments. The chapter concludes with Part VIII.

3. THE 1994 CPS-SSA MATCHED DATA

In January 1994, the Current Population Survey (CPS) began to identify immigrants in each monthly survey. We use longitudinal Social Security Administration (SSA) earnings data matched to the 1994 March CPS to track the annual earnings of working-age foreign- and native-born men and women.[3] The longitudinal individual earnings data circumvent potential cohort biases associated with cross-sectional analyses, biases due to immigrant emigration, and other factors that potentially affect both cohort and cross-sectional analyses.

We identify immigrants as persons born abroad of non-US parents. An important aspect of our study is the historical nature of the Social Security earnings data. This permits us to separately follow numerous year-of-entry immigrant cohorts over time. For each cohort, immigrant earnings are first measured in the year following a CPS defined year-of-immigration period. We only follow individuals (whether US or foreign-born) who are at least 25 years old in the initial year of earnings measurement and no more than 60 in the final year of earnings measurement.

The samples we track do not change because of emigration—the earnings of the same people are measured at the beginning and end of each year-of-entry, cohort-specific analysis. Nevertheless, who is in these samples is affected by emigration. We observe immigrants who were in the United States in 1994 (as evidenced by their response to the 1994 CPS) but not immigrants who immigrated before 1994 and emigrated prior to the 1994 CPS. Our study provides information on the earnings profiles of persons who immigrated in the past and stayed. This statement is particularly true for the pre-1984 cohorts since emigration declines steeply with time in the United States, with most occurring in the first 10 years following immigration (Duleep, 1994; Warren & Kraly, 1985; Warren & Peck, 1980). Thus, our 10-year earnings growth findings for the 1960–1983 cohorts present accurate earnings profiles for immigrant stayers. As the year of immigration approaches 1994, the cohorts will increasingly include persons who emigrate, and this affects the earnings profiles to an unknown degree. Our theoretical perspective is that permanence increases the propensity to invest and hence earnings growth (Duleep & Regets, 1999); were it possible to limit the more recent cohorts to stayers, the measured earnings growth might be higher.

4. OUR METHODOLOGY VS REGRESSION APPROACHES FOR ESTIMATING IMMIGRANT EARNINGS GROWTH

The typical regression approach underestimates the earnings growth of immigrants who start their US journeys at low earnings relative to US natives of similar age and education. This occurs for two reasons:

(1) The fixed-cohort-effect regression specification generally used by economists ignores a pronounced inverse relationship between entry earning and earnings growth.
(2) Most regression specifications in economics use ln earnings as the dependent variable, thereby excluding zero earners and creating inconsistent sample universes over time.

4.1 The Fixed-Cohort-Effect Methodology

Whether following year-of-entry immigrant cohorts across cross-sections from multiple years or individuals with longitudinal data, economists typically pool immigrants who have entered the host country in different years and estimate a variant of the following stylized model:

$$\ln(y_i) = X'\beta + \alpha \cdot F \cdot \text{YSM} + \gamma' F \cdot C_j + \epsilon_i \quad (1)$$

where y_i denotes the earnings of immigrant i; X is a vector of variables measuring education and experience, and β the corresponding coefficients; $F = 1$ if the individual is an immigrant or 0 if the individual is a US native; YSM measures years since migration. C_j is a set of 0–1 variables representing each year-of-immigration category, j. The coefficients on C_j measure how high initial earnings are for each cohort j; the coefficient on YSM measures earnings growth.

Multiple studies document a systematic inverse relationship between entry earnings and earnings growth.[4] Yet, the fixed-cohort-effect methodology (taught in all economic textbooks) only lets the initial earnings of each cohort change. It assumes that immigrant entry earnings and earnings growth (controlling for age and education) are not systematically related. Averaging earnings growth rates across year-of-entry cohorts hides earnings-growth changes that occur when entry earnings change. Moreover, it understates the earnings growth of immigrants who start with relatively low earnings while overstating the earnings growth of immigrants who start with relatively high earnings.[5]

Following individuals over time, versus cohorts, solves many problems. Nevertheless, the fixed-cohort-effect methodology dominates studies by economists even when researchers use longitudinal data on individuals. Important exceptions among economists include Green and Worswick (2012) and Lin (2013). Using a multivariate analysis that models intercepts and slopes separately, sociologists Hall and Farkas (2008) find significant wage growth for poorly educated immigrants, casting doubt on a segmented labor market theory prediction that low-skill immigrants are permanently consigned to dead-end jobs with no wage appreciation.

In estimating the earnings profiles of immigrants, the simplest and most informative way to let earnings growth change with entry earnings is to examine each year-of-entry cohort separately.

4.2 Using ln Earnings as the Dependent Variable

A staple of labor economics is to use ln earnings for the dependent variable in earnings equations. Economists relate age and education to the logarithm of earnings because using the log allows them to interpret the relationship as a percentage change in earnings for a given change in age or education. An oft forgotten fact, however, is that log of earnings is undefined when earnings are zero. Hence, using ln earnings in any statistical analysis excludes zero earners from the sample. This issue, in addition to ignoring an inverse relationship between entry earnings and earnings growth, underestimates immigrant earnings growth.

Even in cross-sectional regressions using data from a single point in time, excluding zero-earners poses a problem for some analytic purposes since non-earners systematically differ from earners. Nevertheless, while this sample selectivity may bias estimates of the return to education, a sample of "all earners" is at least consistently defined.

A much bigger problem occurs when pooling data across more than one time period. Very different individuals may qualify for the sample in each period. Yet, any estimate of earnings growth from censored pooled data, done by regression or other means, will be based upon the over time difference of these inconsistent samples. Consider one hypothetical individual who is out of the labor market in Period 1 because of low earnings potential and is instead in school. If that person works in Period 2, they will qualify for the sample in Period 2 even if they were ineligible in Period 1. Earning growth would be measured, not by looking at the Period 2 earnings of those in the sample in Period 1, but by comparison of Period 1 earnings to the Period 2 earnings of anyone qualifying for the Period 2 sample. Many such scenarios can be posited where sample restrictions lead to people with very different earnings histories included in different periods of pooled data. In each case, this will lead to biased estimates of earning growth.

Although biases from sample restrictions causing inconsistent sample universes across periods will bias the earnings growth estimate for any group, the problem becomes much worse when comparing the earnings growth of two groups: immigrant earnings are often standardized by the earnings of natives in the same data. Excluding zero earners,[6] as immigrants and natives are followed across censuses over say 10-year periods, US natives become an increasingly select group as the cohort ages and lower wage individuals leave the labor force, a phenomenon that has worsened for natives over time. In comparison, immigrant labor force participation remains high at older ages.

The estimated low relative earnings growth of immigrant men for the post-1970 cohorts (reported in all of the studies of Borjas) and its apparent worsening in recent years (Borjas, 2015) occurs because of the differential native/immigrant selection bias from sample restrictions not because immigrant earnings growth is lower than that of US natives or has worsened. The exclusion of zero earners is the main reason why all of the empirical analyses of Borjas show low earnings growth for immigrant men relative to natives. Using the exact same census data sans sample restrictions reveals high earnings growth for immigrant men relative to natives (Duleep et al., 2021, 2022; Duleep & Regets, 1992, 2002).

A simple solution to avoid a differential sample selection between immigrants and natives when following cohorts is not to impose *any* sample selections. This eliminates the problem and incorporates labor force participation into measures of immigrant economic assimilation. Duleep et al. (2022) show that the effect of imposing sample selections is enormous, changing the high earnings growth that we find for the post-1965 immigrants relative to US natives to low earnings growth. It accounts for the low earnings growth measured by Borjas in all of his works that suggest the quality of US immigrant men fell following the 1965 Immigration Act.

Most often, this type of analysis is done between different years of census data. With pseudo cohorts, it is impossible to know if an individual being included in the sample for one period would have qualified in the other periods being pooled. However, even with longitudinal data on individuals, where one can require an individual to qualify in each period, it is not clear that analysts do this: the use of natural log of earnings will still reject an individual from one period's data without removing them from others.[7]

In longitudinal data, this differential sample selection problem can be avoided by linking individual earnings at one point in time to later earnings for the same individual and measuring earnings growth by the difference between the two points. Duleep and Regets (1997) and Duleep and Dowhan (2002) do this and show high earnings growth for immigrant men relative to natives. This, the simplest and most straightforward approach, avoids selection bias from sample restrictions and from emigration. Nevertheless, it is not commonly pursued despite the problematic effects of age-related changes in immigrant/native sample selections on the measurement of immigrant earnings growth relative to natives, as shown in Duleep et al. (2022).

4.2.1 Avoiding These Problems

Problems with fixed cohort-effect functional forms and with sample restrictions imposed by using the log of earnings can be avoided using simple nonparametric models. Analytic trade-offs are implicit in any model choice. In this case, nonparametric models make sense because of the statistical problems they solve and because of the analytic question being asked wherein neither the return to education nor the return to experience is a primary focus.

With large foreign-born cohort-specific sample sizes, an attractive nonparametric option for controlling for age/education differences between immigrants and natives is to use cross-tabs—compare immigrants and natives within age/education subsets (Duleep & Regets, 1992, 1999, 2002). Constrained by small cohort-specific foreign-born sample sizes, we pursue another nonparametric alternative that uses all of the foreign-born observations in each year-of-entry cohort. Specifically, we compare native and immigrant earnings controlling for age and education by reweighting each native-born observation so that the age and education distribution of each native-born cohort matches the corresponding foreign-born cohort's distribution.[8]

To do this, we describe the age-education distribution of each immigrant and native cohort sample, labeling the percent in each age-education cell $f(i, j)$ for the foreign born and $n(i, j)$ for the native born. We then weight each native-born observation in cell i, j by $f(i, j)/n(i, j)$. With this approach, we estimate the median earnings of immigrants at their own age-education distributions while exploiting the numerous native-born observations to estimate their median earnings at alternative age-education distributions. This approach controls for immigrant/native age and education differences without assuming how education and age affect immigrant and native earnings, or as DiNardo and Tobias (2001, p. 11) quip, "...without the straitjacket of a specific functional form."

Our analyses of immigrant men and women use this approach to track the annual earnings of nine year-of-entry cohorts of immigrants who report coming to the United States in 1960–1964, 1965–1969, 1970–1974, 1975–1979, 1980–1981, 1982–1983, 1984–1985, 1986–1987, and 1988–1989 and compare their earnings with those of US natives. For the analyses presented in this chapter, we first describe the age-education distribution of each immigrant and native cohort sample with a 36-element matrix composed of six age and six education categories: the age categories begin with 25–29 year olds, covering 5 years each; the education categories are 8th grade or less, 8–12 years with no high school diploma, high school diploma, some college short of a bachelor's degree, bachelor's degree, and a graduate degree. Each cell $f(i, j)_k$ of each foreign-born cohort k matrix is the percent of the foreign-born cohort's sample in age category i and education category j. Each cell $n(i, j)_k$ of each US-born cohort k matrix is the percent of the US-born cohort's sample in age category i and education category j. For each native-born cohort k, we weight each native-born age i/education j observation by $f(i, j)_k/n(i, j)_k$.

As noted before, we reweight each cohort of the United States born with the corresponding foreign-born cohort's age-education distribution rather than the reverse. Given small, cohort-specific, foreign-born sample sizes, this permits estimating the median earnings (or other earnings percentile) of immigrants at their own age-education distributions while taking advantage of the plenitude of native-born observations to reliably estimate the median earnings of natives at alternative detailed age-education distributions. Prediction error increases the smaller the sample size and the farther away the forecast is from the sampling experience. Since the sample size for natives exceeds that for immigrants, it makes sense to predict the US native values at the foreign-born schooling and age distribution rather than the reverse.

With this nonparametric methodology, we use the 1994 CPS-SSA Matched data to measure the earnings growth of immigrant men, as reported in Duleep and Dowhan (2002) and discussed in Part V. We use the same methodology and data to measure the earnings growth of immigrant women as discussed in Part VI.

5. IMMIGRANT MEN

In 1965, US immigrant admissions changed from a policy that discriminated against persons from economically developing countries to one that promoted family-sponsored admissions. The 1965 Immigration and Nationality Act also allowed 20% of numerically restricted visas for employer-sponsored immigrants.

According to our analyses of the 1994 CPS-SSA Matched data, the earnings profiles of men coming to the United States in 1960–1964 and in 1965–1969 (before and after the 1965 Immigration and Nationality Act) resemble the earnings profiles of US natives of similar age and education. Then, starting with the 1970–1974 cohort, the entry earnings of immigrant men fell relative to their US-born statistical twins and their earnings growth grew. Indeed, earnings growth exceeding that of US natives characterizes all male immigrant cohorts beginning with the 1970–1974 cohort. Similar results emerge using census data to follow cohorts that do not exclude zero earners (Duleep & Regets, 2002).

The entry-earnings decline of immigrant men likely occurred because of a decline in the proportion of immigrants with transferable skills to the United States, accompanying greater immigration from less-developed countries. But, since immigration policy changed in 1965, why did initial earnings not drop until the 1970–1974 cohort? Two factors may explain this.

By 1965, the 1924 Immigration Act had existed for over four decades. Potential migrants from previously excluded economically developing countries were unlikely to have US family members to sponsor them via the 1965 family admission provisions. Unable to migrate via family ties, migrants with highly transferable skills in the 1965–1969 cohort from economically developing countries likely entered the United States via the employment categories and had initial earnings resembling those of US natives. Once established, their relatives, with less transferable skills, could immigrate through family ties.

Using different datasets, Jasso and Rosenzweig (1995), Duleep and Regets (1996a, 1996b), and DeSilva (1997) find that although family-based immigrants start their host-country lives with lower earnings than their employment-based statistical twins, they have higher earnings growth. This narrative likely explains why the earnings of immigrant men in the 1965–1969 entry cohort resembled the earnings of US natives and why—starting with the 1970–1974 cohort—immigrant entry earnings fell relative to natives' earnings but earnings growth grew.

6. IMMIGRANT WOMEN

The FIH predicts immigrant women will have low earnings growth (relative to US-born women) when immigrant men (investing in human capital with the assistance of their spouses) have high earnings growth. The three panels of Fig. 3 show, for each year-of-entry cohort, the median annual earnings of immigrant women in a specific year, divided by the median annual earnings of US-born women. The native-born observations are weighted to match the age and schooling distribution of the corresponding immigrant cohort.

Earnings are first measured in the year following a CPS defined year-of-immigration period. For instance, earnings are measured in 1965 for women who came to the United States in 1960–1964. Earnings are last measured 9 years later for cohorts followed 10 years and in 1992, for cohorts followed less than 10 years. Positive earnings are required in the year following the last-year earnings to guard against partial-year earnings from emigration or individuals leaving Social Security covered employment. These same requirements were followed for the analyses of men in Part IV.[9]

Besides the final-year-plus-one requirement, the top panel of Fig. 3 requires earnings only in the first and last years, which defines the top panel's lines. The

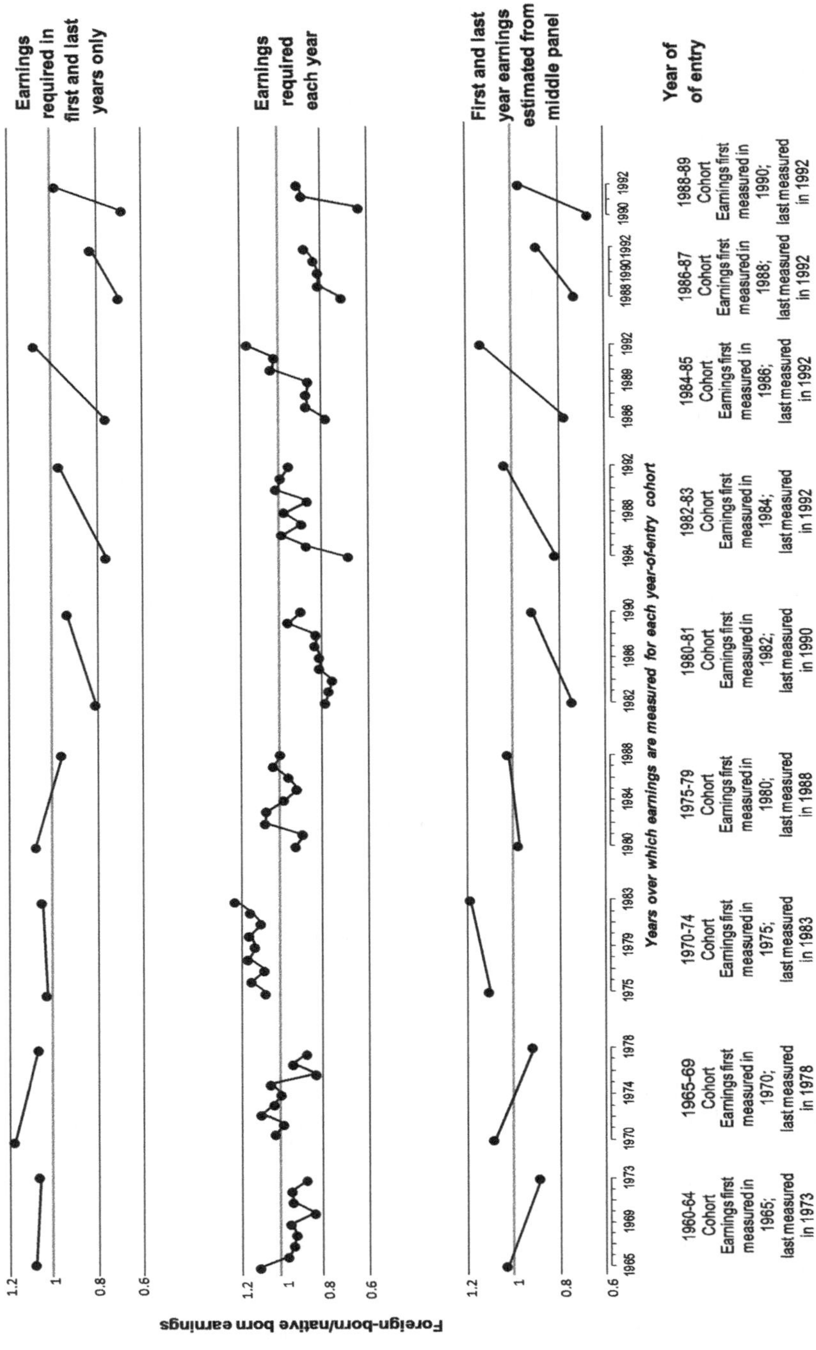

Fig. 3. The Annual Earnings of Foreign-Born Women Relative to US-Born Women. *Source:* Authors' calculations using the 1994 March Current Population Survey matched to the Social Security Administration's administrative record system.

Notes: Each dot is the median annual earnings of foreign-born women, in a specific year, divided by the median annual earnings of US-born women, wherein the individual observations in each US-born sample are weighted to match the age and schooling distribution middle panel, based on samples requiring positive earnings each year, measures earnings each year. Using the points of the middle panel the bottom panel estimates, for each cohort, $\frac{Y_{Ft}}{Y_{Nt}} = \alpha + \beta \text{Year}_t$, where Y_{Ft} is the median earnings of immigrant women for year t and Y_{Nt} is the median earnings of the corresponding weighted native sample.[10] These estimates, evaluated at first and last years, determine the bottom panel's lines and help compare the top and middle panels.

The top panel suggests that immigrant women went from having earnings profiles resembling those of US natives (of similar age and education) to earning profiles with low initial earnings and high earnings growth, relative to their US-born statistical twins. The transformation parallels that for immigrant men except the shift from high-entry-earnings/low-earnings-growth to low-entry-earnings/high-earnings-growth begins with the 1970–1974 cohort for men; for women, it begins with the 1980–1981 cohort.

The male/female divergent earnings patterns for the 1970–1974 and 1975–1979 cohorts might suggest a family investment strategy. However, the middle and bottom panels show that women who work every year have the same transition as men: flat earnings profiles (relative to natives) to low initial earnings and high earnings growth starting with the 1970–1974 cohort. Fig. 4 emphasizes this similarity with cohort-specific ratios of immigrant to native ten-year growth rates for women and men.[11]

Perhaps, the high earnings growth of recent cohorts reflects high earnings growth of unmarried immigrant women while married women—particularly those married to immigrants—have relatively low earnings growth reflecting the FIH. Decreasing marriage rates among immigrants in recent years could yield the overall pattern we observe. If so, then restricting our sample for the most recent cohorts from "all immigrant women" to "married immigrant women" to "married immigrant women with immigrant husbands" should decrease the earnings growth of immigrant women relative to natives.[12] Fig. 5 shows this is not the case.

7. CAVEATS

7.1 Why Do We Not Find Stronger Support for the FIH?

The FIH suggests that the earnings of immigrant women are influenced by their efforts to finance their husbands' human capital investment. Perhaps, our results are not more supportive of the FIH because most women in our study are not married by the year we first measure their earnings?

The CPS asks when immigrants migrated to the United States and whether they are married at the time of the survey but not when they first married. Age of marriage and year of immigration on the 1980 5% Census public use sample permits estimating the percent of immigrant women who were married by or in the first year we measure each cohort's earnings. For women 25–51 years old, 79% of the 1960–1964 cohort (those who immigrated in 1960–1964) were married before 1966; 82% of the 1965–1969 cohort were married before 1971; 82% of

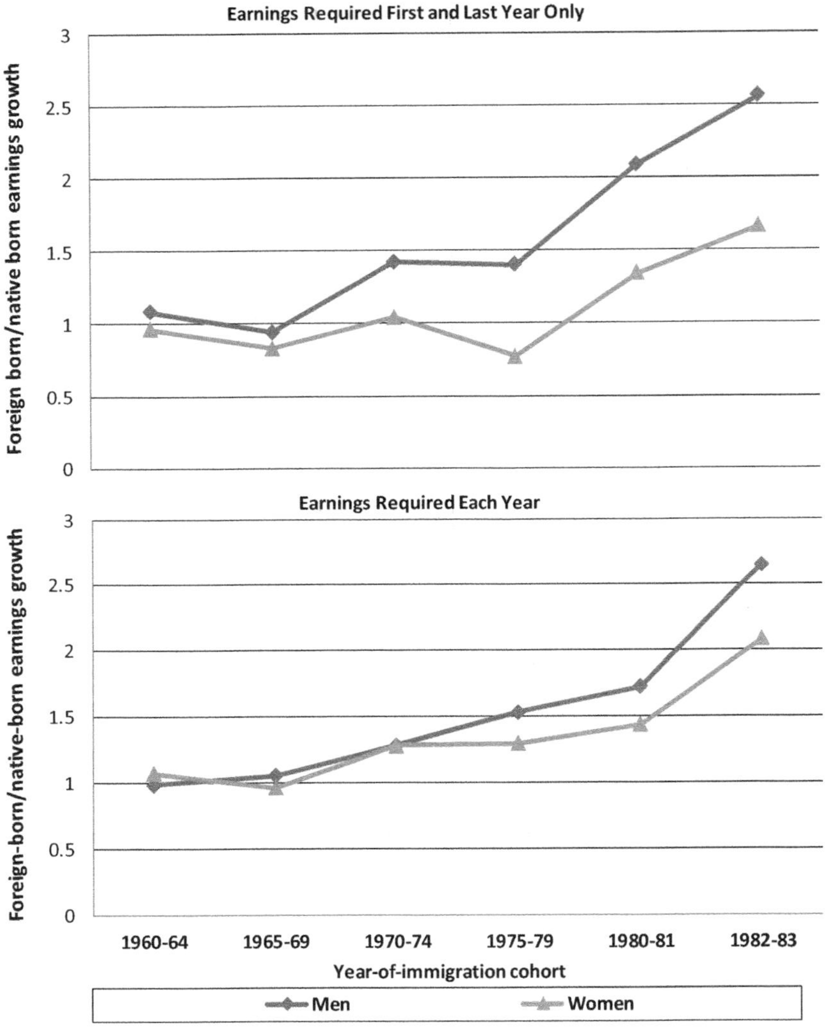

Fig. 4. Cohort-Specific Ratios of Foreign-Born to Native-Born Ten-Year Earnings Growth Rates: Women and Men *Source:* Authors' calculations using the 1994 March Current Population Survey matched to the Social Security Administration's administrative record system.

Notes: Each marker is a cohort-specific ratio of foreign-born to native-born ten-year relative growth rates defined as $[(Y_{\text{END}} - Y_1)/Y_1]_F/[(Y_{\text{END}} - Y_1)/Y_1]_N$ where Y_1 and Y_{END} denote the beginning- and end-year median annual earnings, and F and N denote foreign and native born. Median annual earnings for the US born are estimated on samples weighted to match the age and schooling distribution of the corresponding foreign-born cohort.

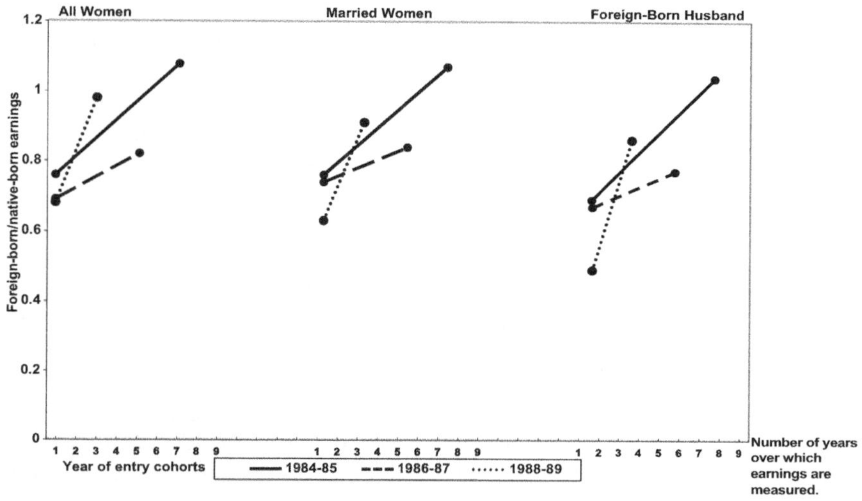

Fig. 5. The Earnings of Foreign-Born Women Relative to US-Born Women, by Marital Status. *Source:* Authors' calculations using the 1994 March Current Population Survey matched to the Social Security Administration's administrative record system.

Notes: Each dot is the median annual earnings of foreign-born women, in a specific year, divided by the median annual earnings of US-born women, wherein the individual observations in each US-born sample are weighted to match the age and schooling distribution of the corresponding foreign-born cohort. The samples that underlie these graphs require earnings in the first and last years, only; the annual median earnings, measured at the first and last years, determine the lines. For the 1984–1985 cohorts (solid lines), earnings are first measured in 1986 and last measured in 1992. For the 1986–1987 cohorts (dashed lines), earnings are first measured in 1988 and last measured in 1992. For the 1988–1989 cohorts (dotted lines), earnings are first measured in 1990 and last measured in 1992.

the 1970–1974 sample were married before 1976; and 79% of the 1975–1979 sample were married before 1981.[13] These statistics suggest that most women in the cohorts we study were married by the year we first measure their earnings.

The FIH predictions pertain to immigrant women who marry immigrant men. Perhaps, most immigrant women in our study did not marry immigrant men. CPS data from 1994 to 2024 reveal that, of married immigrant women aged 25–51 who had been in America for 1–5 years, more than 85% had an immigrant spouse.

The FIH assumptions are less likely to apply if either the woman or their spouse entered with an employment visa. There would then be less reason for either spouse to invest in the career of the other since the employment principal's skills are already highly valued in the US labor market. Our data lack information on the type of visa women or their spouse entered with. However, only about 20% of new green card recipients are employer-sponsored.

Although we fail to find evidence for the FIH, other work underscores the role women play in immigrant family earnings (e.g., Blau et al., 2011; Reimers, 1984, 1985), including family efforts to pursue self-employment (Duleep et al., 2021). In this vein, there are multiple ways our work could be enhanced via variations in marriage patterns and US arrival times. Indeed, one such variation is at the heart of the research of Baker and Benjamin (1997).

7.2 Transition Puzzles

Resonating with the work of Blau et al. (2003), we have stressed the similarity of the earnings profiles of immigrant men and women. There are, however, differences warranting exploration.

An obvious route for further investigation is how children affect the results. A large literature (Mincer & Polachek, 1974, 1978; O'Neill & Polachek, 1993; Polachek, 2004; Polachek & Siebert, 1996) relates optimal human capital investment by women to the skill depreciation that occurs during time taken out of the labor force for child rearing. To the extent this pattern is the same for immigrant women, it is an additional reason we might have expected a flatter earnings profile for immigrant women than for immigrant men. On the other hand, difficulties in the transfer of skills for immigrants may in many ways resemble the effect of skill depreciation during labor market absences yet equally affect both men and women. Whether this helps explain similarities and differences in male and female immigrant earnings calls for further research. It may illuminate why the "transition" from earnings patterns resembling those of US natives to low initial earnings and high earnings growth occurs earlier for men than for women.

7.3 Labor Force Restrictions

Another key issue with policy implications is the effect of labor force restrictions. Our analyses assume that work—type of work and hours of work—are unrestricted. But that is not universally the case. Employment is barred in some of the temporary visa classes and for the unauthorized foreign born. Further, some employment opportunities are for citizens only.

For example, the spouses of those here on temporary work visas can only work under limited circumstances. Spouses of J-1 visa holders (an odd visa class that includes summer carnival workers and biomedical postdocs) can apply for authorization to work (an Employment Authorization Document, or EAD) only if they can demonstrate that their family does not need the money. Spouses of H-1B visa holders (specialty occupations requiring a college degree, or fashion models) can apply for an EAD only after their spouse has an approved application for a permanent visa. Those on student visas are allowed limited off-campus work, but generally their spouses are not allowed to work at all. As confusing as these variations are, their analysis could help elucidate the economic assimilation of immigrants as individuals and as family members.

Of course, whether immigrants have legal status or not affects their employment. We limited our longitudinal earnings analyses to individuals with a CPS-SSA match on Social Security Number, name, age, and gender. The exact match nature of our sample makes it very likely that the earnings we follow are for the correct persons, albeit at the cost of a smaller sample. Reporting errors, name confusions, and other issues cause mismatches between the CPS and Social Security records. These mismatches would affect both the US- and foreign-born samples. In addition, the CPS foreign-born sample includes illegal aliens, who either lack a Social Security number or have a fraudulent one. The percent of the 1994 CPS's foreign-born sample who fail the CPS-SSA exact match test exceeds the corresponding percent for the United States born by the percent of the CPS foreign-born sample that is estimated to be illegal (Passel, 1999). This suggests that the foreign-born sample we analyze provides a good representation of the legal foreign-born population.[14]

7.4 Permanence and Naturalization

Empirical evidence suggests that the US permanence of immigrants from economically developing countries exceeds that of immigrants from economically developed countries and that the decision to invest in human capital and the decision to stay permanently in the United States are jointly determined and positively associated (Duleep & Dowhan, 2008; Duleep et al., 2021).

Another issue is naturalization. Those who seek to be naturalized are more permanently attached to the US and naturalization increases opportunities for Federal employment, employment that requires security clearances, and with employers that discriminate on citizenship status (something illegal only since 1986). To become naturalized, individuals generally have to be in the United States for 5 years, or two years if married to a US citizen. The interplay between permanence and naturalization could be better understood with information about when individuals apply for naturalization. Although the naturalization date is not included on Census or CPS files, it might be possible to add this information in future matches of Social Security and Census data: USCIS (United States Citizenship and Immigration Services) has provided these data to the Social Security Administration when a person's citizenship status changes.

8. EVIDENCE FROM NATURAL EXPERIMENTS

An evolving picture of the role women play in the economic adjustment of immigrants continues to unfurl. Earlier research, mostly based on cross-sectional data, supported the FIH. More recent evidence[15] including our analyses of year-of-entry cohorts in this paper contradict the FIH.

When compared with similar US-born workers, the early cohorts of immigrant women and men have relatively flat earnings growth; more recent cohorts have low initial earnings but high earnings growth. These analyses support Blau et al. (2003) who find similar earnings behavior of US immigrant women and men. Our study also illuminates why scholars found some previous support for diverging earnings patterns for immigrant men and women. Yet, this disappears when we examine women who work every year.

To understand the earnings of immigrant women, Blau et al. (2003) encourage international comparisons. Such pursuits might be aided by using the "rules" guiding our exploration: Follow immigrant cohorts from the beginning of their host-country years. Follow each year-of-entry cohort separately, thus allowing both entry earnings and earnings growth to vary. With large sample sizes consider education and age-defined crosstabs to facilitate international comparisons; with smaller sample sizes consider using weights to control for variables that affect earnings such as education and age. Finally, in studies that do not measure earnings growth by linking individual earnings, consider how results are affected by changes in immigrant and native sample universes caused not only by immigrant emigration but by dramatic immigrant/native differences in the effects of sample restrictions as cohorts age (Duleep et al., 2022).

Two natural experiments are embedded in the broad swath of time we analyze. With a distinct policy change, the United States went from excluding immigrants from economically developing countries to including them. Concomitantly, two programs to admit immigrants were initiated: one where US family members sponsor their relatives and another where employers sponsor immigrants. Almost by definition, immigrants sponsored by employers have skills that are immediately valued in the US labor market and thus have very high skill-transferability.

Consistent with the IHCI model, both natural experiments find high earnings growth associated with low initial earnings. Relative to immigrants from economically developed countries, immigrants from economically developing countries have low initial earnings and high earnings growth (Duleep, Liu, et al., 2018; Duleep et al., 2021). Relative to employment-based immigrants, family-admitted immigrants have low initial earnings and high earnings growth (DeSilva, 1997; Duleep & Regets, 1996a; Jasso & Rosenzweig, 1995).

Several studies provide evidence of immigrants with low initial earnings investing in specific forms of human capital, such as schooling or learning English (Akresh, 2007; Duleep et al., 2021; Duleep, Jaeger, et al., 2018; Duleep & Regets, 2017, Van Tubergen & van De Werfhorst, 2007).[16] Yet, human capital investment takes myriad forms not easily captured by any one type of human capital investment. One group may invest in English proficiency, another in creating businesses not requiring English; Korean immigrants with poor English fluency have high self-employment rates (Duleep et al., 2021). Human capital investment strategies also vary with time and place and reflect how permanently attached groups are to the United States. For all of these reasons, the best indicator of human capital investment is earnings growth, which is affected by all forms of human capital investment observable and unobservable.

9. CONCLUSION

After 1965, America experienced a historic transformation in the countries of origin of her immigrants. As previously found for men, recent cohorts of US immigrant women with low entry earnings relative to similar US natives have high earnings growth. Though limited to a subset of the immigrant population—individuals who are more permanent (given their presence in the United States over a ten-year period)—the high earnings growth of the post-1965 immigrants refutes the idea that post-1965 immigrants, who mostly come from economically developing countries, are of lower quality than immigrants from economically developed countries.

Over the time period we have examined, a transition in immigrant earnings profiles occurred. The earnings profiles of US immigrant men and women changed from earnings resembling those of US natives before the 1965 Immigration Act to lower initial earnings but much higher earnings growth than their US-born statistical twins. This transition underlies the overtime success of immigrant families from economically developing countries (Duleep et al., 2021). The high earnings growth signifies human capital investment that invigorates the economy (Duleep, Jaeger, et al., 2018; Green, 1999; Green & Worswick, 2012).

ACKNOWLEDGMENTS

This chapter has benefitted from useful comments and help from Jason Brown, Patrice Cole, Anya Olsen, Cordelia Reimers, Michael Leonesio, David Weaver, Seth Sanders, Phani Wunnava, Sol Polachek, two anonymous reviewers, and the greatly missed Robert Lalonde and Finis Welch.

NOTES

1. Separate provisions banned Asian immigration (Duleep et al., 2021, Chapter 2). Western Hemisphere immigration continued to be unrestricted, but the same 1924 Act created the Border Patrol and different types of restrictions upon legal Mexican immigration later in the decade.

2. If these immigrants were negatively selected and of lower quality, they would likely have less incentive to invest in US-specific skills as such learning might come harder and have a lesser return. Alternatively, immigrants may be positively selected since the act of migration requires at least a modicum of motivation and personal organization. This would, however, apply to immigrants from all source countries and all admission visa types. The test of the IHCI model comes from connecting differences in immigrant behavior to likely differences in degrees of skill transferability.

3. Refer to Duleep and Dowhan (2002) for comprehensive detailed information about these data.

4. Empirical evidence following cohorts or individuals includes Akresh (2007), Demombynes (2002), DeSilva (1997), Duleep and Dowhan (2002), Duleep, Liu, et al. (2018), Duleep et al. (2021), Duleep and Regets (1992, 1994, 1996a, 1996b, 1997, 1999, 2002), Green and Worswick (2012), Hall and Farkas (2008), Jasso and Rosenzweig (1990a, 1995), LaLonde and Topel (1991, 1997), Schoeni (1997), and Villarreal and

Tamborini (2018). Lin (2013) and Duleep et al. (2021) show this for immigrants from specific countries.

5. Duleep et al. (2022) illustrate this for all-immigrants and Duleep et al. (2021) for country-specific groups. Also refer to Jasso and Rosenzweig (1990b).

6. The same type of issue occurs with many types of sample restriction, such as excluding the self-employed. But the zero-earner exclusion is pervasive since it occurs routinely by the common practice of using ln (earnings) as the dependent variable.

7. Forcing longitudinal data into a functional form developed for regressions on pseudo cohorts also misses the opportunity to measure actual earnings growth over the period for each specific individual and directly relate that to individual characteristics.

8. Kitagawa and Hauser (1973) in their classic study of differential mortality weighted observations to compare groups. Some economists have embraced this approach. See DiNardo et al. (1996) for an elegant extension, and Duleep (1988), Duleep and Regets (1997), Duleep and Dowhan (2002), and Duleep et al. (2021) for applications.

9. For immigrant men, several ways to identify initial earnings are examined in Duleep and Dowhan (2002).

10. For each cohort, the estimated coefficients and t-statistics (in parentheses) for $\frac{Y_{Ft}}{Y_{Nt}} = \alpha + \beta \text{Year}_t$ are as follows: 1960–1964 −0.017 (−2.26); 1965–1969 −0.020 (−2.35); 1970–1974 0.010 (2.07); 1975–1979 0.006 (0.64); 1975–1979 0.006 (0.64); 1980–1981 0.021 (4.02); 1982–1983 0.026 (2.28); 1984–1985 0.058 (6.10); 1986–1987 0.040 (3.79); and 1988–1989 0.149 (2.00).

11. The earnings growth rates shown in Fig. 4 are defined as $[(Y_{\text{END}} - Y_1)/Y_1]_F/[(Y_{\text{END}} - Y_1)/Y_1]_N$ where Y_1 and Y_{END} denote the beginning- and end-year earnings, and F and N denote foreign and native born.

12. For our most recent cohorts, we assume that women who report to the CPS ever having been married in 1994 were married by the year we first measure each cohort's earnings.

13. A similar analysis is not possible for the 1980–1981, 1982–1983, 1984–1985, 1986–1987, and 1988–1989 cohorts because the 1990 census does not ask age of marriage.

14. For further information on measuring the unauthorized via administrative and survey data matches and mismatches refer to Duleep et al. (2025) and Tamborini et al. (2025).

15. See, for instance, Adserà and Ferrer (2014, 2016), Blau et al. (2003), Cohen-Goldner et al. (2009), Cortes (2004), Rashid (2004), and Worswick (1996). Also refer to Tamborini and Villarreal (2024) for information by generation and ethnicity.

16. For a detailed discussion of the difficulties associated with measuring human capital investment with a single form of human capital investment versus earnings growth, representing multiple and varied forms of human capital investment, refer to Part V of Duleep et al. (2022).

REFERENCES

Adserà, A., & Ferrer, A. M. (2014). The myth of immigrant women as secondary workers: Evidence from Canada. *American Economic Review*, *104*(5), 360–364.

Adserà, A., & Ferrer, A. M. (2016). Occupational skills and labour market progression of married immigrant women in Canada. *Labour Economics*, *39*, 88–98.

Akresh, I. R. (2007). U.S. immigrants' labor market adjustment: Additional human capital investment and earnings growth. *Demography*, *44*(4), 865–881.

Baker, M., & Benjamin, D. (1997). The role of the family in immigrants' labor-market activity: An evaluation of alternative explanations. *The American Economic Review*, *87*(4), 705–727.

Blau, F., Kahn, L., Moriarty, J., & Souza, A. (2003). The role of the family in immigrants' labor-market activity. *The American Economic Review*, *93*(1), 429–447.

Blau, F., Kahn, L., & Papps, K. (2011). Gender, source country characteristics, and labor market assimilation among immigrants. *The Review of Economics and Statistics*, *93*(1), 43–58.

Borjas, G. (1987). Self-selection and immigrants. *American Economic Review*, *77*, 531–553.

Borjas, G. (1992). National origin and the skills of immigrants. In G. J. Borjas & R. B. Freeman (Eds.), *Immigration and the work force* (pp. 17–48). National Bureau of Economic Research, University of Chicago Press.

Borjas, G. (2015). The slowdown in the economic assimilation of immigrants: Aging and cohort effects revisited again. *Journal of Human Capital*, *9*(4), 483–517.

Chiswick, B. (1978). The effect of americanization on the earnings of foreign-born men. *Journal of Political Economy*, *86*(5), 897–922.

Chiswick, B. (1979). The economic progress of immigrants: Some apparently universal patterns. In W. Fellner (Ed.), *Contemporary economic problems* (pp. 359–399). American Enterprise Institute.

Cohen-Goldner, S., Gotlibovski, C., & Kahana, N. (2009). The role of marriage in immigrants' human capital investment under liquidity constraints. *Journal of Population Economics*, *22*(4), 983–1003.

Cortes, K. E. (2004). Are refugees different from economic immigrants? *The Review of Economics and Statistics*, *86*(2), 465–480.

Demombynes, G. M. (2002). Three ways of looking at immigrant wage growth. In *Institute for Labor and Employment Conference, January, 2002*.

DeSilva, A. (1997). Earnings of immigrant classes in the early 1980's in Canada: A Re-examination. *Canadian Public Policy*, *23*(2), 179–202.

DiNardo, J., Fortin, N., & Lemieux, T. (1996). Labor market institutions and the distribution of wages, 1973-1992: A semiparametric approach. *Econometrica*, *64*(5), 1001–1044.

DiNardo, J., & Tobias, J. L. (2001). Nonparametric density and regression estimation. *The Journal of Economic Perspectives*, *15*(4), 11–28.

Duleep, H. (1988). *The economic status of Americans of Asian descent*. U.S. Commission on Civil Rights, GPO.

Duleep, H. (1994, Spring). Social security and the emigration of immigrants. *Social Security Bulletin*, *57*(1).

Duleep, H., & Dowhan, D. (2002). Insights from longitudinal data on the earnings growth of U.S. foreign-born men. *Demography*, *39*(3), 485–506.

Duleep, H., & Dowhan, D. (2008). Research on immigrant earnings. *Social Security Bulletin*, *68*(1), 31–50.

Duleep, H., Gesumaria, R., Shoffner, D., & Tamborini, C. (2025). A new way to measure the number of unauthorized immigrants in the U.S. *Social Security Bulletin*. (forthcomnig).

Duleep, H., Jaeger, D., & McHenry, P. (2018). *On immigration and native entrepreneurship*. IZA Discussion. Paper #14188.

Duleep, H., Liu, X., & Regets, M. (2018). *Country of origin, earnings convergence, and human capital investment* GLO Discussion Paper Series 247. Global Labor Organization.

Duleep, H., Liu, X., & Regets, M. (2022). How the earnings growth of U.S. immigrants was underestimated. *Journal of Population Economics*. https://link.springer.com/journal/148/volumes-and-issues/35-2

Duleep, H., & Regets, M. (1992). *The elusive concept of immigrant quality: Evidence from 1960–1980*. American Economic Association presentation.

Duleep, H., & Regets, M. (1994). *Country of origin and immigrant earnings*. Discussion Paper PRIP-UI-28. The Urban Institute.

Duleep, H., & Regets, M. (1996a). Admission criteria and immigrant earnings profiles. *International Migration Review*, *30*(2), 571–590.

Duleep, H., & Regets, M. (1996b). Family unification, siblings, and skills. In H. Duleep & P. V. Wunnava (Eds.), *Immigrants and immigration policy: Individual skills, family ties, and group identities* (pp. 219–244). JAI Press.

Duleep, H., & Regets, M. (1997). Measuring immigrant wage growth using matched CPS files. *Demography*, *34*(2), 239–249.

Duleep, H., & Regets, M. (1999). Immigrants and human capital investment. *American Economic Review*, *89*(2), 186–191.

Duleep, H., & Regets, M. (2002). *The elusive concept of immigrant quality: Evidence from 1970-1990*. IZA Discussion Paper No. 631.

Duleep, H., & Regets, M. (2017). Family-friendly and human-capital-based immigration policy. *IZA World of Labor*. https://doi.org/10.15185/izawol.389

Duleep, H., Regets, M., Sanders, S., & Wunnava, P. (2021). *Human capital investment: A history of Asian immigrants and their family ties*. Palgrave Macmillan.

Duleep, H., & Sanders, S. (1993). The decision to work by married immigrant women. *Industrial and Labor Relations Review*, *46*(4), 677–690.

Green, D. A. (1999). Immigrant occupational attainment: Assimilation and mobility over time. *Journal of Labor Economics*, *17*(1), 49–79.

Green, D. A., & Worswick, C. (2012). Immigrant earnings profiles in the presence of human capital investment. *Labour Economics*, *19*(2), 241–259.

Hall, M., & Farkas, G. (2008). Does human capital raise earnings for immigrants in the low-skill labor market? *Demography*, *45*(3), 619–639.

Jasso, G., & Rosenzweig, M. R. (1990a). *The new chosen people: Immigration in the U.S.* Russell Sage Fdn.

Jasso, G., & Rosenzweig, M. R. (1990b, March). Self-selection and the earnings of immigrants: Comment. *The American Economic Review*, *80*(1), 2980304.

Jasso, G., & Rosenzweig, M. R. (1995). Do immigrants screened for skills do better than family-reunification immigrants? *International Migration Review*, *29*(1), 85–111.

Kitagawa, E., & Hauser, P. (1973). *Differential mortality in the United States: A study in socioeconomic epidemiology*. Harvard University Press.

LaLonde, R. J., & Topel, R. H. (1991). Immigrants in the American labor market: Quality, assimilation, and distributional effects. *The American Economic Review*, *81*(2), 297–302.

LaLonde, R. J., & Topel, R. H. (1997). Economic impact of international migration and the economic performance of migrants. In M. R. Rosenzweig & O. Stark (Eds.), *Handbook of population and family economics* (pp. 800–850). Elsevier.

Lin, C. (2013). Earnings gap, cohort effect and economic assimilation of immigrants from mainland China, Hong Kong, and Taiwan in the United States. *Review of International Economics*, *21*(2), 249–265.

Long, J. (1980). The effect of americanization on earnings: Some evidence for women. *Journal of Political Economy*, *88*(3), 620–629.

Mincer, J., & Polachek, S. (1974). Family investments in human capital: Earnings of women. *Journal of Political Economy*, *82*(2, Part 2), S76–S108.

Mincer, J., & Polachek, S. (1978). An exchange: The theory of human capital and the earnings of women: Women's earnings reexamined. *Journal of Human Resources*, *13*(1), 118–134.

O'Neill, J., & Polachek, S. (1993). Why the gender gap in wages narrowed in the 1980s. *Journal of Labor Economics*, *11*(1, Part 1), 205–228.

Passel, J. S. (1999). Undocumented immigration to the United States: Numbers, trends, and characteristics. In D. W. Haines & K. E. Rosenblum (Eds.), *Illegal Immigration in America* (pp. 27–111). Greenwood Press Ct.

Polachek, S. (2004). *How the human capital model explains why the gender wage gap narrowed*. IZA DP No. 1102.

Polachek, S., & Siebert, W. S. (1996). Family labor market incentives: Men and women working for pay. In *Household and family economics* (pp. 159–194). Springer.

Rashid, S. (2004). *Married immigrant women and employment. The role of family investments* (p. 623). Umeå Economic Studies. http://www.usbe.umu.se/enheter/econ/ues/ues623/

Reimers, C. (1984). Sources of the family income differentials among hispanics, blacks, and white non-hispanics. *American Journal of Sociology*, *89*(4), 889–903.

Reimers, C. (1985). Cultural differences in labor force participation among married women. *American Economic Review*, *75*(2), 251–255.

Reimers, D. (2023). *How America, through immigration, is becoming a multicultural nation, 1848-2016*. forthcoming.

Rivera-Batiz, F., & Sechzer, S. (1991). Substitution and complementarity between immigrant and native labor in the United States. In F. L. Rivera-Batiz, S. L. Sechzer, & I. N. Gang (Eds.), *U.S. immigration policy reform in the 1980s* (pp. 89–116). Praeger.

Schoeni, R. (1997). New evidence on the economic progress of foreign-born men in the 1970s and 1980s. *Journal of Human Resources*, *32*(4), 683–740.

Tamborini, C., Duleep, H., Gesumaria, R., & Shoffner, D. (2025). Measuring unauthorized immigrants in U.S. surveys: Insights on their characteristics. *Social Security Bulletin*. forthcoming.

Tamborini, C., & Villarreal, A. (2024). First- and second-generation women's economic assimilation: An analysis of longitudinal earnings records. *Social Forces*, *103*(4), 655–680.

Van Tubergen, F., & van De Werfhorst, H. (2007). Post immigration investments in education: A study of immigrants in the Netherlands. *Demography*, *44*(4), 883–898.

Villarreal, A., & Tamborini, C. (2018). Immigrants' economic assimilation: Evidence from longitudinal earnings records. *American Sociological Review*, *83*(4), 686–715.

Warren, R., & Peck, J. M. (1980, February). Foreign-born emigration from the United States: 1960 to 1970. *Demography*, *17*(1), 72–84.

Warren, R., & Kraly, E. P. (1985). *The elusive exodus: Emigration from the United States*. Population Reference Bureau.

Worswick, C. (1996). Immigrant families in the Canadian labour market. *Canadian Public Policy*, *22*(4), 378–396.

NACARA: DOES AMNESTY AFFECT MARRIAGES OF UNDOCUMENTED IMMIGRANTS?

Eva Dziadula[a] and Jorgen Harris[b]

[a]*University of Notre Dame, USA*
[b]*Occidental College, USA*

ABSTRACT

This study examines the effect of the Nicaraguan Adjustment and Central American Relief Act (NACARA), a 1997 policy that provided permanent residency in the United States to previously undocumented immigrants, on recipients' choice of whether to marry and whom to marry. Using a difference-in-differences design that defines treatment by country of origin and arrival before 1991 (NACARA eligibility criteria), the authors find that NACARA recipients are more likely to marry and less likely to live in an ethnic enclave. Using a triple-difference design on a sample of married couples that defines treatment by NACARA eligibility and by marriage after NACARA was announced, the authors find that becoming aware of their eligibility for permanent residence led NACARA recipients to be less likely to marry US citizens, more likely to marry immigrants from their country of origin, and more likely to marry younger spouses with fewer years of education. The authors also find some suggestive evidence that NACARA increased intra-household bargaining power for men. These findings reveal that obtaining legal status through nonmarriage channels allows immigrants to choose partners with less consideration for their partner's legal status.

Keywords: Amnesty; immigration; marriage markets; assortative matching; legal status

Migration, Human Capital and the Labor Market
Research in Labor Economics, Volume 53A, 193–230

Published under exclusive licence by Emerald Publishing Limited
ISSN: 0147-9121/doi:10.1108/S0147-91212026000053A006

1. INTRODUCTION

In this chapter, we estimate the effect of receiving permanent legal status on marriage decisions by examining the Nicaraguan Adjustment and Central American Relief Act (NACARA), a 1997 immigration policy enacted with the intention of normalizing the status of Salvadoran and Guatemalan immigrants who had arrived in the United States during their civil wars and had not received an adequate opportunity to plead for asylum. NACARA beneficiaries entered the United States prior to 1991 and lived without legal status until the policy was enacted in 1997. Under the policy, they were issued legal permanent residency and were able to sponsor spouses and children for legal permanent residency regardless of their spouse's form of entry to the United States.

Marriage plays a key role in US immigration policy. Nearly 60% of Legal Permanent Resident (LPR) visas issued in 2022 were family-based, and among these, visas for spouses of US citizens were the largest category (Congressional Research Service, 2023). As a consequence, marriage offers a key pathway to permanent legal status and citizenship for those living in the United States without legal status or with temporary legal status. This population is quite large. Approximately, 11 million undocumented immigrants live in the United States, alongside 1.8 million immigrants without permanent status (Passel & Krogstad, 2023). The United States receives over 35,000 petitions for an alien fiancee each year (US Citizenship and Immigration Services, 2021), and nearly 240,000 LPR visas are issued to spouses of US citizens in the United States (Congressional Research Service, 2023). However, laws providing immigration status to spouses can distort immigrants' choice of marriage partner and create power imbalances within marriages (Balgamwalla, 2013). Spouses with precarious immigration status may marry partners with citizenship or permanent legal status who are less suitable along other dimensions and may have less bargaining power within their relationships.

As a result, it is important to understand how marriages change when immigrants gain legal status for reasons other than marriage. First, legal status may change an immigrant's attractiveness as a spouse. For potential partners without permanent legal status, a spouse with permanent legal status can be a sponsor for immigration status adjustment. Even for those who are ineligible for adjustment, a documented spouse can safely participate in formal interactions with the legal system and financial institutions on behalf of their household, for instance by signing rental contracts and mortgage applications. Potential partners with permanent legal status also benefit from having a spouse who already has permanent legal status. A spouse's legal status eliminates the need for sponsorship, a potentially difficult and lengthy interaction with the immigration system, and may allay fears that a relationship is insincere or transactional.

Likewise, receiving legal status may change an immigrant's preferences over who to marry. Because continued residence in the United States is no longer conditional on finding a partner who can sponsor an immigration application, immigrants may value their partner's citizenship status less after receiving permanent legal status themselves. This allows them to find a partner with greater appeal along other dimensions such as age, education, or cultural background.

These factors suggest that the overall "match surplus" from marrying a spouse without permanent legal status is likely to increase when an immigrant gains legal status. In a transferable utility framework with intra-household bargaining, as in Becker (1973), this is likely to lead to more marriages to spouses without permanent legal status. This prediction is somewhat less clear in a nontransferable utility framework. Because recipients of permanent legal status become higher-value matches for those with and without legal status, they are likely to have more and better options for a spouse. Because legal status is a valuable characteristic, this may increase the likelihood that they will marry a spouse with legal status. On the other hand, they may instead be more likely to marry a spouse without legal status but with other valuable characteristics. In addition, receiving permanent legal status may lead immigrants to live and work outside of ethnic enclaves, increasing their likelihood of marrying citizens. As a result, the question of how legal status affects marriages is an empirical question.

NACARA provides a unique opportunity to understand the effect of legal status on marriage markets. NACARA represents one of only a few times that undocumented immigrants in the United States have received permanent legal status, alongside the Immigration Reform and Control Act (IRCA) of 1986 and the Chinese Student Protection Act of 1989. Unlike these other amnesties, NACARA affected a small subset of Spanish-speaking undocumented immigrants, allowing us to compare recipients to a natural control group. In addition, because NACARA was implemented in 1997 but affected immigrants who entered the country before 1991, we can observe differences between the marriages of recipients who married before the policy went into effect, not knowing that they would receive legal status, and those who married after, with full knowledge that they would receive legal status.

We take advantage of this natural experiment by using the 2008–2012 American Community Surveys (ACS) to estimate two empirical strategies. First, we examine the effect of NACARA on marriage, naturalization, and residence in an ethnic enclave using a difference-in-differences approach. This approach compares immigrants who entered the country between 1988 and 1990 (and were thus eligible for NACARA but not for IRCA) to immigrants who arrived between 1991 and 1997 (prior to the announcement of NACARA). It then compares immigrants from El Salvador and Guatemala—two countries affected by NACARA—to immigrants from other Spanish-speaking countries that were not eligible for NACARA. We find that individuals who were eligible for NACARA were 17% less likely to remain unmarried and lived in areas where 11% fewer residents were from their country of origin.

We then examine the effect of NACARA on the characteristics of respondents' spouses using a triple-difference approach. This approach further divides respondents by the timing of their marriages, comparing marriages that took place after entry into the United States but before NACARA was announced to marriages occurring after NACARA was announced. In doing so, it allows us to see how receiving NACARA affected the characteristics of respondents' spouses. We find that after NACARA went into effect, eligible individuals became less likely to marry citizens and more likely to marry partners who benefit from their permanent legal status. Eligible individuals were 20% more likely to marry a noncitizen, 8% more likely to marry a spouse from their country of origin, and 20% less likely to marry a spouse who was likely eligible for NACARA. At the same time, eligible individuals married spouses who were on average a year younger and who had almost a year less education.

We validate these results in several ways. First, we confirm our triple difference results by estimating event studies relative to the year of marriage. We find no evidence of pretrends and find results consistent with our regression estimates. Next, we carefully defend our choice of control group. We show that our group is comparable to NACARA recipients by showing that the two groups have similar demographic characteristics, both among immigrants who entered the country before 1991 and among immigrants who entered after. Next, we show that our results are unlikely to be biased by differences in sample attrition following the receipt of NACARA by demonstrating that sample attrition rates are very similar for control and treatment groups who arrived before and after 1991. In addition, we show that the relationship between sample attrition and respondents' education, English proficiency, and gender are similar for the treatment and control groups.

This chapter expands a very limited body of evidence on the causal relationship between legal status and marriage. In the absence of legal status, Mexican noncitizens are more likely to marry a US citizen when facing more intense immigration enforcement (Amuedo-Dorantes et al., 2020). Likewise, immigrants who gain legal status are less likely to marry native citizens (Adda et al., 2020; Azzolini & Guetto, 2017; Bansak et al., 2023). Our chapter is in line with this literature and is the only work examining the effect of gaining legal status on the choice of whom to marry for immigrants from Latin America, who constitute two-thirds of undocumented immigrants in the United States (Migration Policy Institute, 2023). In addition, it is the only work that can compare the marriage decisions of the same population before and after receiving legal status due to retroactive implementation in 1997 requiring entry prior to 1991. Our work shows that the insecurity of uncertain legal status profoundly affects even the most intimate life choices.

2. BACKGROUND AND CONTEXT

2.1 NACARA

NACARA was an immigration bill passed in 1997 and implemented in 1999 that intended to retroactively correct decisions made in the 1980s and early 1990s that disadvantaged asylum seekers from countries that had experienced civil war and/or communist control. The policies targeted people who had entered the United States and applied for asylum at a time when the policy of US immigration authorities was less favorable to asylum seekers than it was in later years.

NACARA has two sub-sections: Section 202, which affects nationals of Nicaragua, Cuba, and the former Soviet Union, and Section 203, which affects nationals of El Salvador and Guatemala. This chapter examines the beneficiaries of Section 203. We focus on Section 203 for several reasons. First, because Section 202 applied to immigrants who arrived in 1995 or earlier and went into effect in 1997, there is not a sufficient "pre-period" to perform a triple-difference regression. Furthermore, there is no natural control group for Soviet or Cuban immigrants.

El Salvador and Guatemala both experienced violent and destructive civil wars throughout the 1980s and early 1990s during which US-backed military governments fought Soviet-backed communist insurgencies. In both countries, these civil wars led to mass immigration to the United States by people fleeing violence. However, US immigration officials denied 97% of asylum applications from Salvadoran nationals and 99% of asylum applications from Guatemalan nationals (Bau, 1985). As a result, a coalition of religious organizations and civil rights groups sued the Immigration and Naturalization Service (INS) in 1985, arguing that their treatment of Central American migrants violated the Refugee Act of 1980. The case, American Baptist Churches v. Thornburgh, was ultimately settled in 1990. In the settlement, the INS agreed to offer new asylum hearings for Salvadoran and Guatemalan migrants who had arrived prior to October 1, 1990 (Guatemalans) or September 20, 1990 (Salvadorans). Beneficiaries were given stays of deportation until new hearings could be completed[1] though few hearings were ever scheduled. In addition, they were issued temporary work permits. In total, 190,000 Salvadorans and 50,000 Guatemalans were covered by the settlement.

Shortly thereafter, nationals of El Salvador (but not Guatemala) were issued Temporary Protected Status for 18 months beginning in 1990. Following the expiration of this status, Salvadoran nationals who had arrived prior to 1990 were granted Deferred Enforced Departure—another form of temporary protection from deportation. This status was extended until 1996.

When Section 203 of NACARA was passed on November 19, 1997 as title II of the District of Columbia Appropriations Act for FY1998 (P.L. 105–100), it applied to the same group of Salvadoran and Guatemalan nationals that had been included in the American Baptist Churches v. Thornburgh settlement. In order to be eligible, migrants had to have arrived in the United States before the Fall of 1990 as specified in the settlement, to have applied for asylum prior to 1995, and to have not been apprehended at the border prior to 1990. In addition, Salvadoran recipients had to have applied for benefits through the American Baptist Churches settlement by October 31st, 1991, and Guatemalan recipients had to have applied by December 31, 1990.

NACARA had a few important effects on recipients. For Guatemalan nationals who had been denied asylum, the policy provided legal status to a population that had been at risk for deportation. Meanwhile, for Salvadorans and for Guatemalans whose asylum cases had not been processed, the policy replaced temporary, discretionary legal status through the executive branch with the opportunity to apply for permanent residence. For all eligible individuals, NACARA was the first policy that provided a path to permanent legal status.

In addition, NACARA recipients were able to pass their NACARA status on to their spouses and children, provided that they were married or had the children prior to applying for NACARA. This last benefit distinguished NACARA recipients from other Green Card holders prior to 2000 because US law at that time did not allow spouses of citizens or foreign residents to receive legal status through their spouse if they had illegally entered the United States (as did the majority of NACARA recipients). However, the Legal Immigrant Family Equity (LIFE) Act of 2000 changed this rule to allow any spouses of citizens or permanent residents to apply for legal status in the United States, regardless of their mode of entry into the country.[2] Because only 573 individuals had applied for NACARA prior to 2000, this means that virtually all spouses of NACARA beneficiaries are eligible for Green Cards—either through NACARA for prior marriages or through the LIFE Act for marriages that took place after the primary eligible individual had received NACARA (US Citizenship and Immigration Services, 2001).

Despite these benefits, take-up of NACARA was slow. Only 17% of Salvadorans and Guatemalans eligible for NACARA were granted amnesty in the first three years of implementation, from 1999 to 2002 (Kaushal, 2006). However, over 100,000 individuals applied between 2003 and 2006, and a total of 186,000 people had received benefits by 2014 (approximately two-thirds of all eligible individuals). This slow take-up is likely due to several challenges, including long administrative wait times and relatively high application fees of \$215 per person and \$430 per family (Kaushal, 2006). However, while most recipients had not yet applied for or received NACARA benefits in 1998, beneficiaries were aware that they were eligible for these benefits. As a result, we consider marriages that occurred after 1997 to be "treated" by the policy.

2.2 Immigrant Marriages

Immigrants face several unique decisions and challenges when choosing a marriage partner. Like all people, immigrants search for a compatible partner with complementary characteristics to maximize gains from marriage. However, immigrants' choices of marriage partners are influenced more than non-immigrants by a desire to marry a partner who shares their cultural, ethnic, or national background, and by considerations of legal status. These considerations can be understood from the theory of assortative matching based on the seminal work of Becker (1973, 1974) and expanded by many others since (for an overview, see Mansour & McKinnish, 2017). While all couples sort along traits such as education and race, immigrant couples also sort by country of origin. Immigrants frequently marry other immigrants, often from the same country of origin (Dziadula, 2020). Moreover, relative to natives, immigrant men living in the United States are significantly more likely to have a marriage migrant spouse, i.e. a foreign-born spouse who married within a year of their arrival to the United States (Dziadula & Zavodny, 2023). Intermarriage is often seen as a form of assimilation—immigrants who differ from their spouse in national origin are often more similar in other respects. Furtado (2012) documents that immigrants trade similarities in origin and culture for similarities in education. In fact, several studies point out that intermarriage between immigrants and natives is more likely among those who are highly educated (Choi et al., 2012; Lichter et al., 2015).

The other important consideration in the immigrant marriage market is legal status. The US immigration system strongly favors family ties. In fact, marrying a citizen is one of the shortest and most straightforward paths to gaining citizenship. Kelly (2010) documents that the Legal Immigration and Family Equity (LIFE) Act of 2000 which provided a short window for status adjustment among undocumented immigrants present in the United States is associated with an increase in marriage rates in counties with large immigrant populations. Moreover, the absence of legal status may also change immigrants' marriage choices in response to intensified immigration enforcement (Amuedo-Dorantes et al., 2020; Wang & Wang, 2012). If a potential spouse is a citizen, a desirable characteristic for immigrants without an alternative path, it increases the possibility of tradeoffs along other compatibility characteristics. Dziadula (2022) shows that immigrants from countries with long wait times and those who have been in the United States longer marry less-educated spouses. Furthermore, there is suggestive evidence that these matches which involve tradeoffs result in higher rates of divorce (Dziadula, 2022; Kelly, 2010).

3. CONTRIBUTION TO THE LITERATURE

Our work contributes to three strands of literature. First, we contribute to a very limited body of empirical work examining the effects of NACARA on intended recipients. Kaushal (2006) shows that receipt of NACARA modestly increased weekly earnings by an average of 4% and decreased employment by 0.5%, with benefits concentrated among those with at least a high-school education. We are the first to examine the effects of NACARA on outcomes outside of the labor market using causal methods.

Next, we contribute to the literature on the effect of immigration status on marriage. Four pieces of existing research have found that when immigrants gain legal status, they change their behavior in the marriage market. Gihleb et al. (2023) find that, immediately after receiving legal status, recipients of the Deferred Action for Childhood Arrivals program (DACA) were less likely to marry. Adda et al. (2020) and Azzolini and Guetto (2017) study the effect of EU expansion on the marriage choices of Eastern European guest workers in Italy. They find that after receiving permanent status through EU expansion, guest workers became less likely to marry Italian natives who would have provided a pathway to legal status and more likely to bring a spouse from their country of origin. Likewise, Bansak et al. (2023) study the effect of the Chinese Student Protection Act, which halted deportation and eventually provided permanent legal status to Chinese immigrants living in the United States following the

Tiananmen Square protests of 1989. They find that Chinese immigrants are more likely to marry "marriage migrant spouses"—i.e. spouses who arrived in the United States from China within a year of their marriage. In the absence of permanent legal status, Amuedo-Dorantes et al. (2020) find that Mexican immigrants to the United States are more likely to marry US citizens when faced with intensified immigration enforcement.

Our work contributes to this body of evidence in several ways. First, unlike the legalizations studied by prior literature, NACARA affects a small minority of Spanish-speaking immigrants. As a result, we estimate effects in a context where most people in the relevant marriage market do not experience a change in status. As a result, we are able to account for changes in immigrant marriage markets that are coincident with amnesty in a way that is not possible in previous literature. Second, our population of interest is considerably less educated and lower income than the populations studied by Bansak et al. (2023), Adda et al. (2020) or Azzolini and Guetto (2017). Whereas a majority of the Chinese immigrants studied by Bansak et al. (2023) have at least a bachelor's degree, a majority of immigrants in our sample have less than a high school education. As a result, our population of interest more closely resembles the undocumented population currently present in the United States (Borjas, 2017). While our results are broadly consistent with those of prior work, there are a few differences worth noting. In contrast to Gihleb et al. (2023), we find that receiving legal status increases the likelihood that male immigrants marry. This difference may be a consequence of the fact that while both groups receive legal status, NACARA recipients can sponsor a spouse for legal status while DACA recipients cannot. Thus, NACARA increases recipients' attractiveness for undocumented partners. In contrast to our findings, Bansak et al. (2023) find that less-educated Chinese women become *more* likely to marry US natives after receiving legal status. This difference may be the result of the fact that the Chinese Student Protection Act provided legal status to all Chinese Nationals present in the United States. This may have meant that the value of legal status in the Chinese marriage market following the Chinese Student Protection Act was less than the value in the Central American marriage market following NACARA because many Central Americans present in the United States did not qualify for NACARA and needed legal status whereas few or no Chinese residents did.

Last, we contribute to a small literature examining the non-labor-market effects of immigrant amnesty. This prior work has found that receiving legal status leads to increased well-being and integration into the country of residence across a number of dimensions. Consistent with our findings, Gihleb et al. (2023) find that DACA-eligible immigrants are less likely to live in an ethnic enclave following the implementation of DACA in 2012. Moreover, they find that eligible immigrants become less likely to live with parents or in multigenerational households. Harris and Jerch (2023) find that Salvadoran immigrants to the United States experienced a 25% increase in homeownership following their receipt of Temporary Protected Status, which provided work permits and protection from deportation. Likewise, Ibanez et al. (2022) find that Venezuelan refugees in Colombia experienced improvements in physical and mental health upon gaining legal status through a large-scale government initiative (PEP, Permiso Especial de Permanencia), which provided full access to formal markets as well as social programs. Similarly, Mastrobuoni and Pinotti (2015) exploit legal status change associated with the expansion of the European Union, which is similar to an amnesty as it applies to all immigrants from the new member nations, and they show that there is a 50% reduction in recidivism among immigrants who gain legal status which explains more than half of the observed difference between documented and undocumented immigrant crime rates. We contribute to this literature by showing that receiving NACARA reduces immigrants' likelihood of living in an ethnic enclave.

4. DATA

We use the 2008–2012 American Community Surveys (ACSs). The ACS is a large, nationally representative survey with relatively rich demographic information. Beginning in 2008, it reports the number of times a respondent has been married and their year of marriage. This information, plus the respondent's year of naturalization, allows us to identify whether a foreign-born individual was naturalized at the time of marriage. We restrict our sample to adult immigrants (18–64) from El Salvador and Guatemala (our treatment group, NACARA Section 203) and immigrants from other Spanish-speaking Latin American countries (our control group: Colombia, Costa Rica, Dominican Republic, Ecuador, Mexico, Panama, Peru, and Venezuela).[3] We restrict our sample to those who arrived after 1987 (as earlier arrivers would have qualified for the Immigration Reform and Control Act of 1986) and to those who arrived prior to 1997 when NACARA was announced.

Table 1 presents descriptive statistics of this sample by country of origin and year of entry into the United States. Column 1 presents characteristics of Salvadorans and Guatemalans (treatment countries) who arrived in the United States prior to 1991 and who were thus eligible for NACARA (treated). Column 2 presents characteristics of Salvadorans and Guatemalans who arrived in the

Table 1. Descriptive Statistics by NACARA Eligibility (Pooled Sample).

	Treatment (NACARA)		Control	
	Arrived 88–90 (Treated) (1)	Arrived 91–97 (2)	Arrived 88–90 (3)	Arrived 91–97 (4)
Characteristics at arrival:				
El Salvador	0.643	0.602	0.000	0.000
	(0.479)	(0.489)	(0.000)	(0.000)
Guatemala	0.357	0.398	0.000	0.000
	(0.479)	(0.489)	(0.000)	(0.000)
Female	0.504	0.499	0.515	0.550
	(0.500)	(0.500)	(0.500)	(0.497)
Naturalized	0.297	0.202	0.304	0.210
	(0.457)	(0.402)	(0.460)	(0.407)

(Continued)

Table 1. (Continued)

	Treatment (NACARA)		Control	
	Arrived 88–90 (Treated)	Arrived 91–97	Arrived 88–90	Arrived 91–97
	(1)	(2)	(3)	(4)
Age at arrival	25.236	25.552	25.218	26.033
	(6.205)	(6.901)	(6.247)	(7.168)
Year of immigration	1989	1994	1989	1994
	(0.806)	(1.718)	(0.816)	(1.703)
Arrived married	0.259	0.279	0.435	0.474
	(0.438)	(0.448)	(0.496)	(0.499)
Contemporary characteristics:				
Age	46.126	41.962	46.092	42.311
	(6.354)	(7.218)	(6.418)	(7.383)
Never married	0.204	0.269	0.123	0.162
	(0.403)	(0.443)	(0.329)	(0.369)
Real income (2012 $)	25,394	23,436	23,558	21,086
	(27,250)	(25,142)	(29,743)	(28,650)
Own origin enclave (%)	2.541	2.282	12.366	10.968
	(2.717)	(2.558)	(10.267)	(9.916)
Education:				
Less than high school	0.575	0.578	0.531	0.534
	(0.494)	(0.494)	(0.499)	(0.499)
High school	0.276	0.272	0.292	0.291
	(0.447)	(0.445)	(0.455)	(0.454)
Some college	0.098	0.086	0.102	0.096
	(0.297)	(0.281)	(0.303)	(0.294)
Bachelor's degree	0.036	0.047	0.054	0.055
	(0.186)	(0.212)	(0.225)	(0.228)
Advanced degree	0.015	0.017	0.022	0.025
	(0.120)	(0.128)	(0.146)	(0.156)
N	4,621	5,382	26,443	45,412

Notes: This table reports descriptive statistics on a set of personal and spouse characteristics. The sample is composed of 2008–2012 ACS respondents who arrived in the United States as adults after 1987 and prior to 1997 from El Salvador and Guatemala (NACARA) or from our control group of Spanish-speaking countries, age 18–64. Each column reports sample means for a subgroup of respondents defined by country of origin and date of arrival to the United States.

United States after 1991—too late to be eligible for NACARA. Likewise, Columns 3 and 4 present the characteristics of immigrants from control countries who arrived before and after 1991. Overall, the four groups appear remarkably similar. Consistent with our identification strategy, the differences between those who arrived before and after 1991 are similar for immigrants from NACARA-eligible countries and immigrants from control countries. Approximately 64% of the treated group are from El Salvador and 36% from Guatemala, relative to 60 and 40% of those who are not eligible. Approximately, half of the sample is female. Sample members entered the United States at an average age of 25 and were an average age of 46 (for early arrivers) and 42 (for late arrivers) at the time of the survey. Approximately, 30% of early arrivers and 20% of late arrivers are naturalized. The sample has fairly low formal education, with more than half of the treatment and control group holding less than a high-school education, and is fairly low-income, with average real incomes below $25,000 (in 2012 dollars). The treatment and control groups differ more in marriage patterns—while fewer than 28% of immigrants from treatment countries arrived in the United States married, more than 40% of the control group did. Likewise, while 20% of treatment-group early arrivers and 27% of treatment-group late arrivers were unmarried at the time of the survey, only 12% of control-group early arrivers and 16% of control-group late arrivers were unmarried. These differences may be due in part to the greater difficulty of entering the United States from Central America relative to Mexico, which may discourage migration of families. We also explore the choice of residential location by measuring the percentage of people from the same country of origin in the geographic area, PUMA, an area of at least 100,000 people reported in the ACS. NACARA individuals live in PUMAs with an average of 2.3–2.5% of own nationals whereas our control group (largely composed of Mexican nationals who have a much larger presence in the United States in absolute numbers) lives in PUMAs of 11–12% of own nationals on average. The sample means for the male and female samples are presented in Appendix Tables A1 and A2.

NACARA was announced late in 1997 but required arrival by 1991 for eligibility (see Fig. 1). We use this retroactive feature to identify the differences in behavior using a triple difference estimation. This sample only includes individuals who are married for the first time, who were married after arrival to the United States (i.e.—married individuals who arrived unmarried), and were married prior to 2008.[4] Each column of Table 2 presents the differences in means of those whose marriage took place after 1997, i.e. after the announcement of NACARA, and those who married after arrival to the United States but in 1997 or before. For example, Column 1 shows the difference in mean characteristics for those who married after 1997 compared to those who married in 1997 or before, among immigrants from NACARA-eligible countries who entered the United States before 1991 (treated individuals). We find that among the treated group, those who married after 1997 were on average half a year younger at arrival to the United States than were those who married before 1998. We see this same difference among immigrants from NACARA-eligible countries who entered the United States too late to receive NACARA. Likewise, among the treated group, those who married after the policy announcement were 10 percentage-points less likely to be female and 10 percentage points less likely to

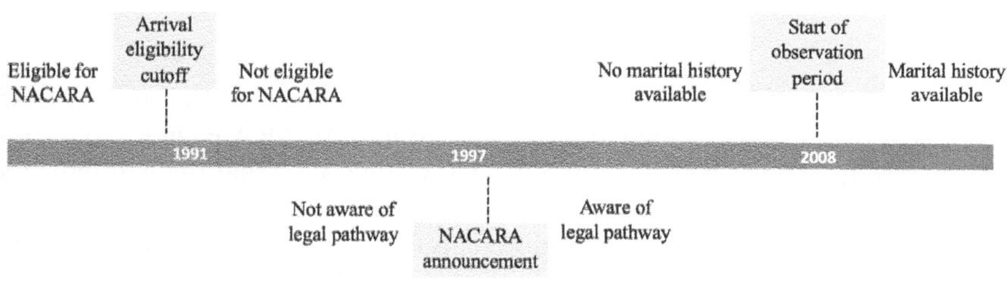

Fig. 1. NACARA Timeline.

Table 2. Difference in Means: Post-1997 Marriages—Arrival-to-1997 Marriages (Pooled Sample).

	Treatment (NACARA)		Control	
	Arrived 88–90 (Treated) (1)	Arrived 91–97 (2)	Arrived 88–90 (3)	Arrived 91–97 (4)
Characteristics at arrival:				
El Salvador	−0.028	−0.032	0.000	0.000
Guatemala	0.028	0.032	0.000	0.000
Female	−0.101	−0.135	−0.055	−0.111
Age at arrival	−0.468	−0.686	−0.051	−0.551
Year of immigration	0.202	1.093	0.177	1.136
Contemporary characteristics:				
Age	−0.632	−1.783	−0.206	−1.746
Real income (2012 $)	−803	1,642	−1,129	588
Own origin enclave (%)	0.323	0.023	0.311	−0.345
Parent(s) live in household	−0.017	−0.005	−0.003	−0.002
Spouse's parent(s) live in household	−0.005	0.006	0.000	0.006
Education:				
Less than high school	0.096	0.049	0.018	0.013
High school	−0.068	0.003	0.004	0.021
Some college	−0.028	−0.033	−0.010	−0.022
Bachelor's degree	−0.001	−0.016	−0.008	−0.010
Advanced degree	0.001	−0.004	−0.006	−0.001
Spouse's characteristics:				
Spouse's age	−2.730	−3.395	−1.495	−3.272
Spouse's education in years	−0.666	0.228	0.055	0.099
Spouse's income	−6,104	−3,920	−3,866	−4,517
Spouse married before	0.042	0.015	0.057	0.028
Spouse NACARA eligible	−0.149	−0.122	0.008	−0.004
Spouse is a marriage migrant	−0.077	−0.076	−0.139	−0.093
Spouse from same country	0.016	−0.031	−0.009	0.010
Spouse's citizenship:				
Spouse US born	−0.030	0.002	−0.009	−0.014
Spouse naturalized prior to marriage	0.021	0.020	0.054	0.022
Spouse naturalized after marriage	−0.197	−0.104	−0.141	−0.099
Spouse noncitizen	0.206	0.082	0.095	0.092

Notes: This table reports the differences in mean characteristics between respondents who married in 1998 or later (after NACARA was implemented) and respondents who married after arriving in the United States but no later than 1997. The sample is composed of 2008–2012 ACS respondents who arrived in the United States as adults after 1987 and prior to 1997 from El Salvador and Guatemala (NACARA) or from our control group of Spanish-speaking countries, age 18–64, and who arrived in the United States unmarried and have been married at least once.

have at least a high-school education. However, as shown in Column 2, these differences are similar among immigrants from NACARA-eligible countries who arrived too late to benefit from NACARA, suggesting that these differences are connected to the timing of marriage for reasons unrelated to the policy announcement. The corresponding differences in descriptive statistics for the male and female samples are in Appendix Tables A3 and A4.

5. EMPIRICAL STRATEGY

Our core empirical strategy exploits two eligibility rules for NACARA: eligible individuals must have entered the United States prior to 1991 and must have arrived from El Salvador or Guatemala. A natural way to use this strategy is to compare Salvadoran and Guatemalan immigrants to a control group in a difference-in-differences estimation, as in Kaushal (2006). However, this strategy faces a conceptual challenge because immigrants from El Salvador and Guatemala who arrived before 1991 were treated differently from immigrants who arrived in 1991 or later prior to the passage of NACARA. As discussed in Section 2, asylum seekers from El Salvador and Guatemala faced rejection rates of over 97% until a successful class-action lawsuit forced the INS to consider the individual merits of asylum cases. Following the lawsuit, Salvadoran and Guatemalan immigrants who had arrived prior to 1991 received some protection from deportation until they received permanent residence through NACARA. In addition, El Salvador and Guatemala experienced civil war and political turmoil throughout this period of migration, with conditions changing on a year-to-year basis. As a result of these factors, it is plausible that Salvadoran and Guatemalan immigrants who arrived before 1991 would be different from those who arrived after 1991 had NACARA never been enacted. Because this history is unique to El Salvador and Guatemala, these differences cannot be fully accounted for with the use of a control group.

We address this challenge in each of our analyses. When examining marriage, naturalization, and residence in an ethnic enclave, we use a standard difference-in-differences strategy but perform a battery of checks to show that our control group is broadly comparable to our treated group, as shown in Section 7. When examining characteristics of marriages, we address this challenge by using a triple-difference design, comparing marriages that occurred after arrival but before 1997 to marriages that occurred after 1997, when NACARA was announced. Because this design includes a control group of pre-1991 Salvadoran and Guatemalan immigrants, it can account for the consequences of asylum rules, civil war, and other factors that would lead to differences between pre-1991 and post-1991 Salvadoran and Guatemalan immigrants.

Our difference-in-differences strategy uses a treatment group consisting of Salvadorans and Guatemalans and a control group consisting of Spanish-speaking migrants from Latin American countries other than El Salvador and Guatemala. Those in our treatment group who arrived prior to 1991 were eligible for NACARA, while those who arrived after were not, as shown in Eq. (1):

$$\begin{aligned} Y_i = {} & \alpha + \beta_1 \text{NACARA}_i + \beta_2 \text{Pre-1991}_i + \beta_3 \text{NACARA}_i * \text{Pre-1991}_i \\ & + \delta_1 \text{Demographics}_i + \delta_c + \delta_t + \epsilon_i, \end{aligned} \tag{1}$$

where Y_i is a measure of naturalization status, never married status, and own country enclave percentage for person i observed in year t. β_3 estimates the treatment effect. Demographics_i includes a set of demographic characteristics that are unlikely to be affected either by receipt of NACARA or by choice of spouse. These characteristics include age, age at arrival to the United States, and education. In pooled estimates, they also include gender. Additionally, we add a broader set of control variables, including English language ability—these controls do not affect our estimates. δ_c and δ_t are year of immigration and survey year fixed effects. We further stratify the sample by sex.

Next, we exclude those who have never been married before and estimate a triple-difference model to evaluate the effect of receiving NACARA on the characteristics of marriages and spouses. In the triple-difference specification, treated individuals are those who were born in El Salvador or Guatemala (NACARA), who entered the United States before 1991 (Pre-1991), and who were married after 1997—after NACARA had been announced (Post-1997 marriage). The regression specification is shown below in Eq. (2):

$$\begin{aligned} Y_i = {} & \alpha + \beta_1 \text{NACARA}_i + \beta_2 \text{Pre-1991}_i + \beta_3 \text{NACARA}_i * \text{Pre-1991}_i \\ & + \beta_4 \text{Post-1997Marriage}_i + \beta_5 \text{NACARA}_i * \text{Post-1997Marriage}_i \\ & + \beta_6 \text{Pre-1991}_i * \text{Post-1997Marriage}_i \\ & + \beta_7 \text{NACARA}_i * \text{Pre-1991}_i * \text{Post-1997Marriage}_i \\ & + \delta_1 \text{Demographics}_i + \delta_c + \delta_t + \epsilon_i, \end{aligned} \tag{2}$$

We also estimate the following event studies of marriage timing using Eq. (3), which replaces Post-1997Marriage$_i$ in Eq. (2) with a series of year-of-marriage indicators. This allows us to evaluate the presence of pretrends and show any dynamic effects:

$$\begin{aligned} Y_i = {} & \alpha + \beta_1 \text{NACARA}_i + \beta_2 \text{Pre-1991}_i + \beta_3 \text{NACARA}_i * \text{Pre-1991}_i \\ & + \textstyle\sum_{t=-4}^{-1} \sigma_4^\tau \cdot 1(M = 1997 + \tau)_i \\ & + \sigma_5^\tau \text{NACARA}_i * \cdot 1(M = 1997 + \tau)_i \\ & + \sigma_6^\tau \text{Pre-1991}_i * \cdot 1(M = 1997 + \tau)_i \\ & + \textstyle\sum_{t=10}^{1} \rho_4^\tau \cdot 1(M = 1997 + \tau)_i \\ & + \rho_5^\tau \text{NACARA}_i * \cdot 1(M = 1997 + \tau)_i \\ & + \rho_6^\tau \text{Pre-1991}_i * \cdot 1(M = 1997 + \tau)_i \\ & + \textstyle\sum_{t=-4}^{-1} \sigma_7^\tau \text{NACARA}_i * \text{Pre-1991}_i * \cdot 1(M = 1997 + \tau)_i \\ & + \textstyle\sum_{t=10}^{1} \rho_7^\tau \text{NACARA}_i * \text{Pre-1991}_i * \cdot 1(M = 1997 + \tau)_i \\ & + \delta_1 \text{Demographics}_i + \delta_c + \delta_t + \epsilon_i, \end{aligned} \tag{3}$$

where Y_i is the outcome for person i. The indicator function: $1(M = 1997{+}\tau)_i$ equals one if the respondent's current marriage took place in the year $1997{+}\tau$. We examine the existence of pretrends up to four years prior to this adoption date as captured by coefficients σ_7^τ. The coefficients ρ_7^τ measure the differential policy dynamics annually for 10 years after the announcement of NACARA.

6. RESULTS

In Table 3, we use a difference-in-differences approach to examine whether Salvadorans and Guatemalans who arrived in the United States prior to 1991, and thus qualified for NACARA, are more likely to be naturalized (Columns 1, 4, and 7), more likely to remain unmarried (Columns 2, 5, and 8), and more likely to live in an ethnic enclave with a higher concentration of immigrants from their own country of origin (Columns 3, 6, and 9). We estimate the model on three samples: pooled, men only, and women only.

Surprisingly, we do not find evidence that NACARA eligibility increased rates of naturalization. This result may be a consequence of slow take-up of permanent residency through NACARA (Kaushal, 2006) combined with hesitancy to naturalize among those who intend to eventually return to Central America.[5] Meanwhile, we find that eligibility for NACARA reduces the likelihood of remaining unmarried by 2.4 percentage points in the pooled sample. This increase in marriage rates is concentrated among men, who experience a 4 percentage point decrease—a 20% reduction relative to the 18.2% of men who are unmarried.[6] This is consistent with NACARA eligibility increasing recipients' attractiveness as a spouse. In addition, we find that NACARA eligibility reduces the likelihood of living in an ethnic enclave (which we define as the percentage of residents in a respondent's PUMA born in the same country as the respondent). This may be a consequence of increased access to the formal labor and housing markets for those with permanent legal status. This result suggests that NACARA eligibility may increase contact between recipients and US natives.

We next analyze the characteristics of marriages and spouses using a triple-difference approach that compares marriages that occurred by the end of 1997, when NACARA was announced, to those that occurred after 1997. In this approach, the "treated" group comprises of Salvadorans and Guatemalans who arrived in the United States before 1991 and were married in 1998 or later. Table 4 presents the triple difference coefficients of interest from separate regression models. Each row represents an outcome variable from a regression estimated on the pooled sample (Column 1), men only (Column 2), and women only (Column 3). Appendix Tables A5, A6, and A7 present the full sets of interactions.

Because receiving permanent legal status likely makes treated individuals more attractive to potential partners and reduces their need to marry a citizen spouse, we expect treated individuals to marry more compatible or desirable spouses relative to control individuals. The spouses of treated individuals do appear to be of higher quality along at least one dimension—their spouses are almost one year younger on average. However, somewhat surprisingly, their spouses are also less educated, less likely to become citizens, and lower-earning, suggesting either that permanent legal status is not helpful in attracting a higher-earning or more highly educated spouse or that these characteristics are not highly valued by this population. These findings present an interesting comparison to the literature. Our finding that permanent legal status increases

Table 3. The Impact of NACARA on Marriage, Naturalization, and Residence in Ethnic Enclave.

	Pooled			Men			Women		
	Naturalized (1)	Never married (2)	Own origin enclave (%) (3)	Naturalized (4)	Never married (5)	Own origin enclave (%) (6)	Naturalized (7)	Never married (8)	Own origin enclave (%) (9)
NACARA	−0.003	−0.024***	−1.153***	−0.015	−0.040***	−1.210***	0.008	−0.008	−1.100***
*Pre-1991	(0.009)	(0.008)	(0.093)	(0.012)	(0.012)	(0.133)	(0.012)	(0.011)	(0.130)
NACARA	0.004	0.094***	−8.615***	0.001	0.098***	−8.329***	0.007	0.087***	−8.887***
	(0.005)	(0.006)	(0.059)	(0.007)	(0.009)	(0.084)	(0.008)	(0.008)	(0.083)
Pre-1991	0.085***	−0.072***	1.089***	0.102***	−0.096***	0.931***	0.069***	−0.045***	1.218***
	(0.011)	(0.009)	(0.235)	(0.015)	(0.013)	(0.340)	(0.015)	(0.012)	(0.326)
Mean	0.245	0.159	10.373	0.225	0.182	10.039	0.262	0.139	10.665
N	90,629	90,629	90,629	42,141	42,141	42,141	48,488	48,488	48,488
R-squared	0.131	0.027	0.126	0.110	0.034	0.120	0.151	0.019	0.132

Notes: This table reports OLS estimation results from the difference-in-differences regression described in Eq. (1) on a respondent's citizenship status, marriage, and the percentage of residents in the respondent's PUMA who were born in the same country as the respondent. Estimates are run on a sample of 2008–2012 ACS respondents who arrived in the United States as adults after 1987 and prior to 1997 from El Salvador and Guatemala (NACARA) or from our control group of Spanish-speaking countries, age 18–64. As described in the text, the regression estimates include controls for age, age at arrival to the United States, education, survey-year fixed effects, and year-of-immigration fixed effects. In the pooled sample, we also control for gender.

Table 4. The Impact of NACARA on the Characteristics of Spouse and Marriage.

	Pooled		Men		Women	
	NACARA* Pre-1991* Post-97 marriage	Mean	NACARA* Pre-1991* Post-97 marriage	Mean	NACARA* Pre-1991* Post-97 marriage	Mean
Spouse's characteristics:						
Spouse's age	−0.774*	40.777	−0.825	38.525	−0.837	43.577
	(0.443)		(0.597)		(0.687)	
Spouse's education in years	−0.773**	8.790	−0.624	8.923	−0.924*	8.623
	(0.334)		(0.459)		(0.497)	
Spouse's income (ln)	−0.166	8.237	0.087	6.236	−0.303	10.724
	(0.282)		(0.490)		(0.219)	
Spouse married before	0.001	0.132	−0.009	0.110	0.001	0.158
	(0.025)		(0.032)		(0.039)	
Spouse NACARA eligible	−0.037	0.070	−0.106***	0.052	0.020	0.093
	(0.031)		(0.039)		(0.048)	
Spouse is a marriage migrant	0.037	0.205	0.072*	0.292	−0.012	0.097
	(0.025)		(0.042)		(0.026)	
Spouse from same country	0.068**	0.742	0.070	0.739	0.058	0.746
	(0.034)		(0.047)		(0.050)	
Spouse's citizenship:						
Spouse US born	−0.040*	0.154	−0.037	0.166	−0.046	0.139
	(0.021)		(0.032)		(0.030)	
Spouse naturalized prior to marriage	−0.030	0.079	−0.016	0.062	−0.041	0.100
	(0.019)		(0.025)		(0.032)	
Spouse naturalized after marriage	−0.048*	0.171	−0.075**	0.143	0.002	0.205
	(0.027)		(0.036)		(0.042)	
Spouse noncitizen	0.118***	0.597	0.128***	0.629	0.086*	0.556
	(0.033)		(0.046)		(0.051)	
Contemporary characteristics:						
Own origin enclave (%)	−0.346	9.813	−0.376	9.703	−0.373	9.951
	(0.343)		(0.457)		(0.537)	
Parent(s) live in household	−0.012	0.037	−0.009	0.030	−0.015	0.046
	(0.013)		(0.016)		(0.021)	
Spouse's parent(s) live in household	−0.005	0.039	−0.035*	0.044	0.037**	0.033
	(0.014)		(0.021)		(0.018)	
N	26,495		14,682		11,813	

Notes: This table reports OLS estimation results from the triple-difference regression described in Eq. (2), on a set of outcomes related to the respondent's spouse's citizenship and nativity the spouse's personal characteristics, and the characteristics of the household at the time of the survey. Estimates are run on a sample of 2008–2012 ACS respondents who arrived in the United States as adults after 1987 and prior to 1997 from El Salvador and Guatemala (NACARA) or from our control group of Spanish-speaking countries, age 18–64, and who arrived in the United States unmarried and have been married at least once. As described in the text, the regression estimates include controls for age, age at arrival to the United States, education, survey-year fixed effects, and year-of-immigration fixed effects. In the pooled sample, we also control for gender.

recipients' likelihood of marrying a younger spouse from their country of origin is consistent with prior work on Chinese immigrants in the United States (Bansak et al., 2023). However, Bansak et al. (2023) find that receiving permanent legal status increased the education and earnings of recipients' spouses among highly educated Chinese immigrants but had less pronounced effects for lower-educated Chinese immigrants. We thus speculate that this difference in findings is a result of the fact that NACARA recipients have on average much less education than did Chinese immigrants affected by the Chinese Student Protection Act.

We find that NACARA-eligible individuals who entered marriages after the announcement of the policy are 4 percentage points less likely to marry a US native and 11.8 percentage points more likely to marry a noncitizen. These findings likely come through two channels. Immigrants value their spouse's citizenship less when they have an independent pathway to permanent residency. Furthermore, the ability to sponsor their spouse for permanent residency likely makes NACARA recipients more attractive to those who do not have an independent pathway to permanent residency. Consistent with the hypothesis that treated individuals are sought out by those without an independent pathway to permanent residency, we find that men who are eligible for NACARA are 10.6 percentage points less likely to marry a spouse who is eligible for NACARA. Perhaps due to a reduced need to marry a citizen, treated individuals are also 6.8 percentage points more likely to marry a spouse from their country of origin. These results are stronger for male beneficiaries, but the coefficients for women are qualitatively similar and in the same direction.

Last, we conduct an exploratory analysis of bargaining power in the household by estimating the probability that a recipient lives with their own parents or with their spouse's parents (in-laws). We hypothesize that most people prefer to care for and live with their own parents than to care for and live with their in-laws. Interestingly, we do not observe any difference in the probability of one's in-laws living in the same household in the pooled sample, but we do, however, observe differences by gender. While NACARA reduces the probability that male beneficiaries live with their in-laws, it increases the probability for female beneficiaries.

We speculate that NACARA eligibility affects the probability of living with in-laws in two ways. NACARA potentially increases the probability that in-laws live with a couple by facilitating parents' immigration to the United States. While permanent residents cannot sponsor parents for immigration visas, holding permanent residency likely makes it easier for parents to enter the United States on a tourist visa and to safely live in the United States without permanent legal status.[7] At the same time, receipt of NACARA potentially decreases the probability that in-laws live in the household by increasing the NACARA-eligible spouse's bargaining power within the marriage.[8] Because, culturally, caring for parents is typically the responsibility of women, we speculate that women may be less likely to use their bargaining power within the household to exclude their in-laws from the household. As a result, while the bargaining power channel may be larger than the immigration channel for men, the opposite may be true for women.

6.1 Treatment on Treated

Because this paper estimates the effects of NACARA by comparing a treatment group that is likely to be eligible for NACARA to a control group that is ineligible, the estimates are likely smaller than the effect of NACARA for those who were directly affected by the policy. Approximately, 290,000 Salvadorans and Guatemalans were eligible to apply for benefits under NACARA, constituting nearly 70% of the 420,000 Salvadorans and Guatemalans who entered the United States between 1980 and 1990 Kaushal (2006). Thus, if NACARA had no effect on ineligible immigrants, the effects of NACARA on the eligible population are likely approximately 40% higher than the estimates reported in this paper. In addition, among eligible immigrants, fewer than 2/3 received benefits by 2012. Thus, if only those who received NACARA benefits were affected by the policy, the effects on recipients would be approximately 2.3 times higher than the estimates reported in the chapter. However, it is plausible that NACARA influenced the marriages of all eligible immigrants, even those who did not receive benefits, because of the knowledge that they could apply for and receive benefits if necessary.

6.2 Event Studies

We show event studies for the three marriage outcomes for which our pooled triple-difference estimates were statistically significant at the 5% level: whether the respondent's spouse is a noncitizen, whether the respondent's spouse is from the same country of origin as the respondent, and the respondent's spouse's years of education. These event studies serve two purposes: they provide suggestive evidence on the dynamics of the triple-difference estimates and they provide evidence for the plausibility of the parallel trends assumption underlying the estimates. Because the sample of marriages occurring in each year is small, our analysis of the timing of effects is speculative.

We present these event studies in Fig. 2. Each figure plots the coefficients on an indicator of whether a person is Salvadoran or Guatemalan, entered the United States before 1991 (and is thus eligible for NACARA) and was married in year *t*, where *t* takes values from 1993 to 2007. Because NACARA was announced in 1997, estimates for marriages between 1993 and 1995 are pretrends while estimates for marriages between 1997 and 2007 are estimated treatment effects. 1996 is the omitted year. We plot 95% confidence intervals around each estimated effect.

Notes: This figure reports OLS estimation results and 95% confidence intervals from the event study regression described in Eq. (3), on a sample of ACS respondents from 2008 to 2012 who arrived in the United States as adults after 1987 and prior to 1997 from El Salvador and Guatemala (NACARA) or from our control group of Spanish-speaking countries, age 18–64. The horizontal axis indexes a respondent's year of marriage, with an omitted year of 1996. Marriages taking place after 1996 were plausibly influenced by the implementation of NACARA while marriages taking place in 1996 or before

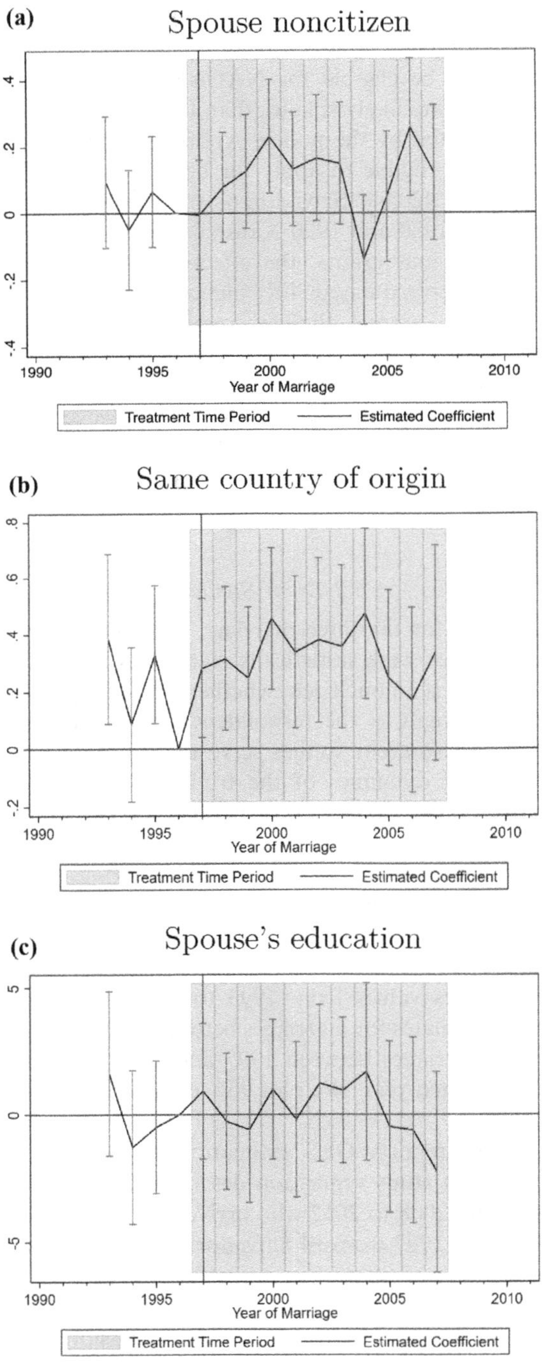

Fig. 2. Event Studies.

could not have been affected by NACARA. Each panel presents event study estimates for one of our primary outcomes of interest.

As shown in Panel A, we see no meaningful trend in event-study estimates of whether respondents' spouses were noncitizens for years of marriage prior to 1997. In 1998 and later, when NACARA was in effect, the estimated effect on marrying a noncitizen spouse was higher in most years than in pretreatment years, consistent with the effect of 0.118 shown in Table 4. We find suggestive evidence that this treatment effect grew in the first three years of enactment—perhaps due to effects being larger for relationships formed after NACARA went into effect.

As shown in Panel B, we find some evidence of a downward trend in event study estimates of whether respondents' spouses were from their country of origin in years prior to 1997.[9] After NACARA went into effect, we see that effect on the probability of marrying a spouse from the respondent's country of origin was higher than the average effect in pretreatment years, consistent with the effect of 0.068 shown in Table 4. We find suggestive evidence that this effect was stable and persistent throughout the post-treatment period.

Last, as shown in Panel C, we see no meaningful trend in event-study estimates of the years of education for the respondents' spouse for years of marriage prior to 1997. After NACARA went into effect, we see estimated treatment effects are close to zero in most years. The decline in spouse's education of −0.773 shown in Table 4 appears to occur only at the end of our sample period.

7. VALIDATION

In this section, we perform two checks to address concerns about the validity of our empirical strategy. First, we address the possibility that effect estimates are driven by differences in sample attrition following the passage of NACARA by estimating the retention rate of our treated and control groups. Next, we address the possibility that the treated groups in our difference-in-differences and triple-difference designs are not comparable to our control groups by performing several placebo regressions on individual characteristics that could not have been affected by NACARA.

7.1 Sample Attrition

We use data from 2008 to 2012 to examine the effect of a policy implemented in 1997; thus, our sample only includes individuals who remained in the United States until 2008 and who responded to the ACS. As a result, the composition of our sample might be influenced by differences between survey respondents and nonrespondents, death, deportation, and voluntary return migration. If these factors lead NACARA-eligible individuals with strong ties to their home country to remain in the sample at higher rates than do NACARA-ineligible individuals, they could account for the higher rate at which NACARA-eligible individuals marry noncitizen spouses and spouses from their home countries.

This figure shows the estimated population of sample members present in the United States in each year from 2000 to 2012 as a percentage of the 2000 population. The figure divides the sample population into four groups on the basis of country of origin and date of arrival to the United States. As described in the text, "early arrivers" entered the United States between 1988 and 1990 while "late arrivers" entered the country between 1991 and 1997. Note that attrition reflects a combination of migration out of the United States and changes in survey nonresponse. As a consequence, it is possible for the estimated population to increase due to increased survey response rates. As discussed in the text, survey response rates increased for likely undocumented immigrants after the 2000 census.

We examine this possibility by measuring the rate of sample attrition for the treatment and control groups from 2000 to 2012. Using the 2000 Census and the 2001–2012 ACS, we count the number of Spanish-speaking respondents who were born in Latin America and entered the United States between 1988 and 1997, weighted by the ACS and Census sample weights. This produces an annual estimate of the number of individuals by country of origin and by year of arrival who are present in the United States and responding to the ACS. To estimate sample retention, we divide these annual estimates of the total population by the estimated total population in 2000. We perform this exercise for four subgroups defined by country of origin (El Salvador and Guatemala vs. control countries) and year of arrival (those arriving between 1988 and 1990 and those arriving between 1991 and 1997).

Fig. 3 shows the percentage of individuals present in 2000 who remained in the sample in each year from 2001 to 2012 for four subgroups: Salvadoran and Guatemalan early arrivers (NACARA-eligible), control-country early arrivers, Salvadoran and Guatemalan late arrivers and control-country late arrivers. Each plotted point represents the ratio of the estimated population of a group in the ACS year to the estimated population of the group in the 2000 census. Because ACS response rates have increased over time, particularly for undocumented immigrants (Van Hook et al., 2014; Warren, 2020), this ratio can increase or decrease over time.[10] The increase in retention rate from 2004 to 2005 is thus likely a result of this increased survey response. We find that those who arrived before 1990 (denoted with solid lines), regardless of NACARA eligibility, had a higher rate of sample attrition than those who arrived after 1990, particularly after 2007. This difference may be a consequence of age differences between early and late arrivers, as early arrivers are five years older than late arrivers on average.

We observe nearly identical patterns of sample retention among late arrivers (dashed lines) from El Salvador and Guatemala and from control countries. Early arrivers from El Salvador and Guatemala (NACARA-eligible—solid black line) were somewhat less likely to remain in the sample compared to the early arrivers from control countries (solid gray line). For instance, in 2011, 39% of Salvadoran and Guatemalan early arrivers remained in the sample, relative to 46% of the control group early arrivers. This difference may be a consequence of receipt of NACARA—because NACARA recipients hold green cards, they can

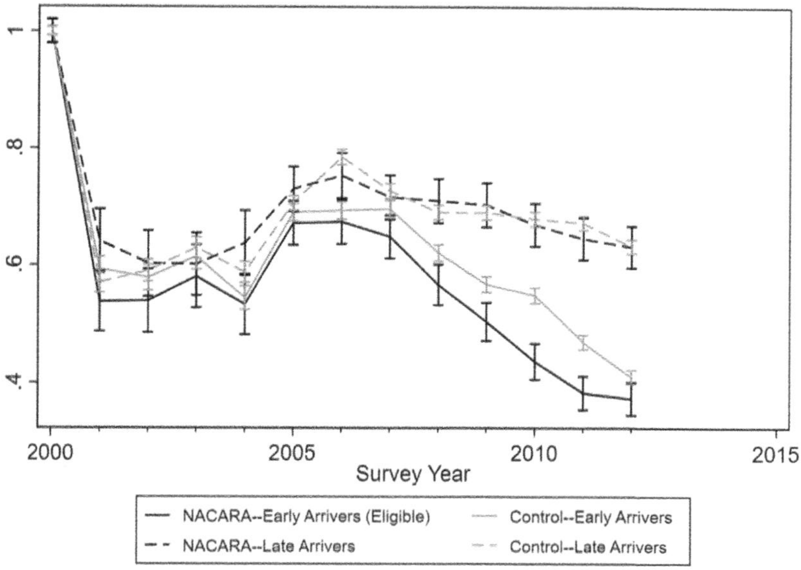

Fig. 3. Sample Retention From 2000 to 2012.

live outside of the United States without compromising their ability to return. Thus, green card-holding households might have been more likely to leave the United States during the 2008 recession. Despite the slight divergence, the overall trend of these two groups of early arrivers is similar.

This figure replicates Fig. 3 for six subgroups defined by gender, education, and English language ability. Panels A and B show attrition rates for female vs male respondents. Panels C and D show attrition rates for respondents without a high school diploma vs respondents with at least a high school diploma. Panels E and F show attrition rates for respondents who reported that they did not speak English or did not speak English well vs respondents who reported speaking English well, speaking English very well, or speaking English exclusively.

These small differences in attrition from the sample only result in bias to our estimates if the characteristics of those remaining in the sample differ from the characteristics of those leaving the sample. We explore this by examining attrition for several subgroups, defined by gender, education, and English language ability. As shown in Fig. 4, we find that the pattern of attrition is broadly consistent across characteristics. We do observe small differences in sample retention between groups by education and English language ability. In particular, we find that among those with at least a high-school education (Panel D), retention is somewhat higher for late-arriving Salvadorans and Guatemalans than for late-arriving control immigrants. In contrast, retention is somewhat lower for early-arriving Salvadorans and Guatemalans (NACARA-eligible) than for early-arriving control immigrants, particularly after 2007. Similarly, we find that the difference in sample retention between eligible and ineligible

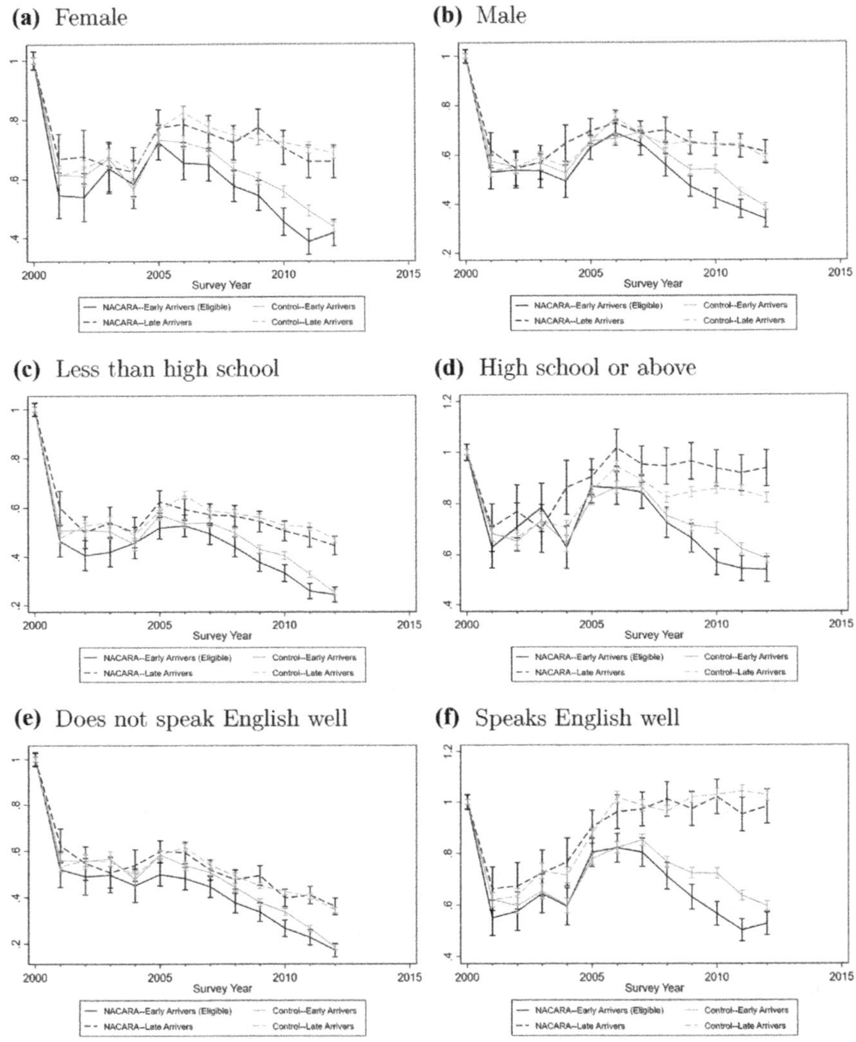

Fig. 4. Sample Retention by Characteristics.

early arrivers (solid lines) is somewhat larger for those who report that they speak English well than for those who report that they do not speak English well. We believe that these small differences in sample retention are unlikely to bias our results because adding controls for education and for English language ability has no effect on our estimated coefficients in our double-difference or triple-difference specifications, as shown in Appendix Tables A8 and A9.

7.2 Placebo Tests

We test the validity of our empirical strategy by examining four fixed characteristics of individuals that could not have been affected by receiving NACARA: whether a respondent was married at arrival to the United States, the respondent's sex, the respondent's age at arrival, and the respondent's years of education. For each of these characteristics, we estimate our double-difference (Equation 1). Because the sample of our triple-difference regression (Equation 2) is limited to those who were unmarried at arrival, we only examine the gender, age, and education of respondents. Since marriage at arrival, sex, and age at arrival were determined prior to entry to the United States, they could only be affected by NACARA if they influenced sample selection through return migration, death, or survey nonresponse, which we discuss in the previous section. Years of education could plausibly be affected by receipt of NACARA, but because our sample has very low average educational attainment and arrived in the United States as adults, sample members are very likely to have completed their education by the time they entered the United States and particularly by the time NACARA was enacted. As a result, we expect NACARA eligibility to have little to no effect on any of these outcomes.

As shown in Table 5, we find that treated respondents in our double-difference analysis are approximately five months older, on average, than control groups and 3 percentage points more likely to be female. However, we find no differences in the likelihood that respondents arrived unmarried, and no differences in education. Some differences between the treated and control groups are unsurprising—as discussed in Section 2, Salvadorans and Guatemalans who arrived in the United States before 1990 and were thus eligible for NACARA faced much higher rejection rates for asylum than those who entered after 1990. These differences are unlikely to substantially influence our estimates both because their magnitudes are small and because our estimates are not sensitive to controls for age or sex.

Table 5. The Impact of NACARA—Placebo Checks.

	Double Difference NACARA*Pre-1991			Triple Difference NACARA*Pre-1991 Post-97 Marriage		
	Pooled	Male	Female	Pooled	Male	Female
Arrived unmarried	0.002	0.006	−0.001			
	(0.009)	(0.012)	(0.013)			
N	83,680	39,274	44,406			
R-squared	0.193	0.246	0.125			
Female	0.033***			−0.021		
	(0.010)			(0.036)		
N	93,609			26,495		
R-squared	0.013			0.025		
Age at arrival	0.430***	0.475***	0.379*	−0.396	−0.191	−0.649
	(0.139)	(0.183)	(0.212)	(0.367)	(0.498)	(0.549)
N	47,946	25,910	22,036	26,495	14,682	11,813
R-squared	0.039	0.029	0.033	0.043	0.040	0.036

(Continued)

Table 5. *(Continued)*

	Double Difference NACARA*Pre-1991			Triple Difference NACARA*Pre-1991 Post-97 Marriage		
	Pooled	Male	Female	Pooled	Male	Female
Years of education	−0.065	−0.151	0.037	−0.127	−0.339	0.286
	(0.069)	(0.094)	(0.103)	(0.200)	(0.271)	(0.300)
N	47,946	25,910	22,036	26,495	14,682	11,813
R-squared	0.015	0.016	0.017	0.017	0.020	0.021

Notes: This table reports OLS estimation results from the regressions described in Eqs. (1) and (2) on a set of outcomes that are unlikely to have been affected by NACARA eligibility. The double-difference columns report estimates of Eq. (1) on a sample of 2008–2012 ACS respondents who arrived in the United States as adults after 1987 and prior to 1997 from El Salvador and Guatemala (NACARA) or from our control group of Spanish-speaking countries, age 18–64. The triple-difference columns report estimates of Eq. (2) on a sample further restricted to respondents who arrived unmarried and have been married at least once. Because the triple-difference estimates use a sample who arrived unmarried, we omit the "arrived unmarried" dependent variable.

In the triple-difference specification, which is our preferred estimation strategy, we find no statistically significant or substantively meaningful differences between NACARA-eligible respondents who married after NACARA was enacted and the control groups. Furthermore, the direction of coefficients is opposite to the double-difference specification for sex and age at arrival. Because this specification includes a control group that arrived in the United States from El Salvador and Guatemala prior to 1991, it is protected from the possible bias from changes in asylum that may affect the difference-in-differences results.

8. CONCLUSION

This paper shows that the insecurity of uncertain legal status profoundly affects even the most intimate life choices. We examine how marriages are impacted by NACARA—a policy that provided permanent legal status to previously undocumented Guatemalan and Salvadoran immigrants. Because NACARA was announced in 1997 but only affected individuals who entered the United States prior to 1991, it provides a unique opportunity to study the choices of undocumented immigrants before and after receiving legal status. After becoming eligible for permanent legal status through NACARA, we find that treated individuals become more likely to marry, suggesting that legal status improves one's prospects in the marriage market.

Moreover, among eligible individuals, spouses of those who married after NACARA was announced differ in several respects from spouses of those who married after entering the United States but before they knew that they would become eligible for permanent residency. These changes in characteristics of the spouse are consistent with eligible individuals choosing a spouse in accordance with their preferences rather than choosing a spouse who can provide them with a pathway to a secure legal status in the United States. For instance, we find that eligible individuals who married after NACARA went into effect were less likely to marry a US citizen than were those who married before knowing that they would qualify for legal status through NACARA. In turn, we find that those who married later marry younger spouses, on average. Likewise, they were more likely to marry a spouse from their country of origin, which may be desirable due to cultural similarity. These results are particularly striking because we find that NACARA-eligible individuals are less likely to live in an ethnic enclave, suggesting that they are marrying within their community of origin at higher rates despite greater exposure to people outside of their community of origin.

These findings suggest that people who do not have a pathway to permanent status are sometimes willing to give up things that they care about in order to obtain legal security by marrying a citizen or permanent resident. Thus, citizens and permanent residents who marry those without permanent legal status are likely to have substantial bargaining power within the household. Because the announcement of NACARA led men to marry noncitizens and women who are not themselves eligible for NACARA at higher rates, we expect NACARA-eligible men to have more bargaining power in marriages that occurred after the announcement of the policy. Consistent with this hypothesis, men are less likely to live with their in-laws if they marry after receiving NACARA. This suggestive finding should encourage further research into the effects of legal status on intra-household dynamics, particularly on dynamics of deep importance to policy such as domestic violence, financial autonomy, and fertility.

NOTES

1. Excepting those who had been convicted of crimes with a more than six-month sentence.

2. The LIFE Act applied to all immigrants who were present in the United States on the day of the amendment (December 21, 2000) and remained in effect until April 30, 2001. The LIFE Act amended Section 245i of the Immigration and Nationality Act of 1994. Section 245i allowed adjustment of immigration status regardless of the mode of entry into the United States provided that applicants had a labor certification or immigrant visa petition filed before a designated deadline. This deadline changed several times before being finalized on January 14, 1998. Thus, illegal entrants to the United States were able to receive permanent legal status by marrying a citizen between 1994 and 1998 and in the four months covered by the LIFE Act in 2001.

3. We exclude Nicaragua and Cuba, which were included in NACARA Section 202. We follow Kaushal (2006) who excludes Hondurans to avoid potential contamination of the analysis, as they were granted temporary protected status in 1999 following Hurricane Mitch. However, our results are robust to using a control group that includes Honduras (not shown here).

4. We want to avoid the issues of censored data with cross-sectional surveys. Those who married in 2009 and are observed in 2008 would appear as not married at the time of the survey, but if they were observed in 2010, they would appear as married. Therefore, we only look at those who married prior to the first survey year.

5. The 2021 Congressional Research Service report identifies these countries as one of the least likely to naturalize (https://crsreports.congress.gov/product/pdf/R/R43366).

6. This effect may be concentrated among men because men's probability of marriage is more dependent than women's on "marriageability." For instance, Gibson-Davis (2009) finds that low-income men are more likely to marry following an increase in income, but low-income women are not.

7. Consistent with this hypothesis, we find that the positive effect for women on living with a spouse's parent is driven entirely by noncitizen spouses. In addition, more than 90% of co-resident parents were born outside of the United States.

8. Consistent with this hypothesis, we find that sample members are less likely to live with their spouse's parents when their spouse is a noncitizen and thus has less bargaining power in the relationship.

9. This downward trend may be due to the increase in immigration from Mexico during the mid-1990s (Cohn & Gonzalez-Barra, 2017). This may have increased the pool of potential spouses from the same country of origin for Mexicans who arrived in the United States after 1991 more than it did for Mexicans who arrived prior to 1991 or for Guatemalans and Salvadorans who arrived after 1991.

10. In particular, a larger share of the sample is retained in 2005 than in the years 2001 through 2004. This is likely due to the fact that the early years of the ACS had relatively low response rates and were not nationally representative.

REFERENCES

Adda, J., Pinotti, P., & Tura, G. (2020). *There's more to marriage than love: The effect of legal status and cultural distance on intermarriages and separations*. CEPR Discussion Paper No. DP14432, London.

Amuedo-Dorantes, C., Arenas-Arroyo, E., & Wang, C. (2020). Is immigration enforcement shaping immigrant marriage patterns? *Journal of Public Economics*, *190*, 104242.

Azzolini, D., & Guetto, R. (2017). The impact of citizenship on intermarriage: Quasi-experimental evidence from two European Union Eastern enlargements. *Demographic Research*, *36*, 1299–1336.

Balgamwalla, S. (2013). Bride and prejudice: How the u.s. immigration law discriminates against spousal visa holders. *Berkeley Journal of Gender, Law, and Justice*, *29* (02).

Bansak, C., Dziadula, E., & Zavodny, M. (2023). The value of a green card in the U.S. marriage market: A tale of chain migration? *China Economic Review*, *82*(C).

Bau, I. (1985). *This ground is Holy: Church sanctuary and central American refugees*. Paulist Press. Original from University of Texas, Digitized Mar 7, 2008.

Becker, G. S. (1973). A theory of marriage: Part I. *Journal of Political Economy*, *81*(4), 813–846.

Becker, G. S. (1974). A theory of marriage: Part II. *Journal of Political Economy*, *82*(2, Part 2), S11–S26.

Borjas, G. (2017). The labor supply of undocumented immigrants. *Labour Economics*, *46*(C), 1–13.

Choi, K. H., Tienda, M., Cobb-Clark, D., & Sinning, M. (2012). Immigration and status exchange in Australia and the United States. *Research in Social Stratification and Mobility*, *30*(1), 49–62.

Cohn, P., & Gonzalez-Barra. (2017). *Rise in u.s. immigrants from El Salvador, guatemala and honduras outpaces growth from elsewhere*. Technical report.

Congressional Research Service. (2023). *Nonimmigrant and immigrant visa categories: Data brief*. Technical Report R45938.

Dziadula, E. (2020). Marriage and citizenship among US immigrants: Who marries whom and who becomes a citizen? *Eastern Economic Journal*, *46*(1), 34–52.

Dziadula, E. (2022). Match quality and divorce among naturalized US citizens. *Southern Economic Journal*, *89*(1), 37–61.

Dziadula, E., & Zavodny, M. (2023). Finding love abroad: Who marries a migrant and what do they gain? *Review of Economics of the Household*, 1–26.

Furtado, D. (2012). Human capital and interethnic marriage decisions. *Economic Inquiry*, *50*(1), 82–93.

Gibson-Davis, C. M. (2009). Money, marriage, and children: Testing the financial expectations and family formation theory. *Journal of Marriage and Family*, *71*(1), 146–160.

Gihleb, R., Giuntella, O., & Lonsky, J. (2023). Dreaming of leaving the nest? Immigration status and the living arrangements of dacamented. *European Economic Review*, *156*, 104447.

Harris, J., & Jerch, R. (2023). *The long-run effects of temporary protection from deportation*. The Center for Growth and Opportunity.

Ibanez, A., Moya, A., Shieber, W., Rozo, S., & Urbina, M. (2022). *Life out of the shadows: Impacts of amnesties in the lives of migrants*.

Kaushal, N. (2006). Amnesty programs and the labor market outcomes of undocumented workers. *Journal of Human Resources*, *41*(3), 631–647.

Kelly, C. S. (2010). The influence of a change in immigration law on us marriage rates. *Eastern Economic Journal*, *36*, 500–522.

Lichter, D. T., Qian, Z., & Tumin, D. (2015). Whom do immigrants marry? Emerging patterns of intermarriage and integration in the United States. *The Annals of the American Academy of Political and Social Science*, *662*(1), 57–78.

Mansour, H., & McKinnish, T. (2017). Marriage-market search and sorting: Explanations and evidence. In S. D. Averett, L. M. Argys, & S. D. Hoffman (Eds.), *Oxford handbook of women and the economy* (pp. 35–54). Oxford University Press.

Mastrobuoni, G., & Pinotti, P. (2015). Legal status and the criminal activity of immigrants. *American Economic Journal: Applied Economics*, *7*(2), 175–206.

Migration Policy Institute. (2023). *Unauthorized immigrant population profiles*. Accessed 11 16, 2023.

Passel, J. S., & Krogstad, J. M. (2023). *What we know about unauthorized immigrants living in the U.S.* Accessed 11 16, 2023.

U.S. Citizenship and Immigration Services. (2001). *Ins annualreport legalimmigration 2001* Technical report. U.S. Department of Homeland Security.

U.S. Citizenship and Immigration Services. (2021). *All forms report, fiscal year 2021, quarter 4* Technical report. U.S. Department of Homeland Security.

Van Hook, J., Bean, F. D., Bachmeier, J. D., & Tucker, C. (2014). Recent trends in coverage of the mexican-born population of the United States: Results from applying multiple methods across time. *Demography*, *51*(2), 699–726.

Wang, C., & Wang, L. (2012). The effects of 9/11 on intermarriage between natives and immigrants to the us. *Review of Economics of the Household*, *10*, 171–192.

Warren, R. (2020). Reverse migration to Mexico led to us undocumented population decline: 2010 to 2018. *Journal on Migration and Human Security*, *8*(1), 32–41.

APPENDIX

Table A1. Descriptive Statistics by NACARA Eligibility—Male Sample.

	Treatment (NACARA)		Control	
	Arrived 88–90 (Treated) (1)	Arrived 91–97 (2)	Arrived 88–90 (3)	Arrived 91–97 (4)
Characteristics at arrival:				
El Salvador	0.633	0.578	0.000	0.000
	(0.482)	(0.494)	(0.000)	(0.000)
Guatemala	0.367	0.422	0.000	0.000
	(0.482)	(0.494)	(0.000)	(0.000)
Naturalized	0.272	0.176	0.293	0.183
	(0.445)	(0.381)	(0.455)	(0.387)
Age at arrival	24.801	24.755	24.911	25.503
	(6.180)	(6.567)	(6.237)	(7.075)
Year of immigration	1989	1994	1989	1994
	(0.802)	(1.722)	(0.825)	(1.689)

(Continued)

Table A1. *(Continued)*

	Treatment (NACARA)		Control	
	Arrived 88–90 (Treated) (1)	Arrived 91–97 (2)	Arrived 88–90 (3)	Arrived 91–97 (4)
Arrived married	0.222	0.232	0.352	0.378
	(0.416)	(0.422)	(0.478)	(0.485)
Contemporary characteristics:				
Age	45.663	41.056	45.811	41.683
	(6.328)	(6.895)	(6.408)	(7.293)
Never married	0.205	0.303	0.135	0.193
	(0.404)	(0.460)	(0.342)	(0.395)
Real income (2012 $)	33,405	30,457	32,974	31,052
	(30,496)	(26,678)	(34,665)	(34,055)
Own origin enclave (%)	2.460	2.215	12.086	10.637
	(2.721)	(2.508)	(10.202)	(9.787)
Education:				
Less than high school	0.581	0.580	0.526	0.534
	(0.494)	(0.494)	(0.499)	(0.499)
High school	0.275	0.274	0.300	0.300
	(0.447)	(0.446)	(0.458)	(0.458)
Some college	0.094	0.082	0.099	0.089
	(0.292)	(0.274)	(0.299)	(0.285)
Bachelor's degree	0.036	0.048	0.052	0.049
	(0.187)	(0.214)	(0.222)	(0.217)
Advanced degree	0.014	0.016	0.023	0.027
	(0.119)	(0.125)	(0.150)	(0.161)
N	2,291	2,694	12,815	20,434

Notes: This table reports descriptive statistics on a set of personal characteristics. The sample is composed of 2008–2012 ACS respondents who arrived in the United States as adults after 1987 and prior to 1997 from El Salvador and Guatemala (NACARA) or from our control group of Spanish-speaking countries, age 18–64. Each column reports sample means for a subgroup of respondents defined by country of origin and date of arrival to the United States.

Table A2. Descriptive Statistics by NACARA Eligibility—Female Sample.

	Treatment (NACARA)		Control	
	Arrived 88–90 (Treated) (1)	Arrived 91–97 (2)	Arrived 88–90 (3)	Arrived 91–97 (4)
Characteristics at arrival:				
El Salvador	0.653	0.626	0.000	0.000
	(0.476)	(0.484)	(0.000)	(0.000)
Guatemala	0.347	0.374	0.000	0.000
	(0.476)	(0.484)	(0.000)	(0.000)
Naturalized	0.321	0.229	0.315	0.231
	(0.467)	(0.420)	(0.464)	(0.421)
Age at arrival	25.664	26.351	25.507	26.467
	(6.201)	(7.132)	(6.242)	(7.215)
Year of immigration	1989	1993	1989	1994
	(0.810)	(1.709)	(0.804)	(1.711)
Arrived married	0.295	0.326	0.513	0.553
	(0.456)	(0.469)	(0.500)	(0.497)
Contemporary characteristics:				
Age	46.581	42.869	46.355	42.825
	(6.348)	(7.419)	(6.416)	(7.417)

Table A2. (*Continued*)

	Treatment (NACARA)		Control	
	Arrived 88–90 (Treated) (1)	Arrived 91–97 (2)	Arrived 88–90 (3)	Arrived 91–97 (4)
Never married	0.204	0.235	0.113	0.137
	(0.403)	(0.424)	(0.316)	(0.344)
Real income (2012 $)	17,517	16,399	14,705	12,933
	(20,817)	(21,299)	(20,611)	(19,895)
Own origin enclave (%)	2.621	2.349	12.629	11.239
	(2.712)	(2.605)	(10.322)	(10.013)
Education:				
Less than high school	0.570	0.576	0.536	0.533
	(0.495)	(0.494)	(0.499)	(0.499)
High school	0.278	0.270	0.284	0.283
	(0.448)	(0.444)	(0.451)	(0.451)
Some college	0.102	0.090	0.104	0.101
	(0.302)	(0.287)	(0.306)	(0.301)
Bachelor's degree	0.035	0.046	0.055	0.060
	(0.184)	(0.210)	(0.228)	(0.237)
Advanced degree	0.015	0.017	0.021	0.023
	(0.122)	(0.131)	(0.142)	(0.151)
N	2,330	2,688	13,628	24,978

Notes: This table reports descriptive statistics on a set of personal characteristics. The sample is composed of 2008–2012 ACS respondents who arrived in the United States as adults after 1987 and prior to 1997 from El Salvador and Guatemala (NACARA) or from our control group of Spanish-speaking countries, age 18–64. Each column reports sample means for a subgroup of respondents defined by country of origin and date of arrival to the United States.

Table A3. Descriptive Statistics by NACARA Eligibility and Timing of Marriage—Male Sample.

	Difference in Means: Post-1997 Marriages—Arrival-To-1997 Marriages			
	Treatment (NACARA)		Control	
	Arrived 88–90 (Treated) (1)	Arrived 91–97 (2)	Arrived 88–90 (3)	Arrived 91–97 (4)
Characteristics at arrival:				
El Salvador	0.000	−0.018	0.000	0.000
Guatemala	0.000	0.018	0.000	0.000
Age at arrival	−0.441	−0.812	−0.180	−0.661
Year of immigration	0.216	1.034	0.185	1.186
Contemporary characteristics:				
Age	−0.646	−1.894	−0.330	−1.902
Real income (2012 $)	−4,225	544	−2,761	−3,163
Own origin enclave (%)	0.262	0.091	−0.020	−0.441
Parent(s) live in household	−0.007	0.002	0.004	0.004
Spouse's parent(s) live in household	−0.016	0.016	0.008	0.005
Education:				
Less than high school	0.104	0.053	0.003	0.011
High school	−0.058	−0.006	−0.001	0.014
Some college	−0.045	−0.036	0.002	−0.019
Bachelor's degree	0.007	−0.014	−0.004	−0.005

(*Continued*)

Table A3. *(Continued)*

	Difference in Means: Post-1997 Marriages—Arrival-To-1997 Marriages			
	Treatment (NACARA)		Control	
	Arrived 88–90 (Treated) (1)	Arrived 91–97 (2)	Arrived 88–90 (3)	Arrived 91–97 (4)
Advanced degree	−0.008	0.004	0.002	0.000
Spouse's characteristics:				
Spouse's age	−2.685	−2.898	−1.606	−2.900
Spouse's education in years	−0.675	0.048	0.086	0.001
Spouse's income	−2,836	1,031	−1,150	−1874
Spouse married before	0.052	0.038	0.055	0.032
Spouse NACARA eligible	−0.156	−0.050	0.003	0.000
Spouse is a marriage migrant	−0.107	−0.133	−0.206	−0.149
Spouse from same country	0.026	−0.018	−0.012	0.018
Spouse's citizenship:				
Spouse US born	−0.022	−0.007	−0.006	−0.027
Spouse naturalized prior to marriage	0.007	0.009	0.043	0.025
Spouse naturalized after marriage	−0.191	−0.081	−0.100	−0.076
Spouse noncitizen	0.206	0.079	0.063	0.078

Notes: This table reports the differences in mean characteristics between respondents who married in 1998 or later (after NACARA was implemented) and respondents who married after arriving in the United States but no later than 1997. The sample is composed of 2008–2012 ACS respondents who arrived in the United States as adults after 1987 and prior to 1997 from El Salvador and Guatemala (NACARA) or from our control group of Spanish-speaking countries, age 18–64, and who arrived in the United States unmarried and have been married at least once.

Table A4. Descriptive Statistics by NACARA Eligibility and Timing of Marriage—Female Sample.

	Difference in Means: Post-1997 Marriages—Arrival-To-1997 Marriages			
	Treatment (NACARA)		Control	
	Arrived 88–90 (Treated) (1)	Arrived 91–97 (2)	Arrived 88–90 (3)	Arrived 91–97 (4)
Characteristics at arrival:				
El Salvador	−0.060	−0.034	0.000	0.000
Guatemala	0.060	0.034	0.000	0.000
Age at arrival	−0.323	−0.305	0.239	−0.234
Year of immigration	0.185	1.146	0.182	1.084
Contemporary characteristics:				
Age	−0.423	−1.411	0.059	−1.382
Real income (2012 $)	−756	−2083	−1822	−465
Own origin enclave (%)	0.467	0.025	0.876	−0.176
Parent(s) live in household	−0.026	−0.007	−0.010	−0.004
Spouse's parent(s) live in household	0.007	−0.015	−0.013	0.004
Education:				
Less than high school	0.085	0.050	0.042	0.006
High school	−0.082	0.011	0.011	0.027

Table A4. *(Continued)*

	Difference in Means: Post-1997 Marriages—Arrival-To-1997 Marriages			
	Treatment (NACARA)		Control	
	Arrived 88–90 (Treated) (1)	Arrived 91–97 (2)	Arrived 88–90 (3)	Arrived 91–97 (4)
Some college	−0.001	−0.030	−0.027	−0.021
Bachelor's degree	−0.016	−0.021	−0.012	−0.011
Advanced degree	0.014	−0.010	−0.014	−0.001
Spouse's characteristics:				
Spouse's age	−1.825	−2.662	−0.613	−2.494
Spouse's education in years	−0.667	0.269	−0.027	0.125
Spouse's income	−5,868	−2,853	−4,401	−1809
Spouse married before	0.034	0.002	0.067	0.035
Spouse NACARA eligible	−0.087	−0.128	0.017	−0.006
Spouse is a marriage migrant	−0.069	−0.062	−0.070	−0.079
Spouse from same country	−0.004	−0.032	−0.005	0.005
Spouse's citizenship:				
Spouse US born	−0.037	−0.002	−0.015	−0.010
Spouse naturalized prior to marriage	0.045	0.036	0.080	0.028
Spouse naturalized after marriage	−0.188	−0.117	−0.193	−0.116
Spouse noncitizen	0.179	0.083	0.127	0.099

Notes: This table reports the differences in mean characteristics between respondents who married in 1998 or later (after NACARA was implemented) and respondents who married after arriving in the United States but no later than 1997. The sample is composed of 2008–2012 ACS respondents who arrived in the United States as adults after 1987 and prior to 1997 from El Salvador and Guatemala (NACARA) or from our control group of Spanish-speaking countries, age 18–64, and who arrived in the United States unmarried and have been married at least once.

Table A5. The Impact of NACARA on the Characteristics of Spouse and Marriage—Pooled Sample.

	Spouse's Age	Spouse's Education in Years	Spouse's Income (ln)	Spouse Married Before	Spouse NACARA Eligible	Spouse is a Marriage Migrant	Spouse From Same Country	Spouse US Born	Spouse Naturalized Prior to marriage	Spouse Naturalized After Marriage	Spouse Noncitizen	Own Origin Enclave (%)	Parent(s) Live in Household	Spouse's Parent(s) Live in Household
	(1)	(2)	(3)	(4)	(5)	(6)	(7)	(8)	(9)	(10)	(11)	(12)	(13)	(14)
NACARA	0.402	−0.456**	0.388**	0.004	0.322***	−0.065***	−0.098***	−0.076***	0.011	0.019	0.046**	−8.658***	0.001	0.001
	(0.245)	(0.194)	(0.154)	(0.014)	(0.018)	(0.016)	(0.020)	(0.013)	(0.011)	(0.017)	(0.020)	(0.176)	(0.008)	(0.008)
Pre-1991	−2.206***	−0.032	0.419**	0.043***	0.024**	0.004	0.066***	−0.046***	0.026**	0.016	0.004	1.354***	−0.014	−0.001
	(0.289)	(0.230)	(0.197)	(0.016)	(0.010)	(0.020)	(0.021)	(0.018)	(0.013)	(0.018)	(0.023)	(0.441)	(0.010)	(0.010)
NACARA* Pre-1991	−0.213	0.244	−0.008	−0.007	0.185***	−0.028	−0.074***	0.028*	−0.020	0.038*	−0.046*	−1.073***	0.005	0.004
	(0.302)	(0.242)	(0.195)	(0.017)	(0.023)	(0.020)	(0.025)	(0.016)	(0.013)	(0.022)	(0.025)	(0.231)	(0.010)	(0.010)
Post-97 marriage	−1.497***	0.048	−0.375***	0.045***	0.005**	−0.132***	0.015*	−0.025***	0.033***	−0.079***	0.071***	−0.143	−0.000	0.004
	(0.108)	(0.087)	(0.073)	(0.006)	(0.002)	(0.008)	(0.008)	(0.007)	(0.005)	(0.007)	(0.009)	(0.177)	(0.004)	(0.004)
NACARA* Post-97 marriage	0.017	0.176	0.316	−0.009	−0.118***	0.014	−0.048**	0.020	0.001	−0.001	−0.020	0.245	−0.000	0.000
	(0.309)	(0.239)	(0.195)	(0.017)	(0.022)	(0.019)	(0.024)	(0.016)	(0.014)	(0.019)	(0.024)	(0.220)	(0.010)	(0.010)
Pre-1991* Post-97 marriage	0.381**	0.068	0.084	0.014	0.007	−0.015	−0.025**	0.016	0.024***	−0.054***	0.013	0.424	−0.001	−0.004
	(0.177)	(0.134)	(0.118)	(0.010)	(0.004)	(0.011)	(0.012)	(0.010)	(0.008)	(0.010)	(0.014)	(0.285)	(0.006)	(0.006)
NACARA* Pre-1991* Post-97 marriage	−0.774*	−0.773**	−0.166	0.001	−0.037	0.037	0.068**	−0.040*	−0.030	−0.048*	0.118***	−0.346	−0.012	−0.005
	(0.443)	(0.334)	(0.282)	(0.025)	(0.031)	(0.025)	(0.034)	(0.021)	(0.019)	(0.027)	(0.033)	(0.343)	(0.013)	(0.014)
Controls	x	x	x	x	x	x	x	x	x	x	x	x	x	x
Mean	40.777	8.790	8.662	0.132	0.070	0.205	0.742	0.154	0.079	0.171	0.597	9.813	0.037	0.039
Observations	26,495	26,495	26,495	26,495	26,495	26,495	26,495	26,495	26,495	26,495	26,495	26,495	26,495	26,495
R-squared	0.464	0.113	0.250	0.037	0.281	0.093	0.067	0.044	0.023	0.056	0.074	0.146	0.009	0.005

Notes: This table reports OLS estimation results from the triple-difference regression described in Eq. (2), on a set of outcomes related to the respondent's spouse's citizenship and nativity the spouse's personal characteristics, and the characteristics of the household at the time of the survey. Estimates are run on a sample of 2008–2012 ACS respondents who arrived in the United States as adults after 1987 and prior to 1997 from El Salvador and Guatemala (NACARA) or from our control group of Spanish-speaking countries, age 18–64, and who arrived in the United States unmarried and have been married at least once. As described in the text, the regression estimates include controls for age, age at arrival to the United States, education, survey-year fixed effects, and year-of-immigration fixed effects. In the pooled sample, we also control for gender.

	Spouse's Age	Spouse's Education in Years	Spouse's Income (ln)	Spouse Married Before	Spouse NACARA Eligible	Spouse is a Marriage Migrant	Spouse From Same Country	Spouse US Born	Spouse Naturalized Prior to Marriage	Spouse Naturalized After Marriage	Spouse Noncitizen	Own Origin Enclave (%)	Parent(s) Live in Household	Spouse's Parent(s) Live in Household
	(1)	(2)	(3)	(4)	(5)	(6)	(7)	(8)	(9)	(10)	(11)	(12)	(13)	(14)
NACARA	0.769**	−0.477*	0.984***	0.005	0.171***	−0.087***	−0.111***	−0.080***	0.032**	0.021	0.026	−8.727***	0.003	0.004
	(0.375)	(0.288)	(0.303)	(0.019)	(0.023)	(0.029)	(0.030)	(0.022)	(0.016)	(0.024)	(0.030)	(0.251)	(0.011)	(0.013)
Pre-1991	−2.275***	−0.241	0.283	0.024	0.023**	0.050*	0.098***	−0.082***	0.018	−0.018	0.082***	1.219**	−0.000	−0.004
	(0.363)	(0.308)	(0.338)	(0.020)	(0.012)	(0.030)	(0.029)	(0.025)	(0.016)	(0.022)	(0.031)	(0.595)	(0.012)	(0.014)
NACARA* Pre-1991	0.022	0.126	−0.280	0.007	0.249***	−0.057*	−0.053	0.012	−0.032*	0.053*	−0.034	−0.905***	−0.006	0.010
	(0.439)	(0.350)	(0.371)	(0.023)	(0.031)	(0.035)	(0.037)	(0.026)	(0.019)	(0.031)	(0.037)	(0.323)	(0.013)	(0.016)
Post-97 marriage	−1.532***	−0.017	−0.490***	0.042***	0.005*	−0.170***	0.027**	−0.042***	0.031***	−0.064***	0.075***	−0.231	0.004	0.005
	(0.142)	(0.122)	(0.135)	(0.008)	(0.003)	(0.012)	(0.012)	(0.011)	(0.006)	(0.009)	(0.013)	(0.248)	(0.005)	(0.005)
NACARA* Post-97 marriage	−0.012	0.135	0.164	0.008	−0.050*	0.022	−0.040	0.024	−0.016	−0.005	−0.003	0.488	−0.000	0.013
	(0.447)	(0.342)	(0.362)	(0.023)	(0.026)	(0.032)	(0.036)	(0.026)	(0.020)	(0.027)	(0.035)	(0.305)	(0.013)	(0.016)
Pre-1991* Post-97 marriage	0.124	0.097	0.018	0.012	−0.001	−0.027	−0.031*	0.032**	0.011	−0.032**	−0.011	0.298	−0.001	0.004
	(0.224)	(0.179)	(0.201)	(0.012)	(0.005)	(0.017)	(0.017)	(0.015)	(0.010)	(0.013)	(0.019)	(0.380)	(0.007)	(0.008)
NACARA* Pre-1991* Post-97 marriage	−0.825	−0.624	0.087	−0.009	−0.106***	0.072*	0.070	−0.037	−0.016	−0.075**	0.128***	−0.376	−0.009	−0.035*
	(0.597)	(0.459)	(0.490)	(0.032)	(0.039)	(0.042)	(0.047)	(0.032)	(0.025)	(0.036)	(0.046)	(0.457)	(0.016)	(0.021)
Controls	x	x	x	x	x	x	x	x	x	x	x	x	x	x
Mean	38.525	8.923	6.236	0.110	0.052	0.292	0.739	0.166	0.062	0.143	0.629	9.703	0.030	0.044
Observations	14,682	14,682	14,682	14,682	14,682	14,682	14,682	14,682	14,682	14,682	14,682	14,682	14,682	14,682
R-squared	0.402	0.107	0.028	0.022	0.213	0.054	0.053	0.035	0.019	0.052	0.059	0.137	0.007	0.006

Notes: This table reports OLS estimation results from the triple-difference regression described in Eq. (2), on a set of outcomes related to the respondent's spouse's citizenship and nativity the spouse's personal characteristics, and the characteristics of the household at the time of the survey. Estimates are run on a sample of 2008–2012 ACS respondents who arrived in the United States as adults after 1987 and prior to 1997 from El Salvador and Guatemala (NACARA) or from our control group of Spanish-speaking countries, age 18–64, and who arrived in the United States unmarried and have been married at least once. As described in the text, the regression estimates include controls for age, age at arrival to the United States, education, survey-year fixed effects, and year-of-immigration fixed effects. In the pooled sample, we also control for gender.

Table A7. The Impact of NACARA on the Characteristics of Spouse and Marriage—Female Sample.

	Spouse's Age (1)	Spouse's Education in Years (2)	Spouse's Income (ln) (3)	Spouse Married Before (4)	Spouse NACARA Eligible (5)	Spouse is a Marriage Migrant (6)	Spouse From Same Country (7)	Spouse US Born (8)	Spouse Naturalized Prior to Marriage (9)	Spouse Naturalized After Marriage (10)	Spouse Noncitizen (11)	Own Origin Enclave (%) (12)	Parent(s) Live in Household (13)	Spouse's Parent(s) Live in Household (14)
NACARA	0.045	−0.422	−0.060	0.005	0.439***	−0.045***	−0.094***	−0.069***	−0.006	0.015	0.060**	−8.649***	−0.000	−0.001
	(0.328)	(0.265)	(0.128)	(0.020)	(0.026)	(0.017)	(0.025)	(0.016)	(0.016)	(0.024)	(0.027)	(0.251)	(0.012)	(0.010)
Pre-1991	−2.104***	0.218	0.638***	0.065**	0.018	−0.071***	0.028	−0.007	0.035	0.065**	−0.093***	1.437**	−0.029*	0.001
	(0.466)	(0.348)	(0.130)	(0.026)	(0.017)	(0.023)	(0.031)	(0.025)	(0.022)	(0.029)	(0.035)	(0.659)	(0.016)	(0.014)
NACARA* Pre-1991	−0.530	0.350	0.097	−0.024	0.165***	0.020	−0.085**	0.041*	−0.013	0.018	−0.045	−1.191***	0.017	−0.003
	(0.426)	(0.339)	(0.152)	(0.025)	(0.033)	(0.022)	(0.034)	(0.021)	(0.019)	(0.032)	(0.035)	(0.337)	(0.016)	(0.013)
Post-97 marriage	−1.467***	0.089	−0.196***	0.048***	−0.001	−0.090***	0.005	−0.010	0.034***	−0.099***	0.076***	−0.040	−0.004	0.005
	(0.165)	(0.124)	(0.049)	(0.010)	(0.004)	(0.009)	(0.011)	(0.009)	(0.008)	(0.010)	(0.013)	(0.254)	(0.006)	(0.005)
NACARA* Post-97 marriage	−0.091	0.257	0.135	−0.030	−0.126***	0.017	−0.050	0.019	0.012	0.004	−0.034	−0.008	−0.002	−0.018
	(0.444)	(0.337)	(0.156)	(0.026)	(0.033)	(0.019)	(0.033)	(0.021)	(0.022)	(0.028)	(0.034)	(0.327)	(0.015)	(0.012)
Pre-1991* Post-97 marriage	0.798***	0.082	0.163*	0.021	0.020**	0.018	−0.025	0.007	0.046***	−0.086***	0.033	0.652	−0.004	−0.017**
	(0.285)	(0.204)	(0.084)	(0.017)	(0.008)	(0.013)	(0.018)	(0.015)	(0.015)	(0.017)	(0.021)	(0.437)	(0.009)	(0.007)
NACARA* Pre-1991* Post-97 marriage	−0.837	−0.924*	−0.303	0.001	0.020	−0.012	0.058	−0.046	−0.041	0.002	0.086*	−0.373	−0.015	0.037**
	(0.687)	(0.497)	(0.219)	(0.039)	(0.048)	(0.026)	(0.050)	(0.030)	(0.032)	(0.042)	(0.051)	(0.537)	(0.021)	(0.018)
Controls	x	x	x	x	x	x	x	x	x	x	x	x	x	x
Mean	43.577	8.623	10.724	0.158	0.093	0.097	0.746	0.139	0.100	0.205	0.556	9.951	0.046	0.033
Observations	11,813	11,813	11,813	11,813	11,813	11,813	11,813	11,813	11,813	11,813	11,813	11,813	11,813	11,813
R-squared	0.415	0.124	0.030	0.058	0.365	0.025	0.105	0.075	0.027	0.061	0.097	0.166	0.013	0.009

Notes: This table reports OLS estimation results from the triple-difference regression described in Eq. (2), on a set of outcomes related to the respondent's spouse's citizenship and nativity the spouse's personal characteristics, and the characteristics of the household at the time of the survey. Estimates are run on a sample of 2008–2012 ACS respondents who arrived in the United States as adults after 1987 and prior to 1997 from El Salvador and Guatemala (NACARA) or from our control group of Spanish-speaking countries, age 18–64, and who arrived in the United States unmarried and have been married at least once. As described in the text, the regression estimates include controls for age, age at arrival to the United States, education, survey-year fixed effects, and year-of-immigration fixed effects. In the pooled sample, we also control for gender.

Table A8. The Impact of NACARA on Marriage, Naturalization, and Residence in Ethnic Enclave With English Ability Controls.

	Naturalized (1)	Never Married (2)	Own Origin Enclave (%) (3)
Panel A: Pooled			
NACARA*Pre-1991	−0.005	−0.024***	−1.107***
	(0.008)	(0.008)	(0.095)
NACARA	−0.007	0.096***	−8.403***
	(0.005)	(0.006)	(0.061)
Pre-1991	0.088***	−0.072***	1.024***
	(0.010)	(0.009)	(0.230)
Mean	0.245	0.159	10.373
N	90,629	90,629	90,629
R-squared	0.184	0.031	0.156
Panel B: Men			
NACARA*Pre-1991	−0.022*	−0.037***	−1.043***
	(0.012)	(0.012)	(0.136)
NACARA	−0.004	0.100***	−8.230***
	(0.007)	(0.009)	(0.087)
Pre-1991	0.109***	−0.098***	0.773**
	(0.015)	(0.013)	(0.333)
Mean	0.225	0.182	10.039
N	42,141	42,141	42,141
R-squared	0.151	0.040	0.150
Panel C: Women			
NACARA*Pre-1991	0.013	−0.009	−1.167***
	(0.012)	(0.011)	(0.133)
NACARA	−0.011	0.090***	−8.574***
	(0.008)	(0.008)	(0.085)
Pre-1991	0.067***	−0.045***	1.246***
	(0.014)	(0.012)	(0.319)
Mean	0.262	0.139	10.665
N	48,488	48,488	48,488
R-squared	0.214	0.020	0.162

Notes: This table reports OLS estimation results from the difference-in-differences regression described in Eq. (1), on a respondent's citizenship status, marriage, and the percentage of residents in the respondent's PUMA who were born in the same country as the respondent. Estimates are run on a sample of 2008–2012 ACS respondents who arrived in the United States as adults after 1987 and prior to 1997 from El Salvador and Guatemala (NACARA) or from our control group of Spanish-speaking countries, age 18–64. As described in the text, the regression estimates include controls for age, age at arrival to the United States, education, English ability, survey-year fixed effects, and year-of-immigration fixed effects. In the pooled sample, we also control for gender.

Table A9. The Impact of NACARA on the Characteristics of Spouse and Marriage With English Ability Controls.

	Pooled		Men		Women	
	NACARA* Pre-1991* Post-97 marriage	Mean	NACARA* Pre-1991* Post-97 marriage	Mean	NACARA* Pre-1991* Post-97 marriage	Mean
Spouse's characteristics:						
Spouse's age	−0.756*	40.777	−0.852	38.525	−0.779	43.577
	(0.444)		(0.598)		(0.688)	
Spouse's education in years	−0.652**	8.790	−0.480	8.923	−0.821*	8.623
	(0.332)		(0.457)		(0.496)	
Spouse's income (ln)	−0.101	8.237	0.200	6.236	−0.280	10.724
	(0.282)		(0.492)		(0.219)	
Spouse married before	0.007	0.132	−0.004	0.110	0.009	0.158
	(0.025)		(0.032)		(0.039)	
Spouse NACARA eligible	−0.038	0.070	−0.107***	0.052	0.019	0.093
	(0.031)		(0.039)		(0.048)	
Spouse is a marriage migrant	0.029	0.205	0.059	0.292	−0.014	0.097
	(0.025)		(0.042)		(0.026)	
Spouse from same country	0.042	0.742	0.044	0.739	0.031	0.746
	(0.033)		(0.047)		(0.049)	
Spouse's citizenship:						
Spouse US born	−0.018	0.154	−0.015	0.166	−0.025	0.139
	(0.021)		(0.031)		(0.029)	
Spouse naturalized prior to marriage	−0.027	0.079	−0.015	0.062	−0.037	0.100
	(0.019)		(0.025)		(0.032)	
Spouse naturalized after marriage	−0.045*	0.171	−0.070*	0.143	0.004	0.205
	(0.027)		(0.036)		(0.042)	
Spouse noncitizen	0.090***	0.597	0.100**	0.629	0.057	0.556
	(0.033)		(0.045)		(0.050)	
Contemporary characteristics:						
Own origin enclave (%)	−0.862**	9.813	−0.999**	9.703	−0.874	9.951
	(0.351)		(0.470)		(0.544)	
Parent(s) live in household	−0.012	0.037	−0.008	0.030	−0.015	0.046
	(0.013)		(0.016)		(0.021)	
Spouse's parent(s) live in household	−0.005	0.039	−0.036*	0.044	0.038**	0.033
	(0.014)		(0.021)		(0.018)	
N	26,495		14,682		11,813	

Notes: This table reports OLS estimation results from the triple-difference regression described in Eq. (2), on a set of outcomes related to the respondent's spouse's citizenship and nativity the spouse's personal characteristics, and the characteristics of the household at the time of the survey. Estimates are run on a sample of 2008–2012 ACS respondents who arrived in the United States as adults after 1987 and prior to 1997 from El Salvador and Guatemala (NACARA) or from our control group of Spanish-speaking countries, age 18–64, and who arrived in the United States unmarried and have been married at least once. As described in the text, the regression estimates include controls for age, age at arrival to the United States, education, English ability, survey-year fixed effects, and year-of-immigration fixed effects. In the pooled sample, we also control for gender.

LINGUISTIC PROXIMITY AND THE INEQUALITY IN RETURNS TO MIGRANTS' SKILLS

Jonas Feld[a] and Joanna Tyrowicz[b]

[a]*Trier University, Germany*
[b]*GRAPE, Poland*

ABSTRACT

The authors provide novel evidence on the inequality of returns to immigrant skills in hosting economies. Although migrant wage gaps are well established in the literature, less is known about the origins of their heterogeneity. The authors propose a potential rationale for this gap related to the linguistic proximity (LP) between the destination and origin countries. The authors exploit individual-level data from nine diverse destination countries, with migrants from a highly heterogeneous group of origin countries, for both recent and long-term migrants. The authors find that lower LP between origin and destination is associated with a higher average wage penalty for highly skilled migrants and a substantially lower position in the wage distribution.

Keywords: Migration; linguistic proximity; returns to education; human capital transferability; wage inequality

1. INTRODUCTION

We study the inequality in returns to tertiary education for migrants from various origin countries in nine diverse destination countries. A rich array of studies documents migrant wage gaps that remain even after adjusting for socioeconomic characteristics. In line with the human capital framework, numerous studies have emphasized the role of skill portability from the origin to the destination economy for immigrant wage assimilation (e.g. Bazzi et al., 2016; Friedberg, 2000, both these studies also provide a thorough overview of the empirical literature in the field).[1] Considerably less attention has been devoted to

Migration, Human Capital and the Labor Market
Research in Labor Economics, Volume 53A, 231–265

ISSN: 0147-9121/doi:10.1108/S0147-91212026000053A007

the *inequality* of the immigrant-native wage gap between destinations and origins. Our study aims to fill this gap.

To conceptualize the dispersion of returns to tertiary education among migrants, we emphasize the costs associated with assessing migrants' qualifications. We leverage information asymmetry in employment to hypothesize that employers face costs inspecting the qualifications of job candidates with foreign education and certification (imposing a friction). Before actual employment, employers cannot fully assert job candidates' qualifications due to this information asymmetry, and they typically rely on references, diplomas, and certificates to bridge the gap. Linguistic proximity (LP) facilitates the comparability of this information for migrants and natives, reducing friction. When LP is high, it is easier for employers to assess qualifications, leading to fewer costs. Conversely, lower LP increases these costs, potentially influencing hiring decisions. We expect LP to be particularly relevant for individuals with tertiary degrees, as their credentials often require closer scrutiny (e.g. Peri & Sparber, 2009).

Thus, we obtain a testable empirical hypothesis: *LP reduces the wage gaps of high-skilled migrants*. Note that our hypothesis is not a foregone conclusion. First, it has been empirically demonstrated that LP drives migration flows (e.g. Adsera & Pytlikova, 2015; Caragliu et al., 2013; Chiswick & Miller, 1994). This selectivity of migration patterns could imply that there is no variation in LP in our data or that it is insufficient to estimate any meaningful relations. Second, the frictions for the employers related to LP can be too low for any relation to emerge from observational data. Finally, these frictions may be quantitatively dominated by mechanisms that are not related to LP, such as network effects.

We address our hypothesis by providing a comprehensive set of measures of returns to human capital (tertiary education) across a diverse group of origin and destination countries. We harmonize individual-level data for nine popular migrant destination countries: Argentina, Brazil, Mexico, Germany, United Kingdom, France, Israel, the United States and Canada. These countries are located on four continents, cover six language families, and feature a strong representation of migrants from many different origin countries. Together, they host about 36% of the total international migrant population worldwide.[2] Our analysis draws on origin- and destination-specific data on returns to tertiary education for migrants, derived from rich, harmonized wage information. Both natives and migrants report wages in our dataset, enabling us to estimate the wage gap between migrants and natives in each destination country, both with and without a tertiary degree. These estimates are obtained in different origin countries and for each destination country separately. They are adjusted for individual characteristics such as age, gender, marital status, and time since arrival in the destination country, as well as for job-related characteristics, such as occupation and industry.

Once we establish the dispersion of returns to tertiary education for migrants in each country pair, we relate it to the bilateral measures of LP for these country pairs. Our measures of LP draw on the experience of international economics and capture the *ease of communication* between random individuals from two countries (Melitz & Toubal, 2014). They reflect the inherent similarity of languages in these countries per se, as well as the knowledge of common languages among the two populations. Our findings indicate that, *ceteris paribus*, greater LP between origin and destination countries is associated with an improved position of migrants in the wage distribution of the destination country. Furthermore, we observe that the (adjusted) wage gap for highly skilled migrants is smaller for origin countries that are linguistically closer, *ceteris paribus*.

Our paper contributes to two distinct strands of the literature. First, we build on the rich literature that studies the role of LP in explaining bilateral worker flows. Earlier studies, such as Chiswick and Miller (1994), Caragliu et al. (2013), and Adsera and Pytlikova (2015), show that migrants tend to select destination countries that are culturally *and* linguistically closer to their origin (see also Sprenger, 2024), complementing migration networks (Bredtmann et al., 2020). Second, we contribute to the literature highlighting that LP not only helps securing employment (Ghio et al., 2023; Wong, 2023), and a type of job obtained by migrants (Adsera & Ferrer, 2021). We show that the wage gaps and position in the wage distribution in the hosting economy are lower for immigrants from linguistically close countries. Our result is not explained away by language skills of the immigrants (Berman et al., 2003; Chiswick, 1991; Chiswick & Miller, 1995,2012; Dustmann & Fabbri, 2003, among others).

Against this literature, our study offers several important innovations. First, we focus on highly skilled migrants whereas most of the existing literature focuses on low-skilled workers. This is relevant because highly skilled migrants often speak some of the most important global languages as second languages (such as English, Spanish, and French; as documented by e.g. Dustmann, 1994; Dustmann & Fabbri, 2003; LaLonde & Topel, 1992). Also, most existing studies on immigrant-native wage gaps relate to destination countries with one of the main global languages as a native language whereas our sample also comprises less popular destination languages. Second, unlike existing studies that typically focus on a single destination country, our analysis spans many destination countries. This broader scope allows for the disentanglement of LP from destination-specific conditions and is complemented by our application of a rich, multidimensional measure of LP.[3] Third, we document the remarkable dispersion of returns to tertiary education among migrants across diverse origin and destination countries and show that this dispersion correlates with LP.

Our chapter is structured as follows. Section 2 summarizes the literature on immigrant-native wage gaps in the context of language proximity. In Section 3, we discuss our methodology, and in Section 4, we cover data and stylized facts emerging from this study. Section 5 presents the results. Finally, the last section offers a summary of the results, discusses policy implications, and outlines avenues for further research.

2. RELATED LITERATURE

Even after adjusting for individual characteristics, wage gaps persist between natives and migrants (Borjas, 1985, 1992, 1994; Chiswick, 1978, 1986; Jasso & Rosenzweig, 1988). These gaps are attributed to migrants' challenges as job seekers (e.g., limited knowledge of the local labor market) and the costly, time-consuming process of skill transfer and assimilation.[4] Chiswick and Miller (2013) argue that what matters is not merely host country language skills, but the match between an immigrant's language proficiency and the language requirements of the job. Imai et al. (2019) find that in Canada, migrants with limited language skills tend to self-select into manual occupations, even if they held jobs demanding cognitive skills in their origin countries. Yao and van Ours (2015) show that in a rarely learned language (Dutch), where migrants usually lack prior exposure, wage gaps prevail particularly among disadvantaged groups.

In addition, Bleakley and Chin (2004, 2010) demonstrate that labor market success hinges on an immigrant's ease of learning the destination country's language; familiarity with similar languages facilitates this learning process (Beenstock et al., 2001). Moreover, extent literature suggests that not just language proficiency but also LP to the host country's language significantly impacts migrants' labor market success (e.g., Chiswick & Miller, 1998, 2001; Crystal, 1987; Espenshade & Fu, 1997; Isphording, 2014; Isphording & Otten, 2013; Wong, 2023).

Measuring language proximity is challenging, though. Early studies, such as Chiswick and Miller (2005), focused on proximity to English, based on how easily Americans could learn a language. They classified migrants into English speakers and non-native speakers, further dividing the latter into groups whose languages are close to, distant from, or intermediate to English. This admittedly crude measurement has been refined with advances in linguistic science. *Ethnologue* measures language proximity on a six-level scale based on linguistic lineage, ranging from full proximity (identical languages) to zero (completely different languages) (e.g., Adsera & Ferrer, 2021; Adsera & Pytlikova, 2015). Dyen's lexicostatistical measure assesses Indo-European languages' similarity based on 200 common words (Belot & Ederveen, 2012; Dyen et al., 1992). The Levenshtein distance, applied to the expert-judged Automatic Similarity Judgment Program (ASJP) data, compares languages using the wording, length, and phonetics of 40 basic words. We report an overview of measures used in economic literature in Table A1.

Many of these economic studies exploit heterogeneity across origin countries but within a single destination country. They thereby confound the role of language proximity with the role of characteristics of the labor market, and cultural factors in a given destination country with factors for a given origin-destination country pair. To obtain meaningful information about the role of LP in isolation from these other factors, it is imperative to take advantage of the heterogeneity of the destination countries in addition to the heterogeneity of origin countries.

Language learning difficulties in the host economy may be less relevant for highly skilled migrants (those with tertiary degrees from their origin countries) for several reasons: First, they often possess proficiency in the languages of major host economies before immigrating.[5] Second, their educational background typically involves exposure to multiple foreign languages, facilitating easier acquisition of the host country's language (Beenstock et al., 2001). Finally, highly educated migrants are more likely than low-educated ones to select destination countries with a common or similar language (Adsera & Pytlikova, 2015; Beine et al., 2011; Belot & Ederveen, 2012; Belot & Hatton, 2012; Clark et al., 2007; Grogger & Hanson, 2011; Pedersen et al., 2008).

Despite the unique characteristics of highly skilled migration and persistent wage gaps among this group, the systematic drivers of these gaps remain underexplored. For highly skilled migrants, factors like cultural distance or limited language proficiency are unlikely to be exclusive or dominant explanations. A crucial but overlooked factor may lie with employers: while highly skilled migrants often communicate well in the host country's language, employers might find it costly to assess credentials or educational quality from linguistically distant countries of origin.

This mechanism is especially relevant for occupations without standardized international certification. In these fields, skills are often highly portable (e.g., analysts, engineers, and creative professionals), but verifying them can be challenging for employers. Unlike fields with strict certification, such as medicine[6] or IT,[7] many other professions require employers to evaluate university curricula or portfolios. When these are in linguistically distant languages, assessing skill content and educational quality becomes costly. This can lead to wage gaps for migrants from linguistically distant countries, as the cost of verifying their qualifications may outweigh the perceived benefit.

To sum up, empirical literature shows that LP influences migration flows. Building on this, we hypothesize that LP between origin and destination economies affects screening costs (e.g. acquiring information in a distant language). This issue is particularly relevant in the case of jobs for which verifying qualifications is essential and language proficiency per se is not a barrier. We empirically test the hypothesis that LP contributes to migrant wage gaps. By leveraging multiple destination languages and destination-by-origin fixed effects, we isolate the role of LP, distinct from simple language proficiency.

3. METHODS

To study the role of language in explaining immigrant wage gaps, we utilize a measure of LP based on *ease of communication*. LP varies between country pairs. It can also vary over time within a country pair, as an effect of migration flows and increased command of foreign languages in either of the country pairs. This measure has previously been used in trade literature (Melitz & Toubal, 2014). It is suitable for capturing the proposed mechanism: the costs to an employer of assessing the quality of a job seeker's credentials. Our measure of *ease of communication* begins with the Automated Similarity Judgment Program (ASJP), which indexes language similarities between 200 common words between country pairs, based on an assessment by ethnologists and ethno statisticians. In subsequent steps, this measure is adjusted for common spoken and official languages and standardized to produce a common language index (CLI), which has a bounded distribution within our sample: between 0 for the most linguistically distant country pair and 1 for the highest LP (see Section 4 in this chapter as well as the original paper of Melitz, 2008; Melitz & Toubal, 2014, for a detailed description on how to construct the measure).[8] More details are presented in Appendix B.

To investigate the determinants of immigrant wage gaps, we pursue two empirical strategies. First, we work directly with the individual-level data as explained in Section 3.1. We refer to this approach as the *one-step approach.* We exploit the richness of 40 million individual-level observations, but this choice poses some econometric challenges. Therefore, we present a second empirical strategy the *two-step approach*: we obtain measures of the immigrant wage gaps across countries of origin and destination from individual-level data (the first step), which we then relate to LP for origin-destination country pairs (the second step). The first step, the process of obtaining the immigrant wage gaps, is described in Section 3.2 whereas the second step, the method for linking wage gaps and LP, is described in Section 3.3.

3.1 Individual-Level Analysis

This section outlines our one-step approach. The benefit of this procedure is that it takes direct advantage of the richness of our data at the individual-level. We convert the individual measure of wages into a percentile measure (denoted by $\widehat{\omega}$) within each destination country to maintain comparability of the estimates across the samples. We then estimate the contribution of language proximity measured by common language index (CLI) from:

$$\widehat{\omega}_i = \alpha + \beta X_i + \gamma \mathrm{TE}_i \times \mathrm{CLI}_{d,o} + \mu M_i + \delta_Z Z_o + \delta_{d,o} Z_{d,o} + \delta_d + \delta_o + \epsilon_i, \quad (1)$$

where the superscript d denotes destination country, o superscript denotes origin country, index i denotes individual. TE_i identifies the educational status of the individual i: it is a dummy variable that takes on a value of 1 if an individual has tertiary education and 0 otherwise. M_i identifies the migrant status of an individual i: it is a dummy variable taking on the value of 1 if an individual is an immigrant in a given destination country, and 0 if an individual is a native.[9] X_i is a vector of individual demographic control variables (personal, job and household characteristics, including information on years since immigration). The country-level controls included in Z_o consist of population size, GDP per capita, fertility, and mortality rates. Country pair controls included in $Z_{d,o}$ consist of geographical variables (geographical distance, contiguity) and historical variables (years at war, common colonizer, common religion, common legal system). These controls are required by Head et al. (2010), because they adjust for cultural barriers important for selectivity of migrations and integration patterns (e.g., Adsera & Pytlikova, 2015; Mayda, 2010; O'Rourke & Sinnott, 2006; Wong, 2023).

The one-step procedure represented by Eq. (1) estimates a well-known Mincerian wage regression, jointly with the role of LP in determining wage inequality. The specification in Eq. (1) allows the returns to tertiary education to vary by country of origin (COO) but is restricted to be common between destination countries. Hence, the term $\text{CLI}_{d,o}$ is the only variable specific to a COO *jointly* with a country of destination. Our main research hypothesis implies a positive estimate of γ, that is, the wages of migrants increase with language proximity. Note that given the specification of the explained variable—percentile of the wage distribution within the destination country—the interpretation of the γ estimate refers to immigrant wage gaps in relative terms (position in income distribution) rather than in absolute terms (percent of the wage).

The strategy proposed in Eq. (1) has a significant advantage: the entire variation in our sample is exploited in one step. But it also has two limitations. First, there is no way to obtain correct estimates of the standard errors for characteristics related to several levels of variation: individual, country of destination, COO, and origin-destination country pairs. Second, the destination countries differ in the level of development and structure of the labor market, and the destination countries' datasets differ in sampling design and sample sizes. We introduce destination country fixed effects (δ_d) to account for country-level characteristics, and we introduce sample weights from the original sampling design in the estimation. Thus, the estimates reflect the relative size of the populations in the destination countries, not the sample sizes for the data utilized.

Given the limitations of the one-step approach, we also propose a two-step approach. In the first step, we estimate the returns to tertiary education by COO, separately for each destination country. Specifically, we obtain deviations of returns to tertiary education specific to a given COO. This step is described in Section 3.2. In the second step, we relate these estimated deviations to LP at the country-pair level. This step is described in Section 3.3.

3.2 Estimating the Returns to Skills by COO

We begin our two-step approach by estimating the country-of-origin-specific returns to skills, separately for each destination country. In other words, for each destination country, we estimate the systematic wage deviation by education level that results from an individual's origin in a given country. The goal is to find out, for instance, whether the returns to skills for Norwegian migrants in Germany differ from those experienced by Swedes in Germany. We seek to obtain a dataset that lists the returns for skills for all destination countries *and* all origin countries that are sufficiently covered in our micro-level data (i.e., we seek to obtain an $m \times n$ matrix in which migrants' destinations are in the rows and their places of origin are in the columns, and the entries in the matrix represent the estimated wage variances for each of these combinations).

For this purpose, we first estimate destination-specific Mincerian wage regressions using individual-level data. We denote by $\log(w_i)$ the log of the hourly wage of individual i:

$$\log(\omega_i) = \alpha + \beta X_i + \eta \text{TE}_i + \mu M\_\text{COO}_i + \rho \text{TE}_i \times M\_\text{COO}_i + \epsilon_i, \qquad (2)$$

where X_i is a vector of individual demographic control variables (personal, job, and household characteristics, including information on migrant status and years since immigration). In this notation, TE_i is a dummy variable for the tertiary education status of individual i (taking on the value of 1 if completed, and 0 otherwise), and M_COO_i is a sequence of dummy variables taking on the value of 1 if an individual i is an immigrant arriving from the given COO and zero otherwise. Accordingly, parameter η measures the average returns to tertiary education for natives in that destination country. Analogously, the vector of parameters μ captures the average effect of an immigrant from a given origin in a given destination for individuals without tertiary education. Finally, the vector of parameters ρ captures the additional effect (positive or negative) of tertiary education for migrants migrating from a particular COO to a particular destination.[10]

We estimate Eq. (2) with two samples of migrants: recent migrants with less than 5 years since immigration (the first sample), and nonrecent migrants, i.e. those who have resided in the destination country for at least 5 years (the second sample). We identify samples using subscript t. This modeling choice has two advantages. Splitting the estimates for recent migrants and nonrecent migrants allows us to tackle the potential bias stemming from selectivity in return migration: we cannot capture the size of the bias, but when estimated among individuals with similar duration of stay in the hosting economy, the bias should be homogeneous (Dustmann & Görlach, 2016). Second, estimating the two subsamples allows us to control for general differences of recent migrants relative to those who had the chance to fully explore the local conditions, as described by Chiswick and Miller (2012).[11]

Using the estimates of $\widehat{\mu}$ and $\widehat{\rho}$, we create a database of estimates for each COO o in each destination country d and for every available sample t. In analogy to the approach in Section 3.1, we construct a vector $\widehat{\gamma}_{d,o,t}$. This vector contains estimates for individuals without tertiary education in the vector of $\widehat{\mu}$ and with tertiary education from the vector of $\widehat{\rho}$. This set of estimates becomes a vector $\widehat{\gamma}_{d,o,t}$ used as a dependent variable in the second stage, in Section 3.3 below.

To ensure that each $\widehat{\gamma}_{d,o,t}$ element can be reliably estimated, sufficient degrees of freedom are needed. Given the number of variables in Eq. (2), we impose a sample restriction that in each destination country, at least 10 individuals from a given origin country are available for each level of education and duration of stay in the destination country.

3.3 Immigrant Wage Gaps and Language Proximity

Section 3.2 described the first step of our two-step approach, i.e. the methodology for determining average returns to tertiary education by destination and COO. The second step in this approach, laid out in the following, tests the relevance of LP in explaining differences in these returns. For this purpose, we estimate the following equation:

$$\widehat{\gamma}_{d,o,t} = \lambda \mathrm{TE}_{d,o} \times \mathrm{CLI}_{d,o} + \delta_Z Z_{d,o} + \delta_d + \delta_o + \delta_t + \epsilon_{d,o,t}, \qquad (3)$$

where the dependent variable $\widehat{\gamma}_{d,o,t}$ is the estimated systematic dispersion in returns to tertiary education for migrants from Eq. (2), for a given destination (d) and origin (o) country and time since migration (t, a dummy variable which determines if a sample comprised recent migrants or long-term migrants); TE dummy identifies whether a given estimate concerns migrants with a tertiary degree from a given COO in a given destination country; Z is a vector of controls for both the COO (population size and GDP per capita) and country-pair unique factors (geographical distance, contiguity, common legal system, religion, and historic past), and δ_d, δ_o and δ_t capture fixed effects for destination, origin and migrant sample type, respectively. The key variable of interest is λ vector of parameters for LP ($\text{CLI}_{d,o}$).

We estimate Eq. (3) with several specifications. First, we account for the sample size used to estimate a given $\widehat{\gamma}_{d,o,t}$ estimate. Not only do larger immigrant groups in a given destination country give more confidence in the robustness of the $\widehat{\gamma}_{d,o,t}$ estimates but the size of the migration flows is also typically proportional to the sample size of a population of migrants from a given COO in a given destination country. In our case, the sample sizes differ between destination countries for methodological reasons (for instance, the sampling size of the US data is much larger than that of Germany), so the sample weights are inappropriate. We thus use migrant stocks for country pairs from the United Nations as weights. Second, since $\widehat{\gamma}_{d,o,t}$ is an estimated parameter, we bootstrap standard errors in estimating Eq. (3). An alternative approach to addressing the measurement error of $\widehat{\gamma}_{d,o,t}$ is to apply weighted regression using, for example, t-statistics or the inverse of the standard errors derived from the estimation of Eq. (2) as weights. However, such re-weighting for precision excludes re-weighting for migration flows. We adopt both re-weighting and bootstrapping to test the robustness of our results.

4. DATA

We acquire individual-level data from around the world. The following criteria are applied: First, the data source has to report wages and individual characteristics relevant to estimating the Mincerian regression. Second, the data source has to refer to a popular migrant destination country. Third, the data sources should be linguistically diversified to exploit variation in LP across country pairs, holding constant the destination country fixed effects and the origin country fixed effects. Data sources for nine migration destination countries meet these basic criteria: Encuesta Permanente de Hogares (*EPH*) for Argentina, IPUMS-published census data for Brazil, Canada, Israel, and Mexico (IPUMS-I, 2020), Labor Force Surveys for France and the United Kingdom, Socio-Economic Panel for Germany and American Community Survey (ACS) data from the United States. These destinations collectively host about 36% of the total migrant population worldwide.[12] We report in Table A2 details of data coverage.

A migrant is defined in the data as a person whose reported country of birth differs from the survey country. Unfortunately, the data do not allow for distinguishing reasons for migration, meaning refugees, asylum seekers, and family-reunification migrants cannot be separated from other groups.

Additionally, the datasets do not include information on migrants' command of the language(s) spoken in the host economy. We construct a variable measuring years since migration to this destination country.[13] Individuals who arrived as children are classified as natives while those reporting their year of arrival no earlier than 5 years prior to the survey are categorized as recent migrants. Those with longer stays are classified long-term migrants. Individuals for whom the implied age of arrival is after obtaining a tertiary degree are considered to have a foreign diploma. The data do not permit to identify the situations, in which an individual left their country of birth before obtaining a tertiary degree, studied in a third country, and later moved to the current destination. If this phenomenon were frequent in the sample, it could bias CLI estimates toward zero due to the absence of informational frictions for employers.

The datasets are harmonized to ensure comparability across countries. For each destination country, waves of data spanning several periods are pooled together. Wages are adjusted for inflation using the consumer price index (CPI) from the World Development Indicators database by the World Bank. Occupations are categorized into five levels: jobs not requiring skills, jobs requiring primary skills, specialists, high-skilled jobs, and managers. Similarly, industries are grouped into four levels: agriculture, manufacturing, construction, and services. More detailed classifications for both industry and occupation could not be obtained in a harmonized manner. Educational attainment is standardized using ISCED categories. Age is measured as a continuous variable while marital status is classified into four levels: single, married, in an informal relationship, and widowed/divorced.

We restrict our full sample to salaried workers aged 18–64. We use hourly wages, calculating them from weekly or monthly wage data, with average hours in the respective period used whenever available. Observations with negative incomes, missing data on hours worked, or hours strictly equal to 0 or exceeding 100 per week are dropped (similar to e.g., Mishel et al., 2012). In cases where earned income or hours worked are reported in intervals, the middle value of these intervals is used. This is the case for the data from Israel. In the case of Brazil and the United States, the middle value for hours was used whenever hours were reported in intervals.

As controls for COO, we include population, mortality, and fertility as well as GDP per capita (adjusted for purchasing power parity), which we take from the World Development Indicators database by the World Bank. We merge country-level variables with the individual-level data using the year relevant for the individual immigrant. For example, if an individual originates from Nigeria and is identified as a resident in the United Kingdom in the 2005 Labor Force Survey, with (self-reported) 11 years since migration, we merge the individual-level observation with the 1994 (=2005 − 11) for the World Bank data on Nigeria.

Some controls unique to a given country pair do not vary over time. These controls include geographical distance between the two countries, contiguity, common legal system, common religion, and measures for common historic past (colonizer, war, etc.). Data on the distance between two countries and their contiguity originally come from the CEPII database. Common colonization history data are taken from Head et al. (2010). Data on common legal systems come from *JuriGlobe*, the University of Ottawa's world legal systems database. The measure on common religion is based on the *CIA World Factbook*, enhanced with information obtained from the International Religious Freedom Report,[14] The www.worldchristiandatabase.org, and the Pew Research Center.[15] Finally, the number of years at war comes from the *CorrelatesOfWar.org* archive. Bilateral migration flows and stocks are taken from the United Nations.

We use the same variables as suggested by Head et al. (2010). To obtain the CLI, which is a measure of the *ease of communication* between individuals from two different countries, we follow the same steps as Melitz and Toubal (2014). We start from the raw data on the ASJP LP measure from Bakker et al. (2009) and combine it with measures of common official language (COL), common spoken language (CSL), and common native language (CNL) from *CIA World Factbook* and European Commission (2006) data.[16] The logic behind the approach is intuitive: If a COL exists for a given pair of countries, individuals from the two countries are likely to communicate fairly easily (and assess one another's credentials effectively). Similarly, suppose that there is some positive probability that two randomly selected individuals, one from each country, are able to communicate in a CNL (for example, many people in the United States report Spanish as their native language) or in another CSL (e.g., via a *lingua franca*). In essence, CNL and CSL can roughly be interpreted as measuring the likelihood that two randomly selected individuals, one from each country, can communicate in their native language (CNL) or another language they both speak (CSL). See Melitz and Toubal (2014) for a detailed description of the underlying methodology. To obtain the CLI, we standardize the original language proximity index (*ease of communication*) by our sample, bounded by the values of 0 and 1 for the lowest and highest LP in our data, respectively.[17]

Table 1 reports the summary statistics of our data. Note that we use several sources of data, each with multiple variables. In the interest of brevity, we report in Table 1 key variables of interest for three groups of variables: data that we are able to recover from individual data in our sample, data on migration from the United Nations which are matched at the country level, and economic data matched at the country or country pair level.

Our sample consists of a large number of observations from Brazil (32% of observations) and the United States (48% of observations). This is because these two data sources are essentially censuses. Meanwhile, data for Israel, Germany, France, and the United Kingdom come from representative population surveys. To adjust for these effects in the individual-level regressions, the observations are weighed by the inverse of the destination country sample size.

The sample of destination countries allows us to study quite diverse cases in terms of immigration prevalence, years since migration, and sociodemographic characteristics such as education and age. We have countries with long and short traditions of immigration (high average value of years since immigration indicator), attracting mostly highly skilled migrants and quite the opposite. Even in terms of age, there are countries where migrants are younger than native salaried

Table 1. Summary Statistics.

	Total	Argentina	Brazil	Canada	France	Germany	Israel	Mexico	UK	USA
Individual-level data										
# of obs.	42,852,038	1,117,908	13,555,036	1,076,098	402,225	301,969	192,622	5,095,568	568,277	20,542,335
# of natives	39,359,351	1,075,475	13,523,179	910,651	369,750	253,229	109,488	5,081,264	528,039	17,508,276
# of migrants	3,492,687	42,433	31,857	165,447	32,475	48,740	83,134	14,304	40,238	3,034,059
# of recent migrants	532,987	38,523	11,278	28,820	2,976	3,352	15,891	10,884	9,830	411,433
% of recent migrants	0.153	0.908	0.354	0.174	0.092	0.069	0.191	0.761	0.244	0.136
Years since immigration	19.620	3.495	9.315	18.902	28.247	19.959	23.279	3.195	19.951	19.868
% of TE natives	0.368	0.333	0.145	0.619	0.308	0.313	0.329	0.195	0.169	0.588
% of TE migrants	0.505	0.196	0.446	0.657	0.237	0.160	0.352	0.449	0.235	0.518
Age of natives	37.25	38.72	34.19	37.49	39.42	40.45	32.96	33.53	39.60	40.46
Age of migrants	40.97	43.90	42.24	41.88	43.88	40.31	43.36	35.30	38.76	40.83
Country-level data: migration (from United Nations)										
# of migrants in DC	-	1,749,013	781,583	4,487,372	5,969,137	7,058,662	1,632,704	516,352	3,766,946	27,571,091
(SD of OCs in DC)	-	(136,592)	(48,342)	(89,099)	(282,479)	(225,947)	(50,543)	(6,751)	(96,272)	(242,630)
Country-level data (World Bank, Barro and Lee (2013) and Melitz and Toubal (2014))										
Common language index (CLI)	-	0.686	0.476	0.555	0.629	0.416	0.348	0.688	0.541	0.462
	-	(0.351)	(0.331)	(0.300)	(0.206)	(0.267)	(0.169)	(0.343)	(0.299)	(0.284)
Common official language	-	0.462	0.071	0.391	0.316	0.044	0.056	0.516	0.338	0.291
	-	(0.503)	(0.259)	(0.493)	(0.471)	(0.206)	(0.232)	(0.504)	(0.475)	(0.455)
Common spoken language	-	0.458	0.076	0.392	0.429	0.239	0.138	0.520	0.372	0.302
	-	(0.454)	(0.197)	(0.299)	(0.236)	(0.251)	(0.073)	(0.454)	(0.339)	(0.324)
Common native language	-	0.371	0.043	0.100	0.047	0.025	0.054	0.423	0.101	0.112
	-	(0.429)	(0.175)	(0.183)	(0.106)	(0.124)	(0.074)	(0.412)	(0.257)	(0.233)
Log of distance	-	8.704	8.891	8.831	6.998	7.920	7.448	8.547	8.257	8.858
	-	(1.052)	(0.653)	(0.653)	(0.952)	(1.031)	(0.773)	(0.782)	(0.982)	(0.562)

% of DC-contiguous OCs	-	0.192	0.190	0.043	0.316	0.103	0.111	0.065	0.014	0.015
% of common colonizer OCs	-	0.000	0.000	0.000	0.000	0.000	0.056	0.000	0.000	0.000
Common religion	-	0.499	0.373	0.199	0.349	0.147	0.057	0.447	0.122	0.151
GDP pc in OC (as % of DC)	-	267%	269%	43%	76%	31%	33%	357%	44%	29%

Notes: Individual-level descriptive statistics obtained for sample of salaried workers aged 18–64 years old. Migrants defined as recent if resident in hosting economy for less than 5 years. Our linguistic proximity index follows Melitz and Toubal (2014), with one modification: we standardize the distribution by common spoken language indicators rather than common native language indicators. All estimations were obtained also for the original Melitz and Toubal (2014) specification standardized by common native language; these robustness results are reported in Appendix 10. Standard errors in parentheses (where applicable).

workers, as well as the opposite. Perhaps more relevant for this study, the sample of destination countries is characterized by quite diverse migration patterns in terms of geographic proximity (e.g. contiguity or geographical distance) and common culture (proxied here by religion and common colonial past).

5. RESULTS

We present results in four substantive parts: the dispersion of returns to tertiary education among migrants, the estimates at individual level, which reflect the link between LP and the position of migrants with tertiary education in the wage distribution, and the estimates at country level, which reflect the link between LP and the magnitude of deviation of return to tertiary education among migrants (enhanced with a robustness check for effect sizes across the wage distribution). These analyses look only at the population of salaried workers, aged 18–64. Note that individuals who obtained their education in the hosting economy are considered native workers, regardless of their country of birth. Our estimates therefore purposefully identify the foreign origin of a tertiary degree.

5.1 The Dispersion of Returns to Tertiary Education Among Migrants ($\widehat{\gamma}_{d,o,t}$ Estimates)

The first step in our two-step approach, i.e. the estimation of Eq. (2), yields estimates of returns to skills for individuals with tertiary education, across origin countries, relative to natives in the respective destination countries. Since we estimate the wages in logs, the coefficients have a clear interpretation: It is the percentage wage deviation of migrants from the average wage of native university graduates, broken down by COO. Tertiary education per se is estimated relative to individuals without tertiary education. For example, consider that a tertiary-educated native earns 20% more than a native without a tertiary degree. Further, consider that for a specific COO in the given destination country, the estimate $\widehat{\gamma} = -10\%$ is equivalent to stating that an immigrant earns 10% less than a native with the same education. We do not interpret the estimates of $\gamma_{d,o,t}$ as causal measures of wage discrimination against particular groups of migrants—we treat them as what they are analytically: measures of the dispersion of wages across the migrants' origin countries.

Table 2 reports the basic features of the obtained $\widehat{\gamma}_{d,o,t}$ estimates from Eq. (2) on nine utilized individual-level datasets. We obtain in total 1,570 estimates of $\widehat{\gamma}_{d,o,t}$ for 153 different countries of origin. Overall, roughly 89% of these $\widehat{\gamma}_{d,o,t}$ estimates are statistically significant, i.e. the estimated $\widehat{\gamma}_{d,o,t}$ coefficient has a p-value lower than 10%. Note that there are two reasons for an insignificant estimate: it is either insufficiently precisely estimated (true $\gamma_{d,o,t} \neq 0$, but we fail to reject the null hypothesis due to insufficient power relative to the variation in the data) or it is actually zero (true $\gamma_{d,o,t} = 0$). The latter implies that there is no wage premium/penalty for workers (of certain education level) from a given COO in a given destination country. The former implies that estimations with significant $\widehat{\gamma}_{d,o,t}$ will be missing distribution mass around 0. This bias may not be large, though, as indicated by the overwhelming majority of estimates that are statistically significant. The outcome of the first step in our two-step procedure thus suggests that indeed for the vast majority of origins and destinations, there seem to be systematic deviations of migrant wages relative to the wages of native workers.

The deviations we find are not only statistically significant but also economically relevant. Fig. 1 visualizes the raw distribution of the $\widehat{\gamma}_{d,o,t}$ estimates obtained from Eq. (2). In line with the results reported in Table 2, the distributions are remarkably dispersed and skewed toward negative values. We report two distributions: the one on the left-hand side provides the distribution of all estimates we obtained while the graph on the right-hand side visualizes the significant estimates of $\widehat{\gamma}_{d,o,t}$ only. Consequently, the estimates in the graph on the right-hand side are more dispersed since there are fewer estimates to be

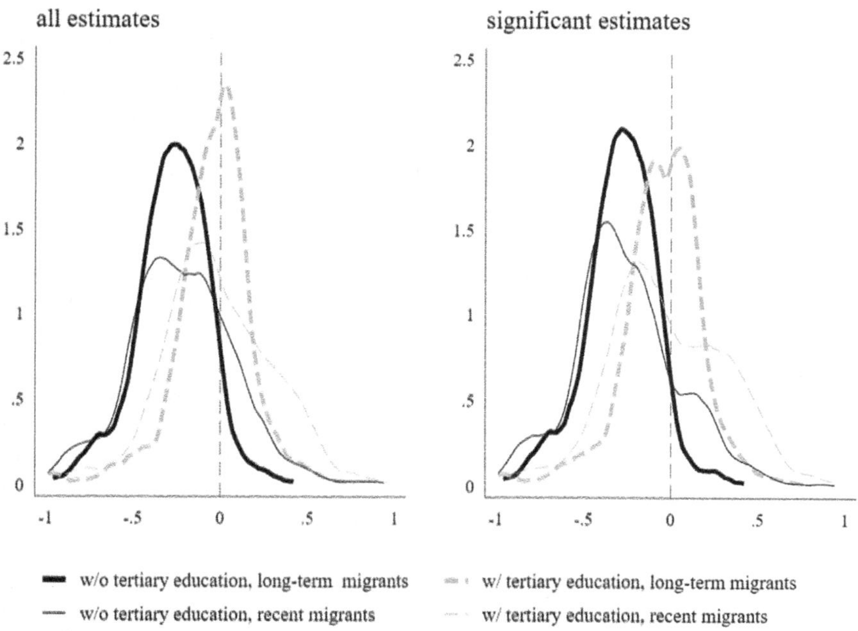

Fig. 1. The Returns to Tertiary Education for Migrants ($\widehat{\gamma}_{d,o,t}$) are Dispersed.

Notes: The figures report the kernel density estimates for the distribution of $\widehat{\gamma}_{d,o,t}$ from Eq. (2) for the full sample reported in Table A2. The gray dotted lines represent the distribution of estimates for highly educated migrants (i.e., those with tertiary education), while the black lines represent the distribution for migrants without tertiary education. Bold lines represent the estimates for nonrecent migrants, thin lines the ones for recent migrants. Recent migrants are individuals who report residing in the country of destination for less than 5 years. Long-term migrants refer to individuals residing for 5 years or longer in the given destination country.

Table 2. Number of $\widehat{\gamma}_{d,o,t}$ Estimates by Country of Destination.

Destination	# of Estimates			# of Significant Estimates			# of Countries of Origin
	Total	Positive	Negative	Total	Positive	Negative	
Argentina	151	36	115	96	11	85	28
Brazil	245	121	124	227	112	115	44
Canada	146	70	76	141	68	73	25
France	117	46	71	92	30	62	20
Germany	396	85	311	255	34	221	72
Israel	118	55	63	106	50	56	22
Mexico	164	24	140	143	17	126	33
United Kingdom	454	159	295	437	150	287	77
USA	839	143	696	831	138	693	140
Total	2,630	739	1891	2,328	610	1718	153

Notes: This table reports the number of estimates of the $\widehat{\gamma}_{d,o,t}$ for the full sample reported in Table A2. The reference group is a native worker with a tertiary degree; thus, a positive coefficient signifies that a migrant worker with a tertiary degree earns more than an otherwise identical native worker. We report jointly the estimates for recent migrants and long-term migrants. In principle, the total number of estimates should be six times the number of the countries of origin (with and without a tertiary degree, for recent migrants, long-term migrants, and for both groups together). For example, in the case of Brazil, 44 countries of origin imply 264 estimates in total. For some countries of origin and education levels, the coefficient $\widehat{\gamma}_{d,o,t}$ could not be identified (insufficient degrees of freedom), which reduces the final sample to 245 estimated coefficients.

found in the range close to zero. Our results confirm that the vast dispersion in terms of wages between origin countries is not a unique feature of the United States (Butcher, 1994) but is a fairly general phenomenon.

Incidentally, Fig. 1 also documents that the dispersion of $\widehat{\gamma}_{d,o,t}$ is smaller for migrants without tertiary education than for migrants with tertiary education: kernel density estimates for migrants without tertiary education (marked in black) are thinner than those for migrants with tertiary education (marked in blue). We quantify this observation with the use of ANOVA analysis. We perform two independent variance decompositions: on the coefficient of the migrant dummy (*M*_COO) and on the estimates $\widehat{\gamma}_{d,o,t}$. In both cases, we use the same set of components: origin country fixed effects, destination country fixed effects, and migrant sample (long-term vs recent vs jointly estimated for all migrants). We report these results in Table A4, which illustrates the following observations. First, the variance of immigrant dummy estimates is considerably lower than for the migrants with tertiary education, but it is also more idiosyncratic. In fact, there is a high fraction in the variation of the estimates of $\widehat{\gamma}_{d,o,t}$ originating from destination countries, almost 56% (compared to 34% on a lower total variation for the immigrant dummy). We also show that destination-by-origin variation essentially trumps the effects attributable to destination countries, but not due to the origin countries. We interpret this analysis of variance as an indication that even if some hosting economies have particular tastes for migrants from some origin countries, this preference is certainly not enough to explain the dispersion of the estimates obtained.

Our destination countries differ in their historical patterns of migration. In a similar manner, data from destination countries span periods of diverse duration. One potential explanation for migrant wage gap is their command of local language, with research showing that successful integration into the hosting labor market usually involves learning the local language. This channel is independent of the ones proposed in our study: LP generating lower frictions for the employers to inspect the qualification of migrant job applicants. In Fig. 2, we scatter the estimates of the migrant wage gap as discussed above against the characteristic of the migrant population in a given destination country from a given COO. We particularly focus on the duration of stay in the destination country. We rely on binned scatters, residualizing both the wage gaps and the average year since migration on country pair fixed effects. There appears to be no correlation on average between the average length of stay of migrants from a given origin country in a given destination country and the wage gaps experienced in the job market by these migrants. In other words, there can be important effects of duration of stay on individual wages, but there is no

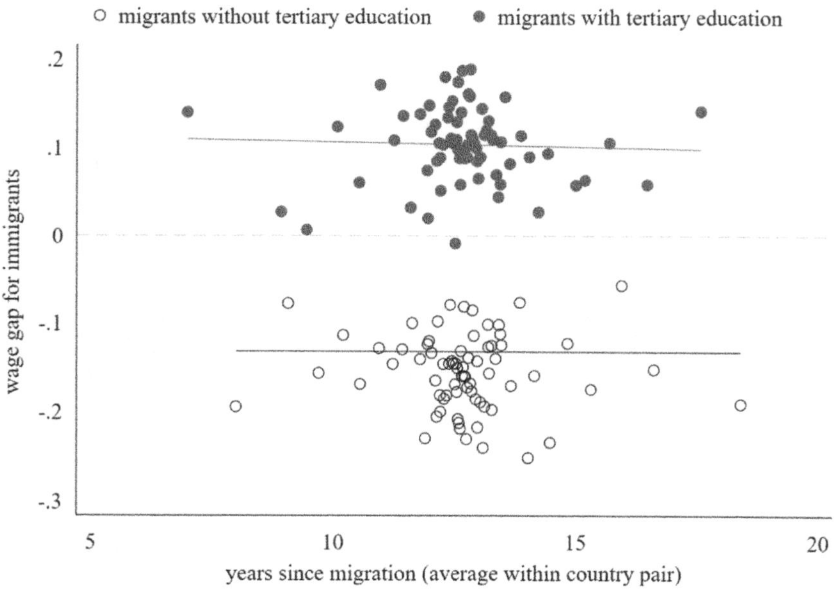

Fig. 2. There is No Link Between Migrant Wage Gap and Duration of Stay.
Notes: The figure reports the binned scatter of $\widehat{\gamma}_{d,o,t}$ from Eq. (2) for the full sample reported in Table A2 against a measure of average number of years since migration to a destination country for each country of origin. The scatters are residualized for country pairs.

correlation between the average duration of stay in a country pair and the estimated migrant wage gap.

Stereotyping and mental accounting lead to a form of a "halo effect," where migrants from a given COO are lumped together to represent one stereotype—distinct from natives as well as migrants from another origin (e.g. Guiso et al., 2009; Rydgren & Ruth, 2013). In Fig. 3, we portray on the horizontal axis the coefficient on the *M_COO* migrant dummy (i.e., the estimated effect for migrants without a tertiary degree for a given country pair) and on the vertical axis the estimated $\widehat{\gamma}_{d,o,t}$ that is the estimated effects for tertiary educated migrants from the same pair. In fact, we find no significant correlation for long-term migrants and a weak positive correlation of 0.17 for recent migrants (with a standard error of 0.039).[18] The strength of the correlation is heterogeneous between the nine countries of destination studied.

5.2 Individual-Level Analysis

We estimate Eq. (1) with a linear model. $\text{TE}_i \times \text{linguistic proximity}_{d,o}$ is the variable of interest in our study. While the variation in TE_i occurs at the

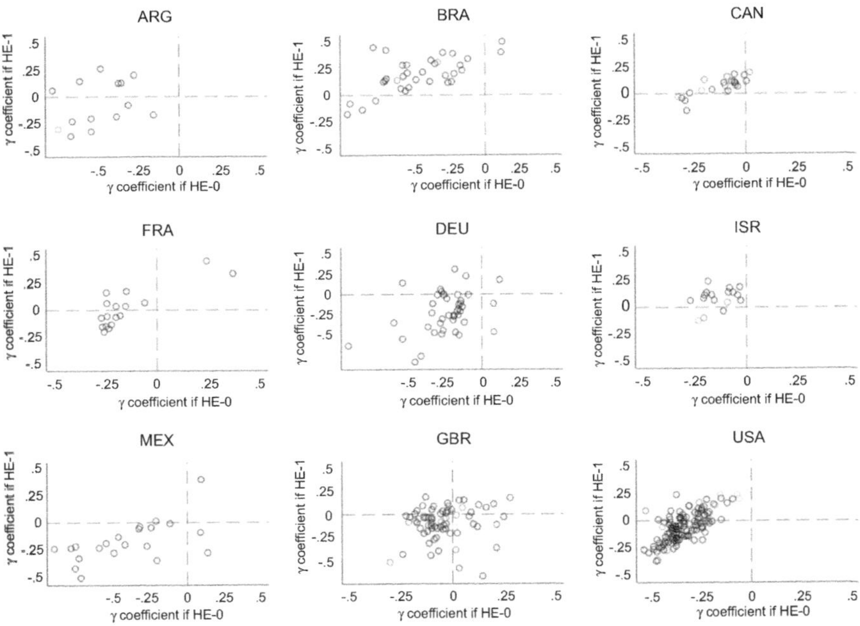

Fig. 3. The Correlation Between Wage Gaps for TE Migrants and Migrants Without TE is Weak.

Notes: The figures report the significant estimates $\widehat{\gamma}_{d,o,t}$ from Eq. (2) for the full sample reported in Table A2, obtained jointly for recent and long-term migrants. The reference level for the two reported dummy coefficients is a tertiary-educated native. The shade of the circles denotes linguistic proximity (darker shade akin to more similar languages).

individual level, $CLI_{d,o}$ has only the variation at the country pair level. To trust the standard errors of the parameter estimates for $CLI_{d,o}$ we need to cluster standard errors at the level of country pair, but then the standard errors are overstated for all the parameters that are characterized by variation at the level of the individual, the origin country, or the destination country. Note that this modeling choice does not affect the estimates of the parameters, but only their standard errors. Table 3 reports our results.

We find that among native workers, tertiary education is associated with a wage percentile roughly 9.4 points higher than with secondary education or less, after adjusting for occupation and sector of employment. This result is roughly consistent with standard estimates of Mincerian wage regressions, which typically report approximately 20% wage gain due to tertiary education. Column (2) shows that among migrants, LP improves the position in wage distribution. The effect is stronger for migrants with tertiary education. This result is robust to clustering standard errors at a country-pair level. In Columns (3)–(4), we add a battery of origin and destination country controls, and the results remain of the same economic magnitude and statistical significance. In the bottom panel of Table 3, we compare migrants, using natives without tertiary education as the reference group. Note that in our specifications, the *M* dummy is insignificant, which can be attributed to the inclusion of adjustment for the number of years since immigration. This variable equals age for natives and measures time since arrival in the destination country for migrants, capturing differences in wage distribution positions between migrants and natives. LP proves significant in the most demanding specification in Column (4) of the bottom panel. We find positive effects for migrants without tertiary education and additional positive effects for migrants with tertiary education. Note that our estimates adjust for industry and occupation, which implies that the interpretation of these two estimates is *within* the same occupation and industry rather than on average.

We find that greater LP between the origin and destination country is associated with a significantly higher percentile position in the wage distribution, in particular for migrants with a tertiary degree (though the effects are not very precisely estimated).

To interpret the magnitude of 7.5 percentiles for the LP (as measured by CLI) from our preferred specification in Column (4), we perform the following exercise: With a wave of migration from Russia to Israel in the 1990s, Russian has become a significant CSL for the country-pair: an estimated 12.25% of the population in Israel can communicate effectively in Russian as a spoken language.[19] The CLI value we observe for the country pair is 0.138. We evaluate a counterfactual value of CLI in our sample, as if this wave of immigration had not occurred, i.e. as if the share of Russian speakers in Israel would be essentially close to zero. In other words, we calculate the country-pair CLI value for a scenario in which Russian would be an irrelevant language in Israel. We obtain the value of CLI = 0.018. Our estimates in Table 3 on the influence of CLI then imply that, on average, migrants from Russia with a tertiary degree can expect to be about 1 percentile higher in Israel's wage distribution in Israel nowadays, once one in eight citizens in Israel can easily communicate with them. Note that

Table 3. One-step Individual Level Regression.

Variables	(1)	(2) (1) + $CLI_{d,o}$	(3) (2) + Z_0	(4) (3) + $Z_{d,o}$
Panel A: Sample of immigrants only				
TE	9.987***	8.781***	8.923***	8.963***
	(0.051)	(0.858)	(0.853)	(0.847)
Linguistic proximity				
for migrants w/o TE		5.668***	5.823***	7.453***
		(1.402)	(1.404)	(1.739)
additionally for migrants w/TE		3.451**	3.221**	3.097**
		(1.388)	(1.391)	(1.385)
Observations	1,490,240	1,490,240	1,490,240	1,490,240
R-squared	0.385	0.388	0.389	0.390
Panel B: Full sample				
TE	9.423***	9.423***	9.519***	9.708***
	(0.013)	(0.735)	(0.735)	(0.711)
Migrants	−0.374***	−0.374	−0.274	−0.050
	(0.012)	(0.468)	(0.465)	(0.485)
Linguistic proximity				
for migrants w/o TE		0.016	0.232	3.326**
		(1.795)	(1.800)	(1.625)
additionally for migrants w/TE		2.400**	2.276**	1.543+
		(1.133)	(1.129)	(1.006)
Observations	42,513,808	42,513,808	42,513,808	42,513,808
R-squared	0.364	0.364	0.365	0.367
Marital status, YSI, gender	Yes	Yes	Yes	Yes
COO FE	Yes	Yes	Yes	Yes
COD FE	Yes	Yes	Yes	Yes
Origin X's	No	No	Yes	Yes
Pair X's	No	No	No	Yes

Notes: Linguistic proximity measured as common language index, following Melitz and Toubal (2014), with the exception that we standardize the final measure by common spoken language rather than common native language. Sensitivity analysis with common native language as standardizing variable reported in Table A5 in the Appendix D. The full set of estimates is available upon request. Standard errors clustered at the level of destination-by-origin country pairs in parentheses. $\widehat{w}$ is the dependent variable, which is the destination country-specific wage percentile for individual i as per Eq. (1). Individual controls (available upon request) include age, age squared, gender, marital status, no. of children, occupation, industry, and years since immigration. Origin country controls (available upon request) include GDP per capita (PPP adjusted), fertility, mortality, and population size, merged by the year of arrival at a destination country for each individual i. Country-pair controls (available upon request) include the geographical distance between origin and destination countries, as well as contiguity dummy, common colonizer dummy, years at war measure, common religion, and common legal system (constant over time). Conventional levels of statistical significance are denoted by asterisk: ***, **, *, and + denote $p < 0.01$, $p < 0.05$, $p < 0.10$, and $p < 0.15$, respectively.

in this regard, our estimates are in line with the study of Eckstein and Weiss (2004).

Another intuitive example is provided by the differences among Nordic languages: we compare Norwegian, Swedish, and Danish relative to contemporaneous German. The ASJP measure of LP reports a relative LP of 0.43 for Norwegian and roughly 0.36 for Swedish and Danish. If Swedish or Danish were linguistically as similar to German as Norwegian is, then the average wages of migrants with a university degree from those two countries would rank roughly 1 percentile higher in the relative wage distribution in Germany, *ceteris paribus*.

The migrant dummy continues to be negative in the more comprehensive specifications, but in terms of magnitude, it declines by roughly a factor of two. The same holds for the relative wages of migrants with a tertiary degree, relative to natives without a tertiary degree. Naturally, these estimates should be evaluated against standard errors of the magnitudes similar to those reported in Column (1) because these are individual-level dummy variables whereas Columns (2)–(4) cluster standard errors at origin-by-destination country level.

5.3 Country-Level Analysis

The country-level analysis is based on a two-step procedure: we first obtained estimates of returns to tertiary education in each destination country for each observed origin country (see Section 5.1) and subsequently utilize these obtained measures of dispersion in rewards to human capital as explained variables. Whereas in Table 3 the explained variable was in percentiles of (within the destination country) wage distribution, in our two-step country analysis the explained variable is the immigrant wage gap, expressed in percent of average wages. The results are reported in Table 4. The estimated coefficients report the effects relative to natives without tertiary education. We find that migrants with the same level of educational attainment earn less than natives if they come from countries with higher LP whereas migrants with tertiary education earn more. The premium for LP among tertiary educated migrants does not fully compensate the gap between tertiary educated natives and tertiary educated migrants, but it helps to narrow it.

Since the explained variable itself is estimated from individual-level data, we apply bootstrapping to adjust the estimators; these bootstrapped specifications are denoted by *a* in Table 4. The procedure of bootstrapping addresses the random nature of the explained variable but still treats all observations equally. Meanwhile, highly statistically significant estimates of $\gamma_{d,o,t}$ are naturally more reliable than the insignificant ones. In a similar spirit, the estimates of $\gamma_{d,o,t}$ which refer to large migration flows may be of more policy relevance than those that refer to rare and quantitatively negligible migration flows. We thus introduce two separate weighting mechanisms: by t-statistic of the obtained $\gamma_{d,o,t}$ estimator and by the size of the bilateral migration flow (scaled by the size of the sending country).

While weighting by t-statistic leverages our certainty about our estimates, weighting by migration flows yields a picture of reality that adjusts for the

Table 4. Migrant Wage gaps: two-step Country-Level Regression.

			p - value < 0.15	w = [t-stat]		w = [$migr_{o,d}$]	
Specification	(1)	(1a)	(2)	(3)	(3a)	(4)	(4a)
TE	0.206***	0.206***	0.232***	0.251***	0.251***	0.216***	0.216***
	(0.021)	(0.023)	(0.022)	(0.016)	(0.024)	(0.020)	(0.026)
Linguistic proximity							
migrants w/o TE	−0.025	−0.025	0.001	−0.052	−0.052	0.003	0.003
	(0.045)	(0.053)	(0.048)	(0.048)	(0.072)	(0.044)	(0.066)
migrants w/TE	0.108***	0.108***	0.098***	0.103***	0.103***	0.068***	0.068*
	(0.036)	(0.040)	(0.038)	(0.028)	(0.044)	(0.033)	(0.044)
Observations	1,447	1,447	1,260	1,447	1,447	1,447	1,447
R-squared	0.521	0.521	0.576	0.767	0.767	0.552	0.552
OC X's	Yes	Yes	Yes	Yes	Yes	Yes	Yes
DC FE	Yes	Yes	Yes	Yes	Yes	Yes	Yes
Country pair X's	Yes	Yes	Yes	Yes	Yes	Yes	Yes
Country pair FE's	Yes	Yes	Yes	Yes	Yes	Yes	Yes

Notes: Linguistic proximity measured as common language index, following Melitz and Toubal (2014), with the exception that we standardize the final measure by common spoken language rather than common native language, a robustness check with common native language standardization reported in Table A6 in the Appendices. Standard errors clustered at the level of the destination country. $\widehat{\gamma}_{o,d,t}$ is the dependent variable, which is the destination-by-origin country-specific wage gap for migrants, with and without tertiary education, relative to natives without tertiary education, as per Eq. (3). Origin country controls (available upon request) include GDP per capita (PPP adjusted) and population size, merged by the year of arrival at a destination country for each individual i. Country-pair controls (available upon request) include the geographical distance between origin and destination countries, as well as contiguity dummy, common colonizer dummy, years at war measure, common religion, and common legal system (constant over time). Conventional levels of statistical significance are denoted by asterisk: ***, **, and * denote $p < 0.05$, $p < 0.10$, and $p < 0.15$, respectively. Standard errors in parentheses.

importance of migration flows: it weighs our estimates by the relative number of migrants from a certain COO in a COD, i.e. mirroring the actual migrant counts reported by the United Nations. This should further minimize any potential biases due to differences in the sampling techniques used in the underlying datasets—further increasing overall reliability. Our preferred specification is reported in Column (4a) of Table 4. The other specifications permit identifying the role of weighing and bootstrapping against the raw estimation in Column (1). All specifications include control factors for the origin countries, fixed effects for the destination countries, and control factors for origin-by-destination country pairs. Finally, in all specifications, we cluster standard errors by origin country.

Generally, migrants with a tertiary degree earn approximately 20% more than migrants without it, as reported in the first row of Table 4 (the reference level for both groups is native workers). There is no effect of LP for the estimates of the wage gaps of migrants without tertiary education and a large positive correlation for individuals with tertiary education. In other words, wages of migrants with a tertiary degree increase in LP (relative to native workers). The effect is relatively large, approximately 10%. The estimates fall to 7%, when we reweigh the estimation by the size of bilateral migration flows. To put this number in perspective, an immigrant with a tertiary degree from a linguistically close country (CLI close to 1) will earn 7% more than an immigrant with an equal educational achievement obtained in a linguistically distant country (CLI close to 0), according to our preferred specification (4a).

6. DISCUSSION AND CONCLUSION

Immigrant wage gaps are well documented in the literature, but their variation across origin countries has been less studied. Two hypotheses were offered in the literature, related to skill portability and knowledge of the hosting country language. We propose to distinguish between skills (which can be positively correlated with the duration of stay in the hosting economy) and the LP between the origin and destination country. We propose that employers may find it harder to assess foreign credentials of job candidates from linguistically distant countries. We tested this hypothesis empirically. We exploit individual-level data from nine destination countries for many origin countries and document the inequality in returns to education between origin countries. We relate this inequality to LP between the origin and destination countries, finding that lower LP between origin and destination correlates with higher wage gaps for skilled migrants.

Our results demonstrate that LP partially explains the dispersion of returns to foreign tertiary education among migrants. In other words, the costs to employers of inspecting the qualifications of job candidates who obtained their education in a foreign country prove to be non-negligible, and their variation correlates with LP. Employers may struggle to assess the qualifications of job candidates educated abroad. This friction is separate from previously considered frictions such as language skills of job candidates or the pure portability of skills across borders.[20]

Our study is not without other caveats. First, we work with worker-level data, unable to study employers and their behavioral patterns. We work with wages, thus employment contracts where the friction was not prohibitively high. Further research would help validating the role of the frictions on the side of the employer. Second, *migrant selectivity* could be relevant on several levels: self-selection in destination countries (Adsera & Pytlikova, 2015; Bredtmann et al., 2020), return migration decision (Dustmann & Görlach, 2016), and task specialization (Peri & Sparber, 2009). Addressing these selectivity patterns is notoriously difficult, as it requires data from both sending and origin country for the same individuals. Third, we cannot address the hypothesis of *enclaves* because our data are insufficient for geographical location. Fourth, although our two-step approach delivers estimates of the migrant wage gap, the gaps used in this study do not have a direct causal interpretation. We merely argue that methodologically comparable gaps adjusted for individual characteristics are lower for migrants arriving in linguistically closer countries *ceteris paribus*. So long as the destination countries' selectivity bias is constant across the sending countries, our estimates remain reliable. If destination country selectivity was pair-wise rather than destination-wise, our estimates could potentially confound selectivity with LP. Migrants may also self-select into production tasks that tend to be less linguistically intensive than typical tasks preformed by native workers (Peri & Sparber, 2009). This division of labor may be the basis for the migrant wage gap per se (D'Amuri & Peri, 2014).

Our results lend tentative support to several policy implications. For sending countries, in order to improve emigration outcomes of their citizens, it is useful to provide rigorous and well-structured curriculum in international language to the graduates. For receiving countries, labor market efficiency could be improved if information friction related to inspecting skills of foreign educated individuals is eliminated. Identifying effective ways to do so remains a fruitful area of further research.

ACKNOWLEDGMENTS

The authors are grateful for inspiring comments to Michel Beine, Ben Elsner, Tomasso Frattini, Harry Ganzeboom, Laszlo Goerke, Sven Hartmann, Konstantin Homolka, Pawel Kaczmarczyk, Yoshihiro Kitamura, Eva Markowsky, David McKenzie, Alberto Palermo, Nazareno Panichella, Solomon Polachek, Panu Poutvaara, Mariola Pytlikova, Laura Renner, Dominik Sachs, Yannik Schenk, Gabriel Schultze, Katrin Sommerfeld, Nicolas Ziebarth, and the anonymous referees. We thankfully acknowledge the feedback from the audiences at Paris School of Economics, WEAI 2019, VfS Annual Conference 2020, ESCR Workshop 2020, ESPE 2021, and Waseda University Tokyo. Joanna Tyrowicz gratefully acknowledges the support of National Science Center (grant # 2021/43/B/HS4/03241). Any remaining errors are ours.

NOTES

1. Speaking the language of the host economy is a prerequisite for being able to communicate one's knowledge and thus transfer the existing human capital, which is why language skills have been at the core of empirical research on the immigrant wage gap. Empirical research on the migrant wage gap is based on the assimilation hypothesis (Chiswick, 1986), the skill portability hypothesis (e.g. Berman et al., 2003; Bleakley & Chin, 2004, 2010; Chiswick, 1991; Chiswick & Miller, 1995; Dustmann, 1994; Rivera-Batiz, 1990) as well as the segmentation/discrimination of the labor market (Doeringer & Piore, 1985; Piore, 1972; Reich et al., 1973). The existing literature typically finds that in various hosting economies, competence in the language of the hosting economy mitigates—but does not eradicate—the wage penalty (e.g. Chiswick, 1991; Chiswick & Miller, 1995; Dustmann, 1994; Dustmann & Fabbri, 2003; Ferrer et al., 2006; Goldmann et al., 2015; Kossoudji, 1988; McManus, 1985; McManus et al., 1983; Rivera-Batiz, 1990). In addition, learning the language of the host economy is associated with lower wage penalties (Berman et al., 2003).

2. Data sourced from "International Migrant Stock," which is periodically disseminated by the United Nations.

3. Wong (2023) explores the random assignment of asylum seekers to cantons in Switzerland and takes advantage of the fact that cantons differ in terms of dominant language.

4. Early studies on the United States include Borjas (1987), LaLonde and Topel (1992), Borjas and Friedberg (2009), and Borjas (2015) while wage gaps have also been documented for the Netherlands (Kee, 1995), Israel (Friedberg, 2000), and Canada (Fortin et al., 2016; Schaafsma & Sweetman, 2001).

5. For example, university entry or high school exit exams in many countries require knowledge of a major global second language.

6. Medical doctors are subject to strict certification, which makes skills portability an issue, but LP is less relevant given the high degree of standardization of certification in this occupation.

7. IT specialists rely on internationally recognized certificates rather than national ones, so neither skill portability nor LP poses a significant obstacle.

8. The online appendix to their study also distributes the data on the ASJP, as well as on common spoken and official languages around the world.

9. We consider individuals who obtained education in the destination economy as natives, regardless of their ancestry. See Section 4 for detailed coverage of the variable definitions and data sources.

10. We explain in detail in Section 4 that for tertiary-educated individuals if the age at arrival in the destination country is below the customary graduation age, we re-code those individuals to be natives in a sense that their highest achieved education had been obtained in the destination country.

11. Also Lubotsky (2007) offers several arguments for why to estimate immigrant-native wage gaps for recent and nonrecent migrants separately.

12. We obtain this value using "International Migrant Stock" data disseminated by The United Nations.

13. For natives, this variable takes the value of the individual's age.

14. See https://www.state.gov/international-religious-freedom-reports/.

15. The data comes from "Mapping the Global Muslim Population. A Report on the Size and Distribution of the World's Muslim Population" available at https://www.pewforum.org/2009/10/07/mapping-the-global-muslim-population/.

16. The missing data on CNL and CSL fractions were hand collected by Melitz and Toubal (2014) and can be found in the online appendix of their paper.

17. Refer to the appendix B for a technical description of the CLI. Note that our measure of LP departs from Melitz and Toubal (2014) in one minor detail, namely we standardize the ASJP measures by CSL rather than CNL; see Fig. A1 for comparison. This form of standardization is closer to the mechanisms we propose in our model: the ability of an employer to inquire about the qualifications of a candidate employee with a foreign diploma. In the interest of transparency, we estimate our model also with the original CLI by Melitz and Toubal (2014), as reported in Appendix D.

18. This is an unconditional correlation coefficient, with fixed effects for the destination country.

19. The Russian diaspora in Israel accounts for almost all of the reported CSL value of the country pair.

20. Our mechanism is distinct also from discrimination per se or cultural and social norms. Some earlier literature has argued that migrants' employment prospects depend on natives' trust towards origin countries (Keita & Valette, 2019), which is typically lower the greater the geographic distance (Cettolin & Suetens, 2019). Earlier literature argues that social, ethnic, and cultural distance shape natives' attitudes towards migrants from certain origin countries (O'Rourke & Sinnott, 2006). In the labor context, the authors report discrimination in hiring decisions based on the geographic origin of migrants (e.g.

Bertrand & Duflo, 2017; Lancee, 2021; Neumark, 2018; Pager, 2007). Our study proposes an additional source of immigrant wage gaps.

21. Any language considered in the measure must be spoken by at least 4% of the respective local populations.

22. For simplicity, if there is more than one native language in a country, a weighted measure of the two most CNLs of a country were used. In the case of Canada, for instance, English has a weight of 0.70 and French a weight of 0.30 in constructing the measure, indicating both languages' relative domestic relevance in terms of population counts. Other illustrative examples include the United States (weight of 0.85 for English and 0.15 for Spanish), Israel (weight of 0.87 for Hebrew and 0.13 for Russian), or Switzerland (weight of 0.74 for German, 0.26 for French).

23. Note that LP is denoted 0 either when two countries have no linguistic similarity or (following the above argumentation) when CSL is 1 (as in this case LP is completely irrelevant).

REFERENCES

Adsera, A., & Ferrer, A. (2021). Linguistic proximity and the labour market performance of immigrant men in Canada. *Labour*, *35*(1), 1–23.

Adsera, A., & Pytlikova, M. (2015). The role of language in shaping international migration. *Economic Journal*, *125*(586), 49–81.

Bakker, D., Müller, A., Velupillai, V., Wichmann, S., Brown, C. H., Brown, P., Egorov, D., Mailhammer, R., Grant, A., & Holman, E. W. (2009). Adding typology to lexicostatistics: A combined approach to language classification. *Linguistic Typology*, *13*(1), 169–181.

Bar-Haim, E., & Birgier, D. P. (2024). Language distance and labor market integration of migrants: Gendered perspective. *PLoS One*, *19*(4), e0299936.

Barro, R., & Lee, J.-W. (2013). A new data set of educational attainment in the world, 1950–2010. *Journal of Development Economics*, *104*, 184–198.

Bazzi, S., Gaduh, A., Rothenberg, A. D., & Wong, M. (2016). Skill transferability, migration, and development: Evidence from population resettlement in Indonesia. *American Economic Review*, *106*(9), 2658–2698.

Beenstock, M., Chiswick, B. R., & Repetto, G. L. (2001). The effect of linguistic distance and country of origin on immigrant language skills: Application to Israel. *International Migration*, *39*(3), 33–60.

Beine, M., Docquier, F., & Ozden, C. (2011). Diasporas. *Journal of Development Economics*, *95*(1), 30–41.

Belot, M., & Ederveen, S. (2012). Cultural barriers in migration between OECD countries. *Journal of Population Economics*, *25*(3), 1077–1105.

Belot, M., & Hatton, T. J. (2012). Immigrant selection in the OECD. *Scandinavian Journal of Economics*, *114*(4), 1105–1128.

Berman, E., Lang, K., & Siniver, E. (2003). Language-skill complementarity: Returns to immigrant language acquisition. *Labour Economics*, *10*(3), 265–290.

Bertrand, M., & Duflo, E. (2017). Field experiments on discrimination. In A. V. Banerjee & E. Duflo (Eds.), *Handbook of economic field experiments* (Vol. 1, pp. 309–393). Elsevier.

Bleakley, H., & Chin, A. (2004). Language skills and earnings: Evidence from childhood immigrants. *The Review of Economics and Statistics*, *86*(2), 481–496.

Bleakley, H., & Chin, A. (2010). Age at arrival, English proficiency, and social assimilation among US immigrants. *American Economic Journal: Applied Economics*, *2*(1), 165–192.

Borjas, G. J. (1985). Assimilation, changes in cohort quality, and the earnings of immigrants. *Journal of Labor Economics*, *3*(4), 463–489.

Borjas, G. J. (1987). Self-selection and the earnings of immigrants. *American Economic Review*, *77*(4), 531–553.

Borjas, G. J. (1992). National origin and the skills of immigrants in the postwar period. In G. J. Borjas & R. B. Freeman (Eds.), *Immigration and the workforce: Economic consequences for the United States and source areas* (pp. 17–48). University of Chicago Press.

Borjas, G. J. (1994). The economics of immigration. *Journal of Economic Literature*, *32*(4), 1667–1717.

Borjas, G. J. (2015). The slowdown in the economic assimilation of immigrants: Aging and cohort effects revisited again. *Journal of Human Capital*, *9*(4), 483–517.

Borjas, G. J., and Friedberg, R. M. (2009). *Recent trends in the earnings of new immigrants to the United States.*

Bredtmann, J., Nowotny, K., & Otten, S. (2020). Linguistic distance, networks and migrants' regional location choice. *Labour Economics*, *65*, 101863.

Brown, C. H., Holman, E. W., Wichmann, S., & Velupillai, V. (2008). Automated classification of the world's languages: A description of the method and preliminary results. *STUF–Language Typology and Universals*, *61*(4), 285–308.

Butcher, K. F. (1994). Black immigrants in the United States: A comparison with native blacks and other immigrants. *ILR Review*, *47*(2), 265–284.

Caragliu, A., Del Bo, C., de Groot, H., & Linders, G.-J. (2013). Cultural determinants of migration. *Annals of Regional Science*, *51*(1), 7–32.

Cettolin, E., & Suetens, S. (2019). Return on trust is lower for immigrants. *The Economic Journal*, *129*(621), 1992–2009.

Chen, M. (2013). The effect of language on economic behavior: Evidence from savings rates, health behaviors, and retirement assets. *American Economic Review*, *103*(2), 690–731.

Chiswick, B. (1978). The effect of americanization on the earnings of foreign-born men. *Journal of Political Economy*, *86*(5), 897–921.

Chiswick, B. (1986). Is the new immigration less skilled than the old? *Journal of Labor Economics*, *4*(2), 168–192.

Chiswick, B. (1991). Speaking, reading, and earnings among low-skilled immigrants. *Journal of Labor Economics*, *9*(2), 149–170.

Chiswick, B., & Miller, P. (1994). Language choice among immigrants in a multi-lingual destination. *Journal of Population Economics*, *7*(2), 119–131.

Chiswick, B., & Miller, P. (1995). The endogeneity between language and earnings: International analyses. *Journal of Labor Economics*, *13*(2), 246–288.

Chiswick, B., & Miller, P. (1998). English language fluency among immigrants in the United States. *Research in Labor Economics*, *17*, 151–200.

Chiswick, B., & Miller, P. (2001). A model of destination-language acquisition: Application to Male immigrants in Canada. *Demography*, *38*(3), 391–409.

Chiswick, B., & Miller, P. (2005). Linguistic distance: A quantitative measure of the distance between English and other languages. *Journal of Multilingual and Multicultural Development*, *26*(1), 1–11.

Chiswick, B., & Miller, P. (2012). Negative and positive assimilation, skill transferability, and linguistic distance. *Journal of Human Capital*, *6*(1), 35–55.

Chiswick, B., & Miller, P. (2013). The impact of surplus skills on earnings: Extending the over-education model to language proficiency. *Economics of Education Review*, *36*, 263–275.

Clark, X., Hatton, T. J., & Williamson, J. G. (2007). Explaining U.S. immigration, 1971-1998. *Review of Economics and Statistics*, *89*(2), 359–373.

Crystal, D. (1987). *The Cambridge encyclopedia of language*. Cambridge University Press.

Dale-Olsen, H., & Finseraas, H. (2020). Linguistic diversity and workplace productivity. *Labour Economics*, *64*, 101813.

D'Amuri, F., & Peri, G. (2014). Immigration, jobs, and employment protection: Evidence from Europe before and during the great recession. *Journal of the European Economic Association*, *12*(2), 432–464.

Desmet, K., Weber, S., & Ortuño-Ortín, I. (2009). Linguistic diversity and redistribution. *Journal of the European Economic Association*, *7*(6), 1291–1318.

Doeringer, P., & Piore, M. J. (1985). *Internal labor markets and manpower analysis*. ME Sharpe.

Dustmann, C. (1994). Speaking fluency, writing fluency and earnings of migrants. *Journal of Population Economics*, *7*(2), 133–156.

Dustmann, C., & Fabbri, F. (2003). Language proficiency and labour market performance of immigrants in the UK. *Economic Journal, 113*(489), 695–717.

Dustmann, C., & Görlach, J.-S. (2016). The economics of temporary migrations. *Journal of Economic Literature, 54*(1), 98–136.

Dyen, I., Kruskal, J. B., & Black, P. (1992). An indoeuropean classification: A lexicostatistical experiment. *Transactions of the American Philosophical Society, 82*(5), iii–132.

Eckstein, Z., & Weiss, Y. (2004). On the wage growth of immigrants: Israel, 1990–2000. *Journal of the European Economic Association, 2*(4), 665–695.

Espenshade, T. J., & Fu, H. (1997). An analysis of english-language proficiency among US immigrants. *American Sociological Review*, 288–305.

European Commission. (2006). *Europeans and their languages*. Report.

Ferrer, A., Green, D. A., & Riddell, W. C. (2006). The effect of literacy on immigrant earnings. *Journal of Human Resources, 41*(2), 380–410.

Fortin, N., Lemieux, T., & Torres, J. (2016). Foreign human capital and the earnings gap between immigrants and Canadian-born workers. *Labour Economics, 41*, 104–119.

Friedberg, R. M. (2000). You can't take it with you? Immigrant assimilation and the portability of human capital. *Journal of Labor Economics, 18*(2), 221–251.

Ghio, D., Bratti, M., & Bignami, S. (2023). Linguistic barriers to immigrants' labor market integration in Italy. *International Migration Review, 57*(1), 357–394.

Ginsburgh, V., & Weber, S. (2020). The economics of language. *Journal of Economic Literature, 58*(2), 348–404.

Goldmann, G., Sweetman, A., & Warman, C. (2015). The portability of new immigrants' human capital: Language, education and occupational matching. *Canadian Public Policy, 41* (Supplement 1), S64–S79.

Grogger, J., & Hanson, G. H. (2011). Income maximization and the selection and sorting of international migrants. *Journal of Development Economics, 95*(1), 42–57.

Guiso, L., Sapienza, P., & Zingales, L. (2009). Cultural biases in economic exchange? *The Quarterly Journal of Economics, 124*(3), 1095–1131.

Head, K., Mayer, T., & Ries, J. (2010). The erosion of colonial trade linkages after Independence. *Journal of International Economics, 81*(1), 1–14.

Hutchinson, W. K. (2005). Linguistic distance as a determinant of bilateral trade. *Southern Economic Journal, 72*(1), 1–15.

Imai, S., Stacey, D., & Warman, C. (2019). From engineer to taxi driver? Language proficiency and the occupational skills of immigrants. *Canadian Journal of Economics/Revue Canadienne d'économique, 52*(3), 914–953.

IPUMS-I. (2020). *Integrated public use microdata series, international* Version 7.3 [Dataset]. Minnesota Population Center. https://doi.org/10.18128/D020.V7.3

Isphording, I. E. (2014). Disadvantages of linguistic origin – Evidence from immigrant literacy scores. *Economics Letters, 123*(2), 236–239.

Isphording, I. E., & Otten, S. (2013). The costs of babylon – Linguistic distance in applied economics. *Review of International Economics, 21*(2), 354–369.

Isphording, I. E., & Otten, S. (2014). Linguistic barriers in the destination language acquisition of immigrants. *Journal of Economic Behavior & Organization, 105*, 30–50.

Jasso, G., & Rosenzweig, M. (1988). How well do U.S. immigrants do? Vintage effects, emigration selectivity, and occupational mobility. *Research in Population Economics, 6*, 229–253.

Karemera, D., Oguledo, V. I., & Davis, B. (2000). A gravity model analysis of international migration to North America. *Applied Economics, 32*(13), 1745–1755.

Kee, P. (1995). Native-immigrant wage differentials in the Netherlands: Discrimination? *Oxford Economic Papers, 47*(2), 302–317.

Keita, S., & Valette, J. (2019). Natives' Attitudes and Immigrants' unemployment durations. *Demography, 56*(3), 1023–1050.

Kossoudji, S. A. (1988). English language ability and the labor market opportunities of Hispanic and East Asian immigrant men. *Journal of Labor Economics, 6*(2), 205–228.

LaLonde, R. J., & Topel, R. H. (1992). The assimilation of immigrants in the US labor market. In G. Borjas & R. Freeman (Eds.), *Immigration and the workforce: Economic consequences for the United States and source areas* (pp. 67–92). University of Chicago Press.

Lancee, B. (2021). Ethnic discrimination in hiring: Comparing groups across contexts. Results from a cross-national field experiment. *Journal of Ethnic and Migration Studies*, *47*(6), 1181–1200.

Lohmann, J. (2011). Do language barriers affect trade? *Economics Letters*, *110*(2), 159–162.

Lubotsky, D. (2007). Chutes or ladders? A longitudinal analysis of immigrant earnings. *Journal of Political Economy*, *115*(5), 820–867.

Mayda, A. M. (2010). International migration: A panel data analysis of the determinants of bilateral flows. *Journal of Population Economics*, *23*(4), 1249–1274.

McManus, W. S. (1985). Labor market assimilation of immigrants: The importance of language skills. *Contemporary Economic Policy*, *3*(3), 77–89.

McManus, W. S., Gould, W., & Welch, F. (1983). Earnings of Hispanic men: The role of English language proficiency. *Journal of Labor Economics*, *1*(2), 101–130.

Melitz, J. (2008). Language and foreign trade. *European Economic Review*, *52*(4), 667–699.

Melitz, J., & Toubal, F. (2014). Native language, spoken language, translation and trade. *Journal of International Economics*, *93*(2), 351–363.

Mishel, L., Bivens, J., Gould, E., & Shierholz, H. (2012). *The state of working America* (12th ed.). Cornell University Press. http://stateofworkingamerica.org/

Neumark, D. (2018). Experimental research on labor market discrimination. *Journal of Economic Literature*, *56*(3), 799–866.

O'Rourke, K. H., & Sinnott, R. (2006). The determinants of individual attitudes towards immigration. *European Journal of Political Economy*, *22*(4), 838–861.

Ortega, F., & Peri, G. (2013). The effect of income and immigration policies on international migration. *Migration Studies*, *1*(1), 47–74.

Pager, D. (2007). The use of field experiments for studies of employment discrimination: Contributions, critiques, and directions for the future. *The Annals of the American Academy of Political and Social Science*, *609*(1), 104–133.

Pedersen, P. J., Pytlikova, M., & Smith, N. (2008). Selection and network effects – Migration flows into OECD countries 1990–2000. *European Economic Review*, *52*(7), 1160–1186.

Peri, G., & Sparber, C. (2009). Task specialization, immigration, and wages. *American Economic Journal: Applied Economics*, *1*(3), 135–169.

Piore, M. J. (1972). *Notes for a theory of labor market stratification.*

Reich, M., Gordon, D. M., & Edwards, R. C. (1973). A theory of labor market segmentation. *American Economic Review*, *63*(2), 359–365.

Rivera-Batiz, F. L. (1990). English language proficiency and the economic progress of immigrants. *Economics Letters*, *34*(3), 295–300.

Rydgren, J., & Ruth, P. (2013). Contextual explanations of radical right-wing support in Sweden: Socioeconomic marginalization, group threat, and the halo effect. *Ethnic and Racial Studies*, *36*(4), 711–728.

Schaafsma, J., & Sweetman, A. (2001). Immigrant earnings: Age at immigration matters. *Canadian Journal of Economics*, *34*(4), 1066–1099.

Sprenger, E. (2024). What makes us move, what makes us stay: The role of language and culture in Intra-EU mobility. *Journal of International Migration and Integration*, *25*, 1825–1855.

Strom, S., Piazzalunga, D., Venturini, A., & Villosio, C. (2018). Wage assimilation of immigrants and internal migrants: The role of linguistic distance. *Regional Studies*, *52*(10), 1423–1434.

Swadesh, M. (1952). Lexico-statistic dating of prehistoric ethnic contacts: With special reference to North American Indians and Eskimos. *Proceedings of the American Philosophical Society*, *96* (4), 452–463.

Wong, L. (2023). The effect of linguistic proximity on the labour market outcomes of the asylum population. *Journal of Population Economics*, *36*(2), 609–652.

Yao, Y., & van Ours, J. C. (2015). Language skills and labor market performance of immigrants in the Netherlands. *Labour Economics*, *34*, 76–85.

A. SUMMARY OF LANGUAGE MEASURES USED IN MIGRATION LITERATURE

Table A1. Concepts and Datasets of Linguistic Measures Used in Economics Literature.

Dataset	Coverage	Data provided	Examples of Literature
World Fact Book[a]	267 world entities (mostly countries)	Lists official and spoken languages in a country (and sometimes the percentage of speakers)	[CL] (Mayda, 2010; Ortega & Peri, 2013)
Ethnologue: Languages of the World[b]	7,111 known living languages	Linguistic lineage, i.e., the language family	[CL] for (Karemera et al., 2000; Pedersen et al., 2008); [LP] (Adsera & Ferrer, 2021; Adsera & Pytlikova, 2015; Belot & Hatton, 2012; Desmet et al., 2009)
World Atlas of Languages (WALS)[c]	2,679 languages	Linguistic lineage, i.e., the language family	[LP] (Chen, 2013; Isphording & Otten, 2013; Lohmann, 2011)
Dyen percentage cognate matrix of linguistic distances (Dyen et al., 1992)	Indo-European languages	Language-pairwise linguistic proximity information, based on the vocabulary-wise cognation of 200 words from each language (see Swadesh, 1952)	[LP] (Adsera & Pytlikova, 2015; Belot & Ederveen, 2012)
Levenshtein Linguistic Distance Matrix (Bakker et al., 2009; Brown et al., 2008)	(approx.) 3,500 languages	Language-pairwise linguistic proximity information, based on the ASJP	[LP] (Adsera & Pytlikova, 2015; Bredtmann et al., 2020; Dale-Olsen & Finseraas, 2020; Ghio et al., 2023; Isphording, 2014; Isphording & Otten, 2013, 2014; Strom et al., 2018; Wong, 2023)
Linguistic Distance to English (Chiswick & Miller, 1998)	43 languages	Information on linguistic proximity to English (based on the difficulty Americans have in learning thesce languages)	[LP to English] (Chiswick & Miller, 2001, 2005; Hutchinson, 2005; Isphording & Otten, 2013)
CEPII[d]	195 countries	Country-pairwise language information, including common official, spoken and native language, and two measures of linguistic proximity	[CL] (Beine et al., 2011; Grogger & Hanson, 2011); [LP] (Bar-Haim & Birgier, 2024; Melitz & Toubal, 2014), *our paper*

[a]https://www.cia.gov/library/publications/the-world-factbook/

[b]https://www.ethnologue.com/

[c]https://wals.info/

[d]http://www.cepii.fr/CEPII/en/welcome.asp, see Melitz (2008) and Melitz and Toubal (2014).

Notes: CL denotes common language. LP denotes language proximity. Isphording and Otten (2013) provide an intuitive illustration of the methodology used by Bakker et al. (2009). The algorithm that calculates the minimal Levenshtein distance is based on pronunciation and vocabulary of 40 (or 100) words (ASJP code) from each language. See also Ginsburgh and Weber (2020) on a short examination of the different measures, main advantages and shortcomings of the methods, and on more economic literature applying linguistic proximity measures.

B. CONSTRUCTION OF CLI

To examine the relevance of linguistic proximity, we draw on the CLI measure conceptualized by Melitz (2008) and Melitz and Toubal (2014). It measures the *ease of communication* between individuals originating from two different countries (in our case, between migrant's origin and destination countries). Basically, it is based on, and adjusts for, the varying relevance of four different measures: Common official language (COL), CNL, CSL, and linguistic proximity (LP). CNL provides the likelihood that two randomly picked persons, one from each country, share a common mother tongue. Similarly, CSL captures the likelihood that the two persons share any CSL (i.e. languages not necessarily their mother tongue, but for instance a global language like English, or other).[21] LP denotes the relative linguistic closeness of two countries' native languages, based on the ASJP index.[22]

Remind that our goal is to have a measure of *ease of communication*, intended to proxy for the role of language in transferring credentials from one country to another. If two countries share a COL, the role of the remainder measures becomes relatively less relevant, as institutional factors likely provide for sufficient transferability of skills. Likewise, if either CNL or CSL is substantially high, LP should be relatively less relevant (Melitz and Toubal (2014) provide some empirical evidence for this argumentation).[23] The CLI reflects these assumptions.

The CLI is bounded by the values of 0 and 1 for the lowest and highest linguistic proximity in our data. For constructing the index, strictly following Melitz and Toubal (2014), LP and COL are first normalized to each equal one at the sample mean. Then, we normalize COL + LP by dividing it with the highest observed value among the country pairs in our sample. We multiply this series' normalized values by 1 − CSL. Finally, we construct CLI as the sum of CSL and the adjusted sum of COL and LP (this ensures CLI cannot exceed 1 − CSL):

$$CLI_{o,d} = \left(1 - CSL_{o,d}\right) * \left(\left(COL_{o,d} + LP_{o,d}\right)/\max_{\text{sample}}(COL + LP)\right) + CSL_{o,d} \tag{4}$$

Note that we deviate from Melitz and Toubal (2014) in that we use the CSL index rather than the CNL index. In Table A3, we provide an overview of the top five origin countries per destination country in our sample, together with information on COL, CSL, and LP for these country pairs.

C. DATA SUMMARY

Table A2. Individual Level Datasets Used in This Study.

Country	Dataset	Years
Argentina	Encuesta Permanente de Hogares (*EPH*)	2004–2018
Brazil	IPUMS-published census data	1991, 2000, 2010
Canada	IPUMS-published census data	1981, 1991, 2001, 2011
France	Labor Force Survey (*LFS*)	2003–2012
Germany	Socio-Economic Panel Study (*SOEP*)	1984–2016
Israel	IPUMS-published census data	1983, 1995
Mexico	IPUMS-published census data	1990, 2000, 2010
United Kingdom	Labor Force Survey (LFS)	1992–1998, 2000–2007
USA	American Community Survey (*ACS*)	2001–2018

Table A3. Top Sample Origin Countries by Destination.

				Linguistic Measures		
Destination	Origin (Top 5)	# of Obs.	Share in Destination Migrant Sample	COL	CSL	LP
Argentina	Chile	12,687	0.30	1.00	0.98	1.00
	Paraguay	9,028	0.21	1.00	0.69	0.09
	Bolivia	7,583	0.18	1.00	0.87	0.57
	Peru	3,886	0.09	1.00	0.86	1.00
	Uruguay	2,865	0.07	1.00	0.98	1.00
Brazil	Portugal	7,455	0.23	1.00	1.00	1.00
	Paraguay	2,812	0.09	0.00	0.11	0.08
	Uruguay	2,136	0.07	0.00	0.07	0.42
	Argentina	2,053	0.06	0.00	0.06	0.42
	Italy	1,912	0.06	0.00	0.02	0.37
Canada	United Kingdom	29,141	0.18	1.00	0.85	0.74
	Philippines	14,809	0.09	1.00	0.47	0.03
	Italy	12,672	0.08	0.00	0.30	0.19
	India	11,674	0.07	1.00	0.20	0.00
	USA	11,301	0.07	1.00	0.82	0.66
France	Portugal	5,634	0.17	0.00	0.34	0.29
	Morocco	4,446	0.14	1.00	0.36	0.09
	Algeria	3,969	0.12	1.00	0.57	0.09
	Türkiye	1,318	0.04	0.00	0.07	0.11
	Tunisia	1,310	0.04	1.00	0.64	0.09
Germany	Türkiye	9,518	0.20	0.00	0.15	0.09
	Italy	5,016	0.10	0.00	0.25	0.16
	Poland	4,578	0.09	0.00	0.36	0.09
	Kazakhstan	3,460	0.07	0.00	0.16	0.10
	Greece	3,282	0.07	0.00	0.35	0.09

Table A3. *(Continued)*

Destination	Origin (Top 5)	# of Obs.	Share in Destination Migrant Sample	Linguistic Measures		
				COL	CSL	LP
Israel	Russia	19,143	0.23	0.00	0.12	0.16
	Morocco	13,625	0.16	0.00	0.16	0.24
	Romania	9,448	0.11	0.00	0.15	0.10
	Ukraine	5,972	0.07	0.00	0.08	0.13
	Iraq	5,514	0.07	0.00	0.13	0.24
Mexico	USA	5,962	0.42	0.00	0.20	0.26
	Guatemala	1,875	0.13	1.00	0.85	1.00
	Spain	860	0.06	1.00	0.98	1.00
	Argentina	481	0.03	1.00	0.98	1.00
	El Salvador	462	0.03	1.00	0.99	1.00
United Kingdom	India	3,910	0.10	1.00	0.23	0.00
	Ireland	3,755	0.10	1.00	0.97	1.00
	Germany	2,674	0.07	0.00	0.61	0.32
	South Africa	1,667	0.04	1.00	0.29	0.00
	Kenya	1,417	0.04	1.00	0.07	0.05
USA	Mexico	776,056	0.25	0.00	0.20	0.26
	Philippines	172,739	0.06	1.00	0.53	0.05
	India	154,140	0.05	1.00	0.22	0.00
	China	121,734	0.04	0.00	0.01	0.05
	Vietnam	98,229	0.03	0.00	0.00	0.03

Notes: The table lists the top five immigrant origin countries in each destination country sample used in our study. It provides the absolute number of observations for each origin country within the destination country sample, their share among all migrants in the respective sample, and the COL, CSL, and LP values for each country-pair. We do not report CLS and CLN here, as these are specific to estimation samples.

Table A4. ANOVA Decomposition of Variance in Estimated Coefficients.

	TE = 1		TE = 0	
Estimate if immigrant = 1 and	(a)	(b)	(a)	(b)
Residual variance	29.11	13.33	26.39	8.73
Captured variance	50.16	65.93	34.54	52.20
due to destination country	56%	1%	34%	1%
due to origin country	40%	18%	51%	11%
due to destination-by-origin	-	24%	-	34%
due to migrant sample	1%	0%	4%	2%

Notes: Specifications denoted by (a) include destination country effects and origin country effects. Specifications denoted by (b) include destination-country effects and origin-country effects as well as destination-by-origin country effects. All specifications include the migrant sample, which has one of the three levels across all specifications: (i) recent migrants; (ii) long-term migrants; and (iii) joint estimation for all migrants. Recent migrants are defined as residing shorter than 5 years in a destination country. All components shown are highly significant (bootstrapped standard errors available upon request).

D. SENSITIVITY ANALYSIS – ESTIMATION FOR LINGUISTIC PROXIMITY STANDARDIZED BY CNL

Fig. A1. Common Language Index Measures: Comparing the Standardization by CNL and CSL. *Notes:* The figure portrays the correlation between CLI measures, standardized by CNL, and by CSL. Melitz and Toubal (2014) standardize by CNL.

Table A5. Robustness Check: Table 3, Full Set of Estimates, Standardization by CNL.

Variables	(1)	(2) (1) + $CLI_{d,o}$	(3) (2) + Z_0	(4) (3) + $Z_{d,o}$
Panel A: Sample of immigrants only				
TE	9.987***	9.509***	9.619***	9.671***
	(0.051)	(0.767)	(0.763)	(0.756)
Linguistic proximity				
for migrants w/o TE		5.905***	6.061***	7.012***
		(1.620)	(1.619)	(2.076)
additionally for migrants w/TE		2.065	1.847	1.745
		(1.621)	(1.622)	(1.609)
Observations	1,490,240	1,490,240	1,490,240	1,490,240
R-squared	0.385	0.387	0.388	0.389

Table A5. *(Continued)*

Variables	(1)	(2) (1) + $CLI_{d,o}$	(3) (2) + Z_0	(4) (3) + $Z_{d,o}$
Panel B: Full sample				
TE	9.658***	9.658***	9.744***	9.913***
	(0.012)	(0.634)	(0.634)	(0.621)
Migrants	−0.405***	−0.405	−0.302	−0.044
	(0.012)	(0.467)	(0.464)	(0.484)
Linguistic proximity				
for migrants w/o TE		−0.966	−0.705	3.362*
		(1.801)	(1.800)	(1.803)
additionally for migrants w/TE		2.653**	2.498*	1.510
		(1.272)	(1.267)	(1.082)
Observations	42,513,810	42,513,810	42,513,810	42,513,810
R-squared	0.364	0.364	0.365	0.367
Marital status, YSI, gender	Yes	Yes	Yes	Yes
COO FE	Yes	Yes	Yes	Yes
COD FE	Yes	Yes	Yes	Yes
Origin X's	No	No	Yes	Yes
Pair X's	No	No	No	Yes

Notes: See note under Table 3.

Table A6. Robustness Check: Table 4 With Common Language Index Standardized by Common Native Language.

			p value < 0.15	w = [t-stat]		w = [$migr_{o,d}$]	
Specification	(1)	(1a)	(2)	(3)	(3a)	(4)	(4a)
TE	0.206***	0.206***	0.232***	0.251***	0.251***	0.216***	0.216***
	(0.021)	(0.023)	(0.022)	(0.016)	(0.024)	(0.020)	(0.026)
Linguistic proximity							
migrants w/o TE	−0.025	−0.025	0.001	−0.052	−0.052	0.003	0.003
	(0.045)	(0.053)	(0.048)	(0.048)	(0.072)	(0.044)	(0.066)
migrants w/TE	0.108***	0.108***	0.098***	0.103***	0.103***	0.068***	0.068*
	(0.036)	(0.040)	(0.038)	(0.028)	(0.044)	(0.033)	(0.044)
Observations	1,447	1,447	1,260	1,447	1,447	1,447	1,447
R-squared	0.521	0.521	0.576	0.767	0.767	0.552	0.552
OC X's	Yes	Yes	Yes	Yes	Yes	Yes	Yes
DC FE	Yes	Yes	Yes	Yes	Yes	Yes	Yes
Country pair X's	Yes	Yes	Yes	Yes	Yes	Yes	Yes
Country pair FE's	Yes	Yes	Yes	Yes	Yes	Yes	Yes

Note: See note under Table 4. These estimates use the measure of linguistic proximity based on CNL.

PERSISTENT OCCUPATIONAL HIERARCHIES AMONG IMMIGRANT WORKER GROUPS IN THE US LABOR MARKET

Agnieszka Postepska[a] and Francis Vella[b]

[a]*University of Groningen, The Netherlands*
[b]*Georgetown University, USA*

ABSTRACT

This chapter examines the phenomenon of occupational hierarchies among immigrant labor groups in the United States. Using census data for 1940–2011, the authors identify and document the existence of hierarchies among immigrant labor in major metropolitan areas as reflected by their position in the empirical distribution of occupations based on the Duncan Socioeconomic Index (SEI) values. Having established the existence and persistence of these hierarchies across regions and over time, the authors explore whether the observed data can be explained via a simple model, which allocates immigrant labor to the occupational distribution on the basis of employers' perception of their productivity. The results suggest that while human capital characteristics are relevant determinants of location in the occupational distribution, the key factor, and the cause of persistence, is the presence of immigrant networks in regional labor markets.

Keywords: Occupational hierarchies; immigrants; networks; empirical distribution of occupations; indirect inference

1. INTRODUCTION

An examination of national and regional patterns in US Census data reveals that some immigrant worker groups were consistently more frequently employed in

---

Migration, Human Capital and the Labor Market
Research in Labor Economics, Volume 53A, 267–328

ISSN: 0147-9121/doi:10.1108/S0147-91212026000053A008

"higher ranked" occupations than others. For example, Italian and Polish workers had different rates of white-collar employment in Chicago and Buffalo in 1940 and 2011. Initially, Italy outperformed Poland in both regions. By 2011, both groups had higher rates of white-collar employment in both regions, but the relative ranking between the groups remained constant. Similarly, in 1940, in New York, 12% more Canadian than German workers were employed in white-collar employment; by 2011, both countries had almost doubled their shares while preserving their ranking. This chapter aims to explore the persistence of these hierarchies.

As human capital differences might explain these patterns, we examine the corresponding shares for individuals without post-high school education (referred to as *unskilled* workers), noting that the share of immigrants with at most high school degree decreased from 83% in 1940 to 36% in 2011. In 1940, 25% of Canadian, 30% of English, 16% of Italian, and 19% of Polish unskilled workers had white-collar jobs. In 2011, Canadian and English workers continued to exhibit the highest shares, 47 and 49%, respectively, compared to 32% of Italians and 19% of Polish workers. While the initial disparity might partially reflect differences in literacy rates and educational attainment, it is unclear why this pattern has persisted.

The above discussion is based on a very simple characterization of the labor market. However, it suggests that immigrants from certain countries are located higher in the occupational distribution than those from other countries, and the ranking persists across years and regions. We explore the observed spatial variation in occupational distributions to explain this phenomenon with a simple model approximating the occupational sorting process among immigrant workers. We do not explicitly model employers' and workers' behavior but propose a simple but plausible model that explains the data well and offers insight into drivers of the persistent hierarchical patterns.[1]

Our investigation uncovers clear evidence of persistent occupational hierarchies among immigrant labor groups in the US labor market. Moreover, the key features of the data can be produced via a simple model in which employers rank workers partially based on the immigrant group to which they belong and their associated networks. Our results also suggest that while human capital characteristics are an essential determinant of the hierarchical structure among immigrant labor groups, the presence of immigrant networks is mainly responsible for its persistence. Simulations of the model suggest that a group's rank in the local labor market depends on the group's history in the region, and for the least skilled workers, the ranking appears resilient. Similarly, individual success hinges upon the individual's group's success in the local labor market.

Economic investigations of the labor market activity of immigrants in the United States have primarily focused on their impact on the native born (Altonji & Card, 2018; Borjas, 1994a, 2006b, Borjas et al., 1997; Card, 2001, 2005; Dustmann et al., 2013, 2016; Ottaviano & Peri, 2008, 2012; Peri & Yasenov, 2019). These studies have investigated the effect of immigration on native-borns' labor market activity as measured by wages (Borjas, 2006b; Borjas et al., 1997; Card, 2001; Dustmann et al., 2013; Foged & Peri, 2016; Ottaviano & Peri, 2008, 2012; Peri, 2014; Peri & Yasenov, 2019), employment opportunities (Altonji & Card, 2018; Card, 2005; Cortes, 2008; Foged & Peri, 2016), and internal migration (Borjas, 2006b; Card, 2001; DiNardo & Card, 2000). Studies on immigrants generally examine how they or they children perform relative to the native born (Abramitzky et al., 2014; Borjas, 1994b; Potochnick & Hall, 2021). This work typically views immigrants as homogeneous although they differ on a number of dimensions including from where and when they came (Borjas, 1985, 1994b), their capacity to speak English, and other features which reflect their capacity to perform in the labor market.[2] We examine how these various features influence their position in the occupational distribution of migrants.

Previous studies have examined aspects of immigrants' occupational choices. Bohon (2005) shows that the occupational attainment of Latino immigrants in the United States is influenced by their place of origin and their destination. Waldinger (1996, 1994), Beaman (2012), and Laschever (2013) studied the emergence of immigrant niche economies and the presence of networks in the labor market. These networks influenced the labor market outcomes of generations of immigrants. The choice of occupations of the early cohorts of immigrants was determined by both immigrant and regional characteristics, and initial differences in ethnic composition may have long-lasting effects on career choices (Munshi & Wilson, 2011). Patel and Vella (2013) provide evidence that the occupational choices of recent immigrants differ by destination and are affected by those of the previous cohorts of immigrants located in that destination. More specifically, they find that immigrants from specific countries cluster in particular occupations in different regions and that this allocation generally does not depend on observed or unobserved skills.

Patel and Vella (2013) assign the persistence in occupational choice to network effects. We investigate whether these effects also contribute to the creation of occupational hierarchies. Consider two countries, A and B. From Patel and Vella (2013), we know that if immigrants from these two countries locate in the same region, they are likely to be employed in different occupations. Moreover, if the same groups locate in a second region, they are likely to locate in different occupations than in the first region. We investigate whether if immigrants from Country A are generally doing better than immigrants from Country B in one region are they also doing better in another region. Moreover if we consider three groups or more, do hierarchical patterns emerge?

Our focus is location in the occupational distribution rather than the actual occupational choice. We do this to examine whether a hierarchy exists. Accordingly, by looking at the range of different locations in different periods, we can exploit occupational variation across regions and time to establish whether certain immigrant groups are ranked above others irrespective of the occupational composition of an area at a certain time. If all regions had the same occupational distribution, it would be more difficult to establish the existence of hierarchies as the rankings may simply reflect occupation-specific skills or reflect the impact of occupation-specific immigrant networks. By looking across regions, we can examine whether the same immigrant hierarchies arise even in the absence of different occupational distributions.

We are motivated by the earlier literature that find immigrants are employed in different occupations depending on the region in which they are located. We examine whether the ranking of immigrant labor is invariant to the occupational composition of the region, which varies across regions and accounts for the "quality" of the workers in the region. Moreover, while uncovering the existence and the determinants of immigrant occupational hierarchies is itself interesting, it has implications for the welfare of new immigrants and their offspring through intergenerational transmission of socioeconomic status (Borjas, 1992, 2006a; Postepska, 2019). Persistent occupational hierarchies may lead to stagnation in the socioeconomic standings of immigrant workers and their subsequent generations even though evidence shows that children of immigrants do not suffer the same degree of occupational downgrading as their parents (Potochnick & Hall, 2021). We document the high persistence of the occupational hierarchies over time and regions which can foster an understanding of the limited mobility in the income distribution (Chetty et al., 2014a,b). Chetty et al. (2014a) document that intergenerational mobility varies substantially across areas within the United States. Occupational hierarchies may contribute to this variation as this phenomenon reflects that workers from certain immigrant groups will have greater challenges to move up the occupational distribution. This will have an impact on mobility. This will also preserve hierarchies in other important welfare determining processes such as housing location or school choice. It also has clear implications for wages and, most likely, nonpecuniary benefits associated with jobs.

While an individual's relative location in the occupational and wage distributions are likely to be similar, we focus on the former for the following reasons. First, while identifying a hierarchy in wages is interesting, it does not provide any insight into the mechanisms underlying it. Second, while a hierarchy in wages does not appear to have any obvious implications for occupational choice, occupational hierarchies have clear implications for wages. In fact, it is likely that the observed hierarchy in immigrant wages is partially the result of the hierarchy in immigrant occupational location. Third, one of our objectives is to analyze the role of networks in maintaining the persistence of hierarchies, and this appears to arise more naturally in occupational choice. Finally, in our view it is more economically interesting to establish that occupational hierarchies arise and persist across time and regions in the face of different occupational compositions rather than focusing purely on whether some immigrant groups are consistently paid more than others.

The next section describes the data and presents evidence on the occupational choice of immigrants in the United States as captured by a measure of socioeconomic standing. Section 3 provides evidence on the existence of occupational hierarchies of immigrant groups in the US labor market. Section 4 presents a descriptive regression analysis while Section 5 introduces an empirical model of occupational hierarchies, which sorts workers into sectors based on productivity and provides a discussion of the model estimates. Section 6 investigates the implications of these estimates while Section 7 provides concluding comments.

2. EMPIRICAL DISTRIBUTION OF OCCUPATIONS

We employ data from 1940–2000 US Census and the 2011 five-year sample from the American Community Survey (Steven Ruggles et al., 2010).[3] We begin by identifying the immigrant groups with a substantial and consistent presence in the United States. To reduce concerns related to selection bias associated with labor force participation and unemployment, we restrict our sample to males aged 16–70 years who are employed in an identified occupation in an identified metropolitan area. We require at least 50 other immigrants from their country in that metropolitan area, and as we investigate a country's relative position, we exclude metropolitan areas with less than two different groups satisfying our size requirement. This reduces the sample of individuals by 20%, producing a final sample of 115 metropolitan areas noting that very few have large numbers of immigrants from multiple origins throughout the period of our analysis.[4] The final sample consists of individuals from Canada, Mexico, Cuba, England, Italy, Germany, Poland, Russia, China, Korea, Philippines, Vietnam, India, Africa, and the Middle East (the sample composition is presented in Table 8 Appendix C).[5] These 15 origins represent 68% of the total immigration of males in the considered age group into the United States in the period we examine. The groups in our resulting sample represent 11% of all males aged 16–70 years and 70% of all immigrants of this age.

To characterize the occupational distribution, we employ the Duncan socioeconomic index, hereafter SEI (Duncan, 1961).[6] Appendix A contains a detailed discussion of this measure. In determining an individual's position in the occupational distribution, one could rank each occupation by its prestige score and rank workers accordingly. A worker would be in the *p*th percentile of the occupational distribution if they were in the occupation corresponding to that location. This, however, does not capture regional differences in occupational composition. That is, the occupations in the *p*th percentile may differ across regions depending on regional demand factors and the other groups present. An alternative is to compute the empirical occupational distribution separately for each region and for each time period. An individual in the *p*th percentile of the occupational distribution has a job in the *p*th percentile of the occupational distribution for that region in that time period. This is a more accurate characterization of the hierarchy phenomenon.

We adopt this latter approach and rank workers based on the SEI. We then consider changes in the shares of workers employed in the *top* sector of each region over time. We define a "sector" as a specific location of the empirical regional occupational distribution. As this distribution is estimated for each region, the sector's composition of occupations may vary by metropolitan area and time period. Specifically, for each metropolitan area in each time period, we rank all workers based on the SEI. We then examine the share of workers from each country located in the top 50% of the regional empirical distribution. The results are summarized in Fig. 1 and provide clear evidence that some immigrant groups have consistently higher shares of workers employed in the top part of the empirical distributions. This is true for both the *all* and *unskilled* samples. For example, fewer than one-quarter of all Mexican immigrants in 1940 were employed in the *top* sector; meanwhile, nearly nine-tenths of unskilled English immigrants in 2011 were employed in that sector.

One suspects these patterns reflect educational differences by immigrant group. Fig. 2 shows that while the relationship between years of schooling and occupational standings is linear and positive, the slope is rather flat, particularly for the less skilled workers. For example, in 1970 an average worker from Canada or Germany completed 11.4 years of schooling and was employed in an occupation with a prestige score of 43. At the same time, the average worker from the Philippines completed almost one year of schooling more but was employed in a job with a 6-point lower prestige score. Similarly, in 2000 the

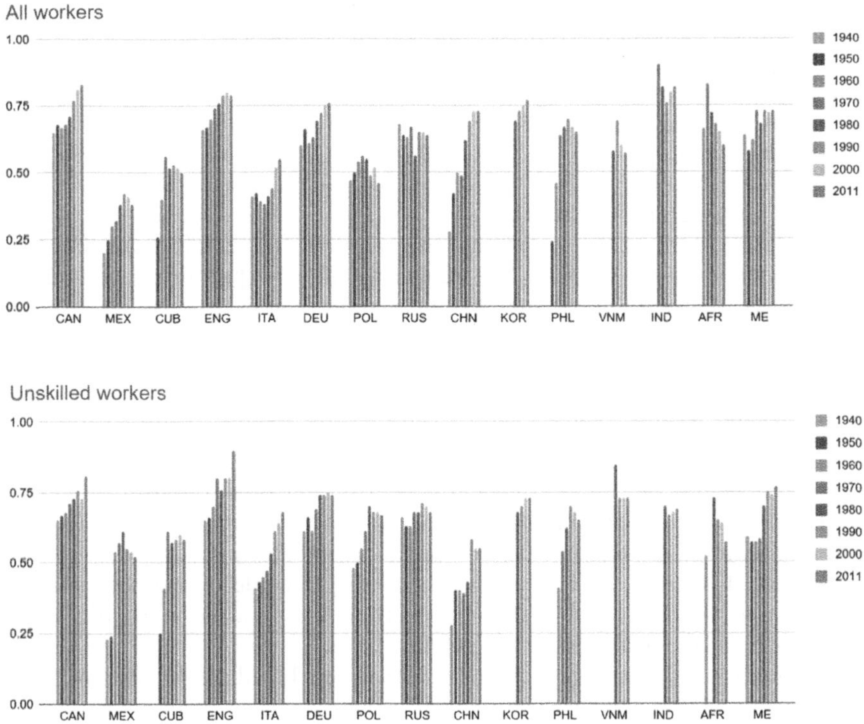

Fig. 1. Share of Workers Employed in the *Top* Sector by Origin 1940–2011. *Notes: Top* sector comprises occupations in the top 50% of the empirical distribution of occupations. Each bar represents an average computed over all regions in which a group is present in given census year.

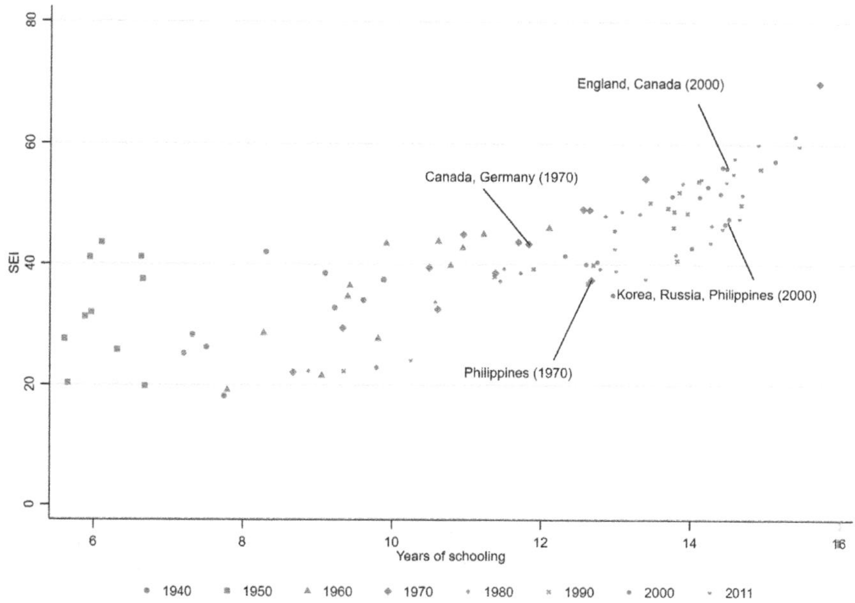

Fig. 2. Relationship Between Years of Schooling and Occupational Standings (SEI).

average worker from England or Canada had 14.5 years of education and an occupation score of 56. Average workers from Korea, Russia, and the Philippines also completed about 14 years of schooling but were employed in jobs with prestige scores 4, 9, and 14 points lower, respectively.

Fig. 1 indicates that the shares of individuals employed in the top sector increased over time. Similarly, the increasing average SEI scores shown in Table 9 suggest that groups substantially improved their occupation. However, Fig. 3 illustrates that increases in a group's average SEI score do not necessarily improve its position in the occupational distribution. For instance, the average prestige score of Italian workers almost doubled between 1940 and 2011 while the share of workers employed in the top sector increased by only 30%. Vietnamese workers have relatively low average SEI scores while having a relatively high share of their workers in the upper part of the occupational distribution (54–64%).[7] Since the occupational composition of the sectors vary across regions, a ranking based on average SEI score does not account for the variation in regional occupational composition.[8]

These patterns do not capture information regarding the type of work associated with the occupations into which different immigrant groups sort. One explanation of occupational hierarchies is that within regions, workers from different countries sort into different occupations. This could be driven by regional labor markets characteristics and/or by country of origin specific skills. In the former case, we should observe groups sorting into different occupations

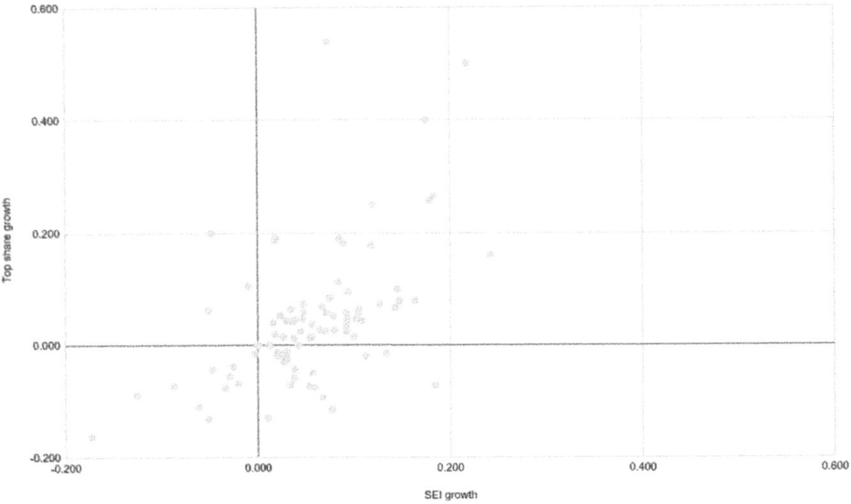

Fig. 3. Relationship Between the Decennial Growth Rates of the Average Prestige Scores and the Shares of Workers Employed in the Top Sector.

across regions while in the latter immigrants from the same countries should generally sort into the same occupations across regions. Patel and Vella (2013) provide evidence that the occupations of low-skilled immigrant workers vary by metropolitan areas suggesting that the immigrants' skills do not drive the allocation to occupations.

However, even if workers sort into different occupations in different regions, there could be substantial overlap between popular occupations among groups within regions. The observed hierarchies would then reflect differences in shares in each occupation within a region. To investigate this, we identify each country's most popular occupational location in the United States. An occupation is defined to be "popular" among workers of a given origin if the share of those workers employed in it is at least 5%. With this characterization in mind, we now examine two issues. First, how frequently does a country develop large networks in the same occupations across metropolitan areas in the same census year? In the time period, we consider the probability that a popular occupation in one metropolitan area is also popular in at least one other region in the same census year is about 50% in the *all* and 61% in the *unskilled* sample suggesting that there is less spatial variation in popular occupations in the *unskilled* sample. A second issue is the frequency at which immigrant groups share popular occupations within metropolitan areas. Around 56% of all the popular occupations in all regions and time periods considered are unique to one group in a given metropolitan area in a given year. This is remarkable given that popular occupations include very broad categories. These two facts suggest that occupational hierarchies arise from workers sorting into different occupations within regions and that occupational networks might play a role in maintaining them.

However, since these patterns might conceal that the sorting of groups into occupations depends on others in the region, we analyze the popular occupations for each pair of countries across regions in which a given pair appears. We find that especially among unskilled workers, countries often establish networks in the same occupations across such regions suggesting that the choice of occupations depends on the ethnic composition of the local labor market.

3. OCCUPATIONAL HIERARCHIES OF IMMIGRANT WORKERS

To identify the presence of occupational hierarchies, we now focus on pairwise comparisons of countries. We initially split workers into two sectors, top and bottom, and examine the shares in the top sector. We first assign each occupation a score based on its place in the empirical occupational distribution. Individuals employed in occupations above the 70th percentile of the empirical distribution are assigned to the *top* sector.[9] For each metropolitan area and year, we calculate the empirical frequency of each country having a larger share of workers employed in the top sector than each of the other countries. Table 10 in Appendix C presents the results for detailed comparisons for all pairs of countries. Fig. 4 summarizes these results by showing the distribution of the empirical frequency of each country having a larger share of workers employed in the *top* sector than each of the other countries. The U-shaped distributions for both the *all* and the *unskilled* sample confirm the consistent ranking of groups. Many entries in Table 10 are consistently high (or low), indicating that some countries are relatively more (or less) likely to maintain large networks in occupations in the same part of occupational distributions over time (about 60% of all entries are either smaller than 0.2 or larger than 0.8). In other words, Fig. 4 shows that the dissimilarities in occupational standings on the basis of membership in a particular immigrant group persist over time.

For each pair of countries, we also compute the difference in the average SEI scores in each metropolitan area for which a given pair is present, and we average these differences over all regions in a given year. In 67% of the *all* sample and 65% of the *unskilled* sample, the ordering remained unchanged over the entire time period. This implies that if the first time we observe immigrants from two origins in the same region those from Country A were, on average, doing better than those from Country B, they are generally doing better in the last year we observe them. Moreover, in many instances, and particularly for the *unskilled*, the average difference remains relatively constant. For example, in 1980 in metropolitan areas where unskilled Canadian and Vietnamese workers appear together, the latter were employed in occupations with an average prestige score lower by 7.2 points. By 2011, this gap was almost unchanged at 7.7 points.

Despite this persistence, some groups improved their position substantially while others fell behind. Regardless of the direction in which the share moved, it appears that the initial location in the distribution determines the outcome in

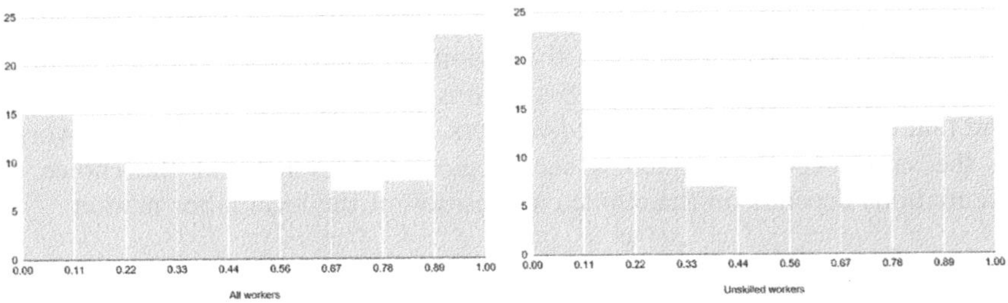

Fig. 4. Distribution of Empirical Frequency of Each Country Having a Larger Share of Workers Employed in the Top Sector than Each of the Other Countries. *Notes:* The comparisons are made on the basis of year and metropolitan area calculations. The figure summarizes the results of all possible pairwise comparisons (each pair is only considered once).

later years. This is particularly so for the least skilled migrants from Mexico and Vietnam. Between 1990 and 2011, the share of Vietnamese workers in the top sector in Oklahoma remained stable at about 50% while in Boston less than 20% enjoyed top sector jobs. In both metropolitan areas, *Operative and kindred workers* are the most popular occupations. Similarly, the share of Mexican workers in the top part of the empirical distribution of occupations in Chicago and Los Angeles was below 15% throughout the time period considered while in newer destinations, such as Fresno, CA and Reno, NV the share exceeded 25%. In Fresno, one in every three Mexican immigrants works as a *Farm laborer* while in Reno as *Operative and kindred worker*. In Chicago and Los Angeles, they seem to face better occupational prospects with a 65% chance of employment in occupations of higher status than *Operative and kindred worker*.

The above examples highlight the need for a more detailed labor market characterization; therefore, we extend the analysis to four sectors. Individuals employed in occupations above the 90th percentile of the empirical distribution are assigned to *Sector A* (top sector); those between the 70th and the 90th percentile are allocated into *Sector B;* those between the 40th and 70th percentiles are allocated into *Sector C*. The remaining workers are employed in *Sector D*. We stress that the choice of cutoff points for these sectors is arbitrary. Our goal is purely to generate a ranking of sectors which seems reasonable.

Fig. 5 presents the shares of *all* and *unskilled* in the four sectors[10] averaged over metropolitan areas and further confirms that the distribution of workers into sectors varies significantly across the origins. These crude patterns suggest that some countries are relatively more likely to maintain large networks in occupations in the same region of the occupational distributions even when we consider a higher level of labor market disaggregation. It appears this is usually true for the more recent immigrant groups. The countries that most increased

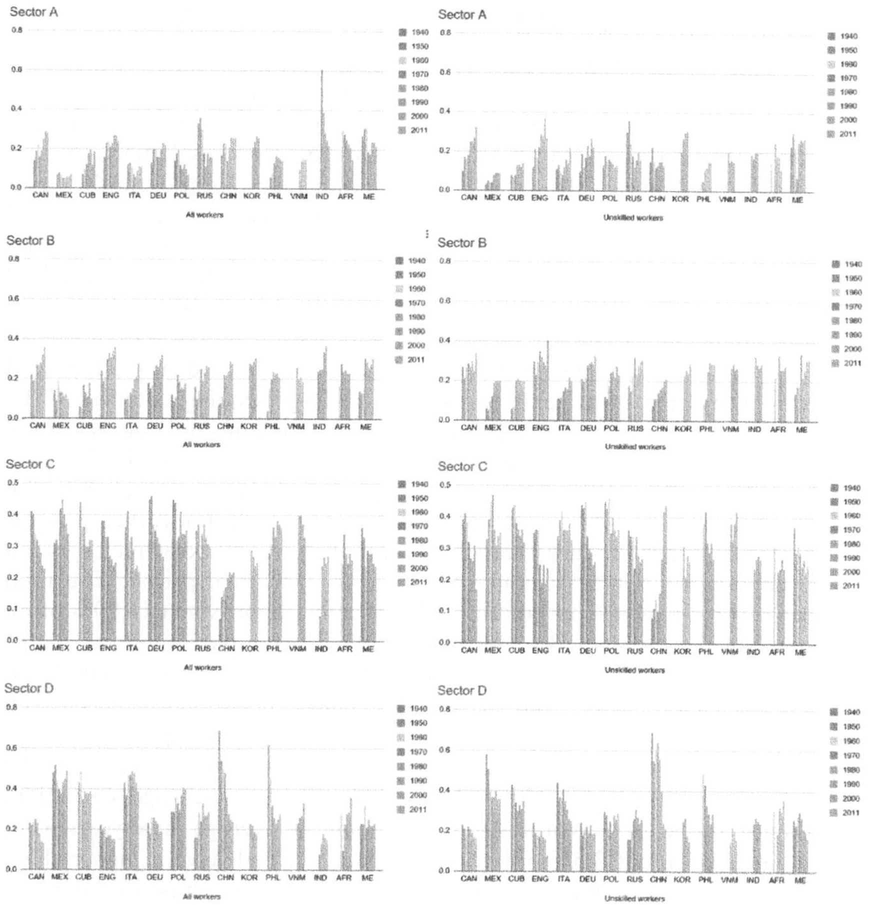

Fig. 5. Share of Workers Employed in the Four Sectors by Origin 1940–2011. *Notes: Sector A* comprises occupations above the 90th percentile of the empirical distribution of occupations (top sector); *Sector B* comprises occupations between the 70th and the 90th percentile; *Sector C* comprises occupations between the 40th and 70th percentiles; *Sector D* comprises occupations below the 40th percentile. Each bar represents an average over all regions in which a group is present in given census year.

their shares in the top two sectors generally did so between 1940 and 1980.[11] For the majority of the countries, the recent changes in shares are relatively small. This is also suggestive of occupational hierarchies. Tables 11 and 12 (Appendix C) present the pairwise comparisons at this higher level of labor market disaggregation and confirm the presence of consistent rankings within sectors.

4. DESCRIPTIVE REGRESSION ANALYSIS

We now present a descriptive regression analysis of the co-variation between the observed hierarchies and some worker observable characteristics. We highlight that the goal of this exercise is to find variables that co-vary with an individual's location in the occupational distribution and not to draw causal inference from the results. As it appears that a potential determinant of location in the occupational distribution is the existence of networks, we examine the occupational location of newly arrived immigrants. We examine the behavior of those who have arrived in the United States within 10 years of each census year and examine the role of existing networks. We maintain our focus on regions where the same immigrant groups are observed with regularity and restrict our sample to metropolitan regions where there are at least 50 (individuals) established migrants from each of at least two of the 15 large sending countries.[12] To account for the presence of all new immigrants, we combine individuals born in all other countries into one category referred to as "Others". As a likely determinant of occupational location is English proficiency, we limit the empirical investigation to post-1980 as this variable is unavailable for earlier periods. These considerations produce a sample of four time periods and 80 metropolitan areas, noting that not all regions contribute to each time period. The total number of time-region data points is 226 reflecting approximately 20% of all metropolitan areas in the 1980–2011 time period. The sample comprises 378,283 individuals representing about 29% of the immigrant population of employed males in the respective age group between 1980 and 2011. Recent migrants from the 15 large sending countries constitute about 70% of our sample.

The summary statistics presented in Table 1 suggest that individuals in the two top sectors differ to all other workers with respect to their age, education, and English proficiency. Workers in Sector A are on average three years older have completed about 3.5 more years of education and have a higher share proficient in English than those in lower ranked sectors. A comparison of those in Sector B with those in Sectors C and D finds similar differences. The differences between those in Sector C and Sector D are smaller. To examine how individual characteristics explain the location in the empirical distribution of occupations, for each Sector $o = \{A, B, C\}$, we estimate the following linear probability model

$$d_{io} = x_i \xi_o + \eta_{io}$$

where d_{io} is a binary variable that equals 1 if individual i is employed in Sector o and x_i is a vector of the individual characteristics *age*, *education* and *English proficiency*; ξ_o is a vector of coefficients and η_{io} is an error term. We plot the relationship between the models' predicted and actual values for the top and two middle sectors in the left panels of Fig. 6. These plots indicate that, especially for Sectors A and B, the model does not predict well suggesting that the individual characteristics alone cannot explain the location in occupational distribution of immigrant workers.

Table 1. Individual Characteristic by Sector 1980–2011.

	Sector A	Sectors B, C, and D	Sector B	Sectors C and D	Sector C	Sector D
Age	36.00	33.00	35.00	32.00	32.00	32.00
Education	15.30	11.50	14.40	10.90	11.60	10.40
English	0.89	0.58	0.87	0.52	0.60	0.45
Arrival year	2.90	2.76	3.12	2.70	2.60	2.70
Tenure in a region	32.00	35.00	31.00	36.00	36.00	36.00
Network in Sector A	0.24	0.14	0.19	0.13	0.15	0.11
Network in Sector B	0.23	0.19	0.26	0.18	0.18	0.17
Network in Sector C	0.30	0.34	0.30	0.35	0.36	0.33

Notes: Columns 2 and 3 compare workers in *Sector A* with all other workers. Columns 4 and 5 compare workers in *Sector B* with workers in *Sector C* and *D*. Columns 6 and 7 compare workers in *Sector C* to workers in *Sector D*. *Sector A* comprises occupations above the 90th percentile of the empirical distribution of occupations (top sector); *Sector B* comprises occupations between the 70th and the 90th percentile; *Sector C* comprises occupations between the 40th and 70th percentiles; *Sector D* comprises occupations below the 40th percentile.

Table 1 suggests the presence of networks and the worker group's history in the region may also be relevant. The variables capturing these factors are the *network size* in the relevant sector, the *tenure* of the group in the metropolitan area, and the *arrival year*. The *network size* is the share of immigrants from a given group employed in a particular sector in a given year. The *networks* do not correspond to a particular occupation or industry but to the location in the empirical distribution of occupations in a region. The *arrival year* denotes the decade in which a group first appears in a region in large numbers. It takes integer values from 1 to 6, where 1 corresponds to the arrival year between 1940 and 1949, 2 corresponds to the arrival year between 1950 and 1959, etc. The *tenure* variable captures a group's tenure in the region and is measured in decades with 1 denoting the most recent arrival. Workers employed in occupations in Sector A have 10% larger networks in Sector A occupations compared to everybody else. Workers employed in Sector B occupations have 8% larger networks in that sector than those in the bottom two sectors. The role of the network appears smaller in Sector C. Tenure in the region and the arrival year also appear more important for the probability of employment in the top sectors (Sectors A and B). We include these factors, and for each Sector *o*, we estimate the following model via OLS:

$$d_{ijo} = \begin{cases} x_{ij}\xi_{jo} + z_j\mu_{jo} + \eta_{ijo} & \text{for } j = 1, \ldots, J \\ x_{ij}\xi_{jo} + \eta_{ijo} & \text{for } j = 0 \end{cases} \tag{1}$$

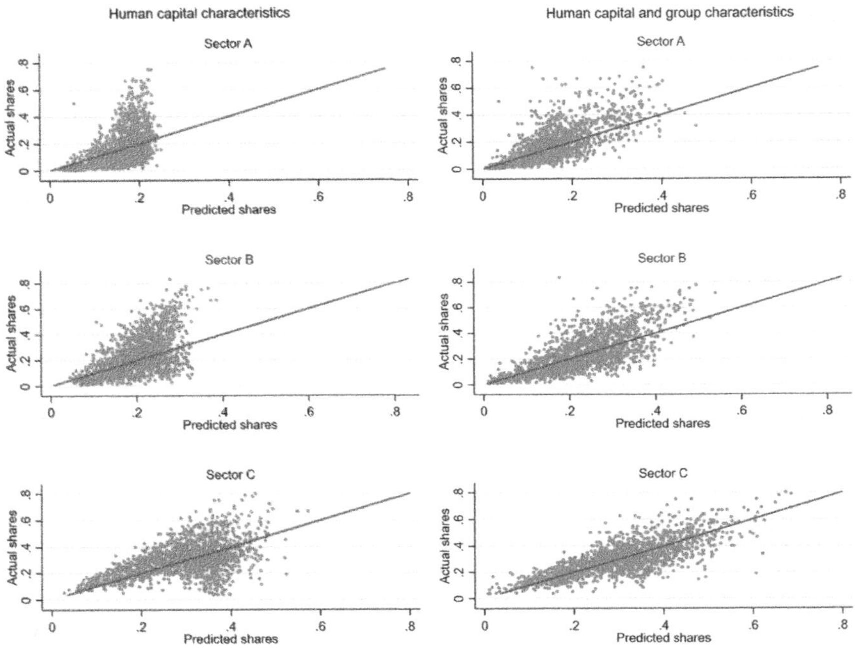

Fig. 6. Predicted Shares From the Linear Probability Models in the Top Three Sectors. *Notes:* Left panels present the relationship between the actual and predicted shares for the top three sectors (A, B, C) for regression with only human capital characteristics. The right panels show the results for regressions including human capital and group characteristics. Top panels correspond to *Sector A*; middle panels to *Sector B* and bottom panels to *Sector C*. *Sector A* comprises occupations above the 90th percentile of the empirical distribution of occupations (top sector); *Sector B* comprises occupations between the 70th and the 90th percentile; *Sector C* comprises occupations between the 40th and 70th percentile; *Sector D* comprises occupations below the 40th percentiles.

where z_j is a vector of group level characteristics including *arrival year*, (*arrival year*)^2, *tenure* and *network size* in Sector o and $j = 1,\ldots,J$ corresponds to the large 15 groups considered while $j = 0$ denotes all other migrants in the region. Given the composition of the last group the construction of the group level variables is not plausible. The right panels of Fig. 6 reveal a clear improvement in the accuracy of predicted shares in all three sectors, highlighting the importance of group characteristics in determining an individual's location in the empirical distribution of occupations.

5. ECONOMIC MODEL OF OCCUPATIONAL HIERARCHIES

5.1 The Model

The descriptive regression analysis suggests the hierarchical patterns are correlated with worker's own characteristics and those of their country of origin. However, this cannot be interpreted as evidence of causal relationships due to endogeneity and reverse causality. We provide insight into these relationships by estimating a model which we consider a plausible mechanism responsible for the observed data.

Our model aims to approximate the economic processes behind workers' sorting into the regional distribution of occupations. It does not aim to reflect the underlying workers' and employers' decision processes. We focus on explaining the spatial and time variation in the location in the occupational distribution of immigrant workers. More specifically, our goal is to estimate a simple model generating the sorting process of immigrants into occupations. We then use the model for three purposes. First, we examine if the model is able to explain the data via in and out of sample prediction exercises. Second, we use the model to evaluate "partial effects" to examine how the ranking may change in response to changes in the values of the conditioning variables. Finally, we perform simulations corresponding to the placement in the distribution of occupations of newly arrived immigrants to highlight the persistence of the hierarchies due to predetermined group characteristics.

As our goal is to explain the variation in the data, we make strong assumptions that allow us to abstract from complex economic processes generating the data. Nevertheless, we still develop a model that is plausible and explains the patterns in the data well. We assume that each region has an exogenous number of jobs for immigrants and an exogenous number of immigrants. Moreover, we assume that these jobs, as reflected by the occupation type, are exogenous. Given the existence of these jobs and immigrants, the employers evaluate the productivity of each worker in each job and rank workers. They then allocate the workers to various jobs. We continue to refer to a collection of jobs as a "sector". In each region, the occupations are ranked according to the SEI index and aggregated into sectors to make the model feasible to estimate.

We divide each region into the four sectors described above with shares s_A, s_B, s_C, and s_D respectively. We also assume that there are j immigrant groups with n_j workers each. If there are $N = \Sigma_{j=1}^{J} n_j$ workers, the employers rank the workers on the basis of their productivity in Sector A and assign the top s_A*N workers to that sector. The employers then rank the remaining workers on the basis of their productivity in the second rank sector and assign the next s_B*N workers to that sector. The remaining workers are then ranked on the basis of their productivity in the third rank sector, and the employers assign the next s_C*N workers to that sector. The remaining workers are allocated to Sector D. As noted earlier, we only consider employed individuals, and while the model allows for unemployment, we impose that each individual is employed. The objective of the empirical work is to estimate the weights the employers put on worker characteristics in determining this allocation.[13]

We acknowledge that these various assumptions regarding exogeneity are contentious but endogenizing these aspects of the model is beyond the scope of this paper. However, the assumptions are not entirely unrealistic. First consider the assumption regarding the number of workers. Jasso and Rosenzweig (1986, 1995) document that the primary justification for immigration is family reunification;[14] thus, it seems plausible to assume that a sample of newly arrived migrants have located in a certain region for reasons unrelated to the distribution of occupations or relative wages. We also assume that the number of jobs is exogenous. This also does not seem unrealistic since the jobs we are considering are generally low-skilled. The exogeneity of the number of jobs assumes that the presence of immigrants does not change the wage distribution in a manner that affects the distribution of jobs across sectors. This seems less important since we focus on rank in the occupational distribution rather than the demand for certain occupations.

We assume that the worker's objective is to be employed in the highest ranked occupation. This does not appear to be unreasonable as the majority of the workers are unskilled, and the evidence in Patel and Vella (2013) suggests immigrants generally do not have occupation specific skills as they tend to be employed in different occupations across regions. Moreover, since an individual's relative location in the occupational and wage distribution are likely to be similar, we are implicitly assuming that the worker's objective is to be employed in the occupation that offers the highest wage in a given region.

Each individual i from country j is characterized by a set of latent variables y_{ijo} capturing their productivity in Sectors A, B, and C. Let:

$$y_{ijo} = \begin{cases} \exp\left(x_{ij}\gamma_{jo} + z_j\alpha_{jo} + u_{ijo}\right) & \text{for } j = 1,\ldots,J;\ o = A \\ \exp\left(x_{ij}\gamma_{jo} + z_j\alpha_{jo} + \zeta_o u_{ijo} + v_{ijo}\right) & \text{for } j = 1,\ldots,J;\ o = B, C \\ \exp\left(x_{ij}\gamma_{jo} + u_{ijo}\right) & \text{for } j = 0;\ o = A \\ \exp\left(x_{ij}\gamma_{jo} + \zeta_o u_{ijo} + v_{ijo}\right) & \text{for } j = 0;\ o = B, C \end{cases}$$

where $\{u_{ijo}\}_{i=1}^{N}$ and $\{v_{ijo}\}_{i=1}^{N}$ are *i.i.d* sequences of $N(0, \sigma_{jo}^2)$ random variables.[15] Recall that $j = 0$ corresponds to a category that comprises all new immigrants originating in countries other than the ones represented in large numbers in a given region ("Others"). Therefore, the composition of this group differs between regions. Our model implies that employers derive no information based on workers' origins for individuals in this category. This is not an unreasonable assumption as it is unlikely that network effects are present for small communities.[16] The inclusion of this group into the estimation makes counterfactual analysis plausible. Moreover, omitting this group from the model necessarily implies redistribution into a sub-sample of available occupations within a particular region and dismisses a large group of available workers.

We do not observe a worker's productivity y_{ijo}, but we observe the occupation in which they are employed. Let d_{io} denote a set of binary variables, indicating an individual i is employed in Sector o. Then:

$$d_{io} = \begin{cases} 1 & \text{if } y_{ijo} \geq s_o \text{ and } d_{il} \neq 1 \text{ where } l < o \\ 0 & \text{otherwise} \end{cases}$$

where s_o denotes the minimum productivity such that an individual is employed in Sector o. As $o = A$ corresponds to the sector comprising the highest ranked occupations $d_{io} = 1$ if individual's i productivity in Sector o exceeds the threshold productivity s_o provided they are not employed in a higher ranked sector, $d_{il} \neq 1\ \forall l < o$.[17] The vectors x and z (defined in the previous section) reflect the likely determinants of a worker's productivity and the impact of networks. An individual's age is a measure of experience and *years of education* and *English proficiency* are the two available measures of skills. Evidence exists suggesting employers rely on observed characteristics they believe are correlated with unobserved attributes, such as worker's productivity, in the absence of complete information about workers (Eriksson & Lagerström, 2012; Phelps, 1972). Employers may also assess the productivity of workers based on the information about their group's productivity (Schwab, 1986). Additional uncertainty also arises from the difficulty in evaluating the measures of skills making employers rely on observable characteristics (Aigner & Cain, 1977; Altonji & Pierret, 2001; Lundberg & Startz, 1983; Phelps, 1972) such as the presence and strength of networks and the group's history in the region.

The model's coefficients differ by sector and by country of origin, allowing the determinants of productivity to be different across sectors and countries of origin. We also allow for the error variance to differ across sectors, noting that the correlation between the error terms in the three sectors accounts for the unobserved correlation between the unobserved productivity in the three sectors. We do not make any assumptions regarding worker productivity in the fourth sector as this is the residual sector.

The coefficients vary by location in the occupational distribution and not necessarily by occupation. Within each region, workers are ranked based on their productivity index; therefore, their location in the occupational distribution depends on the distribution of productivities in the region. Identical individuals can therefore assume different positions in the occupational distribution across sectors depending on the "quality" of other workers and the job types in the region. This implies that the value that employers place on certain characteristics depends on the distribution of these characteristics in the local labor market. For instance, a college degree might be valued more in regions with a smaller fraction of individuals with a college degree. The implication of this allocation mechanism is that the weight of each characteristic in the productivity index is determined by the distribution of the characteristics of all workers and not by the characteristics of the occupations.

While the model has some attractive features, it also has shortcomings. For example, in addition to the issues related to the exogeneity concerns discussed above, it does not incorporate equilibrium behavior by workers and employers. Ideally, the model would allow the number of workers and jobs to vary depending on the quality of the workers, wages and local demand conditions. The model might also allow the employers and workers to move across regions. While these would be positive extensions, the results suggest that even when failing to allow for this behavior, the model provides an insightful description of the data.

5.2 Estimation Procedure

The model's parameters are difficult to directly estimate due to the productivities being latent, the multinomial outcomes, and the sequential nature of the allocation process. Even if we exploit the distributional assumptions to construct a likelihood function, the multiple integrals involved would make estimation challenging due to the correlation of the error terms across sectors. However, it is straightforward to simulate data for given parameter values under our model assumptions. Thus, we estimate the model via the indirect inference procedure (Gourieroux et al., 1993). We first specify an auxiliary model and estimate its parameters. We then simulate data from our model for given values of the model parameters. We choose the parameters of the model such that the corresponding parameters for the auxiliary model estimated over the simulated data are "close" to the parameters for the auxiliary model for the true data.

Let β denote the parameters of the model and k_1 and k_2 the number of individual and group variables in the productivity index. The β vector contains the parameters in the productivity index, $\{\gamma_{jo}\}_{j=0}^{J}$, $\{\alpha_{jo}\}_{j=1}^{J}$, $\{\sigma_{jo}^2\}_{j=0}^{J}$ and ζ_o in each Sector o. Let $\widehat{\theta}$ denote the estimates of the auxiliary model for the real data, and $\tilde{\theta}^m(\beta)$ denote the corresponding estimates on the simulated data where $m = 1, \ldots, M$ denotes the number of simulations. The simulated data are generated using observed data on the exogenous variables and an assumed value of β. For each of the simulated data sets, we estimate the auxiliary model and obtain $\tilde{\theta}^m(\beta)$. Let $\tilde{\theta}(\beta) = \frac{1}{M}\sum_{m=1}^{M}\tilde{\theta}^m(\beta)$ equal the average vector of the estimated parameters of the auxiliary model. We choose the values of β such that:

$$\widehat{\beta} = \underset{\beta}{\operatorname{argmin}}\big(\widehat{\theta} - \tilde{\theta}(\beta)\big)'W\big(\widehat{\theta} - \tilde{\theta}(\beta)\big)$$

where W is a positive definite weighting matrix.[18]

An important feature of indirect inference is that the auxiliary model need not be "correctly specified," and the estimates of the auxiliary model's parameters do not need to have the usual desirable properties. While the choice of the moments to match between actual and simulated data is theoretically unimportant, subject to issues related to identification, the indirect inference procedure seems most attractive when the auxiliary model describes the primary features of interest of the data. Our choice of the moments is directly related to the features of the data, which motivate our interest. Since we are interested in the shares of immigrant workers in each sector in each region, we will focus on the parameters in a reduced form explanation of those shares. Accordingly, we use the auxiliary model outlined in Eq. (1) that predicts the shares. This yields $3(k_1 + k_2 + 1) = 36$ parameters. To aid identification of the error variances and covariances, we add the estimates of the covariance matrix of the OLS residuals obtained from estimation of Eq. (1), and this yields 10 additional parameters. In sum, 46 parameters are being matched in the estimation process.

In estimating models with endogenous discrete variables using indirect inference, small changes in the model's parameters can cause jumps in the simulated data which make the objective function change discretely (Bruins et al., 2018). The objective function is thus not a smooth function of the parameters, and it is not possible to use gradient based methods to estimate the model. To overcome this we follow Bruins et al. (2018) and substitute d^m_{ijo} with a continuous function of the latent productivity, $g(y^m_{ijo}(\beta);\lambda)$, such that:

$$g\left(y^m_{ijo}(\beta);\lambda\right) = \frac{\exp\left(\left(y^m_{ijo}(\beta) - s_o\right)/\lambda\right)}{1 + \exp\left(\left(y^m_{ijo}(\beta) - s_o\right)/\lambda\right)}$$

where λ is the smoothing parameter and s_o is the minimum productivity guaranteeing employment in Sector o.[19] The choice of the smoothing parameters is important as larger values of λ result in a smoother objective function but may introduce a large bias. Based on the Monte Carlo simulations, we use $\lambda = 0.05$ and set the number of simulations (M) equal to 10, noting that increasing the number of simulations appears to have little effect on the estimates while increasing the time burden significantly.[20]

5.3 Results

Within each sector, we restrict the coefficients to be the same for the 15 "Large" groups but allow them to differ for the category of "Others". Therefore, in each sector o, $\gamma_j = \gamma_1$ and $\alpha_j = \alpha_1$ for $j = 1,\ldots, J$ and $\gamma_j = \gamma_0$ and $\alpha_j = \alpha_0$ for $j = 0$.[21] For identification purposes, we normalize the coefficient on education in all three sectors to 1 for the "Large" group. We also normalize the variances in Sector A for the group of "Large" and "Others" to 1 leading to 33 parameters to be estimated. All explanatory variables are scaled to ensure that the entries in the Hessian are of the same order of magnitude to aid the performance of the search algorithms. The covariance matrix is estimated following Gourieroux et al. (1993) and is explained in Appendix B, noting that since our auxiliary model consists of additional moments the estimated standard errors are underestimated.[22]

Before proceeding to the main results, consider the estimates from the auxiliary model. The right panels of Fig. 6 illustrate the capacity of our auxiliary model to reproduce the shares of immigrant workers in each sector. The model performs very well. This is not surprising as the conditioning set of variables is rich and includes the individual's age, educational attainment, English proficiency as well as characteristics of the group defined as country of origin of an individual, such as the *network size*, *arrival year*, *arrival year* squared, and the *tenure*.[23] Almost all regressors in the three sectors for the "Large" groups and the category of "Others" have a statistically significant role in predicting the shares. Only when immigrants from "Large" groups are considered, time of arrival and the group's tenure in the region do not play an important role in explaining the placement in Sector C.

Table 2 presents the parameter estimates of our economic model. Recall that for the "Others" category, we do not include the variables describing the characteristics of the country of origin. Due to the employed normalizations, one cannot directly interpret the coefficients. Below we examine the impact of changes in the values of the explanatory variables by simulating the model for different values of the explanatory variables. However, from a visual inspection of Table 2 we can directly interpret the change's direction via the coefficient's sign. This provides insight into what individual features positively affect employers' evaluation of productivity.

Focus on the "Large" groups first. Assuming that *education* positively affects the employers' assessment of worker's productivity most of the explanatory variables appear to have a positive effect on the evaluation of worker's productivity in all three sectors. Employers value experienced workers, those with a better knowledge of English, and those with established networks in the relevant part of the distribution. Employers appear to more highly value workers with longer histories and positively value group's tenure in the region (with the exception of Sector C). English proficiency, relative to years of education, plays a smaller role in the top two sectors than in Sector C. This suggests that in more skilled jobs which are more likely to be located in the top part of the empirical distribution, formal skills are essential whereas in occupations requiring less formal skills, language skills can be seen more of a substitute for schooling. The importance of networks relative to education is largest in Sector B, suggesting that employers in this region of the empirical distribution more highly value the information derived from the appropriate networks.

When evaluating the productivity of workers with no "Large" group affiliation, all the individual characteristics have positive weights in all three sectors with the exception of age in Sector C. As for workers from "Large" groups, English proficiency plays a smaller role in Sector A, while the weight on years of education is the biggest in this sector in comparison to the two sectors, comprising occupations in the middle part of the empirical distribution.

Contrasting the relative magnitudes of the estimated parameters within sectors delivers additional evidence. The weights associated with educational attainment are substantially higher for workers without a "Large" group affiliation in all three sectors. The same is true for the weights on English proficiency in Sectors B and C. Both results suggest that workers without "Large" group affiliation need to demonstrate significantly higher skills to compensate for the lack of a network.

5.4 Model Fit

We evaluate the model's within-sample predictive performance on the basis of 100 simulations. For each simulation, we calculate the shares of workers from each origin in each region in each sector.[24] We then compute the occupational

Table 2. Parameters Estimates.

Sector A		
Large Groups		
Age	0.758	(0.287)
English proficiency	0.240	(0.542)
Arrival	−0.803	(10.265)
Arrival squared	1.172	(1.687)
Tenure in a region	0.044	(0.821)
Size of the network in Sector A	1.871	(0.387)
Others		
Age	0.559	(1.859)
Education	1.647	(4.494)
English proficiency	0.179	(1.111)
Sector B		
Large Groups		
Age	0.069	(2.594)
English proficiency	0.288	(1.881)
Arrival	0.265	(1.162)
Arrival squared	0.051	(0.596)
Tenure in a region	0.254	(1.302)
Size of the network in Sector B	3.076	(0.248)
Others		
Age	0.720	(3.502)
Education	1.471	(0.341)
English proficiency	0.424	(3.241)
Sector C		
Large Groups		
Age	0.428	(1.914)
English proficiency	0.372	(1.341)
Arrival	−0.216	(0.962)
Arrival squared	0.502	(0.342)
Tenure in a region	−1.267	(2.104)
Size of the network in Sector C	1.509	(0.187)
Others		
Age	−0.185	(2.786)
Education	1.474	(0.421)
English proficiency	0.471	(2.549)
$\sigma^2_{Large,\ Sector\ B}$	0.471	(0.667)
$\sigma^2_{Others,\ Sector\ B}$	0.630	(0.795)
$\zeta_{SectorA-SectorB}$	1.684	(0.476)
$\sigma^2_{Large,\ Sector\ C}$	1.432	(0.759)
$\sigma^2_{Others,\ Sector\ C}$	1.107	(0.981)
$\zeta_{SectorA-SectorC}$	2.665	(0.579)

Notes: Standard errors in parentheses. *Large groups* correspond to the 15 sending countries while *Others* to all other migrants in regions under investigation. *Sector A* comprises occupations above the 90th percentile of the empirical distribution of occupations (top sector); *Sector B* comprises occupations between the 70th and the 90th percentile; *Sector C* comprises occupations between the 40th and 70th percentiles; *Sector D* comprises occupations below the 40th percentile.

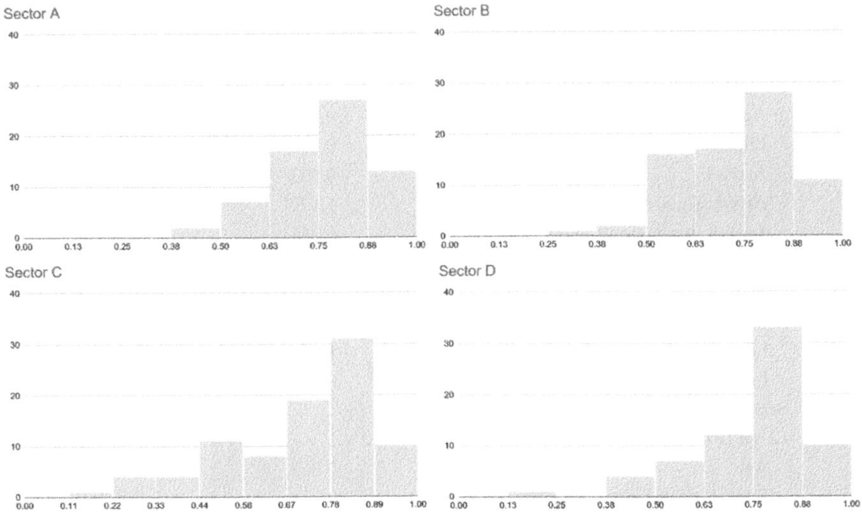

Fig. 7. Model Fit. *Notes:* Frequency of the share of the correctly predicted rankings based on predicted shares in each sector between each pair of countries. *Sector A* comprises occupations above the 90th percentile of the empirical distribution of occupations (top sector); *Sector B* comprises occupations between the 70th and the 90th percentile; *Sector C* comprises occupations between the 40th and 70th percentiles; *Sector D* comprises occupations below the 40th percentile.

distribution based on the averaged shares for each of the group and rank countries within each region based on the average fraction of workers employed in each sector. Fig. 7 summarizes the results by showing the distribution of the correctly predicted rankings.[25]

The model correctly predicts the pairwise ranking of countries in 80% of the comparisons. Two factors appear to influence the model's predictive capacity. The first issue is related to the relative magnitude of the shares of workers employed in a sector. When both groups have roughly equal shares the model does not predict the pairwise ranking well. The second issue is the sample size. If we only observe a pair of countries in a small number of regions, the average performance of the model is relatively low. For example, there are only 6 regions with large groups of newly arrived Cuban and Vietnamese workers, and in 3 of these regions, the shares of each group in Sector C are almost the same. Thus, the model predicts correctly only 50% of the rankings between Cubans and Vietnamese workers.

The predictions are generally more accurate in Sectors A and D, averaging 84% of correctly predicted pairings. Eighty percent of the parings in Sector B are correctly predicted while in Sector C, the average is 75%. The loss in average performance is driven by the decline in the accuracy of predicting the shares in regions with relatively small numbers of new migrants from a given group. Overall, the model's predictive capacity suggests it performs well.

To examine the model's capacity to predict pairwise rankings out of sample, we estimate the model omitting selected regions. We perform two exercises. First, we omit three metropolitan areas (Atlanta, Boston, and Sacramento) in all time periods. This results in a 5% decrease in sample size. In the second exercise, we exclude New York in all years resulting in a 12% smaller sample. Using the estimated coefficients and observed data, we compute the occupational distribution of workers in each of the omitted regions. The computations are based on 100 simulations, and the results are summarized in Table 3. In both instances, the model's out of sample performance is good. In the first case, 69, 90, 74, and 83% of pairwise rankings in Atlanta, Boston and Sacramento in Sectors A, B, C, and D, respectively, are predicted correctly. In New York, the fraction of correctly predicted rankings in Sectors A, B, C, and D are 0.66, 0.75, 0.69, and 0.76, respectively.

Table 3. Out of Sample Predictions.

Omitted Regions	Sector A	Sector B	Sector C	Sector D
Atlanta, Boston, Sacramento	0.69	0.90	0.74	0.83
New York	0.66	0.75	0.69	0.76

Notes: Each entry represents the share of correctly predicted rankings in an omitted region. *Sector A* comprises occupations above the 90th percentile of the empirical distribution of occupations (top sector); *Sector B* comprises occupations between the 70th and the 90th percentile; *Sector C* comprises occupations between the 40th and 70th percentiles; *Sector D* comprises occupations below the 40th percentile.

6. QUANTITATIVE IMPACT OF CONDITIONING VARIABLES

To assess the quantitative impact of the exogenous variables in the model, we perturb each in isolation for each group and evaluate the consequences for the rankings. As we take averages over individuals within regions, we limit the sample to regions with large groups of new migrants. We first simulate the outcomes using the parameter estimates and the actual values for the conditioning variables. We then change the value of a specific characteristic for all individuals from a specific origin and repeat the simulations to generate a new allocation of workers.[26]

Since there is no obvious metric to compare the magnitude of these effects, we examine what changes in characteristics would result in similar changes in rankings.[27] To illustrate the magnitude of changes required to improve the group's standings in the empirical distribution of occupations, we consider two examples: China in Sector A (Table 4) and Korea in Sector B (Table 5). In both cases, we examine what type of changes in educational attainment and the shares of established migrants in the relevant part of empirical distribution of occupations would induce similar changes in the rankings as increasing English proficiency of all individuals from a specific country of origin.

Table 4. Fraction of Affected Rankings Between China and Selected Countries in Sector A.

	ME	AFR	IND	KOR	DEU	ENG	CAN
English proficiency*	0.13	0.25	0.14	0.40	0.10	0.10	0.14
Extra year of schooling	0.25	0.38	0.40	0.40	0.22	0.30	0.35
Extra year of schooling to less than HS	0.13	0.13	0.13	0.00	0.11	0.00	0.13
Extra 2 years of schooling to less than HS	0.13	0.38	0.20	0.20	0.00	0.10	0.17
10% increase in network size in the top sector**	0.13	0.00	0.10	0.00	0.11	0.00	0.09
15% increase in network size in the top sector	0.15	0.05	0.13	0.00	0.15	0.05	0.15

Notes: *63% of Chinese workers report speaking English well; **Average share of Chinese workers employed in Sector A jobs is 0.20. *Sector A* comprises occupations above the 90th percentile of the empirical distribution of occupations (top sector).

If all Chinese workers were proficient in English, between 10 and 40% of pairwise comparisons with other countries would be affected. A similar effect would be triggered by an extra year of schooling for all workers or an extra one to two years of schooling to individuals with less than a high school degree, or by increasing the network size in the top sector by 10–15% (2–3% points average increase in the share of workers employed in the top part of the occupational distribution).

Table 5 reveals similar patterns among Korean workers in Sector B. If all Korean workers were proficient in English, 13–43% of pairwise comparisons would be affected. A change of a similar magnitude is induced by an extra year of schooling for all workers, or extra 2–5 years of schooling for workers with less than high school, or a 5–15% increase in the network size in Sector B (0.7–2% points increase). Both examples suggest relatively small absolute changes in the network size in the top sector result in changes of similar magnitude as large increases in skills.

Table 5. Fraction of Affected Rankings Between Korea and Selected Countries in Sector B.

	ME	AFR	IND	CHN	DEU	ENG	CAN
English proficiency*	0.33	0.17	0.19	0.43	0.27	0.33	0.13
Extra year of schooling	0.43	0.17	0.13	0.31	0.27	0.20	0.13
Extra year of schooling to less than HS	0.14	0.00	0.00	0.00	0.00	0.00	0.13
Extra 2 years of schooling to less than HS	0.14	0.17	0.00	0.08	0.00	0.20	0.13
Extra 5 years of schooling to less than HS	0.43	0.33	0.20	0.46	0.27	0.20	0.13
5% increase in network size in Sector B**	0.00	0.17	0.06	0.21	0.18	0.33	0.13
10% increase in network size in Sector B	0.57	0.33	0.07	0.31	0.27	0.20	0.13
15% increase in network size in Sector B	0.57	0.33	0.19	0.50	0.27	0.33	0.13

Notes: *62% of Koreans report speaking English well; **Average share of Korean workers employed in Sector B jobs is 0.14. *Sector B* comprises occupations between the 70th and 90th percentile of the empirical distribution of occupations.

6.1 Occupational Distribution Allocation of Newly Arrived Workers

We now use the model to allocate new migrants from each of the large sending countries to verify how important the group characteristics are in determining the labor market success of newly arrived workers and how persistent the group's ranking is. We first consider each country separately by simulating 30 new migrants from a specific origin in each region in which it has an established presence in 2011. The individual characteristics of these simulated workers reflect the distribution of the individual characteristics for the whole sample in 2011 and is kept constant for all experiments. The simulated workers are between 30 and 45 years old, ranging from no high school degree to some college and 65% of them speak English well.[28] The network size in the three sectors, arrival year, and tenure in the region are set to the actual characteristics of a given group in a region. We evaluate how these simulated workers would sort into the occupational distribution within regions. Since the individual characteristics are kept constant across groups and across regions within groups, the differences between the resulting locations in occupational distribution highlight the role of the group characteristics in determining the success of a new cohort. The results for selected regions, summarized in Table 6, show substantial variation in the shares of workers that would be allocated in all sectors. The shares in Sectors A and B vary between 3–28 and 2–39%, respectively, while in Sector C, the majority of the shares fall between 15 and 25% interval. Groups also exhibit a large variation within sectors and across regions. For example, in Los Angeles 30% of the simulated workers of Chinese origin would find employment in Sector B while only 3% would be employed in this sector in Las Vegas.

Examining each region separately reveals that within the same region workers assume a different position in the occupational distribution depending on their origin. For instance, in San Antonio, 18% of the simulated workers of Indian origin would find Sector A jobs while only 5% of Korean and 8% of Vietnamese workers would do so. In the same region, 36% of Indian workers would find Sector B jobs compared to 20% of Chinese and 18% of Korean workers. In Boston, 8% of Canadian, 17% of Chinese, and 16% of Indian workers from the simulated cohort would find jobs in Sector C jobs. Given that individual characteristics are held constant across groups, these results highlight the role of the group's history in the local labor market.

Now consider the resulting ranking if each of these groups simultaneously arrived in the same region. For each region and for each group with an established presence in 2011, we simulate 30 new workers. The distribution of individual characteristics is the same across groups, and the country of origin characteristics are predetermined. Table 7 presents the allocation of the simulated workers into Sectors A, B, C, and D for selected regions and compares it to the observed shares. Two features of this table are important. First, there is substantial variation in the group's allocation to Sector A despite the identical distribution of individual characteristics across countries. Second, the relative magnitudes of the predicted and actual shares are similar.[29] For example, in Houston the model allocates at most 7% of Filipinos, Vietnamese and Mexican

Table 6. Placement in the Distribution of Occupations.

	CAN	MEX	ENG	DEU	CHN	KOR	PHL	VNM	IND	AFR	ME
Sector A											
Atlanta, GA				0.04							
Chicago-Gary-Lake, IL				0.09					0.11		
Las Vegas, NV	0.16		0.28							0.18	
Los Angeles-Long Beach, CA								0.07			
Philadelphia, PA/NJ	0.23										
San Antonio, TX						0.05		0.08	0.18		
San Francisco-Oakland, CA										0.03	
Sector B											
Boston, MA				0.09	0.07						0.19
Chicago-Gary-Lake, IL							0.01		0.19		0.08
Dallas-Fort Worth, TX									0.08		
Fort Lauderdale-Hollywood, FL							0.03				
Honolulu, HI								0.08			0.39
Houston-Brazoria, TX							0.17				
Las Vegas, NV					0.03						
Los Angeles-Long Beach, CA		0.02			0.30	0.33			0.28	0.27	
Orange County, CA										0.05	0.10
Bergen-Passaic, NJ									0.17		
Middlesex-Somerset, NJ					0.28		0.02				
Phoenix, AZ		0.06									
San Antonio, TX					0.20	0.18			0.36		
Oakland, CA							0.05				
Vallejo-Fairfield-Napa, CA									0.07		
Stockton, CA		0.04									
Tampa-St. Petersburg, FL						0.09					

Sector C											
Boston, MA	0.08				0.17				0.16		
Chicago-Gary-Lake, IL					0.16						0.18
Dallas-Fort Worth, TX		0.38						0.36	0.25		
Fort Worth-Arlington, TX		0.41						0.36			
Houston-Brazoria, TX		0.43					0.30				
Las Vegas, NV		0.35	0.22					0.34		0.29	
Los Angeles-Long Beach, CA								0.22	0.14		
Orange County, CA			0.14								
Orlando, FL					0.11				0.19		
Phoenix, AZ					0.17		0.33		0.17		
San Antonio, TX		0.17			0.18		0.25			0.22	
San Francisco-Oakland-Vallejo, CA								0.21	0.27	0.21	
Tampa-St. Petersburg, FL				0.18				0.18		0.21	

Notes: Each entry represents the simulated share of workers of a given origin employed in a given sector in a selected region. *Sector A* comprises occupations above the 90th percentile of the empirical distribution of occupations (top sector); *Sector B* comprises occupations between the 70th and the 90th percentile; *Sector C* comprises occupations between the 40th and 70th percentiles; *Sector D* comprises occupations below the 40th percentile. The selection of regions does not reflect any underlying patterns. The empty entries in the table imply that a given group was not present in large numbers in given metropolitan area in 2011.

Table 7. Allocation of New Arrivals in the Occupational Distribution.

	Observed Shares				Model Predictions			
	A	B	C	D	A	B	C	D
Houston, TX								
CAN	0.34	0.47	0.14	0.04	0.12	0.00	0.18	0.70
CHN	0.46	0.23	0.18	0.13	0.12	0.00	0.23	0.65
ENG	0.21	0.52	0.28	0.00	0.10	0.03	0.17	0.70
KOR	0.56	0.18	0.12	0.15	0.09	0.00	0.31	0.60
IND	0.28	0.43	0.23	0.06	0.09	0.03	0.27	0.61
DEU	0.23	0.52	0.23	0.03	0.08	0.00	0.28	0.64
AFR	0.14	0.19	0.36	0.31	0.08	0.00	0.31	0.61
PHL	0.18	0.22	0.46	0.14	0.07	0.00	0.37	0.56
VNM	0.05	0.08	0.44	0.43	0.07	0.00	0.34	0.59
ME	0.19	0.32	0.29	0.20	0.07	0.33	0.19	0.41
MEX	0.02	0.06	0.34	0.58	0.06	0.00	0.25	0.69
Orange County, CA								
IND	0.19	0.54	0.17	0.09	0.09	0.18	0.14	0.59
CHN	0.32	0.37	0.18	0.13	0.08	0.06	0.16	0.70
DEU	0.22	0.44	0.11	0.22	0.07	0.03	0.21	0.69
AFR	0.23	0.37	0.26	0.14	0.07	0.03	0.18	0.72
CAN	0.34	0.32	0.29	0.05	0.06	0.31	0.14	0.49
KOR	0.15	0.44	0.30	0.11	0.06	0.04	0.21	0.69
PHL	0.08	0.22	0.40	0.29	0.06	0.00	0.26	0.68
VNM	0.03	0.13	0.34	0.50	0.06	0.00	0.24	0.70
ME	0.12	0.27	0.41	0.20	0.06	0.11	0.17	0.66
MEX	0.00	0.05	0.18	0.76	0.04	0.00	0.21	0.75
Seattle-Everett, WA								
CAN	0.19	0.62	0.13	0.07	0.05	0.00	0.05	0.90
CHN	0.14	0.48	0.11	0.28	0.04	0.06	0.07	0.83
KOR	0.11	0.44	0.21	0.24	0.04	0.00	0.08	0.88
VNM	0.01	0.12	0.19	0.67	0.04	0.00	0.09	0.87
IND	0.09	0.77	0.06	0.08	0.04	0.25	0.07	0.64
AFR	0.06	0.20	0.22	0.52	0.04	0.00	0.08	0.88
Stockton, CA								
MEX	0.03	0.06	0.31	0.60	0.08	0.00	0.29	0.63
PHL	0.15	0.38	0.24	0.24	0.11	0.30	0.14	0.45

Notes: Columns 2–5 present the actual shares of migrants in each sector while Columns 6–9 present the shares of the extra (simulated) workers as predicted by the model. *Sector A* comprises occupations above the 90th percentile of the empirical distribution of occupations (top sector); *Sector B* comprises occupations between the 70th and the 90th percentile; *Sector C* comprises occupations between the 40th and 70th percentiles; *Sector D* comprises occupations below the 40th percentile.

workers are in the top part of the empirical distribution whereas the actual shares among workers of the above origins in Sector A do not exceed 18%. Similarly, in Orange County, more Indian than Mexican workers are employed in the top sector. The model allocates Indian and Mexican workers accordingly. Similarly, in Sectors C and D, the allocation of the simulated workers mimics the observed distribution. For example, in Houston, both Filipino and Vietnamese workers have a relatively high fraction of workers employed in Sector C, and a relatively high fraction of the simulated workers are allocated here. Relatively few Canadian and English migrants are employed in Sector C; therefore, a small fraction of the "extra" workers is allocated to this sector.

Overall, these results suggest that the relative placement in the occupational distribution of future cohorts resembles the allocation of the established migrants irrespective of the individual characteristics and stresses the role of the predetermined group's characteristics. They further highlight the significance of the starting point for labor market outcomes of new cohorts of immigrant workers.

7. CONCLUSION

We provide clear evidence of a persistent hierarchical structure among immigrant labor groups in the United States as measured by their location in the occupational distribution. The evidence suggests the hierarchies do not result from specific immigrant group skills. Rather, our empirical results suggest that employers in labor markets at the metropolitan region level rank the workers partially on the basis of which immigrant group they belong to. The evidence from an estimation of a model in which employers rank workers according to their perceived productivity suggests the effect of membership of a particular immigrant group operates through immigrant networks. Moreover, these network effects are largely responsible for the hierarchy persisting across regions and time.

Although it is remarkable how our simple model can capture the observed occupational hierarchies at a reasonably detailed labor market characterization, its simplicity limits the scope of policy recommendations. Future work should explore relaxing the exogeneity assumptions made in our analysis to understand the behavior of employers and employees and better inform the policymakers. Similarly, increasing the number of sectors would improve our understanding of the mechanisms behind the observed hierarchies. Similarly, our operationalization of network effects is rather broad. Extending the analysis to capture important group-level heterogeneity, such as groups' cohesion or within-group cultural diversity, would provide insight into the group's dynamics contributing to the occupational hierarchies. Last but not least, further research should explore how occupational hierarchies contribute to the persistence of hierarchies in other important welfare-determining processes such as housing location or school choice and how they affect wages and other nonpecuniary benefits associated with jobs.

Our empirical evidence is valuable not only because it is the first to document the existence of a persistent hierarchical structure among immigrant labor. It is also important because it highlights that the persistence reflects network effects. This has implications for future generations of immigrants as the evidence suggests that those from specific countries will be disadvantaged in the US labor market. Moreover, given the recent evidence documenting the lack of intergenerational mobility in the income distribution (Chetty, Hendren, Kline, Saez, et al., 2014), it is clear that the starting point for new immigrants has implications for their offspring and beyond.

NOTES

1. Note that while we do not explicitly model the workers' and employers' behavior our simple model is consistent with models of statistical discrimination and network effects.
2. Some studies also considered how Hispanic and Asian American workers compare to natives (see for example Bohon, 2005; Model, 2002; Tolnay, 2001).
3. For 1980, 1990, and 2000, we use the 1% samples, and for 1940, 1950, 1960, and 1970 the 5% samples. We exclude data prior to 1940 as the individual's educational attainment was not available. The 2010 census used only a short form asking ten basic questions, and these questions did not include relevant information on origins, educational attainment, occupation, and English proficiency. In 2010, all detailed socioeconomic information is collected via the American Community Survey.
4. Boston, Chicago, Detroit, Los Angeles, New York, Philadelphia, and San Francisco have at least five different groups in every time period between 1940 and 2011. Many metropolitan areas have at most three large groups and have experienced large inflows of immigrants from 1980 onward.
5. Russia includes all individuals who declare Russia or the USSR as their country of birth. Moreover, we include some regions, but we will refer to them as countries for simplicity.
6. This index was obtained by regressing occupational prestige ratings on occupational income and education of native men for a limited number of occupations based on the 1950 Census occupational classification and using the estimates to assign scores for all occupations in the 1950 Census classification.
7. India and Africa appear to show different patterns. However, there were only three metropolitan areas with large concentrations of African or Indian workers in 1970, New York and Los Angeles and New York and Chicago, respectively. Immigrants from both groups were frequently employed as Physicians and Managers and Administrators. In addition, Indians built large networks in engineering and African workers in actuarial occupations.
8. For example, in 1990, plumbers in Baltimore and Seattle were in the bottom sector and in Los Angeles and Miami, they were in the top sector. Similarly, in 2011, welders in Boston and Washington DC were in the bottom sector and in Austin and Atlanta, they were in the top sector.
9. The choice of the threshold is arbitrary and the general patterns do not change as we vary the threshold. Nevertheless, we believe that the 70% margin is a good benchmark to isolate the disproportionate sorting of some groups into what might be considered high-rank occupational categories.
10. The sectors are defined for the population of interest, *all* or *unskilled*, meaning that the sectors are not the same for the two tables.

11. Note that since we estimate the occupational distribution in every year in every metropolitan area, these patterns are driven by the disappearance of some low-prestige occupations.

12. Established migrants are individuals who arrived in the United States more than 10 years prior to each census year.

13. Extending the model beyond four sectors is trivial from a simulation point of view. However, it proved to be challenging from an estimation perspective. It would also require a larger data set to reliably compute the network sizes in each sector.

14. Jasso and Rosenzweig (1986, 1995) document that immigrants who come for family reunification reasons constitute the largest group out of all immigrants and even the change in policy in 1990, which put a lower weight on family reunification, did not change this fact. Between 1969 and 1986, the share of adults who were spouses of US citizens and were granted permanent residence increased from 17 to 40%. Similarly, in 1961, 60% of all nonrefugee immigrants were either spouses, parents, children, or siblings of US citizens.

15. The choice of the functional form was driven by the performance of the estimator. It has no implications for identification.

16. Sensitivity analysis regarding the cut-off value for a large group showed that our results are not sensitive to the choice of the cut-off value.

17. This notation is consistent with denoting the highest-ranked sector as A.

18. We use an identity matrix. Our auxiliary model includes additional moments; therefore, we cannot apply the optimal weighting matrix as described in Gourieroux et al. (1993).

19. We follow (Bruins et al., 2018) in the choice of the $g(\cdot)$ function. Provided $g(y^m_{ijo}(\beta); \lambda)$ converges to $d^m_{ijo}(\beta)$ as λ goes to zero, any continuous function of the latent productivity produces consistent estimates of the model's parameters. This function was also used in Altonji et al. (2013).

20. The estimation was implemented in GAUSS using optimum optimization module. Implementation of this estimation strategy proved to be challenging. The objective function exhibits multiple local minima which makes the search for the global solution time intensive. We carefully examined the neighborhood of every parameter estimate to ensure that we have found a global minimum.

21. Allowing the parameters of the productivity index to vary by groups proved to be not feasible due to the large number of resulting parameters.

22. As the analytic standard errors rely on numerical derivatives, therefore allowing the manipulation of their magnitude, the value added from the derivation of the asymptotic covariance matrix in this setting seems low. Therefore, we report the analytic standard errors noting that they are underestimated and also that their magnitude varies with the choice of the delta in the numerical derivatives.

23. We highlight that the moments we match in the model estimation are the auxiliary model coefficient estimates.

24. Region denotes metropolitan area-year combinations.

25. When computing predicted shares, we limit the sample to metropolitan areas with at least 30 new migrants in each group to avoid taking averages over small cells.

26. For all experiments we simulate the model 100 times.

27. Analysis of the quantitative impact of each conditioning variable is presented in Appendix C.

28. Since our focus is on low-skilled workers, the education composition is biased toward individuals with at most high school degree. For English and Canadian workers, we assume that all extra (simulated) workers speak English well.

29. The model allocates very few workers to Sector B due to the relatively large coefficient on education for the category of *Others* for this sector.

30. This index was obtained by regressing occupational prestige ratings on occupational income and education of native men for a limited number of occupations based on the 1950 Census occupational classification and using the estimates to assign scores for all occupations in the 1950 Census classification.

31. The negative sign follows from the fact that OLS minimizes the sum of squared residuals.

32. Since *English proficiency* is measured with an indicator that an individual speaks English well, the experiment we consider is making everyone proficient in English. England and Canada are omitted from the tables.

33. The effect of arrival year is positive in its domain as it takes values between 0.1 and 0.6 where 0.1 corresponds to a group arrival prior to 1940 and 0.6 corresponds to arrival between 1990 and 2000.

REFERENCES

Abramitzky, R., Boustan, L. P., & Eriksson, K. (2014). A nation of immigrants: Assimilation and economic outcomes in the age of mass migration. *Journal of Political Economy*, *122*(3), 467–506.

Aigner, D. J., & Cain, G. G. (1977). Statistical theories of discrimination in labor markets. *Industrial and Labor Relations Review*, *30*(2), 175–187.

Altonji, J. G., & Card, D. (2018). The effects of immigration on the labor market outcomes of less-skilled natives. In *The new immigrant in the American economy* (pp. 137–170). Routledge.

Altonji, J. G., & Pierret, C. R. (2001). Employer learning and statistical discrimination. *Quarterly Journal of Economics*, *116*(1), 313–350.

Altonji, J. G., Smith, A. A., & Vidangos, I. (2013). Modeling earnings dynamics. *Econometrica*, *81*(4), 1395–1454.

Beaman, L. A. (2012). Social networks and the dynamics of labour market outcomes: Evidence from refugees resettled in the US. *The Review of Economic Studies*, *79*(1), 128–161.

Bohon, S. A. (2005). Occupational attainment of Latino immigrants in the United States. *Geographical Review*, *95*(2), 249–266.

Borjas, J. G. (1985). Assimilation, changes in cohort quality, and the earnings of immigrants. *Journal of Labor Economics*, 463–489.

Borjas, J. G. (1992). Ethnic capital and intergenerational mobility. *Quarterly Journal of Economics*, *107*(1), 123–150.

Borjas, J. G. (1994a). The economics of immigration. *Journal of Economic Literature*, 1667–1717.

Borjas, J. G. (1994b). *Assimilation and changes in cohort quality revisited: What happened to immigrant earnings in the 1980s?* Technical report. National Bureau of Economic Research.

Borjas, J. G. (2006a). Making it in America: Social mobility in the immigrant population. *The Future of Children*, *16*(2), 55.

Borjas, J. G. (2006b). Native internal migration and the labor market impact of immigration. *Journal of Human Resources*, *41*(2), 221–258.

Borjas, J. G., Freeman, R. B., Katz, L. F., DiNardo, J., & Abowd, J. M. (1997). How much do immigration and trade affect labor market outcomes? *Brookings Papers on Economic Activity*, (1), 1–90.

Bruins, M., Duffy, J. A., Michael, P. K., & Smith, A. A., Jr. (2018). Generalized indirect inference for discrete choice models. *Journal of Econometrics*, *205*(1), 177–203.

Card, D. (2001). Immigrant inflows, native outflows, and the local labor market impacts of higher immigration. *Journal of Labor Economics*, *19*(1), 22–64.

Card, D. (2005). Is the new immigration really so bad? *The Economic Journal*, *115*(507), F300–F323.

Chetty, R., Hendren, N., Kline, P., & Saez, E. (2014). Where is the land of opportunity? The geography of intergenerational mobility in the United States. *Quarterly Journal of Economics*, *129*(4), 1553–1623.

Chetty, R., Hendren, N., Kline, P., Saez, E., & Turner, N. (2014). Is the United States still a land of opportunity? Recent trends in intergenerational mobility. *The American Economic Review*, *104*(5), 141–147.

Cortes, P. (2008). The effect of low-skilled immigration on US prices: Evidence from CPI data. *Journal of Political Economy*, *116*(3), 381–422.

DiNardo, J., & Card, D. (2000). Do immigrant inflows lead to native outflows? *The American Economic Review*, *90*(2), 360–367.

Duncan, O. D. (1961). A socioeconomic index for all occupations. *Class: Critical Concepts*, *1*, 388–426.

Dustmann, C., Frattini, T., & Preston, I. P. (2013). The effect of immigration along the distribution of wages. *The Review of Economic Studies*, *80*(1), 145–173.

Dustmann, C., Schönberg, U., & Stuhler, J. (2016). The impact of immigration: Why do studies reach such different results? *The Journal of Economic Perspectives*, *30*(4), 31–56.

Eriksson, S., & Lagerström, J. (2012). Detecting discrimination in the hiring process: Evidence from an internet-based search channel. *Empirical Economics*, *43*, 537–563.

Foged, M., & Peri, G. (2016). Immigrants' effect on native workers: New analysis on longitudinal data. *American Economic Journal: Applied Economics*, *8*(2), 1–34.

Gourieroux, C., Monfort, A., & Renault, E. (1993). Indirect inference. *Journal of Applied Econometrics*, *8*(S1), S85–S118.

Jasso, G., & Rosenzweig, M. R. (1986). Family reunification and the immigration multiplier: US immigration law, origin-country conditions, and the reproduction of immigrants. *Demography*, *23*(3), 291–311.

Jasso, G., & Rosenzweig, M. R. (1995). Do immigrants screened for skills do better than family reunification immigrants? *International Migration Review*, 85–111.

Laschever, R. A. (2013, June 15). *The doughboys network: Social interactions and the employment of World War I veterans*. https://ssrn.com/abstract=1205543. https://doi.org/10.2139/ssrn.1205543

Lundberg, S. J., & Startz, R. (1983). Private discrimination and social intervention in competitive labor market. *The American Economic Review*, *73*(3), 340–347.

Model, S. (2002). Immigrants' social class in three global cities. In M. Cross & R. Moore (Eds.), *Globalization and the new city: Migrants, minorities and urban transformation in comparative perspective* (pp. 82–118). Palgrave.

Munshi, K., & Wilson, N. (2011). *Identity, occupational choice, and mobility: Historical conditions and current decisions in the American Midwest* [Unpublished Manuscript]. Brown University.

Ottaviano, G. I. P., & Peri, G. (2008). *Immigration and national wages: Clarifying the theory and the empirics*. Technical report. National Bureau of Economic Research.

Ottaviano, G. I. P., & Peri, G. (2012). Rethinking the effect of immigration on wages. *Journal of the European Economic Association*, *10*(1), 152–197.

Patel, K., & Vella, F. (2013). Immigrant networks and their implications for occupational choice and wages. *The Review of Economics and Statistics*, *95*(4), 1249–1277.

Peri, G. (2014). *Do immigrant workers depress the wages of native workers?* IZA World of Labor.

Peri, G., & Yasenov, V. (2019). The labor market effects of a refugee wave synthetic control method meets the Mariel boatlift. *Journal of Human Resources*, *54*(2), 267–309.

Phelps, E. S. (1972). The statistical theory of racism and sexism. *The American Economic Review*, *62*(4), 659–661.

Postepska, A. (2019). Ethnic capital and intergenerational transmission of educational attainment. *Journal of Applied Econometrics*, *34*(4), 606–611.

Potochnick, S., & Hall, M. (2021). US occupational mobility of children of immigrants based on parents' origin-country occupation. *Demography*, *58*(1), 219–245.

Ruggles, S., Alexander, J. T., Genadek, K., Goeken, R., Schroeder, M. B., & Sobek, M. (2010). *Integrated Public Use Microdata Series: Version 5.0 [Machine-readable database]*. University of Minnesota.

Schwab, S. (1986). Is statistical discrimination efficient? *The American Economic Review*, *76*(1), 228–234.

Tolnay, S. E. (2001). African Americans and immigrants in northern cities: The effects of relative group size on occupational standing in 1920. *Social Forces*, *80*(2), 573–604.

Waldinger, R. D. (1994). The making of an immigrant niche. *International Migration Review*, 3–30.

Waldinger, R. D. (1996). *Still the promised city?: African Americans and new immigrants in post-industrial*. Harvard University Press.

APPENDIX A. OCCUPATIONAL PRESTIGE SCORES

Our analysis below ranks occupations on the basis of their SEI value [30] (Duncan, 1961), as it provides a consistent measure of occupational prestige and allows inter-temporal comparisons. We rely on the 1950 classification and new occupations are assigned scores according to their relevant counterparts in the 1950 classification. The score takes values from 0 to 100 noting that the lowest score in our data is 3 and the highest is 96. While the SEI is useful for our purposes it has some shortcomings. Its values are time invariant and do not capture changes in the occupation's prestige. Such a change might, for instance, manifest itself in large increase in the occupation's average wage. However, the SEI score appears to capture the variation in average wages across occupations. The correlation between the SEI score and average wages in each year in the period considered is between 0.7 and 0.79. Moreover, there are no occupations with a low (high) SEI score and unusually high (low) average income. Another shortcoming is the distance in socioeconomic status is not accurately reflected in this measure. Nevertheless, despite its limitations it has certain advantages given our focus. Occupational hierarchies are a long term phenomena and we prefer a measure unaffected by short term fluctuations. The SEI score is robust to shocks to local economies that temporarily affect a status of an occupation but do not reflect its long term place in occupational distribution. Similarly, since it is based on native workers' wages it does not reflect any sorting into occupations by immigrants and its impact on wages. Furthermore, with the exception of two occupations (*Operative and kindred workers* and *Managers and proprietors*) the variance of individual wages within occupations is relatively low. Thus the observed variance in wages among immigrant workers is due to differences in wages across, rather than within, occupations.

APPENDIX B. ESTIMATION OF THE COVARIANCE MATRIX

The following appendix describes the estimation of the covariance matrix of the indirect inference estimator as explained in Appendices 1 and 2 of Gourieroux et al. (1993).

From Proposition 3 in Gourieroux et al. (1993) it follows that:

$$\sqrt{N}\left(\widehat{\beta_{MN}}(\Omega) - \beta_0\right) \xrightarrow{d} N(0, W(M, \Omega))$$

where N denotes the sample size, M denotes the number of simulations, Ω denotes the weighting matrix and:

$$W(S,\Omega) = \left(1+\frac{1}{S}\right)\left[\frac{\partial b'}{\partial \beta}(\beta_0)\Omega\frac{\partial b}{\partial \beta'}(\beta_0)\right]^{-1}\frac{\partial b'}{\partial \beta}(\beta_0)$$
$$\times\,\Omega\Omega^{*-1}\Omega\frac{\partial b}{\partial \beta'}(\beta_0)\left[\frac{\partial b'}{\partial \beta}(\beta_0)\Omega\frac{\partial b}{\partial \beta'}(\beta_0)\right]^{-1}$$

where $b(\beta)$ denotes the binding function, β_0 denotes the true parameter values and $\Omega^* = J_0 I_0^{-1} J_0$ is the optimal weighting matrix.

To proceed with the estimation of the covariance matrix, we need to introduce some more notation. Let Q_N denote the objective function of the auxiliary model and:

$$\tilde{\theta} = \underset{\theta\in\Theta}{\operatorname{argmax}} Q_N(y,x,\beta)$$

Let $\widehat{\theta}$ denote the estimates of the auxiliary model on the actual data. In our model Q_N is a block diagonal matrix, with diagonal elements equal to $-e_{oj}'e_{oj}$, where e_{oj} denotes the residuals from an OLS regression corresponding to jth group in oth sector.[31]

As stated in Appendix 2 of Gourieroux et al. (1993) J_0 can be consistently estimated by:

$$-\frac{\partial^2 Q_N}{\partial\theta\partial\theta'}\left(y,x,\widehat{\theta}\right)$$

In our model, the above approximation becomes a block diagonal matrix with diagonal elements equal to $2x_{jo}'x_{jo}$. The middle term in the expression of Ω^*, $(I_0 - K_0)^{-1}$, can be consistently estimated by:

$$\frac{N}{S}\sum_{s=1}^{S}\left(W_s-\overline{W}\right)\left(W_s-\overline{W}\right)'$$

Where:

$$W_s = \frac{\partial Q_N}{\partial\theta}\left(y^s\left(\tilde{\beta}\right),x,\widehat{\theta}\right)$$

$$\overline{W} = \frac{1}{S}\sum_{s=1}^{S}W_s$$

and $\tilde{\beta}$ denotes a consistent estimator of β. S denotes the number of simulations in the estimation of $\tilde{\beta}$. Notice, that the optimal indirect inference estimator requires that we can get a preliminary consistent estimator of β to get a preliminary estimate of the optimal weighting matrix. We can obtain these estimates using identity matrix as a weighting matrix.

In our model, W_s can be expressed as block diagonal matrix, with diagonal elements equal to $2x_{jo}^{'}y_{jo}(\tilde{\beta}) - 2x_{jo}^{'}x_{jo}\widehat{\theta}$. In practice, we first estimate the model using identity matrix as weighting matrix and obtain $\tilde{\beta}$. Using $\tilde{\beta}$ we compute $y^s(\tilde{\beta})$ and obtain the matrix of first derivatives of the auxiliary model criterion function w.r.t. θ, so the parameters of auxiliary model.

The last element in the expression of the covariance matrix contains the derivatives of the binding function at the true value. It can be consistently estimated with:

$$\frac{\partial b}{\partial \beta}(\beta_0) = J_0^{-1}\frac{\partial^2 Q_\infty}{\partial \theta \partial \beta^{'}}$$

which can be obtained by numerical derivation of $\frac{\partial Q_N}{\partial \theta}[y(\beta), x, \widehat{\theta}]$ w.r.t. β and evaluated at the $\widehat{\beta}$.

APPENDIX C. SUPPLEMENTARY TABLES AND FIGURES

In all tables we use the 3-letters country codes: CAN (Canada), MEX (Mexico), CUB (Cuba), ENG (England), ITA (Italy), DEU (Germany), POL (Poland), RUS (Russia), CHN (China), KOR (Korea), PHL (Philippines), VNM (Vietnam). AFR refers to Africa and ME to Middle East.

Table 8. Sample Composition 1940–2011.

	1940	1950	1960	1970	1980	1990	2000	2011	1940	1950	1960	1970	1980	1990	2000	2011
	All Workers								*Unskilled Workers*							
CAN	0.11	0.12	0.13	0.14	0.07	0.03	0.03	0.03	0.11	0.11	0.12	0.12	0.05	0.01	0.05	0.00
MEX	0.01	0.04	0.07	0.15	0.32	0.41	0.46	0.44	0.01	0.04	0.08	0.17	0.49	0.63	0.72	0.73
CUB		0.01	0.02	0.06	0.11	0.07	0.04	0.04		0.00	0.02	0.07	0.05	0.09	0.04	0.04
ENG	0.07	0.05	0.06	0.05	0.03	0.02	0.02	0.01	0.06	0.04	0.05	0.03	0.01	0.00	0.00	0.00
ITA	0.29	0.32	0.24	0.20	0.09	0.04	0.02	0.01	0.30	0.33	0.28	0.27	0.14	0.05	0.02	0.01
DEU	0.15	0.12	0.15	0.13	0.08	0.05	0.03	0.03	0.15	0.12	0.14	0.12	0.06	0.01	0.01	0.00
POL	0.16	0.17	0.14	0.10	0.04	0.02	0.02	0.01	0.17	0.17	0.15	0.11	0.05	0.02	0.02	0.01
RUS	0.19	0.16	0.13	0.06	0.01	0.01	0.03	0.03	0.18	0.16	0.12	0.05	0.00	0.00	0.01	0.01
CHN	0.01	0.01	0.03	0.05	0.07	0.08	0.07	0.08	0.01	0.01	0.02	0.04	0.05	0.05	0.04	0.05
KOR					0.03	0.04	0.03	0.03					0.01	0.02	0.01	0.01
PHL		0.01	0.03	0.03	0.06	0.08	0.06	0.07			0.02	0.02	0.03	0.04	0.03	0.03
VNM					0.01	0.04	0.05	0.05					0.01	0.03	0.04	0.04
IND				0.01	0.04	0.06	0.09	0.11					0.01	0.02	0.03	0.03
AFR			0.00	0.01	0.02	0.03	0.04	0.05				0.00	0.00	0.01	0.01	0.02
ME	0.01	0.02	0.01	0.02	0.03	0.03	0.03	0.03	0.01	0.01	0.01	0.01	0.03	0.02	0.02	0.02

Notes: Unskilled workers are defined as individuals with at most high school degree.

Table 9. Summary Statistics by Country of Origin 1940–2011.

	Age	Edu	Eng	SEI	Age	Edu	Eng	SEI	Age	Edu	Eng	SEI
	Canada				*Germany*				*Italy*			
1940	42.90	9.52		34.04	45.35	9.17		32.74	46.14	7.18		25.23
1950	44.58	10.50		37.52	48.49	10.19		37.48	50.91	7.52		27.55
1960	46.29	10.92		42.53	48.54	10.79		39.69	50.93	8.26		28.49
1970	45.78	11.41		43.65	45.35	11.44		43.33	45.59	9.24		29.36
1980	43.68	12.65	0.99	48.39	39.99	12.75	0.99	47.39	43.49	10.37	0.84	33.68
1990	42.07	13.84	0.99	52.00	40.65	13.77	0.99	48.80	46.00	11.37	0.89	37.94
2000	41.69	14.42	0.99	56.08	40.68	14.11	0.99	50.58	48.19	12.31	0.93	41.32
2011	44.46	14.90	0.99	59.97	43.31	14.47	0.99	53.30	51.07	12.97	0.95	45.64
	Mexico				*Poland*				*Korea*			
1940	38.71	7.70		18.15	47.53	7.28		28.29				
1950	44.15	7.64		20.31	52.48	8.13		31.25				
1960	41.53	7.46		19.34	51.09	9.43		36.36				
1970	36.80	8.58		22.10	51.34	10.26		39.40				
1980	32.71	8.76	0.48	22.50	49.09	11.21	0.84	39.21	37.59	13.65	0.69	46.33
1990	32.40	9.35	0.52	22.27	43.84	12.62	0.76	36.80	39.23	13.95	0.70	48.53
2000	33.68	9.79	0.50	22.89	41.39	12.96	0.74	34.91	41.24	14.39	0.72	51.65
2011	38.32	10.25	0.52	24.10	43.61	13.40	0.78	37.61	44.12	14.93	0.76	55.80
	Cuba				*Russia*				*Philippines*			
1940					47.41	8.25		42.00				
1950	36.00	9.83		25.79	52.38	8.98		43.59	43.44	8.98		19.82
1960	38.01	9.81		27.66	55.44	9.92		43.45	47.06	9.06		21.54
1970	40.01	10.28		32.50	56.70	10.67		44.95	39.56	12.35		37.40
1980	42.07	11.32	0.67	38.50	46.93	11.22	0.85	37.18	37.67	13.03	0.96	39.14
1990	44.08	11.89	0.69	39.19	42.17	13.77	0.83	46.17	38.92	13.82	0.96	40.67
2000	44.40	12.59	0.70	39.99	39.34	14.45	0.82	46.72	41.33	14.01	0.96	42.22
2011	46.71	13.00	0.66	38.96	41.62	14.66	0.84	47.63	44.47	14.26	0.96	43.37
	England				*China*				*Africa*			
1940	45.91	9.79		37.43	40.82	7.44		26.22				
1950	49.20	10.32		41.16	42.01	8.00		31.93				
1960	49.55	11.22		44.98	43.59	9.40		34.63	40.49	12.10		46.01
1970	45.21	12.02		49.12	42.36	11.15		38.51	37.81	13.05		54.23
1980	40.60	13.20	1.00	53.00	39.83	12.55	0.72	45.55	36.63	13.83	0.97	51.44
1990	40.08	14.10	1.00	53.84	40.37	13.69	0.74	49.37	37.02	14.68	0.97	49.92
2000	41.91	14.48	0.99	55.85	41.26	14.22	0.76	52.87	39.41	14.51	0.97	47.54
2011	45.40	14.59	1.00	57.52	44.03	14.57	0.77	55.09	42.41	14.42	0.96	45.92
	Vietnam				*Middle East*				*India*			
1940					42.14	9.03		38.51				
1950					50.72	9.31		41.11				
1960					49.78	10.61		43.84				
1970					42.55	12.18		49.00	32.71	15.54		69.99
1980	32.14	12.18	0.73	39.15	36.08	12.39	0.91	47.99	35.80	14.93	0.97	61.20
1990	34.18	12.69	0.77	39.91	37.95	13.46	0.95	50.26	38.09	14.94	0.95	55.87
2000	38.23	12.75	0.73	40.32	39.50	13.75	0.94	51.29	38.53	15.13	0.95	57.17
2011	43.77	12.98	0.73	42.60	43.02	14.14	0.95	54.20	41.15	15.45	0.95	59.71

Notes: For brevity, standard deviations are omitted. *Edu* denotes the average years of schooling. *Eng* denotes the share of individuals who speak English well. *SEI* denotes the average prestige score.

						[illegible]	[illegible]	POL	DEU	ITA	ENG	CUB	MEX	CAN
All Workers														
ME	0.61	0.27	1.00	0.90	0.57	0.45	0.73	0.94	0.63	0.91	0.37	0.90	1.00	0.38
AFR		0.12	0.94	0.78	0.27	0.22	0.59	0.90	0.34	0.81	0.26	0.82	1.00	0.27
IND			0.99	0.95	0.71	0.65	0.90	0.96	0.86	0.94	0.65	0.94	1.00	0.65
VNM				0.35	0.01	0.04	0.12	0.30	0.02	0.18	0.00	0.17	0.98	0.00
PHL					0.08	0.10	0.30	0.65	0.14	0.43	0.05	0.59	0.95	0.05
KOR						0.35	0.85	0.89	0.46	0.90	0.23	0.85	1.00	0.16
CHN							0.70	0.77	0.70	0.89	0.44	0.90	0.99	0.45
RUS								0.76	0.42	0.79	0.26	0.67	1.00	0.28
POL									0.15	0.58	0.06	0.55	1.00	0.11
DEU										0.91	0.17	0.88	1.00	0.17
ITA											0.04	0.55	0.99	0.04
ENG												0.95	1.00	0.42
CUB													0.97	0.06
MEX														0.00
Unskilled Workers														
ME	0.75	0.65	1.00	0.95	0.62	0.97	0.60	0.84	0.52	0.94	0.26	0.94	1.00	0.38
AFR		0.12	0.88	0.33	0.11	0.91	0.50	0.33	0.19	0.60	0.11	0.82	0.97	0.36
IND			0.91	0.67	0.32	0.86	0.64	0.88	0.38	0.79	0.22	0.87	1.00	0.27
VNM				0.26	0.00	0.59	0.06	0.33	0.00	0.07	0.00	0.45	0.97	0.00
PHL					0.09	0.63	0.22	0.25	0.05	0.29	0.08	0.50	0.96	0.00
KOR						0.96	0.67	0.82	0.48	0.78	0.11	0.83	1.00	0.08
CHN							0.04	0.20	0.07	0.42	0.00	0.44	0.94	0.00
RUS								0.81	0.70	0.83	0.44	0.88	1.00	0.40
POL									0.21	0.59	0.06	0.68	1.00	0.14
DEU										0.96	0.22	0.96	1.00	0.18
ITA											0.00	0.61	1.00	0.05
ENG												1.00	1.00	0.54
CUB													0.92	0.00
MEX														0.00

Notes: Comparisons are made based on the share of workers in the top sector in each region in each year where top sector comprises occupations above the 70th percentile of the empirical distribution of occupations in each region. Each entry represents the incidence of a row country being ranked above the column country.

Table 11. Pairwise Comparisons Based on the Share of Workers in the Four Sectors.

	AFR	IND	VNM	PHL	KOR	CHN	RUS	POL	DEU	ITA	ENG	CUB	MEX	CAN
Sector A														
ME	0.55	0.00	1.00	1.00	0.92	0.15	0.86	1.00	1.00	1.00	0.46	1.00	1.00	0.38
AFR		0.00	1.00	1.00	0.60	0.44	1.00	1.00	0.72	1.00	0.47	1.00	1.00	0.45
IND			1.00	1.00	1.00	0.45	1.00	1.00	1.00	1.00	1.00	1.00	1.00	0.73
VNM				0.35	0.00	0.00	0.00	0.66	0.00	0.66	0.00	0.29	1.00	0.00
PHL					0.17	0.00	0.11	0.88	0.17	0.65	0.00	0.96	1.00	0.17
KOR						0.07	0.85	1.00	0.55	1.00	0.38	1.00	1.00	0.08
CHN							0.81	1.00	1.00	1.00	1.00	1.00	1.00	1.00
RUS								1.00	0.49	1.00	0.33	1.00	1.00	0.38
POL									0.06	0.67	0.00	0.60	1.00	0.00
DEU										1.00	0.00	1.00	1.00	0.11
ITA											0.00	0.30	1.00	0.00
ENG												1.00	1.00	0.60
CUB													1.00	0.00
MEX														0.00
Sector B														
ME	0.92	0.70	1.00	1.00	0.16	1.00	0.84	1.00	0.88	1.00	0.06	1.00	1.00	0.37
AFR		0.39	1.00	1.00	0.03	0.43	0.72	1.00	0.09	0.47	0.04	1.00	1.00	0.09
IND			1.00	1.00	0.00	0.65	0.96	1.00	0.29	0.73	0.00	1.00	1.00	0.00
VNM				0.00	0.00	0.00	0.00	0.00	0.00	0.00	0.00	0.00	1.00	0.00
PHL					0.00	0.01	0.00	0.00	0.00	0.00	0.00	0.00	0.99	0.00
KOR						1.00	1.00	1.00	1.00	1.00	0.31	1.00	1.00	0.53
CHN							0.81	0.90	0.00	0.73	0.00	1.00	0.99	0.00
RUS								0.92	0.00	0.60	0.00	0.87	1.00	0.00
POL									0.00	0.50	0.00	0.14	1.00	0.00

DEU										0.81	0.00	1.00	1.00	0.00
ITA											0.00	0.74	0.97	0.00
ENG												1.00	1.00	0.79
CUB													1.00	0.00
MEX														0.00
Sector C														
ME	0.21	0.19	0.62	0.02	0.03	1.00	0.05	0.61	0.00	0.81	0.00	0.28	0.94	0.00
AFR		0.18	0.63	0.00	0.17	1.00	0.18	0.94	0.00	0.95	0.00	0.32	0.97	0.00
IND			0.64	0.35	0.63	0.97	0.63	0.77	0.30	0.92	0.56	0.78	0.96	0.56
VNM				0.00	0.35	0.65	0.32	1.00	0.25	1.00	0.25	0.71	1.00	0.25
PHL					1.00	0.99	0.95	0.97	0.91	0.89	0.87	0.94	0.92	0.85
KOR						0.99	0.41	0.80	0.00	0.96	0.27	0.80	0.97	0.27
CHN							0.00	0.69	0.00	0.68	0.00	0.27	0.87	0.00
RUS								0.56	0.43	0.68	0.52	0.80	0.89	0.33
POL									0.00	0.69	0.00	0.10	0.89	0.00
DEU										1.00	0.73	1.00	1.00	0.72
ITA											0.00	0.07	0.90	0.00
ENG												0.78	0.92	0.19
CUB													0.95	0.00
MEX														0.00
Sector D														
ME	0.23	1.00	0.00	0.00	0.60	0.00	0.22	0.00	0.17	0.00	1.00	0.00	0.00	0.95
AFR		1.00	0.00	0.34	0.83	0.58	0.37	0.00	0.76	0.27	0.96	0.00	0.00	0.80
IND			0.00	0.00	0.00	0.00	0.00	0.00	0.00	0.00	0.00	0.00	0.00	0.00
VNM				1.00	1.00	1.00	1.00	0.19	1.00	0.57	1.00	1.00	0.00	1.00
PHL					1.00	1.00	0.58	0.20	1.00	0.15	1.00	0.05	0.04	1.00
KOR						0.00	0.00	0.00	0.18	0.00	0.98	0.00	0.00	0.96
CHN							0.20	0.22	0.75	0.03	1.00	0.00	0.00	1.00

Table 11. *(Continued)*

	AFR	IND	VNM	PHL	KOR	CHN	RUS	POL	DEU	ITA	ENG	CUB	MEX	CAN
RUS								0.12	0.80	0.00	0.93	0.16	0.00	0.92
POL									1.00	0.47	1.00	0.83	0.00	1.00
DEU										0.00	1.00	0.00	0.00	1.00
ITA											1.00	0.70	0.00	1.00
ENG												0.00	0.00	0.46
CUB													0.00	1.00
MEX														1.00

Notes: Comparisons are made based on the share of workers in each sector in each region in each year. Each entry represents the incidence of a row country being ranked above the column country. *Sector A* comprises occupations above the 90th percentile of the empirical distribution of occupations (top sector); *Sector B* comprises occupations between the 70th and the 90th percentile; *Sector C* comprises occupations between the 40th and 70th percentiles; *Sector D* comprises occupations below the 40th percentile.

Table 12. Pairwise Comparisons Based on the Share of Workers in the Four Sectors: Unskilled Workers.

	AFR	IND	VNM	PHL	KOR	CHN	RUS	POL	DEU	ITA	ENG	CUB	MEX	CAN
Sector A														
ME	1.00	1.00	1.00	1.00	0.34	1.00	0.76	1.00	1.00	1.00	0.42	1.00	1.00	0.58
AFR		0.29	1.00	1.00	0.10	0.62	0.24	0.65	0.38	0.44	0.00	0.72	1.00	0.15
IND			1.00	1.00	0.07	1.00	1.00	1.00	0.00	0.68	0.00	1.00	1.00	0.00
VNM				0.69	0.00	0.00	0.00	0.35	0.00	0.00	0.00	0.33	1.00	0.00
PHL					0.00	0.00	0.00	0.26	0.00	0.00	0.00	0.28	0.83	0.00
KOR						1.00	1.00	1.00	0.88	1.00	0.00	1.00	1.00	0.00
CHN							0.17	1.00	0.20	0.41	0.08	1.00	1.00	0.22
RUS								0.95	0.54	0.75	0.49	0.87	1.00	0.58
POL									0.38	0.65	0.11	1.00	1.00	0.10
DEU										0.76	0.00	1.00	1.00	0.07
ITA											0.00	0.81	1.00	0.00
ENG												1.00	1.00	1.00
CUB													1.00	0.00
MEX														0.00
Sector B														
ME	0.79	0.67	0.88	1.00	1.00	1.00	0.57	0.79	0.00	0.96	0.21	1.00	1.00	0.42
AFR		0.00	1.00	0.19	0.65	1.00	0.24	0.84	0.10	1.00	0.06	1.00	1.00	0.11
IND			1.00	1.00	1.00	1.00	0.52	1.00	0.31	1.00	0.00	1.00	1.00	0.44
VNM				0.12	0.13	1.00	0.12	0.22	0.00	1.00	0.00	1.00	1.00	0.00
PHL					1.00	0.89	0.41	0.67	0.00	0.83	0.00	0.95	0.92	0.00
KOR						1.00	0.12	0.81	0.00	1.00	0.00	1.00	1.00	0.00
CHN							0.00	0.04	0.00	0.03	0.00	0.05	0.11	0.00
RUS								0.90	0.21	1.00	0.26	0.87	1.00	0.36
POL									0.00	1.00	0.00	0.98	1.00	0.00

Table 12. *(Continued)*

	AFR	IND	VNM	PHL	KOR	CHN	RUS	POL	DEU	ITA	ENG	CUB	MEX	CAN
DEU										1.00	0.34	1.00	1.00	0.33
ITA											0.00	0.52	1.00	0.00
ENG												1.00	1.00	1.00
CUB													0.97	0.00
MEX														0.00
Sector C														
ME	0.33	0.13	0.00	0.04	0.24	0.41	0.24	0.00	0.00	0.00	0.32	0.00	0.06	0.51
AFR		0.68	0.00	0.00	0.82	0.36	0.31	0.00	0.56	0.00	0.58	0.00	0.00	0.52
IND			0.00	0.00	0.87	0.28	0.16	0.00	0.00	0.00	1.00	0.00	0.00	0.86
VNM				0.87	1.00	0.58	0.87	0.53	1.00	1.00	1.00	1.00	1.00	1.00
PHL					1.00	0.72	0.80	0.00	0.81	0.33	0.85	0.66	0.13	0.77
KOR						0.16	0.00	0.00	0.22	0.00	0.75	0.21	0.00	0.47
CHN							0.56	0.25	0.54	0.26	0.50	0.33	0.34	0.51
RUS								0.00	0.30	0.13	0.48	0.18	0.16	0.42
POL									0.70	1.00	0.89	1.00	0.76	0.90
DEU										0.43	1.00	0.17	0.06	0.93
ITA											0.81	0.55	0.08	0.83
ENG												0.02	0.06	0.13
CUB													0.25	0.98
MEX														0.94
Sector D														
ME	0.08	0.00	0.00	0.00	0.27	0.00	0.41	0.39	0.67	0.00	1.00	0.00	0.00	0.83
AFR		1.00	0.87	0.60	0.83	0.32	0.81	0.95	0.97	0.51	0.96	0.00	0.00	0.96
IND			0.89	0.00	0.63	0.33	0.00	0.18	1.00	0.31	1.00	0.00	0.00	1.00
VNM				0.00	0.73	0.00	0.00	0.24	0.71	0.00	1.00	0.00	0.00	0.72

PHL	1.00	0.31	0.76	1.00	1.00	0.70	1.00	0.31	0.20	1.00
KOR		0.00	0.00	0.52	0.76	0.00	1.00	0.00	0.00	0.71
CHN			0.77	0.83	1.00	0.80	1.00	0.74	0.45	1.00
RUS				0.45	0.72	0.24	0.88	0.18	0.00	0.91
POL					0.83	0.09	1.00	0.00	0.00	1.00
DEU						0.00	1.00	0.00	0.00	1.00
ITA							1.00	0.31	0.00	1.00
ENG								0.00	0.00	0.09
CUB									0.00	1.00
MEX										1.00

Notes: Comparisons are made for workers with less than a high school degree based on the share of workers in each sector in each region in each year. Each entry represents the incidence of a row country being ranked above the column country. *Sector A* comprises occupations above the 90th percentile of the empirical distribution of occupations (top sector); *Sector B* comprises occupations between the 70th and the 90th percentile; *Sector C* comprises occupations between the 40th and 70th percentiles; *Sector D* comprises occupations below the 40th percentile.

APPENDIX D. QUANTITATIVE IMPACT OF CONDITIONING VARIABLES

This appendix contains a detailed analysis of the quantitative impact of the conditioning variables. We report the frequency of changes in rankings by every pair of countries. These are based on average sector shares and country A is considered ranked above country B in Sector *o* if its share of workers in Sector *o* is higher than those from country B. Table 13 reports the changes from an one year increase in schooling. Table 14 reports the changes corresponding to increasing English proficiency[32] and Table 15 summarizes the changes from a 10 year earlier group arrival and, simultaneously, a 10 year longer tenure in a region. Table 16, Table 17 and Table 18 present the results from a 10% increase in the share of established migrants in Sectors A, B and C respectively. In each table we alter the characteristic for one country at a time (row country) and follow the changes in pairwise rankings between the row country and every other country (column country) in all four sectors.

When the conditioning variable of focus has an unambiguously positive (negative) effect on productivity in a given sector a ranking change can only occur if there are instances where the row country was initially ranked below (above) the column country. Therefore, each entry in Table 13 through Table 18 represents the fraction of such eligible regions in which the ordering between the two countries has changed. The positive (negative) entry implies that the row country is ranked above the column country more (less) often after the change. As reasonable changes in the individuals' ages did not result in meaningful changes we exclude it from the tables and conclude it is not an important determinant of rankings.

For Sector A the direction of the change is always the same as the sign of the variable's coefficient. Since the covariates all have a positive effect on the *Larger* group's productivity in Sector A the change in ordering in this sector always favors the group whose characteristics are enhanced.[33] For the two middle Sectors B and C, however, the change operates through two channels. The first is a direct effect through the productivity index. The second is an indirect effect through the composition of individuals who do not find employment in a higher-ranked sector. Therefore, it is not straightforward to assess the direction of the overall change.

We first consider the role of the individual characteristics. An extra year of schooling to all individuals from given country reverses 14, 1, 6 and 2% of pairwise comparisons in Sectors A, B, C, and D, respectively. German, Chinese, Filipino and African workers appear to most benefit from higher educational attainment in the top sector as it would affect on average more than 20% of rankings with other countries. The role of educational attainment in Sectors B and D appears generally much smaller than for Sectors A and C. For some countries, such as China, it plays an important role in all sectors. English proficiency has a large and consistent effect across the four sectors, affecting on average 9, 8, 9 and 5% of all rankings in Sectors A, B, C, and D, respectively. It is especially important for Chinese, Korean and Vietnamese workers. For example, if all Chinese workers spoke English well, in regions in which they appear with Indian workers, the ranking would be reversed for 95, 71, 23 and 10% of cases in Sectors A, B, C, and D, respectively. Similarly, if all Korean workers spoke English well, in regions where they appear together with African workers, the ranking would change favorably in 12, 59, 59 and 24% of cases respectively. Mexican, Cuban and Polish workers would also improve their positions in Sector C as a result of better command of English. These results suggest that differences in human capital accumulation play an important role in generating the rankings. Even though the results are not surprising, their magnitude has nontrivial policy implications as it appears that promoting the mastering of English skills among disadvantaged immigrant worker groups can generate a long term positive effect on their performance in the labor market.

Now consider the "country of origin" characteristics. Earlier arrival and longer tenure in the region appear to have a large effect on the rankings in Sectors A and C. Only Mexican, Cuban, German and African workers do not notably benefit from earlier arrival and longer tenure. In Sector B arrival year and tenure in the region generally appear not to affect rankings with the exception of a few pairings. Similar patterns with smaller magnitudes occur in Sector D.

Finally, consider the placement of established workers in the occupational distribution. On average, a 10% increase in the share of established migrants in the respective sectors leads to a 12, 14 and 13% of rankings reversed in Sectors A, B and C. Except for the increased network size in Sector B the spillover effects to other sectors are on average of a smaller magnitude. Increases in the share of established workers in Sector A leads to a reversed ranking in 2, 6 and 5% of regions in Sectors B, C and D, respectively. A 10% increase in the share of workers employed in sector B affects rankings in 11 and 13% of regions in Sectors C and D. The same increase in the share of workers in Sector C occupations affects rankings in only 1% of the regions in Sector D.

The impact on the hierarchies varies greatly by characteristic. There is also notable variation in the magnitude of the effects of each of the characteristics across countries of origin. However, the results suggest that the characteristics considered play an important role in generating the hierarchies. Nonetheless, reasonable changes in the characteristics do not have any effect on rankings for some countries. For example, improving the position of Mexican workers in the occupational distribution proved to be difficult. On average, five extra years of education for all Mexican workers is needed to achieve an effect of a similar magnitude as with one year increase of schooling of Italian or Chinese workers in Sectors A and B, respectively. Moreover, such a large increase in schooling of Mexican workers would affect comparisons with only 4 and 5 out of 14 large countries in Sectors A and B, respectively. Similarly, a 20% point increase in the share of established migrants employed in Sector A in all regions still leaves all of the rankings with 14 large countries unaffected in Sector A. These results suggest that a group's position in the distribution of occupations in local labor markets largely depends on the group's historical position in the empirical distribution of occupations. For the lowest-ranked workers this appears resilient to change.

Table 13. The Effect of 1 Year Increase in the Educational Attainment by Sector and Group.

	ME	AFR	IND	VNM	PHL	KOR	CHN	RUS	POL	DEU	ITA	ENG	CUB	MEX	CAN
Sector A															
CAN	0.00	0.15	0.00	0.00	0.00	0.56	0.65	0.10	0.00	0.16	0.00	0.20	0.00	0.00	
MEX	0.00	0.00	0.00	0.00	0.00	0.00	0.00	0.00	0.00	0.00	0.00	0.00	0.00		0.00
CUB	0.00	0.00	0.00	0.00	0.00	0.00	0.20	0.00	0.00	0.00	0.50	0.00		0.00	0.00
ENG	0.11	0.00	0.00	0.00	0.00	0.00	0.00	0.00	0.00	0.00	0.00		0.00	0.00	0.10
ITA	0.25	0.00	0.00	0.00	0.13	0.00	0.13	0.20	0.00	0.14		0.00	0.00	0.00	0.13
DEU	0.67	0.20	0.12	0.00	0.00	0.83	0.53	0.00	0.00		0.00	0.33	0.00	0.00	0.22
POL	0.14	0.00	0.00	0.00	0.00	0.00	0.13	0.20		0.00	0.17	0.00	0.00	0.00	0.00
RUS	0.10	0.11	0.83	0.00	0.20	0.00	0.83		0.00	0.00	0.20	0.00	0.00	0.00	0.10
CHN	0.00	0.12	0.21	0.42	0.79	0.48		0.83	0.25	0.16	0.00	0.20	0.00	0.00	0.13
KOR	0.11	0.00	0.87	0.00	0.53		0.48	0.10	0.00	0.83	0.17	0.00	0.00	0.00	0.00
PHL	0.59	0.56	0.31	0.45		0.15	0.26	0.30	0.00	0.63	0.00	0.00	0.00	0.00	0.71
VNM	0.00	0.00	0.00		0.45	0.00	0.42	0.00	1.00	0.00	0.00	0.00	0.50	0.00	0.00
IND	0.43	0.00		0.00	0.31	0.13	0.21	0.83	0.00	0.18	0.17	0.25	0.00	0.00	0.19
AFR	0.13		0.18	0.00	0.17	0.18	0.12	0.00	0.00	0.13	0.00	0.00	0.00	0.00	0.50
ME		0.63	0.87	0.00	0.12	0.17	0.45	0.30	0.00	0.20	0.25	0.11	0.00	0.00	0.50
Sector B															
CAN	0.00	0.00	0.00	0.00	0.00	0.00	0.00	0.00	0.00	0.00	0.00	0.00	0.00	0.00	
MEX	0.00	0.00	0.00	0.00	0.00	0.00	0.00	0.00	0.00	0.00	0.00	0.00	0.00		0.00
CUB	0.00	0.00	0.00	0.00	0.00	0.00	0.00	0.00	0.00	0.00	0.00	0.00		0.00	0.00
ENG	0.00	0.00	0.00	0.00	0.00	0.00	0.00	0.00	0.00	0.00	0.00		0.00	0.00	0.00
ITA	0.25	0.00	0.00	0.00	0.00	0.00	0.00	0.00	0.00	0.00		0.00	0.00	0.00	0.00
DEU	0.00	0.00	0.00	0.00	0.00	0.00	0.53	0.00	0.00		0.00	0.00	0.00	0.00	0.00
POL	0.00	0.00	0.00	0.00	0.00	0.00	0.00	0.00		0.00	0.00	0.00	0.00	0.00	0.00
RUS	0.10	0.00	0.00	0.00	0.00	0.00	−0.83		0.00	0.00	0.00	0.00	0.00	0.00	0.00
CHN	0.00	0.00	0.00	0.42	0.26	0.00		0.00	0.00	0.53	0.00	0.00	0.00	0.00	−0.32

KOR	0.00	0.00	0.00	0.00	0.53		0.00	0.00	0.00	0.00	0.00	0.00	0.00	0.00	0.00
PHL	0.00	0.00	0.00	0.00		0.00	0.00	0.00	0.00	0.00	0.00	0.00	0.00	0.00	0.00
VNM	0.00	0.00	0.00		0.00	0.00	0.00	0.00	0.00	0.00	0.00	0.00	0.00	0.00	0.00
IND	0.00	0.00		0.00	0.31	0.00	0.00	0.00	0.00	0.00	0.00	0.00	0.00	0.00	0.00
AFR	0.00		0.00	0.00	0.00	0.00	0.00	0.00	0.00	0.00	0.00	0.00	0.00	0.00	0.50
ME		0.00	0.00	0.00	0.00	0.00	0.00	0.00	0.00	0.00	0.00	0.00	0.00	0.00	0.00
Sector C															
CAN	−0.50	0.50	0.00	0.00	0.00	0.00	−0.65	0.00	0.00	0.00	0.00	−0.10	0.00	0.00	
MEX	0.00	0.00	0.00	0.00	0.00	0.00	0.00	0.00	0.00	0.00	0.00	0.00	0.33		0.00
CUB	0.00	0.00	0.00	0.00	0.00	0.00	0.00	0.00	0.00	0.00	0.00	0.00		−0.33	0.00
ENG	0.00	0.00	0.00	0.00	0.00	0.00	−0.10	0.00	0.00	0.00	0.00		0.00	0.00	0.00
ITA	0.00	0.00	0.00	0.00	−0.13	−0.17	0.00	0.00	0.00	−0.14		0.00	0.00	0.00	0.00
DEU	0.00	0.00	0.00	0.00	0.00	0.00	0.00	0.00	0.00		0.00	0.00	0.00	0.00	0.00
POL	0.00	0.00	−0.83	0.00	0.00	−0.20	0.00	0.00		0.00	0.00	0.00	0.00	0.00	−0.10
RUS	−0.32	−0.45	0.00	−0.48	0.00	0.00	−0.48		−0.83	0.00	−0.53	0.00	−0.10	0.00	0.00
CHN	0.00	0.00	0.00	0.00	0.00	0.00		0.00	−0.10	0.00	−0.83	0.00	0.00	0.00	−0.77
KOR	−0.36	−0.12	0.00	0.00	0.00		−0.53	0.00	0.00	0.00	−0.63	0.00	0.00	0.00	−0.36
PHL	0.00	0.00	0.00	0.00		−0.45	0.00	0.00	0.00	0.00	0.00	0.00	0.00	0.00	0.00
VNM	−0.37	0.00	−0.36		0.00	0.00	0.00	0.00	0.00	0.00	−0.59	0.00	0.00	0.00	0.00
IND	0.00	−0.63		0.00	0.00	0.00	0.00	0.00	0.00	0.00	0.00	0.00	0.00	0.00	0.00
AFR	0.00		−0.63	−0.43	0.00	0.00	0.00	−0.45	0.00	0.00	0.00	0.00	0.00	0.00	0.00
ME		0.00	0.00	0.00	0.00	0.00	0.00	0.00	0.00	0.00	0.00	0.00	0.00	0.00	0.00
Sector D															
CAN	−0.05	−0.05	−0.04	0.00	−0.04	0.00	0.00	0.00	0.00	0.00	0.00	−0.10	0.00	0.00	
MEX	0.00	0.00	0.00	0.00	0.00	0.00	0.00	0.00	0.00	0.00	0.00	0.00	0.00		0.00
CUB	0.00	0.00	0.00	0.00	0.00	0.00	0.00	−0.33	0.00	0.00	0.00	0.00		0.00	0.00
ENG	0.00	0.00	−0.13	0.00	−0.22	0.00	0.00	0.00	0.00	−0.22	0.00		0.00	0.00	−0.20
ITA	0.00	0.00	0.00	0.00	0.00	−0.17	−0.13	0.00	−0.17	0.00		0.00	0.00	0.00	0.00

Table 13. *(Continued)*

	ME	AFR	IND	VNM	PHL	KOR	CHN	RUS	POL	DEU	ITA	ENG	CUB	MEX	CAN
DEU	0.00	0.00	−0.06	0.00	−0.13	−0.08	0.00	0.00	0.00		0.00	0.00	0.00	0.00	−0.05
POL	0.00	0.00	0.00	0.00	0.00	0.00	0.00	0.00		0.00	0.00	0.00	0.00	0.00	0.00
RUS	−0.10	0.00	−0.08	0.00	0.00	−0.20	−0.17		0.00	0.00	0.00	0.00	0.00	0.00	0.00
CHN	0.00	0.00	0.00	0.00	0.00	−0.10		0.00	0.00	−0.11	0.00	0.00	−0.20	0.00	−0.03
KOR	0.00	0.00	−0.09	0.00	−0.11		−0.05	−0.10	0.00	0.00	0.00	0.00	0.00	0.00	−0.06
PHL	0.00	−0.06	−0.03	−0.05		0.00	−0.03	0.00	0.00	0.00	0.00	0.00	0.00	0.00	−0.07
VNM	0.00	0.00	0.00		0.00	0.00	−0.04	0.00	0.00	0.00	0.00	0.00	0.00	0.00	0.00
IND	0.00	−0.04		0.00	0.00	0.00	0.00	0.00	0.00	0.00	0.00	0.00	0.00	0.00	−0.04
Africa	0.00		0.00	0.00	−0.06	−0.06	0.00	0.00	0.00	−0.07	0.00	0.00	0.00	0.00	0.00
ME		0.00	−0.22	−0.09	0.00	−0.06	−0.05	−0.20	0.00	0.00	0.00	0.00	−0.20	0.00	0.00

Notes: Each entry denotes the fraction of rankings affected by an extra year of schooling for workers from the row country. *Sector A* comprises occupations above the 90th percentile of the empirical distribution of occupations (top sector); *Sector B* comprises occupations between the 70th and the 90th percentile; *Sector C* comprises occupations between the 40th and 70th percentiles; *Sector D* comprises occupations below the 40th percentile.

	ME	AFR	IND	VNM	PHL	KOR	CHN	RUS	POL	DEU	ITA	ENG	CUB	MEX	CAN
Sector A															
MEX	0.00	0.00	0.00	0.00	0.00	0.00	0.00	0.00	0.00	0.00	0.00	0.00	0.00		0.00
CUB	0.00	0.00	0.00	0.00	0.00	0.00	0.20	0.00	0.00	0.00	0.25	0.00		0.00	0.00
ITA	0.13	0.00	0.00	0.00	0.00	0.00	0.00	0.00	0.00	0.00		0.00	0.00	0.00	0.00
DEU	0.00	0.67	0.00	0.00	0.63	0.00	0.00	0.00	0.00		0.00	0.00	0.00	0.00	0.00
POL	0.00	0.00	0.00	0.00	0.00	0.00	0.13	0.20		0.00	0.17	0.00	0.00	0.00	0.00
RUS	0.10	0.11	0.83	0.00	0.10	0.10	0.83		0.00	0.00	0.20	0.00	0.00	0.00	0.10
CHN	0.45	0.80	0.95	0.83	0.15	0.95		0.00	0.25	0.53	0.00	0.10	0.00	0.00	0.97
KOR	0.11	0.12	0.87	0.67	0.00		0.95	0.10	0.00	0.25	0.33	0.00	0.00	0.00	0.11
PHL	0.00	0.00	0.00	0.00		0.00	0.26	0.00	0.00	0.00	0.00	0.00	0.00	0.00	0.00
VNM	0.00	0.00	0.00		1.00	0.00	0.00	0.00	1.00	0.00	0.00	0.00	0.50	0.00	0.00
IND	0.00	0.36		0.00	0.31	0.43	0.24	0.00	0.00	0.59	0.00	0.00	0.00	0.00	0.00
AFR	0.00		0.00	0.00	0.00	0.00	0.00	0.00	0.00	0.00	0.00	0.00	0.00	0.00	0.00
ME		0.00	0.00	0.00	0.00	0.00	0.00	0.00	0.14	0.00	0.13	0.00	0.00	0.00	0.00
Sector B															
MEX	0.00	0.00	0.00	0.00	0.00	0.00	0.00	0.00	0.00	0.00	0.00	0.00	0.00		0.00
CUB	0.00	0.00	0.00	0.00	0.00	0.00	0.20	0.00	0.00	0.00	0.00	0.00		0.00	0.00
ITA	0.00	0.00	0.00	0.00	0.00	0.00	0.00	0.00	0.00	0.00		0.00	0.00	0.00	0.00
DEU	0.00	0.00	0.00	0.00	0.00	0.00	0.53	0.00	0.00		0.00	0.00	0.00	0.00	0.00
POL	0.00	0.00	0.00	0.00	0.00	0.00	0.13	0.00		0.00	0.00	0.00	0.00	0.00	0.00
RUS	0.00	0.11	0.83	0.00	0.20	0.20	0.17		0.00	0.10	0.00	0.14	0.00	0.00	0.00
CHN	0.00	0.80	0.71	0.42	0.13	0.00		0.83	0.00	0.22	0.00	0.00	0.00	0.00	0.65
KOR	0.11	0.59	0.13	0.00	0.53		0.29	0.50	0.00	0.25	0.00	0.29	0.00	0.00	0.11
PHL	0.00	0.00	0.00	0.00		0.00	0.00	0.00	0.00	0.00	0.00	0.00	0.00	0.00	0.00
VNM	1.00	0.13	0.42		0.45	0.67	0.83	0.00	1.00	0.00	0.00	0.00	0.00	0.00	0.00
IND	0.00	0.36		0.00	0.00	0.00	0.00	0.00	0.00	0.00	0.00	0.00	0.00	0.00	0.00
AFR	0.00		0.00	0.00	0.56	0.59	0.00	0.00	0.00	0.00	0.00	0.00	0.00	0.00	0.00
ME		0.00	0.43	0.00	0.59	0.56	0.00	0.00	0.00	0.00	0.00	0.00	0.00	0.00	0.00
Sector C															
MEX	0.17	0.00	0.00	0.22	0.71	0.77	0.00	0.00	0.60	0.00	0.20	0.00	0.67		0.00
CUB	0.00	0.40	0.33	0.00	0.17	0.00	0.00	0.00	1.00	0.00	0.25	0.00		0.00	0.00

Table 14. *(Continued)*

	ME	AFR	IND	VNM	PHL	KOR	CHN	RUS	POL	DEU	ITA	ENG	CUB	MEX	CAN
ITA	0.00	0.00	0.00	0.00	0.00	0.00	0.00	0.00	0.17	0.00		0.00	0.00	0.00	0.00
DEU	0.00	0.00	0.59	0.00	0.00	0.00	0.00	0.00	0.00		0.00	0.00	0.00	0.00	0.00
POL	0.29	0.60	0.17	0.00	0.13	0.17	0.00	0.00		0.00	0.33	0.00	0.00	0.20	0.00
RUS	0.00	0.00	0.00	0.00	0.00	0.10	0.00		0.20	0.00	0.00	0.00	0.33	0.00	0.00
CHN	0.45	0.00	0.24	0.42	0.00	0.48		0.17	0.00	0.00	0.00	0.00	0.00	0.53	0.65
KOR	0.00	0.59	0.43	0.13	0.00		0.48	0.10	0.00	0.17	0.00	0.00	0.00	0.00	0.10
PHL	0.00	0.00	0.00	0.00		0.00	0.26	0.00	0.00	0.00	0.00	0.00	0.00	0.00	0.00
VNM	0.00	0.13	0.83		0.23	0.13	0.83	0.00	0.00	0.11	0.00	0.00	0.00	0.00	0.00
IND	0.00	0.36		0.00	0.00	0.00	0.24	0.00	0.00	0.00	0.17	0.00	0.00	0.00	0.00
AFR	0.00		0.00	0.00	0.11	0.00	0.40	0.00	0.00	0.00	0.20	0.00	0.00	0.00	0.00
ME		0.00	0.00	0.00	0.00	0.00	0.45	0.10	0.00	0.00	0.00	0.00	0.00	0.00	0.00
Sector D															
MEX	0.00	0.00	0.00	0.00	0.00	0.00	0.00	0.00	0.00	0.00	0.00	0.00	0.00		0.00
CUB	0.00	0.00	0.00	−0.50	0.00	−0.33	−0.40	−0.33	0.00	−0.20	0.00	−0.20		0.00	−0.14
ITA	−0.13	0.00	0.00	0.00	0.00	0.00	−0.13	0.00	0.00	0.00		0.00	0.00	0.00	0.00
DEU	0.00	0.00	0.00	0.00	0.00	0.00	0.00	0.00	0.00		0.00	0.00	0.00	0.00	0.00
POL	−0.14	0.00	0.00	0.00	0.00	0.00	0.00	0.00		0.00	−0.17	0.00	0.00	0.00	0.00
RUS	−0.40	0.00	−0.17	−0.17	−0.10	−0.30	−0.17		0.00	0.00	−0.40	−0.14	−0.33	0.00	0.00
CHN	−0.18	−0.08	−0.10	−0.08	−0.08	−0.19		−0.17	−0.25	−0.32	−0.13	0.00	−0.40	0.00	−0.13
KOR	−0.17	−0.24	−0.13	−0.07	−0.26		−0.29	0.00	0.00	−0.33	0.00	−0.43	0.00	0.00	−0.28
PHL	0.00	0.00	0.00	0.00		−0.05	−0.05	0.00	0.00	0.00	0.00	0.00	0.00	0.00	0.00
VNM	−0.09	−0.06	−0.04		0.00	−0.07	−0.08	−0.17	0.00	−0.11	0.00	0.00	0.00	0.00	0.00
IND	−0.04	−0.04		0.00	−0.03	0.00	0.00	0.00	0.00	0.00	−0.17	0.00	0.00	0.00	0.00
AFR	−0.06		0.00	0.00	0.00	0.00	0.00	0.00	0.00	0.00	0.00	0.00	0.00	0.00	0.00
ME		0.00	−0.13	0.00	0.00	0.00	0.00	−0.10	0.00	0.00	−0.13	−0.11	−0.40	0.00	0.00

Notes: Each entry denotes the fraction of rankings affected by the full English proficiency of workers from the row country. *Sector A* comprises occupations above the 90th percentile of the empirical distribution of occupations (top sector); *Sector B* comprises occupations between the 70th and the 90th percentile; *Sector C* comprises occupations between the 40th and 70th percentiles; *Sector D* comprises occupations below the 40th percentile.

Table 15. The Effect of the Arrival Year and Group's Tenure by Sector and Group.

	ME	AFR	IND	VNM	PHL	KOR	CHN	RUS	POL	DEU	ITA	ENG	CUB	MEX	CAN
Sector A															
CAN	0.00	0.50	0.75	0.00	0.71	0.56	0.32	0.00	0.00	0.22	0.00	0.10	0.00	0.00	
MEX	0.00	0.00	0.00	0.00	0.00	0.00	0.00	0.00	0.00	0.00	0.00	0.00	0.00		0.00
CUB	0.00	0.00	0.00	0.00	0.00	0.00	0.00	0.00	0.00	0.00	0.25	0.00		0.00	0.00
ENG	0.11	0.00	0.00	0.00	0.00	0.00	0.00	0.14	0.00	0.11	0.00		0.00	0.00	0.20
ITA	0.13	0.13	0.40	0.00	0.00	0.13	0.00	0.13	0.20	0.00		0.00	0.00	0.00	0.00
DEU	0.00	0.00	0.00	0.00	0.00	0.00	0.00	0.13	0.20		0.00	0.17	0.00	0.00	0.00
POL	0.20	0.10	0.11	0.83	0.00	0.20	0.10	0.83		0.00	0.00	0.20	0.00	0.00	0.00
RUS	0.16	0.45	0.80	0.24	0.83	0.53	0.00		0.83	0.25	0.53	0.00	0.10	0.00	0.00
CHN	0.56	0.56	0.00	0.43	0.67	0.00		0.95	0.10	0.00	0.17	0.17	0.00	0.00	0.00
KOR	0.00	0.24	0.11	0.31	0.45		0.16	0.26	0.20	0.00	0.00	0.13	0.11	0.00	0.00
PLH	0.00	0.00	0.00	0.00		0.45	0.67	0.00	0.00	1.00	0.00	0.00	0.00	0.50	0.00
VNM	0.75	0.87	0.71		0.00	0.31	0.13	0.17	0.83	0.00	0.12	0.17	0.13	0.00	0.00
IND	0.50	0.63		0.17	0.00	0.11	0.18	0.80	0.00	0.00	0.67	0.00	0.13	0.00	0.00
AFR	0.00		0.13	0.43	0.00	0.18	0.17	0.00	0.40	0.14	0.67	0.25	0.00	0.00	0.00
ME		0.00	0.00	0.00	0.00	0.00	0.00	0.00	0.00	0.00	0.00	0.00	0.00	0.00	0.00
Sector B															
CAN	0.00	0.00	0.00	0.00	0.00	0.00	0.00	0.00	0.00	0.00	0.00	0.00	0.00	0.00	
MEX	0.00	0.00	0.00	0.00	0.00	0.00	0.00	0.00	0.00	0.00	0.00	0.00	0.00		0.00
CUB	0.00	0.00	0.00	0.00	0.00	0.00	0.00	−0.14	0.00	0.00	0.00	0.00		0.00	0.00
ENG	0.00	0.00	0.00	0.00	0.00	0.00	0.00	0.00	0.00	0.00	0.00		0.00	0.00	0.00
ITA	0.00	0.00	0.00	0.00	0.00	−0.83	−0.53	0.00	0.00	0.00		0.00	0.00	0.00	0.00
DEU	0.00	0.00	0.00	0.00	0.00	0.00	0.00	0.00	0.00		0.00	0.00	0.00	0.00	0.00
POL	0.00	0.00	0.00	0.00	0.00	0.00	−0.83	0.00		0.00	0.00	0.00	0.00	0.00	0.00
RUS	0.00	0.00	0.00	0.00	0.00	0.00	0.00		−0.13	−0.53	0.00	0.00	0.00	0.00	0.00

Table 15. *(Continued)*

	ME	AFR	IND	VNM	PHL	KOR	CHN	RUS	POL	DEU	ITA	ENG	CUB	MEX	CAN
CHN	−0.56	0.00	0.00	0.00	0.00	0.00		0.00	0.00	0.00	0.00	0.00	0.00	0.00	0.00
KOR	0.00	0.00	0.00	0.00	0.00		0.00	0.00	0.00	0.00	0.00	0.00	0.00	0.00	0.00
PHL	0.00	0.00	0.00	0.00		0.00	0.00	0.00	0.00	0.00	0.00	0.00	0.00	0.00	0.00
VNM	0.00	0.00	0.00		0.00	−0.43	0.00	0.00	0.00	0.00	0.00	0.00	0.00	0.00	0.00
IND	0.00	0.00		0.00	0.00	0.00	0.00	0.00	0.00	0.00	0.00	0.00	0.00	0.00	−0.50
AFR	0.00		−0.43	0.00	0.00	0.00	0.00	0.00	0.00	0.00	0.00	0.00	0.00	0.00	0.00
ME		0.00	0.00	0.00	0.00	0.00	0.00	0.00	0.00	0.00	0.00	0.00	0.00	0.00	0.00
Sector C															
CAN	−0.50	−0.50	0.00	0.00	−0.17	−0.56	−0.23	−0.20	0.00	−0.16	0.00	−0.40	0.00	0.00	
MEX	−0.17	0.00	−0.56	−0.53	−0.17	−0.77	−0.53	0.00	−0.20	−0.27	−0.20	0.00	−0.33		0.00
CUB	−0.20	0.00	0.00	0.00	−0.17	−0.33	0.00	−0.33	0.00	−0.40	0.00	−0.20		−0.67	−0.14
ENG	−0.22	0.00	−0.13	0.00	−0.11	0.00	0.00	0.00	0.00	−0.22	0.00		0.00	0.00	−0.10
ITA	−0.38	−0.60	−0.17	0.00	−0.25	−0.17	0.00	0.00	−0.50	−0.29		−0.17	−0.25	−0.20	0.00
DEU	−0.13	−0.13	−0.18	−0.11	−0.63	−0.25	−0.16	0.00	0.00		0.00	−0.33	0.00	0.00	−0.26
POL	−0.29	0.00	0.00	0.00	0.00	−0.17	0.00	−0.20		−0.14	−0.33	−0.25	−1.00	−0.60	0.00
RUS	−0.30	−0.11	−0.83	0.00	−0.10	−0.20	−0.17		0.00	−0.20	−0.20	−0.14	0.00	0.00	0.00
CHN	−0.14	−0.80	−0.19	−0.42	−0.53	−0.48		−0.83	0.00	0.00	0.00	−0.50	0.00	0.00	−0.13
KOR	−0.28	−0.18	−0.43	−0.67	−0.15		−0.14	−0.20	−0.33	0.00	−0.17	−0.29	0.00	0.00	−0.11
PHL	−0.18	−0.22	−0.94	−0.27		−0.15	−0.26	0.00	−0.25	−0.63	−0.13	0.00	−0.17	−0.17	0.00
VNM	−1.00	−0.63	−0.13		−0.45	−0.20	−0.17	0.00	0.00	0.00	0.00	0.00	−1.00	−0.22	0.00
IND	−0.13	−0.17		−0.83	−0.31	−0.22	−0.26	0.00	−0.33	−0.59	−0.17	−0.25	−0.33	0.00	−0.75
AFR	−0.19		−0.18	−0.25	−0.56	−0.18	0.00	−0.22	−0.60	−0.27	0.00	0.00	−0.40	0.00	−0.50
ME		−0.13	−0.87	0.00	−0.59	−0.56	−0.14	−0.10	−0.29	−0.33	0.00	−0.11	0.00	−0.83	−0.10
Sector D															
CAN	0.00	0.00	0.00	0.00	0.00	0.00	0.00	0.00	0.00	0.05	0.00	0.00	0.00	0.00	

MEX	0.00	0.00	0.00	0.00	0.00	0.00	0.00	0.00	0.00	0.00	0.00	0.00	0.00		0.00
CUB	0.40	0.00	0.00	0.00	0.00	0.00	0.20	0.33	0.00	0.00	0.00	0.00		0.00	0.00
ENG	0.11	0.00	−0.13	0.00	0.00	0.00	0.00	0.00	0.00	0.00	0.00		0.00	0.00	0.10
ITA	0.00	0.00	0.17	0.00	0.00	0.00	0.00	0.20	0.17	0.00		0.00	0.00	0.00	0.00
GER	0.00	0.07	0.00	0.00	0.00	0.00	0.11	0.00	0.00		0.00	0.11	0.00	0.00	0.00
POL	0.00	0.00	0.00	0.00	0.00	0.00	0.00	0.00		0.00	0.17	0.00	0.00	0.00	0.00
RUS	0.10	0.00	0.00	0.17	0.00	0.00	0.17		0.00	0.00	0.00	0.00	0.00	0.00	0.00
CHN	0.00	0.00	0.00	0.04	0.05	0.00		0.00	0.00	0.05	0.00	0.00	0.00	0.00	0.00
KOR	0.00	0.00	0.04	0.00	0.05		0.10	0.30	0.00	0.00	0.00	0.00	0.00	0.00	0.00
PHL	0.00	0.00	0.03	0.00		0.05	0.03	0.00	0.00	0.06	0.00	0.22	0.00	0.00	0.04
VNM	0.09	0.00	0.00		0.05	0.00	0.08	0.17	0.00	0.00	0.00	0.00	0.50	0.00	0.00
IND	0.09	0.00		0.00	0.00	0.04	0.00	0.08	0.00	0.06	0.00	0.00	0.00	0.00	0.04
AFR	0.00		0.04	0.00	0.06	0.00	0.00	0.00	0.00	0.00	0.00	0.00	0.00	0.00	0.05
ME		0.06	0.04	0.00	0.00	0.06	0.00	0.20	0.00	0.00	0.13	0.00	0.00	0.00	0.05

Notes: Each entry denotes the fraction of rankings affected by the 10 year earlier arrival and 10 year longer tenure of workers from the row country. *Sector A* comprises occupations above the 90th percentile of the empirical distribution of occupations (top sector); *Sector B* comprises occupations between the 70th and the 90th percentile; *Sector C* comprises occupations between the 40th and 70th percentiles; *Sector D* comprises occupations below the 40th percentile.

Table 16. The Effect of the 10% Increase in the Share of Workers in Sector A by Sector and Group.

	ME	AFR	IND	VNM	PHL	KOR	CHN	RUS	POL	DEU	ITA	ENG	CUB	MEX	CAN
Sector A															
CAN	0.00	0.10	0.00	0.00	0.00	0.56	0.32	0.10	0.00	0.15	0.00	0.20	0.00	0.00	
MEX	0.00	0.00	0.00	0.00	0.00	0.00	0.00	0.00	0.00	0.00	0.00	0.00	0.00		0.00
CUB	0.00	0.00	0.00	0.00	0.00	0.00	0.00	0.00	0.00	0.00	0.00	0.00		0.00	0.00
ENG	0.11	0.00	0.00	0.00	0.00	0.00	0.00	0.00	0.00	0.00	0.00		0.00	0.00	0.10
ITA	0.25	0.00	0.00	0.00	0.00	0.00	0.00	0.00	0.00	0.14		0.00	0.00	0.00	0.13
DEU	0.00	0.20	0.12	0.00	0.00	0.83	0.53	0.00	0.00		0.00	0.33	0.00	0.00	0.16
POL	0.00	0.00	0.00	0.00	0.00	0.00	0.13	0.00		0.00	0.00	0.00	0.00	0.00	0.00
RUS	0.10	0.11	0.83	0.00	0.00	0.00	0.00		0.00	0.00	0.20	0.00	0.00	0.00	0.10
CHN	0.00	0.80	0.17	0.42	0.26	0.48		0.83	0.00	0.15	0.00	0.10	0.00	0.00	0.97
KOR	0.11	0.00	0.00	0.00	0.53		0.48	0.10	0.00	0.83	0.17	0.00	0.00	0.00	0.56
PHL	0.59	0.56	0.00	0.45		0.15	0.00	0.20	0.00	0.63	0.00	0.00	0.00	0.00	0.71
VNM	0.00	0.00	0.00		0.45	0.00	0.42	0.00	1.00	0.00	0.00	0.00	0.50	0.00	0.00
IND	0.00	0.00		0.00	0.31	0.13	0.95	0.83	0.00	0.59	0.00	0.13	0.00	0.00	0.19
AFR	0.00		0.17	0.00	0.11	0.59	0.80	0.00	0.00	0.13	0.00	0.00	0.00	0.00	0.10
ME		0.00	0.13	0.00	0.59	0.56	0.45	0.20	0.00	0.67	0.13	0.00	0.00	0.00	0.00
Sector B															
CAN	0.00	−0.50	0.00	0.00	−0.36	0.00	0.00	0.00	0.00	0.00	0.00	0.00	0.00	0.00	
MEX	0.00	0.00	0.00	0.00	0.00	0.00	0.00	0.00	0.00	0.00	0.00	0.00	0.00		0.00
CUB	0.00	0.00	0.00	0.00	0.00	0.00	0.00	0.00	0.00	0.00	0.00	0.00		0.00	0.00
ENG	0.00	0.00	0.00	0.00	0.00	0.00	0.00	0.00	0.00	0.00	0.00		0.00	0.00	−0.10
ITA	0.00	0.00	0.00	0.00	0.00	0.00	0.00	0.00	0.00	0.00		0.00	0.00	0.00	0.00
DEU	0.00	0.00	0.00	0.00	0.00	0.00	0.00	0.00	0.00		0.00	−0.11	0.00	0.00	−0.53
POL	0.00	0.00	0.00	0.00	0.00	0.00	0.00	0.00		0.00	0.00	0.00	0.00	0.00	0.00
RUS	0.00	0.00	0.00	0.00	0.00	0.00	−0.83		0.00	0.00	0.00	0.00	0.00	0.00	0.00

CHN	0.00	0.00	0.00	0.00	0.00	0.00		0.00	0.00	0.00	0.00	0.00	0.00	0.00	−0.32
KOR	0.00	0.00	0.00	0.00	0.00		0.00	0.00	0.00	0.00	0.00	0.00	0.00	0.00	0.00
PHL	0.00	0.00	0.00	0.00		−0.53	0.00	0.00	0.00	0.00	0.00	0.00	0.00	0.00	0.00
VNM	0.00	0.00	0.00		0.00	0.00	0.00	0.00	0.00	0.00	0.00	0.00	0.00	0.00	0.00
IND	0.00	0.00		0.00	0.00	0.00	0.00	0.00	0.00	0.00	0.00	0.00	0.00	0.00	0.00
AFR	0.00		0.00	0.00	0.00	0.00	0.00	0.00	0.00	0.00	0.00	0.00	0.00	0.00	0.00
ME		0.00	0.00	0.00	0.00	0.00	0.00	−0.10	0.00	0.00	0.00	0.00	0.00	0.00	0.00
Sector C															
CAN	−0.50	−0.10	−0.37	0.00	0.00	0.56	0.00	0.00	0.00	0.00	0.00	0.00	−0.14	0.00	
MEX	0.00	0.00	0.00	0.00	−0.36	0.00	0.00	0.00	0.00	0.00	0.00	0.00	−0.33		0.00
CUB	0.00	0.00	0.00	0.00	0.00	0.00	0.00	0.00	0.00	0.00	0.00	−0.20		0.00	0.14
ENG	0.00	0.00	−0.13	0.00	0.11	0.00	−0.10	0.00	0.00	0.11	0.00		0.20	0.00	−0.10
ITA	−0.13	0.00	−0.17	0.00	−0.13	0.00	0.00	0.00	−0.17	−0.14		0.00	0.00	0.00	0.00
DEU	−0.67	0.67	0.00	0.00	−0.63	0.00	−0.53	0.00	0.00		0.00	−0.22	0.00	0.00	−0.16
POL	0.00	0.00	0.00	0.00	0.00	−0.17	0.00	0.00		0.00	0.17	0.00	0.00	0.00	0.00
RUS	0.00	0.00	−0.83	0.00	−0.10	−0.10	0.00		0.00	0.00	0.00	0.00	0.00	0.00	−0.10
CHN	0.00	0.00	−0.24	0.42	0.00	0.00		−0.83	0.00	−0.53	0.00	−0.10	0.00	0.00	−0.13
KOR	0.56	0.00	0.87	0.00	−0.53		−0.48	−0.20	0.17	−0.17	−0.33	0.00	0.00	−0.77	−0.56
PHL	−0.18	−0.56	0.00	0.00		0.00	0.00	0.00	−0.13	−0.63	0.00	−0.11	0.00	0.36	−0.36
VNM	0.00	0.00	0.00		−0.45	0.00	−0.42	0.00	0.00	0.00	0.00	0.00	0.00	0.00	0.00
IND	−0.13	−0.36		−0.42	0.00	−0.87	−0.12	0.00	0.00	−0.12	0.17	0.00	0.00	0.00	−0.37
AFR	−0.13		0.00	0.00	0.00	0.00	0.00	−0.11	0.00	−0.13	0.00	0.00	−0.20	0.00	0.50
ME		0.00	0.43	0.00	0.00	−0.56	−1.00	0.00	0.00	0.00	0.00	0.00	0.00	0.00	0.00
Sector D															
CAN	−0.50	−0.50	−0.37	0.00	−0.36	0.00	0.00	0.00	0.00	−0.53	0.00	0.10	0.00	0.00	
MEX	0.00	0.00	0.00	0.00	0.00	0.00	0.00	0.00	0.00	0.00	0.00	0.00	0.00		0.00
CUB	0.00	0.00	0.00	0.00	0.00	0.00	0.00	0.00	0.00	0.00	0.00	0.00		0.00	0.00
ENG	0.00	0.00	−0.13	0.00	0.00	0.00	0.00	0.00	0.00	−0.11	0.00		0.00	0.00	−0.30

Table 16. *(Continued)*

	ME	AFR	IND	VNM	PHL	KOR	CHN	RUS	POL	DEU	ITA	ENG	CUB	MEX	CAN
ITA	0.00	0.00	0.00	0.00	0.00	0.00	0.00	0.00	0.00	0.00		0.00	0.00	0.00	0.00
GER	0.00	0.00	0.00	0.00	0.00	0.83	−0.53	0.00	0.00		0.00	−0.11	0.00	0.00	0.00
POL	0.00	0.00	0.00	0.00	0.00	0.00	0.00	0.00		0.00	0.00	0.00	0.00	0.00	0.00
RUS	−0.10	0.00	0.00	0.00	0.00	−0.10	−0.17		0.00	0.00	0.00	0.00	0.00	0.00	0.00
CHN	0.00	0.00	0.00	0.00	0.00	−0.48		0.00	0.00	0.53	0.00	0.00	−0.20	0.00	0.00
KOR	−0.56	0.00	−0.43	0.00	−0.53		−0.48	0.00	0.00	−0.83	−0.17	0.00	0.00	0.00	0.00
PHL	0.00	−0.56	0.00	−0.45		0.00	0.00	0.00	0.00	0.00	0.00	−0.11	0.00	0.00	−0.36
VNM	0.00	0.00	0.00		0.00	0.00	0.00	0.00	0.00	0.00	0.00	0.00	0.00	0.00	0.00
IND	0.00	−0.36		0.00	0.00	0.00	0.00	0.00	0.00	0.00	0.00	0.00	0.00	0.00	0.00
AFR	0.00		0.00	0.00	0.00	−0.59	0.00	0.00	0.00	0.00	0.00	0.00	0.00	0.00	0.00
ME		0.00	0.00	−1.00	0.00	0.00	0.00	0.00	0.00	0.00	0.00	0.00	−0.20	0.00	0.00

Notes: Each entry denotes the fraction of rankings affected by the 10 % increase in the share of workers from the row country in Sector A. *Sector A* comprises occupations above the 90th percentile of the empirical distribution of occupations (top sector); *Sector B* comprises occupations between the 70th and the 90th percentile; *Sector C* comprises occupations between the 40th and 70th percentiles; *Sector D* comprises occupations below the 40th percentile.

Table 17. The Effect of the 10% Increase in the Share of Workers in Sector B by Sector and Group.

	ME	AFR	IND	VNM	PHL	KOR	CHN	RUS	POL	DEU	ITA	ENG	CUB	MEX	CAN
Sector B															
CAN	0.50	0.50	0.11	0.00	0.18	0.56	0.97	0.00	0.00	0.15	0.00	0.10	0.00	0.00	
MEX	0.00	0.00	0.00	0.00	0.00	0.00	0.00	0.00	0.00	0.00	0.00	0.00	0.00		0.00
CUB	0.00	0.00	0.00	0.00	0.00	0.00	0.20	0.00	0.00	0.00	0.00	0.00		0.00	0.00
ENG	0.11	0.13	0.00	0.00	0.22	0.14	0.00	0.14	0.00	0.22	0.00		0.00	0.00	0.20
ITA	0.25	0.00	0.00	0.00	0.00	0.17	0.00	0.20	0.17	0.00		0.00	0.00	0.00	0.00
GER	0.67	0.00	0.59	0.00	0.63	0.00	0.16	0.10	0.00		0.00	0.11	0.00	0.00	0.15
POL	0.00	0.00	0.00	0.00	0.00	0.00	0.13	0.00		0.00	0.00	0.00	0.00	0.00	0.00
RUS	0.20	0.00	0.83	0.00	0.20	0.20	0.25		0.00	0.20	0.00	0.14	0.00	0.00	0.00
CHN	0.45	0.00	0.14	0.42	0.15	0.95		0.83	0.00	0.22	0.00	0.00	0.00	0.00	0.32
KOR	0.22	0.12	0.87	0.00	0.53		0.19	0.40	0.00	0.33	0.00	0.14	0.00	0.00	0.11
PHL	0.00	0.11	0.94	0.45		0.53	0.53	0.00	0.00	0.63	0.00	0.00	0.00	0.00	0.71
VNM	0.00	0.00	0.42		0.45	0.00	0.42	0.00	0.00	0.00	0.00	0.20	0.00	0.00	0.00
IND	0.27	0.18		0.00	0.94	0.13	0.48	0.83	0.00	0.18	0.00	0.00	0.00	0.00	0.15
AFR	0.13		0.36	0.00	0.28	0.59	0.80	0.00	0.00	0.67	0.00	0.00	0.00	0.00	0.50
ME		0.13	0.13	0.00	0.12	0.56	0.18	0.30	0.00	0.13	0.00	0.11	0.00	0.00	0.10
Sector C															
CAN	−0.50	−0.50	−0.37	0.00	−0.36	0.00	−0.13	−0.10	0.00	−0.53	0.00	−0.10	0.00	0.00	
MEX	0.00	0.00	0.00	0.00	0.00	0.00	0.00	0.00	0.00	0.00	0.00	0.00	0.00		0.00
CUB	0.00	0.00	0.00	0.00	0.00	0.00	0.00	0.00	0.00	0.00	0.00	0.00		0.00	0.00
ENG	0.00	0.00	−0.13	0.00	0.00	0.00	−0.10	0.00	0.00	0.00	0.00		0.00	0.00	−0.10
ITA	0.00	0.00	−0.17	0.00	0.00	0.00	0.00	0.00	−0.17	0.00		0.00	0.00	0.00	0.00
GER	−0.13	0.00	0.00	0.00	−0.63	0.00	−0.53	−0.10	0.00		0.00	−0.11	0.00	0.00	−0.16
POL	0.00	0.00	0.00	0.00	0.00	0.00	0.00	0.00		0.00	0.00	0.00	0.00	0.00	0.00
RUS	−0.10	0.00	−0.83	0.00	−0.10	−0.10	0.00		0.00	0.00	0.00	0.00	0.00	0.00	−0.10

Table 17. *(Continued)*

	ME	AFR	IND	VNM	PHL	KOR	CHN	RUS	POL	DEU	ITA	ENG	CUB	MEX	CAN
CHN	0.00	−0.40	−0.14	0.00	0.00	0.00		−0.83	0.00	−0.15	0.00	−0.10	0.00	0.00	−0.13
KOR	−0.11	−0.59	0.00	0.00	−0.53		−0.14	−0.10	0.00	−0.17	−0.17	−0.14	0.00	−0.77	−0.56
PHL	−0.18	−0.11	0.00	−0.45		0.00	−0.26	0.00	−0.25	−0.63	0.00	−0.11	0.00	0.00	−0.36
VNM	0.00	0.00	0.00		−0.45	0.00	0.00	0.00	0.00	0.00	0.00	0.00	0.00	−0.53	0.00
IND	−0.13	0.00		0.00	−0.31	−0.17	−0.14	−0.83	0.00	−0.59	0.00	−0.13	0.00	0.00	−0.37
AFR	−0.13		−0.36	0.00	0.00	0.00	−0.80	0.00	−0.20	−0.67	0.00	0.00	0.00	0.00	−0.50
ME		−0.63	−0.43	0.00	−0.59	−0.11	−0.14	0.00	−0.14	−0.67	−0.13	0.00	0.00	0.00	−0.10
Sector D															
CAN	−0.50	−0.50	−0.37	0.00	−0.36	0.00	−0.13	−0.10	0.00	−0.53	0.00	−0.10	0.00	0.00	
MEX	0.00	0.00	0.00	0.00	0.00	0.00	0.00	0.00	0.00	0.00	0.00	0.00	0.00		0.00
CUB	0.00	0.00	0.00	0.00	0.00	0.00	0.00	−0.33	0.00	0.00	0.00	0.00		0.00	0.00
ENG	0.00	0.00	−0.25	0.00	−0.33	−0.14	−0.10	0.00	0.00	−0.33	0.00		0.00	0.00	−0.40
ITA	−0.13	0.00	0.00	0.00	−0.13	0.00	−0.13	0.00	−0.17	−0.14		0.00	0.00	0.00	0.00
GER	0.00	0.00	−0.59	0.00	−0.19	−0.83	−0.15	−0.10	0.00		0.00	−0.22	0.00	0.00	−0.22
POL	0.00	0.00	0.00	0.00	0.00	0.00	0.00	0.00		0.00	0.17	0.00	0.00	0.00	0.00
RUS	−0.50	0.00	−0.17	−0.17	−0.20	−0.20	−0.25		0.00	0.00	−0.20	−0.14	0.00	0.00	−0.10
CHN	−0.14	−0.12	−0.17	−0.42	−0.53	−0.19		0.00	0.00	−0.37	0.00	0.00	−0.40	0.00	−0.19
KOR	−0.22	−0.59	−0.17	−0.67	−0.22		−0.19	−0.10	0.00	−0.25	−0.17	−0.29	0.00	0.00	−0.28
PHL	0.00	−0.22	−0.63	−0.45		0.00	−0.53	0.00	0.00	0.00	0.00	−0.11	0.00	0.00	−0.14
VNM	0.00	0.00	−0.42		0.00	0.00	−0.42	0.00	0.00	−0.11	0.00	0.00	0.00	0.00	0.00
IND	0.00	−0.18		0.00	−0.94	0.00	−0.71	0.00	0.00	−0.59	−0.17	−0.13	0.00	0.00	−0.19
AFR	−0.63		−0.36	0.00	−0.56	−0.12	0.00	0.00	0.00	−0.13	0.00	−0.25	0.00	0.00	0.00
ME		−0.19	−0.35	−1.00	0.00	0.00	−1.00	−0.10	0.00	−0.67	−0.25	−0.22	−0.20	0.00	−0.50

Notes: Each entry denotes the fraction of rankings affected by the 10% increase in the share of workers from the row country in Sector B. *Sector B* comprises occupations between the 70th and the 90th percentile; *Sector C* comprises occupations between the 40th and 70th percentiles; *Sector D* comprises occupations below the 40th percentile.

Table 18. The Effect of the 10% Increase in the Share of Workers in Sector C by Sector and Group.

	ME	AFR	IND	VNM	PHL	KOR	CHN	RUS	POL	DEU	ITA	ENG	CUB	MEX	CAN
Sector C															
CAN	0.50	0.00	0.37	0.00	0.00	0.56	0.13	0.10	0.00	0.15	0.00	0.10	0.00	0.00	
MEX	0.00	0.00	0.00	0.53	0.00	0.77	0.00	0.00	0.20	0.00	0.20	0.00	0.00		0.00
CUB	0.00	0.00	0.00	0.00	0.00	0.00	0.00	0.00	0.50	0.00	0.00	0.00		0.33	0.14
ENG	0.00	0.00	0.00	0.20	0.11	0.00	0.00	0.00	0.25	0.11	0.17		0.20	0.00	0.00
ITA	0.13	0.00	0.00	0.00	0.00	0.17	0.00	0.00	0.17	0.00		0.00	0.00	0.00	0.00
GER	0.67	0.13	0.12	0.00	0.63	0.17	0.15	0.00	0.00		0.14	0.00	0.20	0.00	0.00
POL	0.14	0.20	0.17	0.00	0.25	0.00	0.00	0.00		0.00	0.33	0.00	0.00	0.00	0.00
RUS	0.00	0.00	0.00	0.00	0.00	0.10	0.83		0.00	0.00	0.00	0.00	0.33	0.00	0.00
CHN	1.00	0.40	0.95	0.42	0.26	0.48		0.00	0.00	0.00	0.00	0.10	0.00	0.00	0.00
KOR	0.56	0.00	0.87	0.00	0.53		0.00	0.00	0.17	0.00	0.00	0.00	0.00	0.00	0.00
PHL	0.00	0.56	0.31	1.00		0.53	0.00	0.00	0.00	0.63	0.25	0.00	0.17	0.36	0.00
VNM	0.00	0.63	0.42		1.00	0.00	0.00	0.00	0.00	0.00	0.00	0.00	0.00	0.00	0.00
IND	0.00	0.00		0.00	0.00	0.00	0.00	0.83	0.00	0.00	0.33	0.00	0.00	0.00	0.37
ME	0.00		0.36	0.00	0.11	0.00	0.00	0.00	0.00	0.00	0.40	0.00	0.00	0.00	0.10
AFR		0.63	0.13	0.00	0.59	0.00	0.00	0.20	0.14	0.00	0.00	0.00	0.00	0.00	0.50
Sector D															
CAN	0.00	0.06	−0.09	0.00	0.00	0.00	0.00	0.00	0.00	0.00	0.00	0.00	−0.20	0.00	
MEX	−0.06	0.00	0.00	0.00	0.00	0.00	0.00	0.00	0.00	0.00	0.00	−0.13	0.00		0.00
CUB	−0.04	0.00	0.00	0.00	−0.03	0.04	0.00	0.00	0.00	0.06	0.00	0.13		0.00	0.00
ENG	0.00	0.00	0.00	0.00	0.00	0.00	−0.08	−0.17	0.00	0.00	0.00		0.00	0.00	0.00
ITA	0.00	−0.11	−0.03	−0.05	0.00	−0.05	−0.05	0.00	0.00	0.00		0.00	0.00	0.00	−0.04
DEU	−0.11	−0.06	−0.04	0.00	−0.05	0.00	−0.10	0.00	0.00		0.00	0.00	0.00	0.00	−0.06
POL	0.00	0.00	0.00	0.00	0.00	−0.05	0.00	−0.17		−0.05	0.00	0.10	−0.20	0.00	0.00
RUS	−0.10	0.00	−0.08	0.00	0.00	0.00	0.00		0.00	0.00	0.00	0.00	−0.33	0.00	0.00

Table 18. *(Continued)*

	ME	AFR	IND	VNM	PHL	KOR	CHN	RUS	POL	DEU	ITA	ENG	CUB	MEX	CAN
CHN	0.00	0.00	0.00	0.00	0.00	0.00		0.00	0.00	0.00	−0.17	0.00	0.00	0.00	0.00
KOR	0.00	0.00	−0.06	0.00	0.00		0.00	0.00	0.00	0.00	0.00	−0.11	0.00	0.00	−0.05
PHL	0.00	0.00	0.00	0.00		−0.17	−0.13	0.00	0.00	0.00	0.00	0.00	0.00	0.00	0.00
VNM	0.00	0.00	−0.13		0.00	0.00	−0.10	0.00	0.00	0.11	0.00	0.00	0.00	0.00	0.00
IND	0.00	0.00		0.00	0.00	0.00	0.00	0.00	0.00	0.00	0.00	0.00	0.00	0.00	0.00
ME	0.00		0.00	0.00	0.00	0.00	0.00	0.00	0.00	0.00	0.00	0.00	0.00	0.00	0.00
AFR		−0.05	−0.04	0.00	0.00	0.00	0.00	0.00	0.00	0.05	0.00	−0.10	0.00	0.00	0.00

Notes: Each entry denotes the fraction of rankings affected by the 10% increase in the share of workers from the row country in Sector C. *Sector C* comprises occupations between the 40th and 70th percentiles; *Sector D* comprises occupations below the 40th percentile.

Printed and bound by CPI Group (UK) Ltd, Croydon, CR0 4YY

13/09/2026

14961176-0002